Travels in America

TRAVELS IN AMERICA

From the Voyages of Discovery to the Present

An Annotated Bibliography of Travel
Articles in Periodicals, 1955–1980

By Garold L. Cole

Foreword by Thomas D. Clark

UNIVERSITY OF OKLAHOMA PRESS : NORMAN

Library of Congress Cataloging in Publication Data

Cole, Garold.
   Travels in America from the voyages of discovery to the present.

   Bibliography: p. 247
   Includes index.
   1. United States—Description and travel—Bibliography. 2. Travelers—United States—
Bibliography.
I. Title.
Z1236.C64   1984   [E161.5]   016.9173'04   84–40273
ISBN 0–8061–1791–5

The paper in this book meets the guidelines for permanence and durability of the Committee on Production Guidelines for Book Longevity of the Council on Library Resources, Inc.

Contents

Foreword

By Thomas D. Clark

Few bodies of historical literature have received more attention or raised more questions on the part of scholars and editors than the great mass of travel and contemporary descriptive accounts. In the same vein, no body of source materials is as diverse or difficult of assembly and categorizing as travel accounts. These exist in a diversity of forms ranging from presentation in formal books to brief articles in periodicals, to personal diaries and journals, to letters, to newspaper columns, to commercial and official governmental reports.

Annually scholars discover new fugitive accounts and edit and publish them in almost as many diverse forms as those in which they were originally cast. A standard source of this constant flow of materials has been local and state historical quarterlies and the journals of the various literary and historical disciplines. In most cases the editors of the specific articles edited and annotated the published journals along with descriptive essays giving information about the provenance of the original manuscript.

Garold Cole has performed the staggering task of locating and annotating more than a thousand travel-related articles that have appeared in periodicals between 1955 and 1980. Chronologically, however, the contents of the articles date from the middle of the sixteenth century until well into the first half of the twentieth. Central to the compilation of a travel bibliography is the critical editorial appraisal of the reliability of the contents and an assessment of their potential historical and literary worth. Often the latter becomes largely a matter of relativity, depending almost altogether on the uses individual scholars make of these materials. Garold Cole has done erudite yeoman service in the location of entries and in preparing brief but perceptive analytical appraisals of this great body of descriptive literature. Both tasks demanded a high degree of familiarity with periodical publication in the United States and a prodigious amount of reading. He has been astute in the location of articles and in perceiving the main thrust of the editors.

No attempt was made to appraise the historical worth per se of this voluminous collection of contemporary description and viewpoint, other than supplying a comprehensive guide in readily usable bibliographical form. The comments of the editors comprise an appraisal of the historical worth, or lack of it, of the individual documents. Also, Cole has brought up to date the collective conclusions and widely varying capabilities and accomplishments of travel scholars in the area of historical criticism. As editor of a fairly extensive bibliography of travel accounts, I often had reasons to wonder whether a particular entry was worth the ink for inclusion. Cole's bibliography demonstrates that the answer lies not so much in the worth of an individual entry as in the collective body which gives both a qualitative and a quantitative comprehension of the historical dimensions of travel literature.

In his organization of this diverse mass of material, the editor has used a variable format of general, regional, and purely local classification. Of necessity there are some overlapping instances of regions and localities which dictate more general organization and presentation.

Obviously much of the travel literature produced over the past three centuries has focused upon localities and sections. Much of it was repetitive in that travelers followed commonly traveled routes or took the "Grand Tour." Hundreds of accounts were written not so much by travelers in the sense of being casual visitors but by individuals who sought new homes, or who acted as agents for speculative interests, or carried out official assignments, or made scientific surveys, or who were individuals grasping at a trace of historical immortality by recording their personal experiences of pioneering in a new country. The travel accounts and personal journals traced in essence the constantly evolving process by which immigrants, settlers, backwoodsmen, and adventurers all went through the chrysalis stages from primitivism to sophistication and social maturity. Nowhere in American historical literature has the common man had more abundant opportunity to put himself into the annals of history than in writing travel accounts and descriptions of the plain course of everyday life. Cole's annotations bring into focus the wide panorama of an expanding nation, of personal experiences and reactions, and of social and political views that take in a broad sweep of time and portray rich and varied human responses.

Many entries in this bibliography are those of foreign travelers who came to the United States from older and far more sophisticated cultural backgrounds. This was especially true of those who came during the eighteenth century and the first three-quarters of the nineteenth century from England and France. In this period Englishmen abroad in this land in their hypercritical accounts produced secondary reflections of Victorian customs and mores cast against an American background of immaturity. Some never left home psychologically, or adapted their sense of physical comforts to the limited accommodations of an emerging nation. In the negative aspects of their accounts they demonstrated the shortsightedness and incapabilities of actually penetrating intelligently the realities of time and place of the new national culture.

Running through this massive body of published materials are two interwoven threads, the impact of "progress" in the conquest of the land and the maturing into local and national profiles of a highly divergent American personality. By the fourth decade of the nineteenth century a third element emerged in the areas of social institutions. Inevitably slavery became a central theme of the writings of many travelers who crossed the South in the nineteenth century. There prevails both strong undertones and strong overtones of the sense of the social and political strains that were building up in the country. Often in a negative manner there is revealed in many accounts a comprehension of the impelling influences of geography and sectionalism that fostered divisions of economic and political viewpoints. The Civil War produced legions of involuntary travelers and foreign observers who recorded mountains of firsthand descriptions of the struggle. A surprisingly large number of soldiers possessed enough interest and curiosity that they kept journals describing the country and the social conditions they observed on marches from one battle site to the next. Following the war the number of travelers multiplied throughout the nation. They went to tour battlegrounds, to observe freedmen making adjustments to their new way of life, to ride over the expanded railway systems, and to observe the settlement and maturing of the Far West.

As indicated, this bibliography represents only a quarter century of recent publication and appraisal of contemporary descriptive sources. Compilation of a guide of this nature is a tedious and vexatious undertaking, both in searches for entries and in the formulation of succinct critical and informational annotations. Few if any libraries anywhere possess the multiplicity of sources consulted by the editor. This listing has its rewards in that scholars will now have available a professionally conceived and executed tool that redeems hundreds of published documents from once again becoming fugitive materials. The volume of entries is astounding and raises the question of how much virginal material still lies untouched in private hands and archives.

A reviewer of our *Travels in the Old South* raised the critical point that it did not contain an index of the contents of the entries themselves. Such an undertaking would have involved a lifetime of search and extraction, to say nothing of the cost of publication. This is a task that must be performed by editors who publish new editions of individual travel accounts. In the case of Cole's bibliography, the user is given an overall notion of the general contents of each entry; the precise contents, however, must be examined by the scholar seeking more complete information on specific subjects.

Again, this compilation presents in reasonably compact form an almost unmanageable volume of critical appraisals nowhere else available. This is a scholarly tool that should find an honorable place alongside all the other guides and critical publications in this field.

Whether travel accounts are valid and dependable sources of historical information is a question that can be answered for the most part by comparative use, by evaluation, creditability, and reliability in specific instances, and in the pertinency of individual accounts. Nevertheless, this bibliography adds a fresh critical dimension to the materials. The erudite bibliographical experience and the critical awareness of Garold Cole helps to plug a vital gap in the field of research in contemporary course of the emergence of the American personality and institutions.

Preface

Travels in America is a compilation of articles published between 1955 and 1980 concerning travel accounts written by persons who traveled in the regions presently known as the United States. Although the earliest document included is dated 1540 and the latest is from the 1960s, the majority of accounts are from the eighteenth and nineteenth centuries. In addition to accounts written by actual travelers, syntheses of accounts by present-day scholars are included as illustrations of how they have utilized the travel account as an integral field of study. The period 1955 to 1980 was selected on the assumption that researchers would be most interested in recent scholarship, although certainly a compilation of periodical articles from an earlier period also would be welcomed by travel scholars.

The multitudinous writings of those who traveled throughout the nation when it was young and unsettled represent a valuable historical legacy long treasured by scholars of this country's past. Although travel accounts provide unique eyewitness testimony, bibliographic control over the literature is somewhat haphazard. If a scholar wishes to learn whether accounts exist for a given area or if a specific traveler wrote about his experiences, or if the scholar simply wants to be kept abreast of developments within the genre, he must consult an assortment of reference tools. For example, there are the guides to historical materials and state bibliographies, both of which list travel accounts selectively; there are the several fine specialized bibliographies of travel accounts for a few geographical areas; there are studies in which travel accounts have been used extensively as documentation; and there are periodical indexes. In all probability, though, the scholar would not find listed manuscripts held privately or by libraries, nor the numerous accounts of travel that appeared in contemporary newspapers or magazines, nor even all of the accounts of earlier travel published in scholarly journals during the twentieth century. Perhaps at some future time a comprehensive bibliography that will include published and unpublished travel accounts will be compiled. Until then, this bibliography may be considered a contribution to the overall bibliographic requirements of the genre of travel literature.

PURPOSE

The specific purposes for compiling this bibliography were threefold: One purpose was to draw attention to travel accounts that were previously unpublished or obscurely published many years ago; another was to ascertain recent interest in older accounts of travel; and another was to investigate scholarly usage of the travel account as an integral field of study. Periodical articles about travel are difficult to locate for several reasons. Because travel accounts are consulted by scholars from several disciplines, as well as having popular interest, they may be found in a variety of journals and magazines. In periodical indexes, however, accounts of travel may be scattered under subject headings that emphasize either the kind of traveler, the reason for travel, the areas traveled, or the research themes for which the accounts have been consulted.

PROCEDURE

The procedure for compiling this bibliography was as follows: The tables of contents of 223 periodicals from many disciplines were searched. Accounts also were located in the relevant periodical indexes: *America: History and Life*, *Writings in American History*, *Bibliographic Index*, and the *Social Sciences Index* and the *Humanities Index*, including their earlier titles. Lists of "Recent Articles . . ." that appear in historical society journals were a good source. Some citations were scattered among footnotes in periodical articles and monographs. From such varied sources as these, any article that sounded remotely as if it might contain a travel account or that was a modern synthesis of a travel account was scrutinized. The listing of articles is as extensive as was possible; the users of this bibliography must decide what is significant for their individual research. Because of the travel account's many applications, what may seem trivial to one scholar may be important to another. In selecting the articles, those having material that was abundant or repetitive or simply a popularly written article about a traveler or an exploration were eliminated. Articles dealing with maps and charts, trails and roads, and landmarks of discovery and exploration that did not include descriptions by travelers were not considered. In addition, newspaper reports of lecturers or visiting dignitaries, or any other types of material that did not use or make specific references to personal narratives of travel were excluded. Even with these guidelines, however, many articles still fell in the twilight zone. Although attempting to err on the side of inclusiveness, almost surely some useful items have been excluded, not to mention the ones simply overlooked.

ANNOTATIONS

No critical comments that might discourage users are offered. The comments contained in the annotations are designed to help users evaluate the articles for their own purposes. Where the information was available and in conjunction with the wording of the title, the following are identified: the traveler; his reason or purpose for travel; points of departure and arrival, and the general itinerary when it could be briefly stated; the type of document under consideration and the dates encompassed; and comments that indicate the individual's reaction to his travel experience. Those aspects of the account that the individual editor considered significant are stressed, and information about other themes believed to be of interest have been added. Often the annotations are intended to convey something of the flavor of the account—the human side that might be excluded in a terse summary or ignored by a mere gleaning of the document for "hard" historical facts. Some articles have brief annotations because they were sufficiently explained by their titles or were so pedestrian that it seemed enough to list them. For articles that are syntheses of several travel accounts, the authors' tenets and conclusions as understood by this writer are summarized. One further comment about the itinerary of travel is in order. The precise routes are frequently not made clear by either the traveler or the editor of the account and often the itinerary of travel cannot be traced on modern maps, except perhaps by scholars of that locale. Therefore, the users of this bibliography may well benefit from keeping the *Atlas of American History* (Kenneth T. Jackson, ed. Rev. ed. New York: Charles Scribner's Sons, 1978) close at hand.

ARRANGEMENT

The arrangement of the material is designed to anticipate three questions the scholar of travel literature will ask: What geographic areas were traveled, when, and by whom? Because not all of the articles fit conveniently into a single geographic designation, an article dealing with two or more states (regions) is under either the first mentioned or the state (region) where most of the travel occurred. Because some users of this bibliography may be unfamiliar with the precise boundaries of areas that were not a part of the United States at the time of the travels, states' (regions') names as they now exist are used. For the articles that are syntheses of travel accounts, the theme of the article is in the traveler's position in the entry and an attempt was made to determine the dates under consideration from the author's footnotes when they were not otherwise indicated. The bibliographic citations are as they appear in the articles with these exceptions: conventional capitalization is used when the title was all in upper case letters and punctuation was added where none existed. Where the name of the editor appears at the head of the article without that designation, but his responsibility was clearly that of editor, "ed." was added. When a modern author wrote *about* a traveler or a travel account, however, the article was entered only under the modern author's name. (I found great inconsistency over the term "editor.")

DEFINITIONS

A traveler is defined herein as anyone who visited or lived briefly in the area that presently constitutes the United States, but who at the time of his writing had not stayed long enough to be considered a permanent resident. This definition is derived from a basic assumption about what makes the travel account a unique document: that an individual from another society may be able to observe that which is unfamiliar from a fresh point of view. Thus he may perceive nuances and notice modes of behavior that are so commonplace to permanent residents that they may go unrecorded. Therefore, in order to include accounts that convey that "fresh" point of view and the ambience of the society visited, considered as travelers are those who were actually in transit (emigrants, tourists), those whose reason for being in a particular place was temporary and who expected to have to leave at any time (soldiers, missionaries, traders), and those who wrote about their first impressions of a new place (pioneers, homesteaders), even though they may later have become residents.

The term "travel account" is used to describe any personal narrative of actual travel: letters, journals, diaries, reminiscences, official reports, newspaper and periodical articles, and excerpts from book-length travel accounts are all included.

SUMMARY

While a summary of the 1,028 items contained in this bibliography must be brief, it should explore the purposes for its compilation. Principally it was to draw attention to accounts of past travel that were published for the first time between 1955 and 1980, or that appeared so many years ago they had to be rediscovered. *Travels in America* brings to light many accounts previously available only in manuscript collections of libraries, as well as items that remain in private holdings. The many accounts that first appeared in periodicals and newspapers hint at the relatively untouched mine of travel accounts that exists in those sources, especially for the nineteenth century.

To illustrate briefly who these travelers were, and why and where they traveled, the majority may be grouped in eight overlapping categories by reasons for travel:

   (1) *Travelers and Tourists.* These two are linked together because they traveled for the sake of travel, ostensibly for edification and enjoyment. These accounts indicate, however, that in the early eighteenth century the vicissitudes of travel precluded experiencing very much enjoyment of the journey itself. As the years passed and the modes of transportation, the roads, and the accommodations improved, the reader can see a gradual change from a preoccupation with the hardships of travel and confrontations with nature to the enjoyment and relaxation that were possible for the increasing numbers who could afford the leisure time by the late nineteenth century. During the seventeenth and eighteenth centuries the Northeast and the Southeast were visited most often. By the early 1800s the frontier of the Middle West and Texas were also being observed, and comments about those regions' prospects for advancement, settlement, and land investment predominate. From shortly after the mid-nineteenth century to the turn of the twentieth century, accounts of camping trips, railroad excursions, and automobile rides signal the arrival of tourists.

(2) *Expeditions.* Expeditions were undertaken for reasons that range from Coronado's search for the Seven Cities of Cíbola in the Southwest and the plains (1540–1542), to the march of Portolá's soldiers and priests from Mexico to California to strengthen Spain's sovereignty over the West Coast and establish the mission system (1769), to the American explorations of Lewis and Clark across the Louisiana Territory to the Pacific (1804–1806) and the famous government-sponsored scientific expeditions of the late nineteenth century. Surveys to establish roads, railroads, canals, and boundaries of land may also fit into this category.

(3) *Emigrants.* Although most of the emigrant accounts in this bibliography were written by individuals traveling across the West in the mid-1800s to find new homes (forty-niners excepted), emigrants followed other trails as well. At the end of the eighteenth century and throughout the first part of the nineteenth, pioneers trekked across Ohio, Pennsylvania, and the upper South to reach Indiana, Illinois, and Iowa. Beginning in the 1830s, accounts appear of families traveling across the South to settle on Texas land, and this bibliography contains several reports of foreign colonies being established in Texas.

(4) *Pioneers and Homesteaders.* Although the accounts of those who recently settled new land were written years and miles apart—from the early 1700s to the early 1900s and from New York State to the Dakotas—they present amazingly similar descriptions of backbreaking work, endless routine, helplessness in the face of disease and the natural elements, and loneliness.

(5) *The Military.* The accounts written by soldiers, their wives, contract doctors, and nurses reveal military men of several nationalities involved in combat as well as in peacetime activities. They include accounts of sixteenth-century Spanish action against the French in Florida; the French and the British against the Indians and each other in the eighteenth century; the Americans and the

British in the Revolutionary War; and Americans involved in the War of 1812, the Seminole wars, and the War of the Rebellion. Civil War narratives are so many that only about one-tenth (75) of all those located are included. The ones selected for inclusion contain the kind of insights that are typical of this literature. They express the soldiers' thoughts about their everyday activities: the dirt, grime, and boredom of the camp, the field, and the marches; the carnage, noise, and confusion of battle; rumors of all kinds; hopes for promotion; attitudes toward other soldiers, blacks, and civilians whose lands they were occupying; prison life; and concerns for the loved ones they left behind. Some writings of Civil War soldiers express an appreciation of the tactical aspects of battle, the aims of the war, or the consequences of the final outcome. Just before and after the Civil War, soldiers reported struggles against the Indians to win the West.

(6) *Commerce.* This category includes itinerant peddlers selling their wares and businessmen traveling to conduct their affairs in the Northeast and the South during the eighteenth century. It also includes fur traders in Michigan, the Dakotas, and Oregon between the late 1790s and the Civil War. The gold seekers who flooded California, Idaho, Montana, and Alaska during the middle and last half of the nineteenth century perhaps fit into this category as would-be entrepreneurs.

(7) *Government Service.* From the Revolutionary War to the end of World War II, foreign diplomats and official observers reported on affairs in America for their governments. The British forwarded the greatest number of reports, but also included are French and Russian dispatches.

(8) *Religion.* Religious travelers who left accounts were usually priests, missionaries, or ministers stationed at missions among the Indians or tending their far-flung flocks. They also acted as peace negotiators and as intermediaries for the distribution of land or money to the Indians.

Into the cracks between these eight reasons for travel have slipped many who simply do not lend themselves to such tight categorization, émigrés, roving photographers, hunters, teachers, and health seekers, to name a few. Yet, the one thing that many of these travelers had in common was that they were ordinary people. Sometimes the only evidence of a traveler's existence is his account of travel.

The second purpose for compiling this bibliography was to ascertain recent interest in travelers who previously published accounts. Among those whose writings are discussed and excerpted are the celebrated—Charles Dickens, Fredrika Bremer, Harriet Martineau, and Frances Trollope, and the unsung—Jacques Gérard Milbert and Henri Herz. There does not seem to have been a wholesale pirating of older accounts for the sake of publication, though. Articles appear because the individual was famous for reasons other than travel, because the travel narrative represented fine writing or literary trends, because the traveler's comments about American society have continuing relevance, or because he presented an accurate description of an event or a region. The various accounts of the participants in the Lewis and Clark Expedition have inspired the greatest number of articles. They have been used to investigate nearly every aspect of the trek, its leading figures, and its importance in westward expansion. Between 1955 and 1980 scholars have probed several editions of Alexis de Tocqueville's *Democracy in America* for topics ranging from what Tocqueville did or did not say about the United States to advice on the usefulness of his critique as a historical document. It should also be pointed out that during the past quarter century translations of foreign language accounts have been published that were previously unknown in the English language.

The third purpose was to investigate the travel account as an integral field of study, that is, how scholars have used these accounts as a collection of historical materials, generally to the exclusion of other sources. The most frequent usage scholars have made of travel accounts has been simply to summarize perceptions or descriptions of American society, places, or events. They have searched accounts written by foreign visitors most often and British writings more than those of other nationalities. In addition, accounts of Polish, Hungarian, Japanese, German, and French travelers have been consulted. While most of these summary articles survey the travelers' myriad comments, such specific aspects of American society as religion, children, Indians, and slavery and race relations have inspired individual articles, as have descriptions of cities and regions. Scholars have utilized collections of travel accounts written by Americans to reveal details about overland travel more than any other theme. The prevalence of cholera, the roles of women and families, the activities of children, the replenishment of supplies on the trail, and descriptions of famous landmarks have all been treated.

However useful travel accounts are for discovering the past through the eyes of the travelers, these writings may also be analyzed for intellectual and historiographic trends. For instance, because travelers' accounts abound in inadvertent and purposeful expressions of cultural predilections, they may reveal insights into the travelers' own societies, insofar as the individuals may be deemed representative. Several scholars who have approached travel accounts seeking such insights have found expressions of the typical nineteenth-century American mind in the negative attitudes American travelers of the 1840s and 1850s manifested toward New Mexicans and in the view that California's preterritorial "pastoral paradise" was unrealistic if the region was to progress along the same lines that the Anglo-Saxon, Protestant American civilization had developed. Another intellectual trend that scholars have explored is the idea that travel writings have heavily influenced perceptions about foreign lands within the travelers' countries of origin. Two such articles probe the effect of travel accounts on formulating the American image of New Mexico and California, as well as the impact of British travel writings about Texas and California on Great Britain during the same period.

Scholars also have used travel accounts to revise generally accepted opinions of the past. The reputation that Southern and frontier homes have had as havens for wayfarers is tarnished as travelers indicate that in those homes guests were usually forced to pay for lodging, if not turned away altogether. The familiar thesis that the women of New Mexico were held in high esteem by mid-nineteenth-century American travelers, while New Mexican men were degraded, is rejected as women are shown to have also been viewed in uncomplimentary terms. The idea that the Americans' negative attitude toward "Californios" in the two decades before transition was something uniquely American is challenged as travelers of other nationalities are demonstrated to have expressed similar attitudes. When emigrant writings are gleaned, the threat of the Plains Indians to overland wagon trains appears not to have been so great as it is usually represented in fiction and movies. Finally, the concept of overland travel as being a singularly masculine enterprise has been revised by several studies.

What conclusions can one draw from the uses scholars have made of the travel account as an integral field of study? While a thorough critique is not the purpose of this preface, at least two points are obvious. First, that the themes of several of these synthetic articles—changing ideas about sex roles and the confrontation between Mexican and Anglo cultures—are very much a part of our contemporary scene indicates that the travel account is a versatile resource for students of multidisciplinary studies in understanding the present as well as the past. Second, in these studies where the travel account has been used as a discreet historical resource, one notices an almost total absence of statements of methodology.

Anyone who has ever used the travel account is painfully aware of its limitations. Any truthful statement about its value as a historical resource must admit that all too often it deteriorates into biased, misleading drivel, which, if accepted uncritically, not only results in a distorted view of the past but invites skepticism about the researcher's approach to scholarship. Therefore, anyone consulting the travel account as a historical document must attempt to evaluate the authority and credibility of the traveler, his degree of objectivity, and the conditions of his travel—where he went, how long he stayed, and with whom he traveled. Furthermore, the scholar must employ some fairly systematic pattern of compiling information pertinent to his themes of study to avoid confusion and to ensure that he is arriving at a consensus and not just the first quotable phrase he encounters. But scholars of travel literature describe their procedures of research only occasionally, which is especially frustrating to the initiate into the field who reads their articles in search of advice on method-ology.

Scholars concerned with the travel account as a historical resource might well address themselves to greater usage of the travel account as a tool to probe intellectual trends, as well as to problems of research techniques unique to the genre. Other articles that would be important to the field of travel literature, but which have not been written during the years with which this bibliography is concerned, are surveys of the literature that might demonstrate the ways scholars from different disciplines have approached travel accounts and illustrations of how the travel account may be used as a teaching resource. Additional bibliographies of travel accounts by travelers to specific regions, or by some category of travelers or form of the publication in which the account appeared would also be welcomed.

ACKNOWLEDGMENTS

The compilation of this bibliography took a little longer than three years and was sustained by support and assistance from a variety of sources. Correspondence with travel scholars from several disciplines—Thomas D. Clark, Percy G. Adams, and John Francis McDermott—confirmed my belief that the project was of value to researchers. A sabbatical leave from my position at Milner Library, Illinois State University, allowed time to systematically search many periodical "runs," as well as to discover other titles by simply browsing the stacks. (What a great role serendipity plays in "systematic" research!) A Faculty Research Grant from Illinois State University provided some financial assistance to travel and peruse the collections of libraries at the University of Illinois, the University of Iowa, the Western History Collections at the University of Oklahoma, and the state historical societies of Iowa and Wisconsin. Although aware that trips to far-flung portions of the United States would have resulted in additional accounts for this bibliography, neither the time nor the money for such research trips was available. Many articles to which citations were found in periodical indexes and other scattered sources, held by libraries outside the Midwest, were obtained by Helga Whitcomb of the Interlibrary Loan Department, Illinois State University. Ann Sokan proofread the final draft of the manuscript and saved me from mistakes of syntax both too numerous and too embarrassing to mention. As always, special acknowledgment should be paid to my wife Betsy. She typed and checked and rechecked entries, names, and dates, usually without complaint. Undoubtedly her most important contribution was—at just the right time—to remind me that this bibliography was more important than our family lives and vice versa.

GAROLD L. COLE

Travels in America

1

United States

GENERAL

(1607–1946) **FOREIGN TRAVELERS** 1

Clark, Thomas D. "The Great Visitation to American Democracy." *Mississippi Valley Historical Review* 44 (June 1957):3–28.

An overview of the interests and observations of foreign travelers to the United States. Although early travelers frequently provided fragmentary information that was geographically vague, their writings were popular with Europeans who wanted to read about the New World, or who actually planned to immigrate. Traders, ministers, and scientists were only a few who authored accounts that were readily accepted by publishers. In colonial times foreign observers noticed that differences in agriculture, climate, and distance created sectional diversity in social and political behavior.

Clark says that during this early period some travelers perceived the rising conflict between the Crown and the colonies, and some even recorded sectional differences at an earlier date than historians often assign to the development of this phenomenon. Between 1776 and the Civil War foreign travelers focused their attention on the workings of democracy, the government, and the office of the presidency. Slavery was also a popular topic during this period, and foreigners had difficulty reconciling human servitude based on race with a democracy.

The "Grand Tour" in the South was a must for foreign travelers, and Clark suggests that in their descriptions slavery must have approximated serfdom in the minds of European readers and thus inhibited immigration. After the Civil War, the cities most attracted foreign observers. They were interested in the raw, new cities of the West, as well as in the mass of unabsorbed immigrants that glutted the eastern cities. Foreign travelers criticized the florid style of urban tabloids, but they still recognized that the cities were the centers of learning.

In the twentieth century Clark says that the modes of travel and the kinds of travelers have changed the nature of travel-accounts. Rapid transportation and more officials and lecturers on tour have produced a different kind of account that has its own distinctive characteristics. Clark points out the general limitations of travelers' perceptions and their accounts for the study of American past. He stresses that the degree of accuracy is only one aspect of these accounts to be considered. Another equally important factor is the effect these writings—whether accurate or inaccurate—had on developing European stereotypes of America.

(1700–1775) **COLONIAL AMERICA** 2

Marshall, Peter. "Travelers and the Colonial Scene." *British Association for American Studies Bulletin, New Series* 7 (December 1963):5–28.

Summarizes accounts foreign travelers left of their experiences in colonial America. Marshall emphasizes that after 1750 the value and the variety of their information increased considerably. As transportation modes and roads improved travelers wrote less about the hazards of travel and more about picturesque detail. Marshall says that the travelers focused on the South and Pennsylvania because those areas contrasted with their predominantly English backgrounds. The travelers found that just as they were interested in the curiosities of America, they were also objects of curiosity to the locals. Marshall examines foreign attitudes about American social life, religion, cities, blacks and the institution of slavery, and the differences between the New World and the Old, as well as the differences between the colonies. After 1763 travelers reported that feelings of independence were growing in the colonies because of conflicts with the Crown.

(1770–1830)   CLIMATE AND DISEASE   3

Jones, Michael Owen. "Climate and Disease: The Traveler Describes America." *Bulletin of the History of Medicine* 41 (May/June 1967):254–66.

Prominent in the accounts written by travelers to the Ohio and Mississippi River valleys between 1700 and 1830 were comments about the healthfulness of the region. Jones says that governing their remarks was a belief that climatic or geographic conditions exerted a direct influence on the human constitution, the nature and prevalence of diseases, and the racial and ethnic characteristics of man. The accounts provide contemporary attitudes about disease, etiology, and information about frontier conditions of health and medicine. Those written by foreigners reveal the impression of America's climate and diseases that was projected in Europe.

(1775–1850)   AMERICAN INNS   4

Yoder, Paton. "The American Inn, 1775–1850: Melting Pot or Stewing Kettle?" *Indiana Magazine of History* 59 (June 1963):135–51.

Yoder focuses on the inns found in the region extending from the Appalachian highlands on the East to Missouri, Iowa, and Wisconsin on the West. The inns or taverns might vary from out-of-the-way one- or two-room cabins with doorways so low that it was necessary for one to stoop to enter, to more commodious surroundings built as the population and amount of travel increased. The absence of individual accommodations in American wayside inns have earned them the reputation of being "the American melting pot." From reading the comments of sixty-nine travelers who resisted this kind of forced democracy, Yoder suggests that these inns should more accurately be labeled the "stewing pot."

(1776–1778)   HUGH MCDONALD   5

McDonald, Hugh. "A Teen-Ager in the Revolution." (Part I) *American History Illustrated* 1 (May 1966):25–34.
———. "From Brandywine to Valley Forge." (Part II) *American History Illustrated* 1 (June 1966):38–47.

From the journal of 14-year-old Hugh McDonald, who left his North Carolina home and joined the Continental Army in 1776. He served in North Carolina, South Carolina, Pennsylvania, and Delaware. He relates such incidents as being reprimanded for stealing geese and the tarring and feathering of a loyalist. He describes a British amphibious attack on the defenses of Wilmington, Delaware, as well as the battles of Brandywine (September 11, 1777) and Germantown (October 4, 1777), and the winter at Valley Forge (1777–78). McDonald's diary ends in May, 1778.

(1783–1784)   JOHANN DAVID SCHOEPF   6

Beard, Eva, ed. "Doctor-Naturalist on Tour 1783–1784." *American-German Review* 25 (October/November 1958):27–29.

Dr. Johann David Schoepf, who came to America in 1777 as chief surgeon for the Ansbach mercenaries who were fighting for the British, never left Long Island until peace was declared. Once freed from his medical duties, he toured New Jersey, Pennsylvania, Virginia, South Carolina, and east Florida, describing everything he saw with scientific detachment. Excerpts from his *Travels in the Confederation* (Philadelphia, 1911).

(1783–1876) POLISH TRAVELERS 7

Hoskins, Janina W. "The Image of America in Accounts of Polish Travelers of the 18th and 19th Centuries." *Quarterly Journal of the Library of Congress* 22 (July 1965):226–45.

Though fewer in numbers than English and French travelers, Polish visitors also came to America and recorded their impressions during the nation's first century of independence. Hoskins points out that their understanding of American customs was hampered by an unfamiliarity with the language, backgrounds different from the Americans, and visits to only selected parts of the country. Polish travelers explored the same themes as other foreigners—the workings of government, the future of democracy, the social life of Americans, the conditions of blacks and women, and Americans' preoccupation with material things. Although the Polish travelers were often shocked by strange and uncouth customs, they were generally pleased with the atmosphere of freedom. Hoskins explores the writings of seven travelers between 1783 and 1876, Tomasz Kajetan Wegierski, Julian Ursyn Niemcewicz, Julian Juźwikiewicz, Adam Gurowski, Julian Horan, Krystyna Narbutt, and Henryk Sienbiewicz.

(1790s) JOHN HARRIOTT 8

Fussell, G. E. "An Englishman in America in the 1790s." *Agricultural History* 47 (April 1973):114–18.

A brief overview of the impressions of John Harriott, who came to the United States to engage in farming. He bought farms in Rhode Island and on Long Island and traveled throughout the eastern United States. Fussell says that because Harriott found neither the inhabitants of the New World nor farming to his liking, he returned to England in 1795. As a more complete source of the traveler's experiences, the author cites Harriott's *Struggles Through Life, Exemplified in the Various Travels and Adventures in Europe, Asia, Africa, and America* . . . (3d ed., London, 1815).

(1791) FRANÇOIS AUGUSTE RENÉ DE CHATEAUBRIAND 9

Amelinckx, Frans C. "Exploration and Creativity: Chateaubriand's 'Travels in America'." *Exploration* 4 (December 1976):25–31.

Vicomte François Auguste René de Chateaubriand arrived in the United States on July 11, 1791, and departed for France in November, 1791. He wrote that during the brief time he traveled throughout the Northeast, the Ohio Valley, down the Mississippi River, and to Florida, he encountered many exotic experiences. Historians have been able to substantiate his travel only in the Northeast and discount the validity of many of his experiences. Amelinckx believes that Chateaubriand's fanciful account of his travels in America came about because of his disillusionment with American cities and particularly with the deteriorated condition of the Indians. Amelinckx says that Chateaubriand chose to reconstruct the former glory of the Indians through his imagination because it fit well with his personality, his concept of the past, and his concept of the function of literature, which was "to present the past and to set it against the devalued present to contrast glory and decay." (p. 29)

For Chateaubriand, the American travels influenced the themes of his future works: "Conflict between cultures and glorification of the past." (p. 26) His travels also influenced his creativity: "his American experiences opened to him the possibility of transforming reality and disillusionment into poetic beauty, and taught him that imagination is the mainspring of human experience and literature." (p. 26) Amelinckx consults several sources, but primarily the translation by Richard Switzer, *Travels in America* (Lexington: 1969). (See also item 233.)

(1791–1793)   EDWARD THORNTON   10

Jackman, S. W., ed. "A Young Englishman Reports on the New Nation: Edward Thornton to James Bland Burges, 1791–1793." *William and Mary Quarterly. Third Series* 18 (January 1961):85–121.

Thornton spent these years in Philadelphia as secretary to the British minister to the United States. His letters cover the affairs of the young Republic fully, as well as his impressions of the American people. For instance, Thornton wrote that Thomas Jefferson held a decided preference for France and "bears a strong hatred to the British name." (p. 96) Thornton believed Jefferson's philosophical nature was of the kind that left him indifferent to human feelings or animal suffering. On several occasions Thornton observed an excess of vanity in the American national character and he thought this flaw caused Americans to be unpredictable diplomatically and even to act against their own best interests. That vanity "tinctures the whole of their character; in acts, in arms, in literature, in political economy they think they take the lead, and have pointed out a new road to Europe." (p. 109) Thornton believed Americans were more adapters of European ideas than originators. He saw nothing in the way of political talent, literature, or inventions that compared with those of England. From what he was able to observe, freedom of religion in America simply led to the "wildest fanaticism and the most ridiculous blasphemy," which further convinced him of the sense of having a national religion. (p. 114)

Thornton also wrote many favorable passages about Americans. He thought them to be a generally sensible, reasonable people with respect for public office. He approved of the strong principle of democracy among the common people, although it "displays itself in vulgarity and a perfect absence on all occasions of ceremony or respect." (p. 93) Thornton commented about Indian troubles in Ohio; regional rivalries, especially between Virginia and New England; and the general political atmosphere. While in America, Thornton kept his eye on his own country. He was aghast at the events in France when the royal family was beseiged, and he hoped England would be able to stay out of war. His letters were written between October 9, 1791, and March 5, 1793.

(1794–1797)   FRANÇOIS ALEXANDRE FRÉDÉRIC,   11
DUC DE LA ROCHEFOUCAULD-LIANCOURT

Brandenburg, David J. "A French Aristocrat Looks at American Farming: La Rochefoucauld-Liancourt's Voyage dans les États-Unis." *Agricultural History* 32 (July 1958):155–65.

While in exile François Alexandre Frédéric, duc de la Rochefoucauld-Liancourt, spent the years 1794 through 1797 in Philadelphia and in the middle and northern Atlantic states. In his *Voyages dans les États-Unis de d'Amérique, fait en 1795, 1796, et 1797* (Paris, 1799), Liancourt devoted many pages to American agriculture. Brandenburg evaluates the work as a historical source, discusses American historians' use of the work, and presents several of Liancourt's impressions. Brandenburg believes the work is a good source of agricultural history, and although Liancourt's work has been frequently cited, it has not been used as systematically or as often as it should have been. (See also item 220.)

(1797–1807)   JULIAN URSYN NIEMCEWICZ   12

Kusielewicz, Eugene, and Drzyzanowski, Ludwig, eds. "Julian Ursyn Niemcewicz's American Diary." *Polish Review* 3 (Summer 1958):83–115.

These selections of the Polish poet-patriot's impressions of the United States are grouped under four categories. (1) His arrival in the United States in 1798 in the company of General Thaddeus Kościuszko; his impressions of Philadelphia; and his visit to the home of General Anthony Walter White. (2) His stay at the home of General Horacio Gates; his meeting with President John Adams; and the departure of Kościuzko for France. (3) His visit to Mount Vernon as a guest of George Washington. (4) His tour of New England; his marriage; and his final return to Poland in 1807. (See also items 91 and 111.)

(1800s)   LANDSCAPE DESCRIPTION   13

Bredeson, Robert C. "Landscape Description in Nineteenth-Century American Travel Literature." *American Quarterly* 20 (Spring 1968):86–94.

Bredeson classifies the three common forms of response to the landscape during the nineteenth century as fashionable, informative, and utilitarian. He says all were a result of what the writers expected to find, but were not the product of a genuine, personal experience. Bredeson discusses several travel writers who he believes escaped these three predetermined responses by describing the landscape for their own unique purposes.

(1800–1810)   LOUIS AUGUSTE FÉLIX DE BEAUJOUR   14

Joyaux, Georges J. "De Beaujour's View of America at the Beginning of the Nineteenth Century." *Modern Language Journal* 39 (April 1955):165–73.

Louis Auguste Félix de Beaujour published a small book following his tour of duty as a French official in the United States (*Aperçu des États-Unis, au commencement du XIXe siècle, depuis 1800 jusqu'en 1810 . . .* Paris, 1814). Because it was written early in the nineteenth century, Joyaux believes this work was influential in shaping attitudes in France and England toward the United States. Beaujour portrayed a negative image of America that contrasted with the earlier romantic writings of Crèvecoeur and others. Joyaux believes the change from optimism to pessimism in French writing occurred when the dreams of the French Revolution, which the American Revolution had inspired, were not realized.

Beaujour pointed out weaknesses in the federal-state system of government, Americans' love of money, the absence of cultural achievements, the crudeness of her society, and the lack of creativity in the urban architecture. He thought American men were sturdy but unattractive. Women fared better in his estimation, but he wrote that their beauty tended to fade by the time they reached age twenty-five and had disappeared completely by the age of thirty. Not all of Beaujour's comments were negative. For example, he found Americans clean and thought they dressed well. In his final analysis, though, Beaujour, unlike many of his contemporaries, predicted a gloomy future for the young nation.

(1800–1860)   INDIAN-WHITE CONFLICT   15

Stein, Gary C. "'And the Strife Never Ends': Indian-White Hostility as Seen by European Travelers in America, 1800–1860." *Ethnohistory* 20 (Spring 1973):173–87.

"Numerous European travelers to America from 1800–1860 observed and discussed the conflicts between Indians and whites in the United States. Generally, they wrote about the causes of these conflicts within the context of life in America. Some displayed sympathy for the Indians, others saw him as a hopeless savage, and nearly all predicted his rapid disappearance."—Abstract from journal, p. 173.

(1800–1860)   INDIANS AND LIQUOR   16

———. "A Fearful Drunkenness: The Liquor Trade to the Western Indians as Seen by European Travelers in America, 1800–1860." *Red River Valley Historical Reviews* 1 (Summer 1974):10–21.

Stein says that European travelers were interested in describing "the effect of the liquor trade on the physical and moral well-being of the Indians, the ineffectiveness of laws regulating the trade, and what they considered the causes and eventual outcome of the continued existence of the liquor problem among the tribes." (p. 110)

Europeans came expecting to find a "Noble Savage." Instead, they found the American government attempting to bring the Indian to the level of white civilization. The inordinate use of alcohol was an unfortunate side effect. Most agreed that Indians had an overwhelming passion for liquor. The federal government had passed laws forbidding the sale of alcohol to Indians, but travelers usually reported that the laws were not enforced. Some travelers saw federal officials flout the law by serving alcohol to Indians at official gatherings, and it was commonly believed that the possession of Indian land often occurred when Indians were under the influence of alcohol. Europeans believed alcohol would lead to the destruction of the Indian and that Americans were hastening it along, either because of lax law enforcement or outright greed.

Stein says the travelers failed to take note of several facts: drinking was a widespread problem throughout American society, especially on the frontier; the temperance crusade was a powerful movement during this period; few saw the Indians' need for drink as an escape from their declining status; and Europeans initiated the practice of giving alcohol to the Indians many years earlier.

(1802–1854)   INDIAN REMOVAL   17

————. "Indian Removal as Seen by European Travelers in America." *Chronicles of Oklahoma* 51 (Winter 1973/1974):399–410.

The removal of eastern Indians to lands west of the Mississippi River attracted much criticism from Europeans during the first half of the nineteenth century. One traveler saw the removal as a simple historical process: the Indians were lower on the scale of creation and their lands could not be used for civilized purposes until they were extinguished or expelled. Another felt the removal was for the good of the Indians because it would get them away from the damaging effects of civilization.

Most travelers rejected the reasoning that removal was for the Indians' benefit and simply attributed the action to the white man's greed. The Europeans criticized the way Georgia land was distributed at auctions, as well as the lottery that disposed of Creek land in Florida even before the Indians were removed. The European travelers also criticized the government's refusal to properly fund the physical removal of the Indians, from which they suffered greatly. While some Americans voiced opposition to removal, Stein says the Europeans did not explore the opposition very deeply. The consensus of European travelers was that however much Americans professed the ideals of liberty and human rights, the Indians were being driven westward without adverse public opinion.

(1806–1838)   RELIGION   18

Clements, William M. "Five British Travelers and Religion in Nineteenth-Century America." *Research Studies* 46 (March 1978):44–49.

Summarizes the perceptions of popular religion in the travel writings of Thomas Hamilton, Harriet Martineau, Frederick Marryat, John Melish, and Frances Trollope. All agreed that for women religion served only as a surrogate for more interesting activity and that men employed religion for the sake of appearance. The five travelers had mixed feelings on the lack of an established state church, but the two women believed Protestant Christianity took the place of a national church. All agreed that emotional enthusiasm characterized behavior at religious affairs, and they were unanimous in their condemnation of such response. Clements concludes by illustrating how the travelers' sense of nationalism, social position, and religious persuasions affected their attitudes.

(1820–1970)   **BRITISH TRAVELERS**   **19**

Fairlie, Henry. "English Visitors." *American Scholar* 46 (Winter 1976/1977):43–55.

This British journalist blends his own observations of American society with those of approximately two hundred other English travelers between the 1820s and the 1960s. Fairlie finds several recurring themes in their writings:

(1) The Englishman's awareness of the enormous geographical expanse of the United States and the freedom and independence this living space encouraged. These qualities were often noticed in women and children and in the absence of formality.

(2) The English visitor's sense of being in a country very different from the Old World.

(3) The Englishman's discovery of friendliness and generosity in Americans.

Fairlie attributes much of the pleasantness in American society to women. He comments that some qualities of American life that were frowned upon by early English writers were praised by later travelers as those American qualities also became characteristics of European culture. He cites rapid eating habits as one such quality. Fairlie believes that understanding of Americans is not found so much in weighty, philosophical discussions of equality, liberty, and conformity, such as can be found in Tocqueville, but rather is found in the informality that creates its own patterns and codes. He thinks the English traveler was usually aware of this flexibility which, Fairlie says, forms the rhythm of American life.

(1827–1832)   **FRANCES (MILTON) TROLLOPE**   **20**

Between 1827 and 1832 Mrs. Trollope lived in America, where she first participated in a utopian colony for slaves in Tennessee. She then moved to Cincinnati and invested the family fortune in a store for imported merchandise that ultimately failed. She kept a diary in which she recorded her impressions of daily life, rather than any philosophical discussions of Americans. The publication of her diary (*Domestic Manners of the Americans*, London, 1832) insulted Americans, who were extremely sensitive to British criticism during this period. (See items 21–24.)

(1827–1832)   **21**

Cross, Helen Reeder. "'I Hate America': Frances Trollope." *History Today* 20 (March 1970):163–73.

Summarizes Mrs. Trollope's purposes for coming to the United States, the failure of the utopian venture in Tennessee, and her unsuccessful bazaar in Cincinnati. Cross suggests that it was the combination of frustrated high hopes, her poor treatment by Cincinnatians, and her need for money that provoked her to write an account of American life that, though accurate, was heavy handed and without subtlety.

(1827–1832)   **22**

Fligor, Martha Weber. "Mrs. Trollope's Valentine to Cincinnati." *Bulletin of the Historical and Philosophical Society of Ohio* 18 (January 1960):13–18.

In a letter of February 14, 1828, Mrs. Trollope writes of her disappointment with the utopian colony of Nashoba established by her friend Fanny Wright near Memphis, Tennessee. Instead of being a functioning model community where slaves could work to earn their freedom, as she expected, the colony was totally undeveloped. Mrs. Trollope, who was proceeding on to Cincinnati to establish her store, admits her lack of business expertise.

(1827–1832)   **23**

Heineman, Helen L. "Frances Trollope in the New World: 'Domestic Manners of the Americans'." *American Quarterly* 21 (Fall 1969):544–59.

Describes the circumstances surrounding Mrs. Trollope's years in the United States and evaluates *Domestic Manners* as a literary work. Heineman believes that Trollope made excellent use of the anecdote. She feels the work's strength as social critique lies in its vivid descriptions of Cincinnati, where Trollope lived for twenty-five months. When Trollope left this area, her work degenerates into a standard traveler's account.

(1827–1832)   24

———. "'Starving in that Land of Plenty': New Backgrounds to Frances Trollope's 'Domestic Manners of the Americans'." *American Quarterly* 24 (December 1972):643–60.

Discusses Trollope's original motive in coming to America, which was to engage in the utopian venture with slaves in Tennessee and not for the Cincinnati commercial enterprise, as is often believed. Heineman also discusses Trollope's family situation, her financial setbacks, and her decision to publish what had begun as a highly personal diary.

(1830–1860)   AMERICA, LAND OF PARADISE   25

Fisher, Marvin. "The 'Garden' and the 'Workshop': Some European Conceptions and Preconceptions of America, 1830–1860." *New England Quarterly* 34 (September 1961):311–27.

The overall impression left by the writings of European travelers in the United States between 1830 and 1860 was that this country possessed ideal agricultural conditions and unlimited industrial potential. These eyewitness accounts strengthened the earlier myth that America was a land of paradise.

(1830–1900)   RELIGION   26

Brauer, Jerald C. "Images of Religion in America." *Church History* 30 (March 1961):3–18.

Two key motifs dominated the image of religion held by nineteenth-century Europeans: the beneficial consequences for both political and religious life of the separation of church and state, and the centrality of religion in everyday life. Although the writings of Alexis de Tocqueville, Frances Grund, James Bryce, William Lloyd George, and Hugo Munsterberg provide insights into American religion, Brauer believes their works are more useful for analyzing and interpreting the life of the Christian community than for revealing continuities and discontinuities with the church universal.

(1831–1832)   ALEXIS DE TOCQUEVILLE   27

Between April, 1831 and February, 1832, two Frenchmen, Alexis de Tocqueville and Gustave de Beaumont, visited the United States. While they came ostensibly as official observers of the American prison system, they also resolved to study the phenomenon of democracy. Their travels took them throughout the Northeast, across the South, to the frontiers of Kentucky and Tennessee, and to Michigan and Wisconsin in the Old Northwest. (The full itinerary of their trip has been documented by George W. Pierson in *Tocqueville and Beaumont in America*, New York, 1938).

The culmination of the visit was the publication of four volumes of *De la démocratie en Amérique*, Paris, 1835, vols. 1–2 and 1840, vols. 3–4. In this work Tocqueville views democracy not only as a system of government but as the basic characteristic of American society. From what he observed in the United States, he hoped to be able to forecast the future of France, which he believed was becoming increasingly egalitarian.

The first two volumes discuss the advantages derived from a democratic government, the consequences of unlimited power of the majority, and the factors that tend to perpetuate democracy. The last two volumes are primarily a sociological inquiry into the implications of democracy.

The volume of periodical literature on Alexis de Tocqueville since 1955 is quite large. The following articles (see items 28–43) were selected for this bibliography because they discuss Tocqueville's personal background and aspects of his travels that influenced his writing; the accuracy of his perception of contemporary American society; the fate of his predictions for America's future; and his acceptance by American intellectuals and historians. The translated editions of *Democracy in America* most frequently cited in the following articles are by Phillips Bradley (ed., New York, 1945, 1948, and 1954) and by J. P. Mayer and Max Lerner (eds.), George Lawrence (trans. New York, 1966). Mayer's definitive edition of Tocqueville's *Oeuvres complètes* (Paris, 1951–) is also cited. *Note:* A recent study of Tocqueville's work that contains a more extensive bibliography than is included here is James T. Schleifer, *The Making of Tocqueville's Democracy in America* (Chapel Hill, 1980).

(1831–1832)   **28**

Boesche, Roger. "The Prison: Tocqueville's Model for Despotism." *Western Political Quarterly* 33 (December 1980):550–63.

> Tocqueville's idea of political despotism becomes clearer when we compare it to Tocqueville's long ignored writings on Pennsylvania's prison system, a system he labeled "the most complete despotism." This prison's predominant characteristics were a rigid isolation of prisoners, strict equality, productive labor, and the complete privatization of life. Tocqueville suggests that by using the terror created by this system, especially the despair generated by solitary confinement, the prison often succeeded in reshaping the prisoner's mind and reforming his very "instincts." In a strikingly parallel fashion, Tocqueville chooses the same characteristics to depict the emerging political despotism. The new despotism, too, will rely on isolation, equality, an obsession with the private production and consumption of goods, the eclipse of public life, and the loss of a meaningful future—all of which will render men passive, dominated by a centralized government and a suffocating majority opinion.

Abstract from journal, p. 450.

(1831–1832)   **29**

Chamberlin, William Henry. "The Prophet De Tocqueville." *Modern Age* 10 (Winter 1965–1966):52–58.

> Reviews some of Tocqueville's predictions that Chamberlin believes have been realized. Tocqueville foresaw the possibility of both totalitarian states and a welfare society, as well as the rise of the United States and Russia as world powers. He foresaw the need for taxation within a democracy to support the government; he believed that the peace and prosperity of a democracy rested in the hands of the Supreme Court and that a democracy was not well qualified to conduct foreign policy. As negative consequences of democracy, he foresaw excessive materialism and oppression by the majority.

(1831–1832)   **30**

Colwell, James L. "'The Calamities Which They Apprehend': Tocqueville on Race in America." *Western Humanities Review* 21 (Spring 1967):93–100.

Colwell believes Tocqueville's predictions about race relations were less accurate than those of other areas. For instance, Colwell says that Tocqueville foresaw the permanence of racial prejudice and never believed that blacks and whites could live on an equal footing. Tocqueville predicted that a calamitous race war would result if any compromise was attempted between the continuance of slavery and the full intermingling of the races. Colwell answers charges made by Richard W. Resh that Tocqueville was insensitive to blacks. (See item 39.)

(1831–1832)   **31**

Horwitz, Morton J. "Tocqueville and the Tyranny of the Majority." *Review of Politics* 28 (July 1966):293–307.

While the "tyranny of the majority" had been considered by James Madison and others to be a political problem, Tocqueville perceived it to be a social problem in the United States. Tocqueville did not believe Americans harbored fears of being coerced by dominant forces in the government or of being abused by restrictive laws. He believed that equal political rights and active participation in the political process gave men the "love and respect for the laws of which they considered themselves authors." (p. 299)

Tocqueville saw widespread social equality to be both a blessing and a danger; though it promoted happiness and stability, it also brought uniformity of attitudes and tendencies. This could stifle diversity and shape the actions and character of men. Horwitz points out that Tocqueville's realization that the "tyranny of the majority" was primarily a social problem in America made it difficult for him to illustrate the workings of a democracy to his countrymen because in France the problem was a political one. Horwitz states that this is one of the reasons the work seems confusing; i.e., Tocqueville often seems to be discussing France and the United States at the same time.

(1831–1832)   **32**

Jezierski, John V. "A Fortnight in the Wilds: Alexis de Tocqueville, Michigan and the 'Democracy,' 1831." *Michigan History* 64 (May/June 1980):29–34.

The author believes that in Tocqueville's essay "Quinze jours au desert" ("A Fortnight in the Wilds"), first published posthumously in *Revue de Deux Mondes* (December 1, 1860), it is possible to discern not only Tocqueville's methods but also the interaction between his observations and his preconceptions. Tocqueville expected that it would be easy to locate the stages of the development of civilization. In New York, however, all elements had been leveled by an egalitarian society, and he was forced to travel west to Saginaw, Michigan, before he was plunged into primitive conditions where the Indians had not yet been touched by civilization. As he traveled he noticed how the balance between civilization and the wilderness changed. In Buffalo, New York, the Indians were smaller and degraded, but around the Saginaw Village they were fine physical specimens.

He observed a similar contrast in nature. Tocqueville saw the white inhabitants of Saginaw as the race to whom the frontier belonged, relentlessly pushing the limits of civilization to the Pacific.

(1831–1832)   **33**

Lerner, Max. "Tocqueville's *Democracy in America*: Politics, Law and the Elites." *Antioch Review* 25 (Winter 1965/1966):543–63.

Approaches Tocqueville with the questions of how valid his analysis of democracy was in Andrew Jackson's day and how suggestive it is for modern America. Discusses three themes. (1) The political, military, and economic power systems. Do they allow for governmental effectiveness and individual freedom? (2) Society, class and status, and institutions. How much freedom do they allow for development of the personality and how much content do they give to the life of the people? (3) Culture, including the whole range of social expression. Does it provide diversity and creativity?

(1831–1832)) 34

Marshall, Lynn L., and Drescher, Seymour. "American Historians and Tocqueville's Democracy." *Journal of American History* 55 (December 1968):512–32.

Although *Democracy in America* is considered indispensable to students of the Jacksonian period, the authors point out that Tocqueville's present status was recently achieved. Only since George Wilson Pierson's *Tocqueville and Beaumont in America* (New York, 1938) has Tocqueville been considered a legitimate analyst of a particular period in American history. Historians Marvin Meyers, Clinton Rossiter, and Louis Hartz, among others, have used Tocqueville differently. The authors of this article point out, however, that *Democracy* is neither a primary resource nor, strictly speaking, is it secondary material. It does not easily conform to traditional research methods nor lend itself to revealing "facts." The authors believe "it might more profitably serve as inspiration for broad ranging historical exploration than orthodox primary authority." (p. 517)

Marshall and Drescher believe that to utilize Tocqueville effectively, one must familiarize himself with Tocqueville's personal, social, and intellectual backgrounds, and with his preoccupation with European civilization. Such familiarization helps one understand apparent ambiguities in Tocqueville's concepts, as well as shifts in conclusions between the two publication dates of his volumes, 1835 and 1840. Most of this article is devoted to illustrating these needs.

(1831–1832) 35

Meyers, Marvin. "The Basic Democrat: A Version of Tocqueville." *Political Science Quarterly* 72 (March 1957):50–70.

The author's goal is to take from Tocqueville "a portrait of the democrat as an American, beginning with a brief account of the basic democratic situation; then searching for the American-democratic synthesis as expressed in social character." (p. 53) The most revealing feature that emerges from the portrait is the "joining in dynamic tension of two major tendencies— toward independence, toward dependence." (p. 69) Tocqueville finds these antithetic trends in every aspect of American life. Meyers characterizes this duality as the "venturous conservative." (p. 69)

(1831–1832) 36

Murphy, William J., Jr. "Alexis de Tocqueville in New York: The Formulation of the Egalitarian Thesis." *New York Historical Society Quarterly* 61 (January/April 1977):69– 79.

Tocqueville's observations of antebellum American society have generally been accepted as accurate. Murphy, however, questions Tocqueville's basic premise that because Americans were devoid of rank and privilege, they were equal in opportunity. Murphy cites later studies to show the inaccuracy of Tocqueville's contention and provides three reasons why Tocqueville arrived at his faulty conclusions.

First, he observed in his own country that the French aristocracy and the monarchy had ceased to function as positive political forces, but that the Third Republic seemed to be making some spectacular gains toward equality. Therefore, with what was happening in France and with what he perceived to be the situation in the United States, Tocqueville believed he could see the development of a historic process that was moving toward greater democratization of society. Second, Tocqueville first arrived in New York City and traveled with a group of friends who were among the socioeconomic elite, and he never met representatives of other groups who might have questioned the opinions held by his hosts. Third, once Tocqueville left New York his thesis had been formulated and he accepted substantiating evidence uncritically.

Murphy believes that Americans have readily accepted Tocqueville's statements on egalitarianism because it was an attractive idea that made them appear unique. Murphy expresses the hope that future historians will not accept Tocqueville's interpretation of American society without question.

(1831–1832)   37

Nisbet, Robert. "Many Tocquevilles." *American Scholar* 46 (Winter 1976/1977):59–75.

Nisbet illustrates how tracing the popularity of *Democracy in America* provides insights into the American intellectual scene. After the book was initially published, it continued to be widely read for a quarter century. During those years Americans approved of Tocqueville's praise of this nation's progress. As newer books appeared that praised that spirit even more, *Democracy* faded into the background and for many years was seldom read. Its rebirth began about 1940 and *Democracy* has remained popular since then for three reasons that relate to different phases of American intellectual life. First, in the late 1930s the rise of totalitarianism within popular governments in Europe and despotism through administrative centralization made Tocqueville's warnings about these developments seem pertinent. Second, in the 1950s the deteriorating effects of wealth and affluence on society were topics of concern for Americans. Third, in recent years the concept of equality, Tocqueville's master concept, has become important. Nisbet believes equality will remain important because it will be "the point of reference for an ever-growing number of issues in social policy." (p. 74)

(1831–1832)   38

Pessen, Edward. "The Egalitarian Myth and American Social Reality: Wealth, Mobility, and Equality in the 'Era of the Common Man'." *American Historical Review* 76 (October 1971):989–1034.

Pessen examines the widely accepted concept of the egalitarian nature of American society that forms an integral part of *Democracy in America*. He also refers to popular contemporary thought and recent scholarly works on the period, and illuminates the difficulties of conducting research on this theme. In cities of the Northeast, he examined four axioms of Tocqueville and arrived at these conclusions:

(1) Tocqueville wrote that in a democratic society fortunes are scanty because the equality of conditions that gives some resources to all members of the community also prevents individuals from amassing fortunes. Pessen found that substantial fortunes did exist.

(2) Tocqueville observed that rich men were self-made men, and it was possible for men of humble origin to become rich. Pessen concludes that upward economic mobility, which did occur up to perhaps 1815, had halted by the Age of Common Man.

(3) Tocqueville believed that fortunes were insecure; they were gained and lost overnight. Pessen interprets the evidence to indicate that fortunes accumulated earlier were retained during Jacksonian America.

(4) Tocqueville believed that a general equality of conditions existed among Americans.

Pessen found that the gap between the rich and the poor, which widened during the colonial era, continued to widen in the Age of Equality. To the questions of who got what and why, Pessen concludes that those who had wealth at the start of the period had it at the end. Despite popular belief, affluence and inherited wealth were most important. In his own words, Pessen has measured the measurable. He admits that some areas—the behavior and influence of the rich, and the imagination and feelings of men—escape the quantitative method.

(1831–1832)   39

Resh, Richard W. "Alexis De Tocqueville and the Negro: *Democracy in America* Reconsidered." *Journal of Negro History* 48 (October 1963):251–59.

Resh says that Tocqueville did not understand the plight of the American Negro and that *Democracy in America* contains some misconceptions about blacks that are not generally found in the writings of other contemporary foreign travelers. According to Resh, Tocqueville believed that the black man's skin condemned him to servitude. Because he was born into slavery, the black could not sense his own tragedy. Also, Resh says Tocqueville neglected the physical misery of the slave, misunderstood the economic consequences of bondage, and generally buried social injustice under a "penchant for philosophical abstractions." (p. 257) Resh compares Tocqueville's conclusions with those of thirty-three other foreigners who visited America between 1820 and 1832.

(1831–1832) 40

Riesman, David. "Tocqueville as Ethnographer." *American Scholar* 30 (Spring 1961):174–87.

Riesman says that Tocqueville never meant for his work to contain detailed descriptions of places he traveled, but that it should be a work of interpretation. Among the themes of Tocqueville's writing that Riesman discusses are the value Tocqueville puts on the separation of church and state, newspapers and free associations to ensure political liberty, and Tocqueville's fear that certain groups (lawyers and the military) would gain hegemony in society. Riesman believes Tocqueville's warnings against the meaner aspects of equality have not been realized. For instance, Riesman thinks that Americans of 1961 were less greedy and less individualistic than Americans of Tocqueville's day. Moreover, he believes that the oppressive centralization of federal power that Tocqueville warned of has not come to pass.

Riesman says that Tocqueville desired the "elevation of the mass of men and the disappearance of the abasement of the oppressed." (p. 186) By understanding democracy, he hoped to be able to suggest policies to his countrymen that would make the coming age of democracy in France less despotic and more free. Although Tocqueville often gathered examples for illustration of his concepts in the company of a mixed bag of American conservatives, Riesman believes that Tocqueville liked the United States more than did his American informants. In Tocqueville's "sampling" of society, Riesman points out that the people he observed on his travels were gregarious, active people, not individuals from isolated frontier groups or slaves.

(1831–1832) 41

Schleifer, James T. "Images of America After the Revolution: Alexis de Tocqueville and Gustave de Beaumont Visit the Early Republic." *Yale University Library Gazette* 51 (January 1977):125–44.

An annotated bibliography of eighty-five items displayed by the Beinecke Library, Yale University, that focuses on the travels and the writing of *Democracy in America*. Includes letters, travel notes, and diaries, Beaumont's sketches, draft copies of *Democracy*, and works about the two men.

(1831–1832) 42

Spitz, David. "On Tocqueville and the 'Tyranny' of Public Sentiment." *Political Science* 9 (September 1957):3–13.

Tocqueville asserted that the climate of opinion in a democracy constitutes tyranny because it controls society and promotes conformity, as well as discouraging men from acting. Spitz disagrees. He points out that conformity is enforced in all societies—egalitarian and nonegalitarian—and that it certainly does not apply to a society as heterogeneous as the brand of democracy practiced in the United States. Although public opinion may be the source of the abuse, Spitz says only the denial of democratic rights of free speech and free association constitutes actual tyranny.

(1831–1832)   **43**

Stroud, Cushing. "Tocqueville's Duality: Describing America and Thinking of Europe." *American Quarterly* 21 (Spring 1969):87–99.

Stroud characterizes Tocqueville as a European of aristocratic temperament and democratic convictions who cared deeply about the future of France. In *Democracy in America*, Tocqueville's analytical task was "to describe outlines of egalitarian society which might be Europe's future." (p. 87) Because of his double focus—describing America and thinking of Europe—Tocqueville has been charged with contradicting himself. Stroud says that Tocqueville might have replied that he did indeed describe America while thinking of both America and France, but his observations were not meant to be applied to both and therefore are not contradictory. Stroud considers the subtleties of the three doctrines in Tocqueville's writings that have seemed particularly illuminating to Americans—the tyranny of the majority, individualism, and virtuous materialism—to illustrate that Tocqueville was not confused.

(1831–1863)   **HUNGARIAN TRAVELERS**   **44**

Katona, Anna. "Hungarian Travelogues on the Pre-Civil-War U.S." *Angol Filológiai Tanulmányok/Hungarian Studies in English* 5 (Debrecen 1971):51–94.

Analyzes the interests of ten Hungarian visitors to the United States between 1831 and 1863 who wrote travel accounts. All were from the radical and most intellectual segment of Hungarian nobility. All feared censorship of their writings from the ruling Hapsburg monarchy. Katona informs us that the vogue for travelogues did not start until the 1830s when the Hungarian national awakening caused the people to look to the guidance the United States could provide in rescuing Hungary from its backward condition. The travelers praised the United States—the rapid growth of its cities, the educational level of the people, the freedom and democracy provided by the Constitution, the newspapers, the activeness of the people, an economy that allowed one to progress with hard work—and all contrasted these qualities with the absence of such qualities in their own country.

They also saw flaws in America, the excessive wealth being amassed by the manufacturing aristocracy, a spirit of isolationism that stressed the belief that America was the best of all possible worlds, immigration and the attendant problems of poverty and increasing crime, and the poor treatment of the Indians and the slaves. Nevertheless, Katona characterizes the common tone of these accounts as one of "reverent admiration." (p. 94)

(1833)   **PATRICK SHIRREFF**   **45**

Mingay, G.E. "A Scottish Farmer in North America: Patrick Shirreff's Tour of 1833." *History Today* 13 (October 1963):700–10.

The purpose of Shirreff's six-month tour was to provide advice to his brother who had expressed a desire to become an American farmer. Shirreff visited New York and Massachusetts and went as far west as Chicago. In Illinois he walked across some two hundred miles of prairie before returning east up the Ohio River. He offers a lengthy assessment of the farming potential of the prairies, little of which had been tilled at that time. Shirreff also comments on the accuracy of other British traveler accounts. Based on his *A Tour through North America* . . . (Edinburgh, 1835).

(1834–1836)   **HARRIET MARTINEAU**   **46**

Dentler, Robert A. "The American Studies of Harriet Martineau." *Midcontinent American Studies Journal* 3 (Spring 1962):3–12.

Between September 19, 1834 and August 1, 1836, the British social commentator traveled throughout the Northeast, as far west as Chicago and as far south as Atlanta and New Orleans. She wrote of her observations in *Society in America* (London, 1837) and again in *Retrospect of*

Western Travel (London, 1838). Dentler appraises Martineau's technique as a field observer and her conclusions as those of a trained ethnologist. (See also item 544.)

(1837–1840)   JOSEPH JOHN GURNEY   47

Rawley, James A. "Joseph John Gurney's Mission to America, 1837–1840." *Mississippi Valley Historical Review* 49 (March 1962):653–74.

Gurney was a Quaker minister and humanitarian who came to the United States at a time when English and American reformers communicated widely on ways to improve mankind. In America he spoke out against slavery and inspired Quakers to press the abolitionist movement. When Gurney returned home, he recorded his observations about education, crime and punishment, slavery, democracy, and the American character in a privately published journal that was intended to correct false notions about Americans.

(1842–1868)   CHARLES DICKENS   48

Whitridge, Arnold. "Dickens and Thackeray in America." *New York Historical Society Quarterly* 62 (July 1978):219–37.

Compares the American visits of English novelists Charles Dickens (1842 and 1867–68) and William Makepeace Thackeray (1852 and 1855). Both came to make money on lecture tours and visited the Northeast, the South, and the Middle West. Although both thought the American people warm and generous, and especially enjoyed the company of refined society in New York and Boston, they thought the rest of the country was raw and crude. Dickens riled the American press when he spoke out against slavery and the need for copyright laws that would force American publishers to pay him royalties. He published his sometimes harsh conclusions about American society in *American Notes* (London, 1842). Even though Thackeray held many views similar to Dickens's, he was less vocal and confined his impressions to personal letters. (See also items 163 and 164.)

(1845–1935)   AMERICAN CHILDREN   49

Rapson, Richard L. "The American Child as Seen by British Travelers, 1845–1935." *American Quarterly* 17 (Fall 1965):520–34.

The consensus of British travelers was that American schools were admirable, but the children were detestable. The children were often described as precocious, which was a polite way of saying they were impertinent, impolite, and disrespectful brats who exhibited more adult than childlike characteristics. Some reasons offered for the poor deportment of American children were that schools were too lenient, homes were not friendly places, and parents did not spend enough time or effort in rearing children. British travelers perceived the American character as childlike, and they thought there were too few adults with adult characteristics. They concluded that there was a "cult of youth" in American society.

(1845–1935)   RELIGION   50

———. "The Religious Feelings of the American People, 1845–1935: A British View." *Church History* 35 (September 1966):311–27.

Most nineteenth-century British travelers approved of the separation of church and state in the United States. They saw the integration of the church into the entire fabric of American life as a desirable development. In the twentieth century, as religion adapted itself to an increasingly materialistic society, British travelers perceived a lack of devotion and an absence of religious spirit in America. But was it change or continuity? Rapson examines Seymour Lipset's assertion that religion's evolution reveals its tenacity as the chief value-giving institution in American society.

(1846)   **THOMAS FRANCIS KNOX**   **51**

Ellis, John Tracy, ed. "An English Visitor's Comments on the American Scene, 1846."
Church History 36 (March 1967):36–44.

Presents a letter from Thomas Francis Knox to John Henry Newman that reveals the
hostility of American Catholics to Newman's recently published *Essay on the Development of
Christian Doctrine* (London, 1845). Knox also comments on the religious situations and the
church personalities he met in Massachusetts, Maine, and Canada, as well as on American
Catholics' attitudes toward Protestant religions.

(1846–1850)   **HENRI HERZ**   **52**

Hill, Henry Bertram and Gara, Larry, eds. "Henry Herz's Comments on Musical
Taste in Nineteenth Century America." *Midcontinent American Studies Journal* 1 (Spring
1960):17–22.

The French composer and pianist writes of the customs and buffoonery he encountered
among American audiences during his five-year tour between 1846 and 1850. Extracts from
Mes voyages en Amérique (Paris, 1866). (See also items 53, 165, 281, and 410.)

(1846–1850)   **53**

————— and —————. "More Comments by Henry Herz on Musical Taste in Nineteenth Century America." *Midcontinental American Studies Journal* 2 (Spring 1961):64–
68.

The touring French composer and pianist relates his impressions of the American music
trade and the pianos he found in the United States between 1846 and 1850. Extracts from *Mes
voyages en Amérique* (Paris, 1866). (See also items 52, 165, 281, and 410.)

(1850)   **JOHN CHANDLER**   **54**

Boromé, Joseph A., ed. "John Chandler's Visit to America, 1850." *Bulletin of Friends
Historical Association* 48 (Spring 1959):21–62.

As a representative of the British and Foreign Anti-Slavery Society, Friend John Chandler
was in the New World inspecting the economic and educational results of emancipation in the
West Indies. On his return trip home he visited the United States and Canada. His journal
(June 18–September 24, 1850) relates a voyage from Haiti with disgruntled California forty-
niners. In New York City he commends the Friends' social work with the lunatics. In Washington, D.C., he soon wearied of the "windy debates" by American congressmen whom he thought
"outrage[d] all patience." (p. 35) Chandler traveled by rail to Indiana where, in the company
of Elijah Coffin, he saw Quaker churches, schools, and farms.

(1850–1860)   **BRITISH TRAVELERS**   **55**

Crawford, Martin. "British Travellers and the Anglo-American Relationship in the
1850's." *Journal of American Studies* 12 (August 1978):203–19.

In contrast to the period before 1850, British travel writing produced in the decade preceding the Civil War was less critical of American society. Consequently, it aroused less hostility in
the United States. Crawford offers three possible reasons for the change in tone. By the middle
of the nineteenth century, Americans were more self-confident and less thin-skinned about criticism. Americans also were preoccupied with the growing sectional crisis. Perhaps the British of
the mid-Victorian period, who were largely middle or upper class, wrote with a greater degree
of stability than earlier writers. Crawford stresses that it is obvious that the later travelers were
responding both to American criticism of earlier British travel writing, as well as to the increasing degree of political and social compatibility between the two nations.

(1855–1856) AXEL ADELSWÄRD 56

Scott, Franklin D., ed. "Glimpses from the Travel Letters of Baron Axel Adelswärd, 1855–1856." *Swedish Pioneer Historical Quarterly* 11 (October 1960):145–54.

Adelswärd's travel diary was stolen and these letters are all that remained of his trip to the East, the Middle West, and the South. As he observed slavery in Charleston and New Orleans, Adelswärd believed the blacks in the South looked to be in better condition than the free blacks in the North. He thought Saint Louis to be the most progressive town he visited; Philadelphia appeared the cleanest and its life most idyllic; and in New Orleans the matrimonial market made his head swim. He was astonished at the beauty of American women.

(1860) JAPANESE TRAVELERS 57

Kawashima, Yasuhide. "America Through Foreign Eyes: Reactions of the Delegates From Tokugawa Japan, 1860." *Journal of Social History* 5 (Summer 1972):491–511.

Reviews the travel writings of the first two official Japanese delegations to the United States. One group visited San Francisco and the other spent a longer time in the major eastern cities. The author concedes that the Japanese had little familiarity with American customs and none spoke the English language. He believes their impressions were important because they helped to formulate the Japanese image of America. Generally, they approved of the educational system, the penal institutions, the newspapers, and the applications of technology to the military, to astronomy, to the railroads, and to everyday life.

Despite all this, the Japanese could not tolerate the food. They abhorred the white rice (they were used to brown rice) and what Americans did to it (we added butter and sugar). While the Japanese observed that the United States was a racist society, it was the great degree of democracy that surprised them. They were somewhat puzzled at the limited powers of the president and at the concept of states' rights because Japan was still a unitary feudal state.

(1860–1863) HENRI MERCIER 58

Carroll, Daniel B. "Henri Mercier on Slavery: The View of a Maryland-Born Diplomat, 1860–1863." *Maryland Historical Magazine* 63 (September 1968):299–310.

Although the conservative French minister to the United States from 1860 to 1864 did not favor slavery, neither did he believe that Lincoln should sign the Emancipation Proclamation. Mercier was convinced that rapid abolition would precipitate violence and social chaos. Carroll consults Mercier's diplomatic dispatches of 1860 through 1863.

(1861) JAMES FERGUSSON 59

Doyle, Elisabeth Joan, ed. "A Report on Civil War in America: Sir James Fergusson's Five-Week Visit." *Civil War History* 12 (December 1966):347–62.

Fergusson, a Conservative member of the British Parliament, was one of the earliest of many foreign observers of the Civil War. He traveled in both the North and the South between September 17 and October 23, 1861, and visited the major personalities of the war. Although he professes objectivity, this letter to Lord Palmerston reveals that Fergusson favored the South and predicted its victory.

(1861) FRENCH TRAVELERS 60

Carroll, Daniel B. "America in 1861: A French View." *Journal of the Illinois State Historical Society* 67 (April 1974):133–53.

From the end of July to the end of September, 1861, a party of Frenchmen toured the United States from Niagara Falls to Virginia and as far west as Saint Louis. From the writings of Prince Jerome Napoleon Bonaparte, Lieutenant Colonel Camille Ferri Pisani, Maurice Sand,

and French Ambassador to the United States Henri Mercier, the author has traced the highlights of the visit. The progress of the war, the possibility of an early conclusion, the French government's official posture were all topics of their concern. After being feted in Washington, D.C., the party saw Union encampments, visited with Confederate leaders in Virginia, and walked over the battleground at Bull Run.

Then they traveled west through Pennsylvania and Michigan, and to Chicago and Saint Louis. As they crossed Illinois the Frenchmen were impressed with the vast stretches of middle America, the treeless prairie, and the rough appearance of the hamlets and their inhabitants. After several days in Saint Louis, which was in the midst of the Fremont-Lincoln debate over the General's declaration of martial law, the seizure of rebel property, and the partial emancipation of the slaves, the French party returned to New York and home, via Niagara Falls and Montreal. (See also item 61.)

(1861)   CAMILLE FERRI PISANI   61

Joyaux, Georges J., ed. and tr. "A French Visit to Civil War America." *American Heritage* 8 (August 1957):65–86.

Letters of Lieutenant Colonel Camille Ferri Pisani, who accompanied Prince Napoleon, cousin of Emperor Napoleon III, for two months in the summer of 1861. The party visited President Lincoln, generals of both the Union and the Confederacy and the battleground of Bull Run, and traveled as far west as Saint Louis. (See also item 60.)

(1869)   NILES SEARLS   62

Long, Frances G., ed. "Coast to Coast by Railroad: The Journey of Niles Searls— May, 1869." *New York History* 50 (July 1969):303–15.

The editor believes that this is an account of the first trip across the United States entirely by rail. Searls left New York on May 8, 1869, two days before the golden spike was driven at Promontory Point, Utah, and arrived in California on May 19. There were many celebrations along the way. Sometimes the sleeping accommodations were elegant, but other times inadequate. Food and baggage were also a problem, but the roadbeds were in good condition. Searls also describes the return trip two weeks later.

(1873)   JULES ÉMILE PLANCHON   63

Morrow, Dwight W., Jr. "The American Impressions of a French Botanist, 1873." *Agricultural History* 34 (April 1960):71–76.

Jules Émile Planchon was sent by the French Ministry of Agriculture and Commerce to make a brief survey of the *phylloxera*-resistant grapevines in the eastern United States. The aphid, which was destroying the vineyards of Europe during the last part of the nineteenth century, was eventually eliminated because of the work of such men as Planchon and his American collaborator Charles Valentine Riley. During his tour through the vineyards, nurseries, and botanical gardens of the East and Middle Atlantic states, and as far west as Saint Louis, Planchon made notes about American life which Morrow has excerpted here.

(1873–1874)   FRIEDRICH RATZEL   64

Sauer, C. O. "The Formative Years of Ratzel in the United States." *Annals of the Association of American Geographers* 61 (June 1971):245–54.

The German geographer and anthropologist Friedrich Ratzel toured most of the United States in 1873 and 1874 as a correspondent for the *Kölnische Zeitung*. Sauer summarizes the trip and focuses on Ratzel's impressions of Boston, New York, New Orleans, Richmond, Saint Louis, Chicago, Denver, Salt Lake City, and San Francisco. Ratzel believed that the nature of a people was most clearly expressed in cities. Generally, he approved of the energy Americans expressed, but he deplored their wastefulness. Ratzel thought the wastefulness would pass as America matured and achieved the greatness he expected. From Ratzel's *Städte und culturbilder aus Nordamerika* (Leipzig, 1876). (See also items 170 and 225.)

(1877–1878)   **THOMAS GUNN SELBY**   **65**

Welland, Dennis, ed. "Across the Continent 1877–78." *British Association for American Studies Bulletin, New Series* 9 (December 1964):56–68.

En route to resume his missionary work in China, the English minister Thomas Gunn Selby traveled across the United States by train. He visited major tourist sites in New York City, where he was favorably impressed by a Henry Ward Beecher lecture and by Niagara Falls. In Chicago he was struck by the magnificent buildings surrounded by streets filled with knee-deep mud. After traveling across the Middle West without comment, he arrived in Salt Lake City. Like many other travelers, he contrasted the Chinese and the Indians. He praised the Chinese for being industrious, but described the Indians as dirty and half-dressed in cast-off American clothing. He felt they retained little of their former savage picturesqueness. In San Francisco, he noted anti-Chinese agitation. His journal runs from December 13, 1877, to January 1, 1878.

2
Northeast
(including Great Lakes and North in general)

GENERAL

(1697)   **BENJAMIN BULLIVANT**   66

Andrews, Wayne, ed. "A Glance at New York in 1697: The Travel Diary of Dr. Benjamin Bullivant." *New York Historical Society Quarterly* 40 (January 1956):55–73.

    Records a nine-week horseback journey in the summer of 1697 from Boston to Delaware and back again. Contains lengthy passages on Newport, Philadelphia, and New York City. The editor believes Bullivant's description of New York City is the best of the seventeenth century.

(1725)   **ISAAC NORRIS II**   67

Parsons, William, ed. "'Journey to Rhode Island'." *Pennsylvania Magazine of History and Biography* 85 (October 1961):411–22.

    The diary of merchant Isaac Norris II describes a six-week horseback trip through New Jersey, New York, Connecticut, and Rhode Island in September and October, 1725. Norris comments about the route, especially the bad roads in Connecticut, and his business transactions. He includes an account of his travel expenses and the cargo he purchased in Newport.

(1776–1777)   **HENRY STIRKE**   68

Bradford, S. Sydney, ed. "A British Officer's Revolutionary War Journal, 1776–1778." *Maryland Historical Magazine* 56 (June 1961):150–75.

    Among the many engagements in which Lieutenant Henry Stirke participated are the battles of Long Island (August, 1776), Harlem Heights (September, 1776), and Germantown (October, 1777). His journal (June, 1776–November, 1777) describes these and other military activities in New York, New Jersey, Delaware, and Pennsylvania.

(1777)   **RAYMOND DEMERE**   69

Demere, Raymond. "Journal of Major Raymond Demere." *Georgia Historical Quarterly* 52 (September 1968):337–47.

    Major Demere was dispatched from Charleston in the spring of 1777 with orders for General Washington in Philadelphia. Travel by sea was made hazardous by storms and British ships. In crossing Maryland and Delaware, Demere had to travel out of uniform for fear of being caught by the British. Throughout the journey he observed that feelings of disunity existed among the colonists. In Philadelphia he believed that the Quakers were leaders of discontent in that city. After Demere delivered the orders to General Washington, he participated in several battles in New Jersey.

(1777–1778)   PAUL BRIGHAM   70

Hoyt, Edward A., ed. "A Revolutionary Diary of Captain Paul Brigham; November 19, 1777–September 4, 1778." *Vermont History* 34 (January 1966):2–30.

The editor thinks Brigham's diary betrays a sense of detachment from the larger purpose of the war and the events in which he was engaged. Brigham concentrated more on the small experiences that affected him than on the battles. For example, he wrote more about finding an ox cart in which he could ride when the heat was so intense that he could no longer march, than he did about the Battle of Monmouth (June, 1778). His diary does provide a look at the cold and suffering at Valley Forge the winter of 1777–78, and military actions in New Jersey and New York. Brigham served with the Eighth Regiment of the Continental Army.

(1778–1779)   JAMES PATTISON   71

Ritchie, Carson I. A., ed. "A New York Diary of the Revolutionary War" (Part I). *New York Historical Society Quarterly* 50 (July 1966):221–80.
———. (Part II). *New York Historical Society Quarterly* 50 (October 1966):401–46.

The editor presumes that the diarist was Major General James Pattison of the Royal Artillery, commandant of New York from July, 1779 to August, 1780. The diary (June 17, 1778 through December 3, 1779) covers the British evacuation of Philadelphia and their retreat across New Jersey to New York. It also includes detailed accounts of the Battle of Monmouth (June, 1778) and British operations in Rhode Island during July and August, 1778.

(1785–1819)   WILLIAM COBBETT   72

Brown, Wallace. "William Cobbett in North America." *History Today* 22 (October 1972):685–91.

The English writer and polemicist spent three periods of his life in North America. From 1785 to 1791 he was a soldier in Atlantic Canada; from 1793 to 1800 he was a journalist in Philadelphia; and from 1817 to 1819 he was a farmer on Long Island while in political exile. From this last experience he wrote *A Year's Residence in the United States* (Boston, 1818). Brown says that during the first stay Cobbett discovered his vocation as a journalist, publisher, and writer of political pamphlets. He frequently quarreled with members of both political parties. Brown points out the improvement in Cobbett's attitude toward the United States during the third visit, but warns that Cobbett's praise of America was primarily a means to promote reform in England.

(1794)   WILLIAM STRICKLAND   73

Herndon, G. Melvin. "Agriculture in America in the 1790's: An Englishman's View." *Agricultural History* 49 (July 1975):505–16.

William Strickland was dispatched to the United States in 1794 by the English Board of Agriculture to observe American agriculture. He was to obtain information on the price of land and labor, the demand for sheep and cattle, and the supply of cereal crops. Herndon says most of Strickland's report about the state of agriculture and about the American people, which he observed during travels in the Northeast and Virginia, was negative.

(1796–1815)   TIMOTHY DWIGHT   74

Timothy Dwight was a clergyman, poet, and president of Yale University who traveled throughout New England and New York each autumn between 1796 and 1815 for his health. When he returned to New Haven he wrote up his travel notes for posterity. They were published by his sons as *Travels in New England and New York* (New Haven, 1821–22). His writings contain lengthy descriptions of the topography and local economic and social conditions. They also include numerous biographical and historical sketches. (See items 75 and 76.)

(1796–1815)   **75**

Freimarck, Vincent. "Timothy Dwight's Brief Lives in 'Travels in New England and New York'." *Early American Literature* 8 (Spring 1973):44–58.

A study of Dwight's biographical sketches in *Travels*. Freimarck says that Dwight selected for his sketches individuals whose lives were worthy of remembrance—those whose lives would instruct and improve, such as clergymen, citizen-soldiers, and statesmen mostly from New England. Dwight was biased toward men of action in religion and politics who lived early in the Colonial period. He wrote about revolutionary figures less flatteringly.

Freimarck says a dominant theme in *Travels* is that "there exists a godly society in a great good place (chiefly Connecticut), led by a continuing body of men devoted to its welfare; and this is always threatened." (p. 46) Freimarck illustrates this threat by contrasting Dwight's treatment of such men as Thomas Hooker and Roger Williams, and Sir William Johnson and Major General Phineas Lyman. Freimarck also discusses Dwight's writing about his own forebears (namely Jonathan Edwards), his contemporaries, and notable Indians who, like his white men, are either heroes or villains.

(1796–1815)   **76**

Sears, John F. "Timothy Dwight and the American Landscape: The Composing Eye in Dwight's 'Travels in New England and New York'." *Early American Literature* 11 (Winter 1976/1977):311–21.

Praises Dwight as being one of the first Americans to "take an interest viewing landscapes and registering their emotional and aesthetic impact." (p. 311) Sears examines Dwight's aesthetic concepts, his social and political concerns, and his own psychological needs. Dwight's New England background forced him to look for social and aesthetic harmony, "but often the wild and partially settled American landscape resisted his vision." (p. 313) Sears says it was the tension between what Dwight wanted to see and what was actually there that makes his landscape descriptions possess enduring value.

(1804)   **MANASSEH CUTLER**   **77**

Newcomer, Lee Nathaniel, ed. "The Long Journey Home From Congress." *Essex Institute Historical Collections* 100 (April 1964):85–87.

A terse travel diary that reveals the length of time and the hardships of travel in the early eighteenth century. Reverend Manasseh Cutler took ten days (March 4 to 14, 1804) to travel from Washington, D.C., to Essex County, Massachusetts.

(1811–1813)   **PAUL SVININ**   **78**

Davidson, Marshall B. "Voyage Pittoresque Aux Etats-Unis de L'Amerique." *American Heritage* 15 (February 1964):49–63; 107.

Paul (Pavel Petrovich) Svinin, who was secretary to the Russian consul general in Philadelphia between 1811 and 1813, tried to convey a favorable impression of America to his people. Davidson feels that Svinin was a competent observer and that his watercolors of subjects from Niagara Falls to Virginia made him the most widely traveled foreign artist at that time. Published in English as *Picturesque United States of America, 1811, 1812, 1813 . . .* (New York, 1830).

(1831)   **HART SHELBY**   79

Scott, William Campbell, ed. "Journal of Travels East in 1831: The Same Being the Journal of Major Hart Shelby of Fayette County, Kentucky." *Register of the Kentucky Historical Society* 65 (July 1967):163–86.

   Shelby's journey took him from Kentucky to Cincinnati, up the Ohio River into Pennsylvania, on to Washington, D.C., Baltimore, New York City, Boston, Niagara Falls, and then home through Ohio. On his four-month trip (April 20 to August 4, 1831), he visited William Henry Harrison in Cincinnati, President Andrew Jackson in the nation's capital, the mint in Philadelphia, and took a cruise on Lake Erie.

(1831)   **FRANCIS SILSBEE**   80

Booth, Alan R., ed. "Francis Silsbee's August Odyssey, 1831." *Essex Institute Historical Collections* 100 (January 1964):59–69.

   As a last fling before starting his law apprenticeship, Silsbee and a chaperoned group of young gentlemen and ladies made a two-week tour of Maine, the White Mountains, the Connecticut River Valley, lower New Hampshire, and Massachusetts.

(1838)   **JOHN H. STEELE**   81

Lindenbusch, John, ed. "Journal Kept by John H. Steele on a Journey from Peterborough, N.H. to Salisbury, North Carolina in the Months of November-December 1838." *Historical New Hampshire* 18 (December 1963):3–24.

   On November 19, 1838, Steele left Nashua, New Hampshire, for a visit to his former home in North Carolina. The round-trip journey took him 2,302 miles by seven conveyances (chart included). He passed through Vermont, Albany, New York City, Philadelphia, Lancaster, Harpers Ferry, Washington, D.C., Richmond, and Raleigh, before finally arriving at Salisbury. Steele provides descriptions of these places and lengthier passages about the area around Salisbury and the nation's capital, and he also offers some conclusions about what he saw. For example, the battles he observed between the Whigs and the Democrats in Washington, D.C. caused him to believe that political strife was destroying the nation. In New York harbor, even after viewing the great number of trading ships docked there, Steele was still convinced the country's future lay not in the hands of men of commerce but in free tillers of the soil.

(1851)   **WILLIAM A. HICKOK**   82

Hickok, William A. "Account of a Journey on the Great Lakes." *Journal of the Illinois State Historical Society* 71 (May 1978):143–47.

   During the first week of July, 1851, William Hickok sailed from Chicago to Union, New York. He was plagued with illness which was worsened by the inconvenience of travel over the Great Lakes. He briefly comments on the cities and towns they passed and on traffic on the Lakes, and included some personal family greetings.

(1853)   **EBENEZER GRAVES**   83

Graves, Ebenezer. "Journal of a Peddling Trip Kept by Ebenezer Graves of Ashfield, Massachusetts." (Part I) *Old-Time New England* 56 (January/March 1966):81–90.

———. (Part II) *Old-Time New England* 56 (April/June 1966):108–16.

   The journalist traveled extensively throughout Maine, Massachusetts, and New Hampshire between March 21 and September 3, 1853. Graves kept a daily record of his sales of silk and he jotted down brief comments about the numerous villages and cities he visited. He was especially observant of the commercial activities he saw—the glass and shoe factories, fishing, and farming—and he provides vignettes of the people he met.

(1860)   **WILLIAM DEAN HOWELLS**   84

Price, Robert, ed. "The Road to Boston: 1860 Travel Correspondence of William Dean Howells." *Ohio History* 80 (Spring 1971):84–154.

From Columbus, Ohio, into Canada, then to New England, and finally home to Ohio through New York was Howells's itinerary during the summer of 1860. His writings reveal his personal reactions to travel and to other passengers. He comments on Niagara Falls; Toronto, Montreal, and Quebec; Portland, Maine, and Haverhill, Massachusetts. The editor says that these travel letters to two Ohio newspapers illustrate how mature Howells's writing ability had become for him to be able to produce such smooth writing under the pressures of time and travel.

(1870)   **JAMES BRYCE**   85

Lefcowitz, Alan F., and Lefcowitz, Barbara F. "James Bryce's First Visit to America: The New England Sections of His 1870 Journal and Related Correspondence." *New England Quarterly* 50 (June 1977):314–31.

Although Bryce's later visits more directly influenced his *American Commonwealth* (London, 1888), during this first trip he developed many favorable attitudes about Americans. He also began lifelong friendships with Oliver Wendell Holmes, Jr., and Charles William Eliot.

CONNECTICUT

(1815–1823)   **JACQUES GÉRARD MILBERT**   86

Sherman, Constance D. "A French Naturalist Visits Connecticut." *Connecticut Historical Society Bulletin* 23 (April 1958):40–43.

A brief summary of the favorable comments Jacques Gérard Milbert wrote about Connecticut in his *Itinéraire pittoresque du fleuve Hudson* . . . (Paris, 1828–29). This work was the result of an eight-year stay in the United States following his arrival in New York in 1815. Milbert, who was a French naturalist and artist, traveled from eastern Canada to Virginia, painting and collecting materials for the Museum of Natural History in Paris. (See also items 120, 157, and 173.)

(1919)   **JOHN STAFFORD BROWN**   87

Brown, John Stafford. "A Missourian Discovers Connecticut, 1919." *Connecticut Historical Society Bulletin* 43 (April 1978):54–64.

A young middle western geologist, John Stafford Brown, recorded his impressions of the New Haven area while engaged in a ground-water study. He divides his discussion of people into three categories: the Yankees, who were most noticeable in the rural areas because in the cities they were outnumbered by the immigrants; the foreign population, mostly Italians, who worked in the cities but also in the suburbs; and the officials he met in his sampling of water supplies.

MASSACHUSETTS

(1704–1705)   **SARAH KEMBLE KNIGHT**   88

Medeiros, Patricia. "Sarah Kemble Knight." *New England Galaxy* 18 (Winter 1977):30–36.

Presents the highlights of Mrs. Knight's diary kept while on a business trip from Boston to New York City in 1704 and 1705. Medeiros points out that although the horseback journey was quite an undertaking for a woman of that day, Mrs. Knight accepted the hardships matter-of-factly. Among the hardships were rivers at flood stage and inadequate food and lodging offered at the inns. Mrs. Knight's ability to amusingly characterize people she met and her description of New York City in comparison with Boston overshadow the few discussions of her business transactions.

Note: Alan Margolies traces the authentication process of Mrs. Kemble's diary in "The Editing and Publication of 'The Journal of Madam Knight'." *Papers of the Bibliographical Society of America* 58 (First Quarter 1964):25–32. When *The Journals of Madam Knight, and Rev. Mr. Buckingham* (New York, 1825) were first published, the identities of both the editor and the author were obscured.

(1775–1776)   MOSES BROWN   89

Thompson, Mack E., ed. "Moses Brown's 'Account of Journey to Distribute Donations 12th Month 1775'." *Rhode Island History* 15 (October 1956):97–121.

In the winter of 1775 the New England Friends made their first successful relief expedition in the colonies to the city of Boston, which was suffering from the effects of the American Revolution. The group was led by Moses Brown, whose journal of December 13, 1775, to January 3, 1776, is reproduced here.

(1775–1776)   THOMAS SULLIVAN   90

Bradford, S. Sydney, ed. "The Common British Soldier—From the Journal of Thomas Sullivan, 49th Regiment of Foot." *Maryland Historical Magazine* 62 (September 1967):219–53.

Sullivan relates experiences from February 5, 1775, to April 2, 1776. He describes his enlistment in Cork, Ireland, and his passage to America and includes a list of the soldiers' rations. Although he was not present at the Battle of Bunker Hill (June 17, 1775), he uses official sources to relate the events of that day. Sullivan writes a long passage about Boston; he describes payment of the soldiers and the values of the English and Spanish coinage they received; the increase in British troop strength; ships in Boston Harbor; and military events in Massachusetts for part of 1776. The editor believes this journal to be important because of the small number of extant documents by British enlisted men who fought in the Revolutionary War. The editor also includes a list of other publications from Sullivan's journal.

(1798)   JULIAN URSYN NIEMCEWICZ   91

Budka, Metchie J.E., ed. "A Visit to Harvard College: 1798 From the Diary of Julian Ursyn Niemcewicz." *New England Quarterly* 34 (December 1971):510–14.

In this extract, Niemcewicz describes Harvard College, and observes that the students had too many vacations and wasted up to three months every year. After arriving in the United States in 1797, the Polish poet-patriot spent all but two years in this country before returning to his native country in 1807. (See also items 12 and 111.)

New Hampshire

(1775–1777)   EDWARD PARRY   92

Maguire, James H. "'Elisium and the Wilds': A Loyalist's Account of Experiences in America at the Beginning of the American Revolution." *Historical New Hampshire* 26 (Winter 1971):31–44.

Edward Parry came to America in 1771 as an agent of the Royal Navy and remained loyal to the Crown. Between 1775 and 1777 he was harassed in New Hampshire, imprisoned in Massachusetts, and released only to be again harassed by the Sons of Liberty in New Hampshire. His journal provides a look at how loyalists were treated by committees of safety, as well as other events in New Hampshire and Massachusetts during the first two years of the American Revolution. Parry returned to England in 1777.

(1828)   **THOMAS COLE**   **93**

Campbell, Catherine H., ed. "Two's Company: The Diaries of Thomas Cole and Henry Cheever Pratt on Their Walk through Crawford Notch, 1828." *Historical New Hampshire* 33 (Winter 1978):308–33.

The two painters set out on foot from Concord, Vermont, on October 2, 1828, and after an arduous march through the White Mountains, they parted company at Crawford Notch, New Hampshire, on October 7 or 8.

(1830)   **MARY JANE THOMAS**   **94**

Lacy, Harriet S., ed. "Reminiscences of the White Mountains." *Historical New Hampshire* 28 (Spring 1973):37–52.

Mary Jane Thomas recalls her first trip to the White Mountains in 1830, when the region was still an unspoiled wilderness and travel and accommodations were crude and scarce.

New Jersey

(1634–1968)   **NEW JERSEYMAN**   **95**

Coad, Oral S. "Some Traveler's-Eye Views of the Jerseyman." *Journal of the Rutgers University Library* 35 (June 1972):42–66.

This author believes that New Jersey has not been included on the itineraries of some travelers because it is small and is not dramatically different from its neighboring states. Nevertheless, Coad found in compiling his bibliography, *New Jersey in Travelers Accounts, 1424–1970: A Descriptive Bibliography* (Metuchen, 1972), that many travelers had focused their attention on the character, religion, and social customs of the people. In this article he summarizes the comments chronologically from 1634 to 1968.

(1745–1751)   **THOMAS THOMPSON**   **96**

Shelly, Fred, ed. "'A Letter from New Jersey'; Monmouth County in the Mid-Eighteenth Century." *Proceedings of the New Jersey Historical Society* 74 (October 1956):293–303.

Thomas Thompson spent six years (1745 to 1751) in New Jersey as a missionary for the Society for the Propagation of the Gospel for the Church of England. From that experience he wrote a lengthy letter that was reprinted as a pamphlet. In this portion, Thompson includes several lines about nearly every imaginable phase of life in Monmouth County. For instance, he describes the trees as being so dense that one was likely to become lost traveling on the roads through the forests. He portrays the people as brisk and lively, and he thought the sense of equality among all classes provided a degree of education above that of similar classes in England. He also believed the poor people of the New World lived better than their English counterparts. The few Indians were Christians; the farms did not provide the best of provisions, and the chief food was a maize dish. The beer was bad; religion was divided into many sects; mad dogs were seldom seen; and, although the woods contained a variety of beasts, the people were not afraid of them. Thompson concluded with a page-long description of the rattlesnake.

(1764)   **CARL MAGNUS WRANGEL**   97

Anderson, Carl Magnus, ed. "Pastor Wrangel's Trip to the Shore." *New Jersey History* 87 (Spring 1969):5–31.

Reverend Carl Magnus Wrangel was provost of the Swedish Lutheran congregations in America when he made this ten-day 220-mile trip across New Jersey to Philadelphia and back in October, 1764. In this portion of his diary (October 7 through 16), Wrangel relates the religious services he performed in Swedish communities along the way.

(1775–1777)   **JOSEPH WHITE**   98

White, Joseph. "The Good Soldier White." *American Heritage* 7 (June 1956):74–79.

The author reminisces about wartime experiences in New Jersey between 1775 and 1777, including action at the Battle of Trenton (December, 1776) and the Battle of Princeton (January, 1777). From his *A Narrative of Events as they Occurred From Time to Time in the Revolutionary War . . .* (Charlestown, Massachusetts, 1833).

Shelley, Fred, ed. "Ebenezer Hazard's Diary: New Jersey During the Revolution." *New Jersey History* 90 (Autumn 1972):169–80.

The editor conjectures that Hazard was in New Jersey in his capacity as surveyor of the post roads for the colonies. His diary (August 5–14, 1777) records the effect of the Revolutionary War as he traveled between Trenton, Elizabeth, and Newark. (See also items 288 and 301.)

(1815–1816)   **BARON DE MONTLEZUN**   100

Yeager, Henry J., ed. "By Steamboat Across New Jersey and Back." *New Jersey History* 87 (Summer 1969):105–18.

Baron De Montlezun (Barthælemi Sernin du Moulin de la Barthelle) was an anti-Bonaparte aristocrat who fled France for the New World when Napoleon returned from exile. Using his experiences of three years in the United States and the Caribbean, he wrote two accounts, *Souvenir des Antilles . . .* (Paris, 1818), and *Voyage de New York . . .* (Paris, 1818), from which the New Jersey sections are reprinted here. The first portion of this article relates a trip from New York through New Jersey to Philadelphia in September, 1815, and a return trip from Philadelphia back through New Jersey to New York in October of 1816. He praises the steamboat, on which he traveled, and New Jersey farms, and he describes New Brunswick in some detail. He also noticed attractive ladies and composed an impromptu poem in honor of one brief acquaintance.

(1852)   **KALIKST WOLSKI**   101

Wolski, Kalikst. "A Visit to the North American Phalanx." *Proceedings of the New Jersey Historical Society* 83 (July 1965):149–60.

Kalikst Wolski, a Polish-born Frenchman, visited the agricultural commune at Red Bank, New Jersey, in 1852 at the peak of the establishment's prosperity. He describes the functions of the colony and praises the personal freedom he found there. Translated by Marion Moore Coleman from a Warsaw journal, *Kłosy* (vol. 2, pp. 171–74).

(1913)   **FRED G. STICKEL**   102

Stickel, Fred G. "Through the Morris Canal." *New Jersey History* 89 (Summer 1971):93–114.

Fred G. Stickel was a member of the Morris Canal Commission which toured the old New Jersey waterway to examine its condition and possible uses in July, 1913. The 102-mile trip took them across the state from Jersey City to Port Delaware. Stickel describes the landscape, the cities of Newark, Paterson, Beaverton, and Phillipsburg, as well as the businesses and railroads along the route of the canal.

NEW YORK

(1751)   FRANÇOIS PICQUET   103

Jezierski, John V., ed. and tr. "A 1751 Journal of Abbé François Picquet." *New York Historical Society Quarterly* 54 (October 1970):360–81.

The record of an expedition (June 10 to July 21, 1751) to the Lake Ontario region to gain recruits for the Abbé's mission, and to evaluate the English and French influence among the Six Nations of the Iroquois. These Indians held the balance of power in the Ohio Valley and Great Lakes region. He relates conversations with the Missisaguans and the Senecas and comments on drunkenness among the Indians. He also visited fortifications on Lake Ontario.

(1758)   WILLIAM SWEAT   104

Blanchette, Paul O., ed. "Captain William Sweat's Personal Diary of the Expedition Against Ticonderoga, May 2–November 7, 1758." *Essex Institute Historical Collections* 93 (January 1957):36–57.

Sweat, who was a resident of Newbury, Massachusetts, signed up to fight in the French and Indian War. His diary provides an eyewitness description of backwoods fighting conditions in eighteenth-century New York and an account of the British attack on Fort Ticonderoga.

(1776)   GEORGE COLLIER   105

Tucker, Louis L., ed. "'To My Inexpressible Astonishment': Admiral Sir George Collier's Observations on the Battle of Long Island." *New York Historical Society Quarterly* 48 (October 1964):293–305.

Why Sir William Howe, the supreme commander of British forces, did not pursue the badly beaten American army following the Battle of Long Island in August, 1776, has been widely debated. In his journal, Admiral Sir George Collier also expresses amazement.

(1778)   JOHN BROOKS   106

Blundell, Barbara Adams, ed. "A Revolutionary Letter of John Brooks." *Essex Institute Historical Collections* 112 (April 1976):140–48.

Writing on August 21, 1778, from his encampment at White Plains, Colonel Brooks reveals his support for the American cause and confidence in its ultimate victory. Although pleased with French support, he realistically recognizes the political nature of the act. Brooks ponders future commercial relations between the two countries.

(1779)   MOSES SPROULE   107

Vail, R. W. G., ed. "The Western Campaign of 1779: The Diary of Quartermaster Sergeant Moses Sproule of the Third New Jersey Regiment in the Sullivan Expedition of the Revolutionary War, May 17–October 17, 1779." *New York Historical Society Quarterly* 41 (January 1957):35–69.

Describes the Sullivan-Clinton campaign against the Iroquois Indians, who had been leading war parties against the unprotected farms and poorly garrisoned settlements in eastern Pennsylvania and western New York. The British encouraged the Indian raids as a method of diverting General Washington's military strength. Sproule describes the march from Elizabethtown, New Jersey, north to Easton, Pennsylvania, then on to the shores of Lake Seneca, New York, and then back to New Jersey. He relates such incidents as soldiers being executed for murdering civilians and enticing troops to desert; he describes accidents, illnesses, and skirmishes with the Indians.

(1785–1830) NIAGARA FALLS 108

Anderson, David D. "English Travelers to Niagara, 1785–1830." *New York History* 46 (April 1965):145–61.

Whether English travelers came to the United States for personal edification or profit, a visit to Niagara Falls was usually on their itinerary. In describing the Falls and the places the visitors stopped en route to upstate New York, Anderson says these accounts have left a record of the Great Lakes area during its transition from English to American ownership.

(1790) LOUIS-GUILLAUME OTTO 109

O'Dwyer, Margaret M., ed. "A French Diplomat's View of Congress: 1790." *William and Mary Quarterly. Third Series* 21 (July 1964):408–44.

Louis-Guillaume Otto was chargé d'affaires in the United States for most of 1785 through 1791. These diplomatic dispatches (January 12 through August 12, 1790) report the great interest surrounding the opening sessions of the First Congress under the Constitution. Otto explains that the topics under consideration are the organization of government, the matters of raising an army and finances, and a permanent location for the nation's capital. As he relates the deliberation of these issues, he observed the gap between the Federalists and Anti-Federalists to be widening. He also saw differences along sectional lines that reflected agricultural and commercial interests.

Otto was particularly interested in commercial matters that would affect trade between France and the United States. Another issue that Otto discusses is Congress's relations with the Indians of Georgia. His impressions of American statesmen are brief, but two of the longest are of George Washington, whom Otto holds in high regard, and John Adams, whom he does not.

(1800–1899) NEW YORK STATE 110

Todd, C. Lafayette. "Some Nineteenth Century European Travelers in New York State." *New York History* 43 (October 1962):336–70.

Todd follows the travelers "up the Hudson to Albany and thence to Niagara Falls, with occasional side trips to Saratoga Springs, the Adirondacks and points North and South." (p. 341) He eliminates New York City from his consideration.

(1805) JULIAN URSYN NIEMCEWICZ 111

Budka, Metchie J. E., ed. and tr. "Journey to Niagara, 1805 From the Diary of Julian Ursyn Niemcewicz." *New York Historical Society Quarterly* 44 (January 1960):72–113.

In October, 1805, the Polish patriot-poet traveled from Newark to Niagara Falls on a route the editor has traced on a contemporary map. His diary is filled with details of his travel: the taverns, the inns, and the bills of fare where he stayed; the vegetation and cultivation of the soil; and his visits to towns, Indian lands, and the Niagara region. Niemcewicz does not conceal his democratic spirit. He praises the adventurous nature of the Americans, who, he believed, quickly turned a wilderness into a civilized place. It would not be long, he thought, before the Great Lakes area and the Louisiana Purchase would be populated.

Another aspect of his democratic spirit is obvious as he scorns the extensive retinue in which the governor of New York traveled. Niemcewicz predicts that one day such pomp would be dismissed as fable. A fine piece of travel writing. Niemcewicz came to the United States in 1797 and stayed until 1807, with the exception of two years. (See also items 12 and 91.)

(1806)   HALLIDAY JACKSON   112

Snyderman, George S., ed. "Halliday Jackson's Journal of a Visit Paid to the Indians of New York (1806)." *Proceedings of the American Philosophical Society* 101 (December 1957):565–88.

An account of the visit by a delegation of Quakers in 1806. The editor compares this journal to the one by John Philips (Item 114). Because Philips was a newcomer to Indian ways, his reactions were described colorfully, sometimes at the expense of details. On the other hand, Jackson, who had spent two years working with the Seneca, paid more attention to the problems and progress of the Indians, which was the purpose of the visit. Snyderman believes that when both diaries are utilized, a more complete picture of the trip may be obtained.

(1806)   GOUVERNEUR MORRIS   113

Dill, David B., Jr. "From Cambray to Ogdensburg in 36 Hours with Gouverneur Morris." *The Quarterly; Publication of the St. Lawrence County Historical Association* 21 (April 1976):6–7.

On September 15 and 16, 1806, Morris navigated the Oswegatchie River in northern New York for about seventy miles. Most of the account is concerned with observations about the soil, its drainage, and the potential for agriculture.

(1806)   JOHN PHILIPS   114

Deardorff, Merle H., and Snyderman, George S., eds. "Nineteenth-Century Journal of a Visit to the Indians of New York." *Proceedings of the American Philosophical Society* 100 (December 1956):582–612.

Presents "Some Account of My Journey made to the Indians in the 9th Mo June 1806 by John Philips, Halliday Jackson and Isaac Bonsal." The editors believe Philips's manuscript of a visit by a delegation of Quakers is "a rich source of knowledge regarding life on a Seneca reservation at the beginning of the nineteenth century. . . . The plight of the dispossessed Munsee Delaware is noted in some detail. Rapidly contracting reservations, conflict between the warriors or youth and the chiefs or elders, encroaching whites, and alcoholism are clearly indicated." (p. 582) (See also item 112.)

(1811)   J. B. DUNLOP   115

Wallace, David H., ed. "From the Windows of the Mail Coach: A Scotsman Looks at New York State in 1811." *New York Historical Society Quarterly* 40 (July 1956):264–96.

In 1810 and 1811, J. B. Dunlop visited the northeastern United States, South Carolina, and Georgia, as well as Canada and Cuba. Reproduced here are his impressions of New York gained during two visits from June 24 to July 12 and from August 8 to August 27, 1811. His itinerary of travel was from Philadelphia, to Trenton, to New York City, then up the Hudson River to Albany. He went by mail coach to Niagara Falls, Canada, and back to New York City from Burlington, Vermont, and finally toured eastern New York State. Dunlop mentions something about all the cities he passed through. As the editor points out, occasionally Dunlop's own personality is advertently revealed. For example, his preference for the Federalist party is indicated as he describes the actions of the Democrats and the Federalists after Fourth of July speeches. He says the Democrats spent the rest of the day in taverns, but the Federalists retired to their homes to celebrate in moderation.

Dunlop was dubious about an Independence Day oration in which the speaker denounced in "sacreligious curses and profound epithets . . . all would be enemies of America." (p. 275) His sorrow for the Mohawk Indians was apparent as he saw the Indians in their reduced state celebrate with their former enemies "the independence of lands that they had wrested from them by acts of oppression and injustice." (p. 277) But it was the Shaker community near Albany that aroused his greatest ire. He ridiculed their abstinence from procreation and the religious principles on which the sect was based. (See also items 263 and 306.)

(1814)   JARVIS FRARY HANKS   116

Smith, Lester W., ed. "A Drummer Boy in the War of 1812: The Memoir of Jarvis Frary Hanks." *Niagara Frontier* 7 (Summer 1960):53–62.

Hanks was a 13-year-old boy when he began his service with the Eleventh Regiment of the United States Infantry in 1813. In this portion of his reminiscence he recalls the events of several engagements on the Niagara frontier in 1814—the battles of Chippewa and Lundy's Lane— and the siege of Fort Erie. One specific incident about a soldier being executed for desertion stayed in his memory. Although the soldier had been reprieved, he was made to stand in the execution square to be shot at by a firing squad without bullets. Hanks also remembers how it felt to march into battle playing martial music.

(1814–1815)   JACOB PORTER NORTON   117

Porter, Daniel R., ed. "Jacob Porter Norton, a Yankee on the Niagara Frontier in 1814." *Niagara Frontier* 12 (Summer 1965):51–57.

Norton recorded his opinions about the Niagara frontier in letters and diaries written between October 6, 1814, and June 20, 1815, while serving with the Fourth United States Infantry Regiment during the War of 1812. Most of his correspondence relates military action, but Norton also describes Buffalo as a nest of villains, rogues, rascals, pickpockets, knaves, and extortioners. He opposes the antiwar activities taking place in Boston.

(1815)   GOUVERNEUR MORRIS   118

Dill, David B., Jr. "Gouverneur Morris's 1815 Journey." *The Quarterly; Official Publication of the St. Lawrence Historical Association* 22 (October 1977):17–18; 23.

Morris's journey into the "wilds" of northern New York State during the summer of 1815 took him over a rudimentary network of stage roads and turnpikes. Most of these excerpts from his journals contain entries about the roads and the inns and the conditions of the land.

(1815)   MALTHUS A. WARD   119

Barlow, William, and Powell, David O., eds. "A Physician's Journey Through Western New York and Upper Canada in 1815." *Niagara Frontier* 25 (No. 4, 1978):85–95.

Malthus A. Ward left his home in Vermont because employment for young physicians was scarce in New England. In his first letter during September, 1815, he reports that there was also an overabundance of physicians in western New York. "Doctors are so thick two are obliged to ride on one horse." (p. 86) In the first letter Ward relates travel from Albany to Buffalo. While he liked Buffalo's location, he believed: "Here is the greatest collection of speculators, and extortioners I hope in the United States." (p. 88) His second letter, in November, tells of a trip along the Niagara frontier, including a visit to Fort Erie and the surrounding region, which bore scars of the recent British attacks.

(1815–1823)   JACQUES GÉRARD MILBERT   120

Sherman, Constance D., ed. and tr. "A French Explorer in the Hudson River Valley." *New York Historical Society Quarterly* 45 (July 1961):255–80.

Jacques Gérard Milbert was a French naturalist and artist who collected specimens, painted scenery, and described New York State during his eight-year stay (1815 to 1823) in America. Sherman considers *Itinéraire pittoresque de fleuve Hudson* . . . (Paris, 1828–29) an important document of social history because Milbert's comments and paintings constitute the first record of many of the communities he visited. (See also items 86, 157, and 173.)

(1816)   GEORGE PARISH   121

Lasky, Herbert, ed. "New York State in 1816: The Journal of George Parish." *New York History* 56 (July 1975):264–97.

Parish was a businessman who was en route to Upstate New York to manage his brother's properties. This journal (January 27 to February 29, 1816) relates his travel experiences from Philadelphia to Ogdensburg, New York. Parish uses numerous anecdotes as he describes the mode of travel, the drivers, the roads, the inns, the scenery, the towns (Utica and Albany in detail), and the lands he was to oversee.

(1820–1860)   FOURTH OF JULY   122

Hay, Robert P. "Britons in New York on Brother Jonathan's Birthday." *New York Historical Society Quarterly* 53 (July 1969):273–82.

During the period of this study, 1820 to 1860, the Fourth of July each year was a time for the United States' self-justification for being "the world's only Republic." (p. 282) Hay summarizes the different ways English travelers reacted to the noisy celebrations, which were often expressions of Anglophobia. They observed the fireworks and cannon shots; the drilling of the local militia (which was always compared as second-best to the Briton's own military); the orations that stressed the United States' superiority; and the excessive eating and drinking.

The British wrote conflicting reports on the meaning of the day to Americans. Some thought the merrymaking genuine and the festivities inspirational, while others thought just the opposite. Hay stresses the importance of comparing such favorable or unfavorable remarks with the travelers' overall evaluations of American society.

(1822)   ALPHEUS SHERMAN   123

Schroeder, Peter B., ed. "By Horse and Waggon: The Diary of Alpheus Sherman." *New York History* 37 (October 1956):432–51.

Sherman traveled from New York City to Auburn, New York, by way of Monticello and Ithaca, and returned through Albany and Poughkeepsie between September 28 and October 23, 1822. He kept account of the amounts he spent, and the price and availability of land, the taverns at which he stayed, and the people he visited.

(1822–1828)   ABEL BINGHAM   124

Cumming, John, ed. "A Missionary Among the Senecas: The Journal of Abel Bingham, 1822–1828." *New York History* 60 (April 1979):157–93.

Bingham was in charge of a school and church on the Indian reservation at Tonawanda in western New York. Cumming says that Bingham was not well educated and possibly not a good teacher; he was "a forgotten toiler in the missionary field." (p. 162) His journal does, however, relate the hardships the missionary had to face, as well as the conflict that existed between the Christians and the pagan Indians.

(1824)   SAMUEL HAYNES JENKS   125

Still, Bayrd, ed. "New York City in 1824: A Newly Discovered Description." *New York Historical Society Quarterly* 46 (April 1962):137–69.

Samuel Haynes Jenks was editor of the Nantucket (Massachusetts) *Inquirer*, in which his report of a visit to New York City during the summer and fall of 1824 was originally published. He arrived on the Fourth of July, in time to see "the swarming populace . . . performing all sorts of insurrectionary rites in memory of the act of independence." (p. 144) That same day he attended a banquet at Tammany Hall, where he observed a split among the Tammany Republicans led by the "people's party." (p. 166)

As he evaluates the city's newspapers, he says that six dailies were devoted exclusively to commerce and advertising, and six others were political vehicles. Jenks comments on the city's entertainment facilities. He describes the parks "where half a dozen shrubs are made to grow perpendicularly out of soil harder than marble . . . ; the galleries from "the first European schools down to the indescribable oil-and-ochre flourishes of American barnyard geniuses"; and the Chatham Garden theater, which he praises. (p. 156) Jenks also writes about the many religions to be found in New York City, its schools, arts, and the tumultuous public reception the city afforded the return of the Marquis of Lafayette.

(1826)   ALMIRA HATHAWAY READ   126

Darden, Genevieve M., ed. "A Visit to Saratoga: 1826." *New York History* 50 (July 1969):283–301.

Excerpts from the diary of Almira Hathaway Read, a health seeker who spent two weeks visiting Saratoga Springs in August, 1826. Apparently her condition was not improved by the waters.

(1830)   HENRY SINGER KEATING   127

Posner, Russell M. "An Englishman's Tour of New York in 1830." *New York Historical Society Quarterly* 55 (April 1971):177–84.

Before Sir Henry Singer Keating became a famous judge, he visited the northeastern United States and Canada during the fall and winter of 1830–1831. This portion of his journal describes a trip from New York City up the Hudson River to Albany, and then overland through Schenectady and Buffalo. He was impressed by the equality of the social classes and surprised at how well-informed the lower classes were. He observed excessive tobacco spitting, meals served and eaten too quickly, and Americans' anxiety that strangers express approval of their country. (See also item 159.)

(1832)   "HIRAETHION"   128

Berthoff, Rowland T., ed. and tr. "'Life in America': A Disillusioned Welshman in New York." *New York History* 37 (January 1956):80–84.

In a letter that appeared in the Welsh language newspaper *Cymro America* (New York) in 1832, "Hiraethion" expressed his disappointment at not finding America the new Canaan. Everything was too expensive, the land was poor, workmanship was of poor quality; America was in danger of being filled with Negroes and Irishmen, and it was becoming a haven for English thieves. Although he does not describe the geographical focus of his complaints, the editor points out that there were Welsh settlements in Oneida County, New York, and Cambria County, Pennsylvania.

(1833)   GEORGE WASHINGTON JOHNSON   129

Winner, Julia Hull, ed. "A Journey Across New York State in 1833 as Recounted in His Manuscript Journals, by George Washington Johnson." *New York History* 46 (January 1965):60–78.

Johnson made this journey from Buffalo to New York City in April and May, 1833, to attend a session of the American Lyceum. His journal includes many comments about the conditions of travel, fellow travelers, and incidents along the way. For instance, he "dogged" a noted anti-Mason publisher into a tobacco store and bought some tobacco he did not want just so he could get a close look at the man. He rented a fishing pole from some boys and then proceeded to give them "sundry gratis instructions piscatory." (p. 63) He comments on many towns but offers longer passages on Batavia, Leroy, the state prison at Auburn, and New York City, where he met Aaron Burr. Johnson traveled by stage and packet-boat.

(1837–1839)   SAMUEL J. PARKER   130

Bishop, Morris, ed. "The Journeys of Samuel J. Parker." *New York History* 45 (April 1964):135–50.

Reminiscences of journeys around New York State between 1837 and 1839. Contains "By Stage, Railroad, and Steamer, Ithaca to New York, 1837"; "By Stage, Ithaca to Catskill, 1838"; and "By Stage and Packet-boat, Cayuga to Utica, 1839."

(1840)   LUDVIG MAGNUS HJERTSTEDT   131

Olsson, Nils William, ed. "The Hjertstedt Notes on America in 1840." *Swedish Pioneer History Quarterly* 14 (October 1963):151–62.

Reprints sections from the journal kept by a young Swedish naval officer, Ludvig Magnus Hjertstedt, during his ship's stop in New York Harbor. He visited the churches and museums of New York City and made a trip to Philadelphia. His general impression of American life was favorable, and he placed the physical appearance of American women before those of any other country. He disapproved of slavery and thought the Seminole War in Florida was unjust to the Indians.

(1843)   PERCY R. PYNE   132

Pyne, Percy R. "The 'Grand Tour' to Niagara in 1843; A Diary by Percy R. Pyne." *New York Historical Society Quarterly* 46 (October 1962):383–421.

Pyne's diary (July 3 through 15, 1843) tells of a steamboat ride up the Hudson River to Albany and one of the earliest railroad trips to Niagara Falls. He mentions Albany, Troy, Schenectady, Trenton Falls, Buffalo, Oswego, and Syracuse and provides a lengthy description of the region around Niagara Falls.

(1846)   MINERVA PADDEN   133

White, Philip L., ed. "An Irish Immigrant Housewife on the New York Frontier." *New York History* 48 (April 1967):182–88.

After summarizing the problems of land ownership on New York's frontier, the editor includes three letters written by Minerva Padden in 1846 to the son of a former employer that relate her family's difficulties in attempting to purchase land in Hannibal Township (Oswego County), New York. The son, James W. Beckman, was glad to assist the family financially, but there is no existing biographical evidence that reveals the Paddens' success in establishing themselves as landowners.

(1846)   **ANDREW D. J. PIRET**   **134**

Praus, Alexis A., ed. "Father Piret Lands in New York, 1846." *Mid-America* 37 (October 1955):229–35.

On his way to Michigan's Upper Peninsula to minister to the needs of the Indians, Father Andrew D. J. Piret, a Belgian missionary, kept a journal that describes a trip up the Hudson River from New York to Albany.

(1850s)   **NEW YORK CITY HOTELS**   **135**

Steen, Ivan. "Palaces For Travelers: New York City's Hotels in the 1850's As Viewed by British Visitors." *New York History* 51 (April 1970):269–86.

In the mid-eighteenth century most visitors to the United States disembarked at New York City. Their first impression was likely of the swarm of porters and the hotels they represented. Because the hotels were lavish and catered to the travelers' every need, they were usually among the city's principal attractions.

(1857)   **ANONYMOUS**   **136**

Cameron, Kenneth M. "Going Heavy in the Great North Woods." *Adirondack Life* 4 (Spring 1973):9–11, 38–39.

Cameron uses an anonymous manuscript, "Jottings Down by one of Our Fishing Party," to recapture the character of a city-dweller who confronted the Adirondacks in 1857. From the list of supplies that included many amenities not essential to survival, "¼ box segars, ½ doz. best brandy," and his dependence on a guide to perform all the physical labors, it is obvious that the adventurer met the wilderness on his own terms. (p. 9)

(1860)   **ZOÉ CAMPBELL**   **137**

Doyle, Elizabeth Joan, ed. "Zoé Campbell: A Southern Lady Travels North in 1860." *Louisiana Studies* 13 (Winter 1974):313–44.

This New Orleans lady kept track of her well-to-do group's activities while on a 77-day "Grand Tour" (July 1 to October 10, 1860). They visited Niagara Falls and New York City, but the diary never goes beyond mundane reactions.

(1881)   **GEORGE M. PRICE**   **138**

Shpall, Leo, tr. "The Memoir of Doctor George M. Price." *Publications of the American Jewish Historical Society* 47 (December 1957):101–10.

Dr. Price, a Russian Jewish immigrant, relates what befell him soon after his arrival in New York City in 1881. He describes the poor conditions for immigrants at Castle Garden and Ward's Island, and the inability of the Hebrew Emigrant Aid Society to cope with the immigrants' problems.

(1898)   **VIRGINIA D. YOUNG**   **139**

Marszalek, John F., ed. "A South Carolinian's 1898 Impressions of Buffalo and the Niagara Frontier." *Niagara Frontier* 23 (Spring 1976):22–28.

This letter, written by Virginia D. Young, appeared in the *Charleston News and Courier* on August 14, 1898, and provides a glimpse of Buffalo and its cemetery, an excursion on Lake Erie, and a visit to Toronto, Canada.

(1960s)   **FESTUS MKUNI**   **140**

Tripp, Wendell, ed. "Some Letters of Festus Mkuni." *New York History* 48 (January 1967):54–90.

The author is a native of Zambia who wrote to friends and fellow students about what he observed of American customs and institutions early in the 1960s while a student at Hobart College. He tells about not being accepted by either blacks or whites. He describes his impressions of American sports, our version of liberty, equality of the sexes, food, civil rights, and politics. He says some of his letters made him unpopular.

PENNSYLVANIA

(1722)   **AMBROSE BARCROFT**   **141**

Hancock, Harold B., ed. "Life in Bucks County in 1722/23." *Pennsylvania History* 27 (October 1960):397–402.

Ambrose Barcroft, who had immigrated from England to Pennsylvania in 1722, wrote this letter relating the problems he faced as a frontier farmer. He describes the arduous labors involved in clearing the land, planting the crops, and constructing homes.

(1750–1850)   **PENNSYLVANIA GERMANS**   **142**

Roth, Julia. "Travel Journals As a Folklife Research Tool: Impressions of the Pennsylvania Germans." *Pennsylvania Folklife* 31 (Summer 1972):28–38.

Roth characterizes the impressions of eighteenth- and nineteenth-century observers of the Pennsylvania Germans by saying, "they show a tremendous capacity for getting things wrong and an instinct for automatic praise or censure depending on their preconceptions." (p. 28) She maintains, however, that travel accounts are important to folklore study because they show the life and ways of the Pennsylvania Germans.

(1755)   **HARRY GORDON**   **143**

Stotz, Charles M., ed. "A Letter from Will's Creek: Harry Gordon's Account of Braddock's Defeat." *Western Pennsylvania Historical Magazine* 44 (June 1961):129–36.

On July 9, 1755, Gordon, an uncommissioned engineer with the British army, wrote this eyewitness account of General Braddock's defeat only a few miles from his goal, the French Fort Duquesne.

(1755–1760)   **JAMES SMITH**   **144**

Smith, James. "The Saga of James Smith." (Part I) *American History Illustrated* 5 (July 1970):34–41.

———. (Part II) *American History Illustrated* 5 (August 1970):36–42.

———. (Part III) *American History Illustrated* 5 (October 1970):34–41.

Smith was captured and adopted by the Mohawk Indians during the French and Indian War. This journal describes his captivity in Pennsylvania and Ohio between 1755 and 1760. From *An Account of the Remarkable Occurances in the Life and Travels of Col. James Smith* (Lexington, Kentucky, 1799). *Note*: Another article about Smith's experiences, together with a bibliography of subsequent printings of his account, is Willard Rouse Jillson, "Narrative of a Caughnawaga Captive: A Glimpse of Ohio Under the French Flag, 1755–1760," *Filson Club History Quarterly* 37 (July 1963):201–09.

(1761) **JOHN BARTRAM** **145**

West, Francis D. "John Bartram's Journey to Pittsburgh in the Fall of 1761." *Western Pennsylvania Historical Magazine* 38 (Fall/Winter 1955):111–15.

Although the journal that botanist John Bartram kept of this trip has completely disappeared, the editor pieces together Bartram's experiences from his letters and the journal of James Kenny, who accompanied Bartram. The trip down the Ohio and Monongahela rivers took ten days (September 14–23, 1761).

(1764) **HENRY BOUQUET** **146**

Williams, Edward G., ed. "Orderly Book I of Colonel Henry Bouquet's Expedition Against the Ohio Indians, 1764 (Carlisle to Fort Pitt)." (Part I) *Western Pennsylvania Historical Magazine* 56 (July 1973):281–316.

————. (Part II) *Western Pennsylvania Historical Magazine* 56 (October 1973):383–428.

————. (Part III) *Western Pennsylvania Historical Magazine* 57 (January 1974):51–106.

This first segment of the orderly book describes the march from Carlisle to Fort Pitt between January 7 and October 1, 1764. (See also item 535.)

(1777) **ANONYMOUS** **147**

Echeverria, Durand, ed. "The American Character: A Frenchman Views the New Republic from Philadelphia, 1777." *William and Mary Quarterly. Third Series* 16 (July 1959):376–413.

This unknown Frenchman, who visited Philadelphia for six weeks in 1777, was a firm believer in liberty and he saw much in Philadelphia that he admired. He describes the city's churches and religion (the Quakers most unfavorably), the origins of those who had immigrated to America, the energy of the Americans which he felt had made the country prosper, and the benefits of educating everyone in a democracy. He expresses regret at the bad impressions left by some French travelers which he believed made Americans wary of all Frenchmen.

(1777) **SAMUEL VAUGHAN** **148**

Williams, Edward G., ed. "Samuel Vaughan's Journal: Or 'Minutes Made by S. V., from Stage to Stage, on a Tour to Fort Pitt'." (Part I) *Western Pennsylvania Historical Magazine* 44 (March 1961):51–65.

————. (Part II) *Western Pennsylvania Historical Magazine* 44 (June 1961):159–67.

————. (Part III) *Western Pennsylvania Historical Magazine* 44 (September 1961):261–85.

This English merchant, who recently settled in America, traveled west from Carlisle, Pennsylvania to Pittsburgh, and then east to Fort Cumberland (Maryland), and on to Fredericksburg, Richmond, and Mount Vernon, Virginia. The entire trip of 1,070 miles was taken between June 18 and July (?), 1777. The editor believes the journal is noteworthy because Vaughan describes the route of the Forbes Road and its successor, the Pennsylvania Road, as well as the Braddock Road, which Williams has traced on a modern map. Vaughan's minutes make brief references to the occupations, religion, and appearance of the people, as well as to the buildings and condition of the roads. He also comments on such places of historical importance as George Washington's home.

(1778–1779)   WILLIAM VAN HORNE   149

Van Horne, William E., ed. "Revolutionary War Letters of the Reverend William Van Horne." *Western Pennsylvania Historical Magazine* 53 (April 1970):105–38.

Reverend Van Horne served as a chaplain to the Continental forces between March 4, 1778, and October 27, 1779. His letters are written from Pennsylvania, New York, and Rhode Island. Though they mostly describe military events, Van Horne (and the editor) comment on the disastrous effects of inflation during the war.

(1786)   ALEXANDER MCCLEAN   150

Murphy, James L., ed. "Alexander McClean's Journal of the 1786 Survey of the Western Boundary of Pennsylvania: Volume 2." *Western Pennsylvania Historical Magazine* 63 (October 1980):321–43.

Reproduces the extant volumes of a boundary survey from near Sharon, Pennsylvania, northward to Lake Erie. Except for several vague references to Indians of the area, the journal is totally concerned with the monotonous process of clearing the vista through more than ninety miles of virgin timber and boggy land. This portion covers August 18 to October 6, 1786.

(1787–1788)   MARY DEWEES   151

Blair, John L., ed. "Mrs. Mary Dewees's Journal from Philadelphia to Kentucky." *Register of the Kentucky Historical Society* 63 (July 1965):195–217.

Records a pioneer family's travel in the trans-Allegheny region in 1787 and 1788. After leaving Philadelphia they crossed Pennsylvania on the turnpike, stopping briefly at Lancaster. They went to Pittsburgh by ferry where they paused and waited for the water to rise so they could cross the river before traveling on to Lexington, Kentucky. Mrs. Dewees comments on the roughness of the roads, the weather, the food eaten, Revolutionary War sites, her fear of Indians, the forts and settlements, and the hospitable but poor and dirty mountain people she met. The date of the diary was either September 27, 1787, to February 11, 1788, or those same dates of the following year. See editor's notes, pp. 216–17.

(1790s)   FRENCH AND ENGLISH TRAVELERS   152

Robbins, Caroline. "The Rage for Going to America." *Pennsylvania History* 28 (July 1961):231–53.

Discusses the travel writings left by the French and English who visited Pennsylvania in the 1790s. The traditional incentives for coming to the United States during the last years of the eighteenth century were reinforced by the urgency for Frenchmen to escape from the Revolution and for Englishmen to avoid the controversies it entailed. Because Pennsylvania was a favored asylum, the travelers left many accounts of the landscape, the travel accommodations, the climate, the blacks, and the Indians. Although some travelers were disappointed with Pennsylvania, most saw the state as a fertile land in which many classes could enjoy a good life.

(1793–1794)   JOHN BADOLLET   153

Hunter, William A., ed. "John Badollet's 'Journal of the Time I Spent in Stony Creek Glades,' 1793–1794." *Pennsylvania Magazine of History and Biography* 104 (April 1980):162–99.

The author, who was born in Switzerland as Jean Louis Badollet, records his survey of a portion of the Spiker's-Cherry's mill road in Somerset County, Pennsylvania, between October 24 and December 9, 1793. Much of his writing is concerned with the rigors involved in working through unbroken forest against the rapidly approaching winter. He also had to contend with the pressure applied by local residents to have the road run near their property. Badollet relates his experiences with wildlife, the varying quality of food, and the inhabitants of the region. Particularly interesting are his descriptions of the poverty and the wretched homes of some who lived in the wilderness. He was, however, extremely impressed with the German communities whose farms reminded him of Switzerland.

(1794) **JAMES EMLEN** **154**

Fenton, William N., ed. "The Journal of James Emlen Kept on a Trip to Canandaigua, New York, September 15 to October 30, 1794 to Attend the Treaty Between the United States and the Six Nations." *Ethnohistory* 12 (Fall 1965):279–342.

At President Washington's request, James Emlen, of the Society of Friends of Philadelphia, attended the treaty signing. The horseback journey took Emlen's party through the rugged and sparsely populated country of eastern Pennsylvania and western New York.

(1794) **JACOB EVERLY** **155**

Wallace, Paul A.W., ed. and tr. "Jacob Everly's Journal, 1794: The Survey of Moravian Lands in the Erie Triangle." *Western Pennsylvania Historical Magazine* 45 (March 1962):5–23.

Everly's task was to survey the lands given by the state of Pennsylvania to the Moravians for the purpose of establishing a mission for the Indians. His journal (May 23-June 30, 1794) provides information about the survey, the landscape, and the drunkenness of the Seneca Indians.

(1811) **JOHN WATSON, JR.** **156**

Smith, Dwight L., and Smith, S. Winifred, eds. "The Journey of a Pennsylvania Quaker to Pioneer Ohio." (Part I) *Cincinnati Historical Society Bulletin* 36 (January 1968):3–40.

————. (Part II) *Cincinnati Historical Society Bulletin* 26 (April 1968):174–210.

The diary of John Watson, Jr., records a journey by horseback and riverboat from Bucks County, Pennsylvania, to Miami County, Ohio, and back again. Watson comments on agriculture in the areas he passed through, the people he met, and the state of public transportation. He also provides an itinerary of travel the editors have traced on contemporary maps. The entries run from April 29 to August 7, 1811.

(1819) **JACQUES GÉRARD MILBERT** **157**

Sherman, Constance D., ed. and tr. "A French Artist Describes Philadelphia." *Pennsylvania Magazine of History and Biography* 82 (April 1958):204–16.

Jacques Gérard Milbert, the French artist and explorer, traveled throughout New England and as far south as Virginia between 1815 and 1823. He came to Philadelphia in 1819 and praised the city's physical layout as well as its social and intellectual institutions. Translated from Milbert's *Itinéraire pittoresque du fleuve Hudson* . . . (Paris, 1828–29). (See also items 86, 120, and 173.)

(1819–1820) **MATHIAS HUTCHINSON** **158**

Ryan, Pat M., ed. "Mathias Hutchinson's Notes of a Journey (1819–20)." (Part I) *Quaker History* 68 (Autumn 1979):92–114.

————. (Part II) *Quaker History* 69 (Spring 1980):36–52.

The journey took Hutchinson through central Pennsylvania, Upstate New York, and into Friends' settlements in Ontario, Canada. It covered 1,940 miles, was made on horseback, and took place from September 6, 1819, to January 3, 1820. Contains descriptions of soil, landscape, crops, land prices, climate, and local commerce, as well as the destruction left by the War of 1812 in New York State. Also provides insights into internal discord among the Quakers.

(1830)   HENRY SINGER KEATING   159

Posner, Russell M. "Philadelphia in 1830: An English View." *Pennsylvania Magazine of History and Biography* 95 (April 1971):239–43.

Before Sir Henry Singer Keating became a renowned jurist, he visited New York, New England, and as far south as Washington, D.C. Three weeks of his four-month stay (August 28, 1830, to January 1, 1831) were spent in Philadelphia. Posner says that his journal was written "frankly and sometimes humorously" and that his remarks do not praise Philadelphia as much as other contemporary accounts. (p. 239) (See also item 127.)

(1831)   ALEXANDER FARKAS   160

Hitchins, Keith, ed. "The Visit of Alexander Farkas of Bolon to Pennsylvania in 1831." *Pennsylvania History* 34 (October 1967):395–401.

Farkas toured the Northeast for three months in 1831 (September 3-November 23) looking for social and economic reforms that might improve his native Transylvania. This portion of his journal (*Utazás Észak-Amerikában*. Kolozsvar, 1834) praises institutions and conditions in Pennsylvania. In Erie, he approved of the variety of religious sects and the people who attended church without being forced. He believed that the location of Pittsburgh was desirable for a manufacturing city. Farkas thought Philadelphia was beautiful and different from most other American cities because business and politics did not monopolize the city's interests to the exclusion of philanthropic and intellectual institutions.

(1836)   PHILO E. THOMPSON   161

Tarr, Joel A., ed. "Philo E. Thompson's Diary of a Journey on the Main Line Canal." *Pennsylvania History* 32 (July 1965):295–304.

Although a portion of Thompson's travels was over the Pennsylvania Main Line Canal, this diary (March 28-April 23, 1836) covers the complete journey of 2,200 miles from Ellington, Connecticut, to Payson, Illinois. The editor points out that Thompson's account contains greater technical detail about the Canal than does Charles Dickens's *American Notes*, in which the English novelist described his trip in 1842. After Thompson left the canal at Pittsburgh, he completed the trip on the Ohio and Mississippi rivers.

(1840)   LOUIS RICHARD CORTAMBERT   162

Cortambert, Louis Richard. "The Colony of Economy and the Harmonist Sect." *Bulletin of the Missouri Historical Society* 28 (October 1971):41–46.

After a few brief, critical remarks about the Quakers, this French traveler praises the establishment he found at Economy, Pennsylvania, in 1840. Cortambert describes the sect and the schism that had developed.

(1842)   CHARLES DICKENS   163

Altman, Gail Platt. "Dickens's Journey to Pittsburgh on the Pennsylvania Canal." *Western Pennsylvania Historical Magazine* 59 (July 1976):370–73.

The transportation system from Philadelphia to Erie consisted of 118 miles of railroad, 28 miles of Ohio River, and 397 miles of canal. Quotations from Charles Dickens's *American Notes* (Paris, 1842) are used to describe his reactions to canal travel. (See also items 48 and 164.)

(1842) 164

Hollinshead, Marilyn P. "Dickens in Pittsburgh: A Stereoscopic View." *Dickensian* 74 (January 1978):33–41.

Despite a satiric comment about Pittsburgh in *American Notes* (London, n.d.), Dickens's activities and other comments regarding the city indicate he enjoyed his surroundings during his three-day visit in March, 1842. Hollinshead consulted *American Notes* and Dickens's published letters. (See also items 48 and 163.)

(1846–1850) **HENRI HERZ** 165

Hill, Henry Bertram, and Gara, Larry, eds. "Henri Herz' Description of the American Quakers." *Bulletin of Friends Historical Association* 46 (Autumn 1957):111–14.

Although the editors believe Herz's account of the Quakers was based on little firsthand observation (he said he visited churches in New York) and contains false information, they believe it is representative of French thought about the Quakers in the mid-1800s. Herz was a French musician who toured the United States between 1846 and 1850. This excerpt is taken from *Mes voyages en Amérique* (Paris, 1866). (See also items 52, 53, 281, and 410.)

(1849) **THEODOR FLIEDNER** 166

Fliedner, Theodor. "Journey to North America." (Part I) *Concordia Historical Institute Quarterly* 44 (November 1971):147–56.

————. (Part II) *Concordia Historical Institute Quarterly* 45 (February 1972):31–41.

Contains extracts from the letters written during the German theologian's visit to Pennsylvania in 1849. The purpose of his trip was to escort four Lutheran deaconesses to serve in a hospital in Pittsburgh. Fliedner visited a theological seminary of the German Reformed Church in Mercersburg, a Lutheran seminary in Gettysburg, as well as orphanages, girls' and boys' schools, and a prison, which the editor identifies as the Western Pennsylvania Penitentiary at Pittsburgh. Translated by Bertha Mueller and edited by Frederick S. Weiser.

(1850s) **PHILADELPHIA** 167

Steen, Ivan D. "Philadelphia in the 1850's as Described by British Travelers." *Pennsylvania History* 33 (January 1966):30–49.

British travelers were impressed with Philadelphia. They commented favorably on the city's hotels, which were regarded as tourist attractions as well as lavish resting places; the streets were straight and lined with monotonous but not unattractive brick houses; the public buildings were beautiful; and the public schools, the homes for the mentally deficient, and the prisons were progressive. Steen believes that British travelers felt more at home in clean, quiet Philadelphia than in New York or the western cities they visited.

(1856) **THOMAS ELKINTON** 168

Elkinton, Thomas. "To Ohio One Hundred Years Ago: Excerpts From the Journal of Thomas Elkinton." *Bulletin of Friends Historical Association* 47 (Spring 1958):38–45.

Records the vicissitudes of rail travel in August and September of 1856 encountered by a Philadelphia family en route to Somerton, Ohio, for a wedding.

(1869) **ALFRED PARSONS** 169

Stotz, Charles Morse, ed. "Alfred Parsons' Diary: A Boating Holiday." *Western Pennsylvania Historical Magazine* 43 (December 1960):349–65.

An account of a 300-mile row in August, 1869 that took Parsons and seven others from Pittsburgh west on the Ohio River, north and east up the Beaver River, and then back south on the Allegheny River. The editor says this is an important document because it serves to remind us of the onetime popularity of rowing and of the canal system that existed a century ago. Stotz provides a brief history of the demise of the sport of rowing around Pittsburgh.

(1873–1874) FRIEDRICH RATZEL 170

Stehlin, Stewart A., ed. and tr. "Philadelphia on the Eve of the Nation's Centennial: A Visitor's Description in 1873–74." *Pennsylvania History* 44 (January 1977):25–36.

Friedrich Ratzel, the German geographer and anthropologist, was in the United States to write a series of articles for the *Kölnische Zeitung* about life in America. Here, Ratzel describes the physical design of Philadelphia in the winter of 1873–74 and plans for the nation's centennial celebration. From Ratzel's *Städte und culturbilder aus Nordamerika* (Leipzig, 1876). (See also items 64 and 225.)

RHODE ISLAND

(1780–1781) ALEXANDRE BERTHIER 171

Morgan, Marshall, tr. "Alexandre Berthier's Journal of the American Campaign: The Rhode Island Sections." *Rhode Island History* 24 (July 1965):77–88.

A French captain writes about the progress of the American Revolution. There is an interesting description of the women of Newport. He is surprised at the freedom afforded girls by their parents, especially with regard to the practice of "bundling." Kept between October 4, 1780 and June 22, 1781.

(1785–1787) LUIGI CASTIGLIONI 172

Hough, Samuel, tr. "Castiglioni's Visit to Rhode Island." *Rhode Island History* 26 (April 1967):53–64.

Count Luigi Castiglioni of Milan made a two-year tour of the eastern and southern portions of the United States and Canada between 1785 and 1787. His observations were recorded in *Viaggio negli Stati Uniti dell'America Settentrionale, fatto anni, 1785, 1786, e 1787 . . .* (Milan, 1790). Translated here are portions on Rhode Island. Hough believes the Count's work is as full of information as any account written by a foreigner during the late eighteenth century.

(1815–1823) JACQUES GÉRARD MILBERT 173

Sherman, Constance D., ed. and tr. "The Isle of Rhodes: A French Vignette." *Rhode Island History* 17 (July 1958):65–72.

Between 1815 and 1823, French artist Jacques Gérard Milbert traveled through New England, on to Canada, and as far south as Virginia. Reproduced here are his descriptions of Pawtucket, Providence, and Newport as excerpted from his *Itinéraire pittoresque du fleuve Hudson . . .* (Paris, 1828–29). (See also items 86, 120, and 157.)

(1864) JAMES GRAHAM GOODENOUGH 174

Merli, Frank J., ed. "The Navy at Newport: A British View, 1864." *Rhode Island History* 25 (October 1966):110–16.

Because British foreign office officials thought the recent growth of the American navy might make it a formidable foe of their own maritime interests, it dispatched Captain James

Graham Goodenough of the Royal Navy on a fact-finding mission in late 1863. The portion of his report here concerns the Naval Academy, which had been moved from Annapolis because of its proximity to Confederate forces. Goodenough describes the college and offers the assessment that the academy added useful officers to the American navy.

VERMONT

(1774–1780)   JONATHAN CARPENTER   175

Alexander, John K., ed. "Jonathan Carpenter and the American Revolution: The Journal of an American Naval Prisoner of War and Vermont Indian Fighter." *Vermont History* 36 (Spring 1968):74–90.

Carpenter was aboard an American privateer that was captured by a more heavily armed British vessel. He was shuttled from ship to ship and treated so badly that he says he was glad to be convicted of piracy and placed in an English prison. He tells of escapes and attempted escape plans and of rumors of exchange. After a year and a half of imprisonment he was exchanged in France. Carpenter then went to Vermont to make his fortune, but ended up fighting Indians and their British allies. Journal kept September 27, 1774, to November 15, 1780.

(1776)   PASCAL DE ANGELIS   176

Snyder, Charles M. "With Benedict Arnold at Valcour Island: The Diary of Pascal De Angelis." *Vermont History* 42 (Summer 1974):195–200.

The diary of De Angelis, a 13-year-old American seaman, describes the delaying action that thwarted the British fleet on Lake Champlain in October, 1776. Snyder says that the recently discovered diary poses a question for historians regarding the generally accepted timing of events of the action.

(1778)   ANONYMOUS   177

Murdock, Richard K., ed. "A French Report on Vermont (October) 1778." *Vermont History* 34 (October 1966):217–25.

In anticipation of entering the American Revolution, the French Minister of Foreign Affairs commissioned a series of reports to investigate conditions and events in the colonies. This report summarizes Vermont's history, its problems with the British Crown and New York State, and Vermont's decision to join the colonies in the rebellion.

(1780–1840)   CHAMPLAIN VALLEY   178

Everest, Allan S. "Early Roads and Taverns of the Champlain Valley." *Vermont History* 37 (Autumn 1969):247–55.

The period between 1780 and 1840 saw a marked improvement of the roads in Vermont, with travel and regular stagecoach arrivals and departures increasing. At the beginning of the period travelers complained that the roads were only paths through the wilderness. For food and rest they often had to rely on the already taxed lodgings of poor and overcrowded frontier families. As toll roads were constructed by landowners for profit, conditions improved and taverns sprung up along the clay roads. When municipalities assumed management of the roads, travel improved even more. Nevertheless, as inconvenient as travel in Vermont was during this early period, Everest believes it was comparable to that in other states. The author uses travel accounts to document this improvement.

(1796)   **ANTHONY HASWELL**   **179**

Wood, Virginia Steele, ed. "From Bennington to New York City in 1796: The Journal of Anthony Haswell." *Vermont History* 42 (Fall 1974):287–95.

    Haswell's journal of his trip (June 9-July 5, 1796) reveals his business transactions and the inconveniences of travel during that era.

(1819)   **LEVI WOODBURY**   **180**

Fant, H. B., ed. "Levi Woodbury's Week in Vermont, May 1819." *Vermont History* 34 (January 1966):36–62.

    Between terms of his New Hampshire court, Justice Woodbury took a trip in a one-horse chaise across Vermont and back. His diary (May 11–19, 1819) describes the countryside and the appearance and industries of Middlebury, Rutland, Burlington, Montpelier, Springfield, and Saint Johnsbury. His comments include references to the dress of the people, a ball he attended, complaints to a landlord about noise and the lack of heat, the repetitious diet at taverns, and clay roads that were either too muddy or too hard.

(1832)   **A. B. BANCROFT**   **181**

Bancroft, A. B. "A Traveller's Account of Bellows Falls and Burlington in 1832." *Vermont History* 36 (Autumn 1968):210–13.

    A letter dated September 8, 1832, praises the natural beauty surrounding Bellows Falls and the physical layout of the college at Burlington.

(1840–1900)   **VERMONT**   **182**

Baker, William J. "English Travelers and the Image of Vermont in Victorian England." *Vermont History* 42 (Summer 1974):204–13.

    Although few of the many British travelers who came to the northeastern United States visited Vermont, Baker believes the writings of those who did served to correct two impressions of the region. First, not all of New England was cosmopolitan like Boston, nor were all of its cities industrial and immigrant-filled like Lowell or Fall River. Second, not everyone fit into the travelers' stereotype that Americans were simple and open, overly sensitive to criticism, and conformist. Vermonters were described as shrewd, tough-skinned, and independent.

(1848)   **"BUCKEYE"**   **183**

Broderick, Warren F., ed. "'The Mountains and the Clouds Are in Close Communion': A Traveler's Description of Three Hill Towns in Windham County, Vermont, in 1848." *Vermont History* 38 (Summer 1970):189–91.

    A visitor to Jamaica, Windham, and Londonderry explains that Yankees of these towns managed to survive in a "starving location for a crow" by "skinning" travelers. (p. 190) He also comments on the local opposition toward the war with Mexico. An article from the Lansingburgh (New York) *Gazette* (March 24, 1848) by "Buckeye."

(1864)   **WINCKWORTH ALLEN GAY**   **184**

Mathews, Marcia M., ed. "An Artist Describes His Visit to Mt. Mansfield in 1864." *Vermont History* 39 (Winter 1971):51–54.

    The editor explains that the climax of most visits to Stowe, Vermont, was the ascent of Mount Mansfield. In his letter of July 17, 1864, Winckworth Allen Gay, a prominent New England painter, describes climbing the mountain and the pageant of vacationers to be found at the new Mount Mansfield Hotel.

(1882) **BRADFORD S. CONGDON** **185**

Carter, Joseph C., ed. "Trip to Clarendon Spa: July 4, 1882." *Vermont History* 48 (Fall 1980):239–44.

Ignoring protests by his wife and two children, Bradford S. Congdon of Danby, Vermont, visited his boyhood home in nearby Clarendon Springs, where he had not been in twenty years. Although he was disappointed by how the farm had deteriorated, he renewed some old acquaintances along the way.

(1895–1896) **JOHN G. BOURKE** **186**

Buechler, John, ed. "Two Excursions on Lake Champlain in the 1890's: Excerpts from the Diaries of Captain John G. Bourke." *Vermont History* 39 (Winter 1971):62–71.

A description of a boat ride from Burlington to Vergennes, Vermont, in June, 1895, and a sleigh ride across the frozen lake to Plattsburgh, New York, in February, 1896.

3

South

GENERAL

(1734–1865)   **GERMAN TRAVELERS**   **187**

Thompson, Lawrence S. "German Travellers in the South Through 1865." *South Atlantic Bulletin* 36 (May 1972):64–74.

A bibliography of sixty-one accounts left by Germans who traveled in the South between 1734 and 1865. In his introduction Thompson says that one of the main purposes for writing was to inform prospective immigrants about conditions in America. Texas, Missouri, Kentucky, and Tennessee were most strongly recommended for German settlement. He says that the Germans were not sightseers, except in New Orleans, and that they wrote little about southern literature and the arts. The German visitors did focus attention on slavery and, although they condemned the peculiar institution, Thompson believes that they examined the situation objectively and intelligently.

(1775–1850)   **SOUTHERN HOSPITALITY**   **188**

Yoder, Paton. "Private Hospitality in the South, 1775–1850." *Mississippi Valley Historical Review* 47 (December 1960):419–33.

The reputation that southern and frontier homes have long had as havens for wayfarers is an accepted generalization that was derived from early literary tradition and selected travelers' experiences. Yet as Yoder reviews specific accounts, he concludes that as often as not travelers were forced to pay for their lodging if they were not turned away completely.

(1819–1862)   **TRAVEL IN THE SOUTH**   **189**

Shingleton, Royce Gordon. "Stages, Steamers, and Stations in the Ante-Bellum South: A British View." *Georgia Historical Quarterly* 56 (Summer 1972):243–58.

Shingleton summarizes British travelers' comments regarding conditions of travel on the "Grand Tour" of the South between 1819 and 1862. The route began at Washington and continued by stage (later rail) and steamboat through Virginia and North Carolina to Wilmington. A steamboat took the travelers to Charleston, then directly to Montgomery, Alabama, although some first went to Savannah. The "Grand Tour" was then accomplished by steamboat down the Alabama River to Mobile, along the Gulf Coast to New Orleans, and then back north up the Mississippi and Ohio rivers.

The travelers hated the stagecoach portion of the trip. The coaches were uncomfortable and the travelers complained that they were squeezed together. When rain and mud made roads impassable, the male passengers were forced to get out and push. Bad ticket agents, robbers, and accidents were constant problems.

Wayside stations were usually private homes that travelers often reported served poor food. Although the hospitality varied, the beds were sometimes dirty, the windows broken, and several passengers were frequently forced to sleep together.

Steamboats were regarded as much more pleasant; they were more spacious and elegant and were considered safer. Shingleton points out that some travelers knew navigation was difficult going upstream, that explosions and hitting snags did occur, and that riverboat captains were not always reliable.

(1840)   ANDERSON ROCHELLE MOORES   190

Atkinson, J. H., ed. "Travel in Pioneer Days." *Arkansas Historical Quarterly* 20 (Winter 1961):351–54.

This terse log of Anderson Rochelle Moores is interesting because it indicates how slow travel was for the many who migrated to the Southwest before the Civil War. Each day's entry while traveling through South Carolina, Tennessee, and Arkansas to Bowie County, Texas, lists rivers or streams crossed and the distances traveled. It took his family eighty-eight days (February 27–May 24, 1840) to make the 1,027-mile overland trip.

(1842–1879)   SOUTHERN CHARACTER   191

Wesson, Kenneth R. "Travelers' Accounts of the Southern Character: Antebellum and Early Postbellum Period." *Southern Studies* 17 (Fall 1978):305–18.

Wesson synthesizes the observations of foreign visitors about the average southerner, rather than the less representative wealthy planters and merchants. Wesson focuses on the small farm and the farmer who leased land and paid the rent from the crops he raised. Travelers deplored the exhaustion of soil by extensive cultivation of cotton. They believed cattle and hogs to be poor choices of stock and thought the practice of allowing the animals to roam free indicated the farmer's laziness. The homes were judged to be meager. Women, who were deprived of necessities for homemaking and overburdened with children, were often considered ignorant. Dress was always poor.

Most travelers agreed southern hospitality with respect to lodging was a myth. Travelers were divided on whether southerners were noble, generous, and uncontaminated by wealth, or rash, arrogant, detestable braggarts. They were unanimous in their belief that southerners held women in high esteem, were independent in spirit, religious, and prejudiced toward Yankee institutions. All agreed that excessive gambling, drinking, and lawlessness were discrediting social traits.

(1852)   JOHN E. PARSONS   192

Parsons, John E. "Through the Atlantic States to Cuba in 1852: Excerpts from the Journal and Letters of John E. Parsons." *New York Historical Society Quarterly* 42 (October 1958):367–85.

Parsons traveled by rail from Philadelphia to Baltimore and Washington, D.C., and then to Charleston before sailing to Cuba. On his return trip he took a steamboat up the Mississippi and Ohio rivers, and passed through New Orleans, Nashville, and Cincinnati. He comments on all of these places, including his brief stop at Mammoth Cave. The trip covered March 3 through April 29, 1852.

(1853–1854)   JOHN GEORGE DODSON   193

Wetta, Frank J., ed. "An English Gentleman's Southern Tour: The Recollections and Reflections of John George Dodson, First Baron Monk Bretton." *Southern Studies* 17 (Fall 1978):291–303.

Selections from Dodson's diary, kept between August 23, 1853, and February 14, 1854. While traveling across the South he observed that white people seemed less shy about coming into contact with blacks than did those in the North. He poked fun at one southerner who defended the treatment of slaves. Dodson suggested if it was such a desirable state the man should consider entering into it voluntarily. As he observed slavery, Dodson thought it was more a business than it was depicted in England and the North. He saw an emotionless slave auction and an emotionless advertisement in the paper offering the talents of a dog pack for hunting down runaway slaves. He thought slavery abhorrent and defended *Uncle Tom's Cabin*. He also offers a lengthy description of New Orleans and comments on how Yankee business buildings had surrounded the old French city.

(1856)   WILLIAM JEFFERIES GOODMAN   194

Goodman, William Jefferies. "A Trip to Tyler, 1856 From the Diary of William Jefferies Goodman." *Chronicles of Smith County, Texas* 5 (Spring 1966):25–29.

A return trip from Union District, South Carolina, to Tyler, Texas. Goodman traveled by coach to Montgomery, by steamer to Mobile and New Orleans, and then up the Mississippi and Red rivers. He describes some of the vicissitudes of travel—getting stuck in mud, staying on the lookout for gamblers, suffering from ague—as well as the pleasures of watching a traveling companion referred to only as "a lady in pink" and shooting alligators. The trip took six weeks (March 12–April 28, 1856).

(1857)   ELIJAH SWIFT   195

Wood, Virginia Steel, ed. "Elijah Swift's Travel Journal from Massachusetts to Florida, 1857." *Florida Historical Quarterly* 55 (October 1976):181–88.

In the editor's introduction, which is more interesting than the journal, she explains why Swift dreaded his business trip to Florida. Travel in the South in 1857 was arduous—eight days by railway, steamship, wagon, and stagecoach—and uncertain because there was no standard railroad time. Nevertheless, Swift seems to have endured the trip with a sense of humor.

(1857–1900)   PINEY WOODS FOLKLIFE   196

Cothran, Kay L. "Magazine Travel Accounts of Piney Woods Folklife." *Tennessee Folklife Society Bulletin* 29 (September 1973):80–86.

Warns against accepting travel accounts as historical fact without first considering such factors as travelers' biases, their social status relative to the society being viewed, the social status of the author's audience, and ideas currently in fashion within the society of the writer. In this article Cothran illustrates how opinions of late nineteenth-century travelers have presented a historically inaccurate picture of "cracker" culture. She does believe that travel accounts are valuable historical material if the biases are peeled away and the facts presented are compared against generally accepted historical knowledge. If this is done with travel accounts of piney woods folklife, we can learn a great deal about such cultural aspects as house types, land-use patterns, diet, and social interaction. Cothran further suggests that these accounts present the opportunity to study the travelers themselves as representatives of self-styled high culture in contrast with a lower culture.

(1861)   GEORGE MARCKMANN (MRS.)   197

Darst, Maury, ed. "Six Weeks to Texas." *Texana* 6 (Summer 1968):140–52.

After returning from visiting relatives in Germany, Mrs. George Marckmann recorded in her diary an adventurous trip to La Grange, Texas, in August and September of 1861. For six weeks she waited in a war-excited New York City, afraid to admit her pro-South sympathies. She writes that military considerations were given first priority on transportation facilities, and anyone wanting a pass into the South was labeled a traitor. Finally, she braved a dash to Louisville. The rest of the journey by train, down the Mississippi River to New Orleans, and finally home is filled with incidents that portray the Confederacy readying for war.

Note: Also published as "Six Weeks to Texas," *American History Illustrated* 14 (June 1979): 30–37.

(1862) GEORGE W. BOOTH 198

Booth, George W. "Running the Inland Blockade." *Civil War Times Illustrated* 11 (June 1972):12–19.

A Newark hatmaker recalls his travels from Kentucky to New Orleans early in 1862 to visit his brother's hat factory. During his journey, which was made by wagon and train, Booth observed that the effects of the blockade had reduced the amount of food he was served at taverns. He also noticed southern troop movements and hospitals, heard rumors of the war, and described the backward people with whom he stayed. (See also item 417.)

(1865) RAILROADS 199

Stover, John F. "The Ruined Railroads of the Confederacy." *Georgia Historical Quarterly* 42 (December 1958):376–88.

The accounts of four travelers in the South during the summer and fall of 1865 document the devastation caused by the war. Because rails, roadbeds, and bridges had been torn up and rolling stock and depots destroyed, service was usually slow and often expensive. Nevertheless, Stover believes that the railroads of the Confederacy were running better than anyone had a right to expect. Accounts consulted are: Sidney Andrews, *The South Since the War* (Boston, 1866); John H. Kennaway, *On Sherman's Track: or the South After the War* (London, 1867); Whitelaw Reid, *After the War: A Southern Tour* (Cincinnati, 1866); and John T. Trowbridge, *The South: A Tour of Its Battlefields and Ruined Cities* (Hartford, 1866).

(1865–1880) RECONSTRUCTION 200

McDonald, Archie P. "Travel Notes of Reconstruction Days." *Louisiana Studies* 8 (Fall 1969):268–76.

After summarizing the writings of six travelers to the Reconstructed South, McDonald enumerates their points of agreement. Southern whites were unrepentant. White women were more insulting than white men. Black women were more pushy than black men. Blacks were good laborers when paid regularly. The rebellion might produced good results if genuine reconstruction was executed. The Republican party was the hope for the South (Charles Nordhoff excepted). The South was not yet safe for northerners to live in, but was a good field for investment. McDonald also suggests some factors which should be utilized in the evaluation of these and other travel accounts.

(1865–1914) RACE QUESTION 201

Wynes, Charles E. "The Race Question in the South as Viewed by British Travelers: 1865–1914." *Louisiana Studies* 13 (Fall 1974):223–40.

At the end of the Civil War, British travelers were interested in ascertaining whether the recently freed slaves would work. Evidence that they would came quickly from the travelers' personal observations and from remarks by southerners. But Wynes points out that the work performed was as unskilled laborers with small chance of becoming artisans. By the 1880s and until the First World War, British travelers devoted themselves to analyzing blacks as lesser human beings. For instance, one explained why blacks were not intelligent enough to run machinery. Another stated that the intelligence blacks sometimes exhibited in youth soon faded. Because this stereotyping characterized these later writings, Wynes thinks the value of British travel accounts for presenting the "raw material" of history is lessened, but that the accounts are still of immense value to historians.

(1865–1950)   HISPANIC TRAVELERS   202

Thompson, Lawrence S. "Hispanic Travellers in the South Since the Civil War." *Inter-American Review of Bibliography* 25 (July/September 1975):256–70.

An annotated bibliography of seventy-five travel books produced by Latin-American visitors to the South between 1865 and 1950, although only seven appeared before 1900. In his introduction Thompson points out that though the racial issue was their great concern, there was no attempt to compare the condition of the American black or Indian with those elements in the travelers' own countries. Cities attracted more Hispanic visitors that did rural areas, although agriculture was observed with interest for application at home. American education was scrutinized, but transportation systems and details of social life and customs were ignored. Thompson says these accounts do not provide much that future historians will want to use as references. Their importance lies in their portrait of the South for the reading public in Spain, Portugal, and Latin America. Thompson believes the accounts to be a generally fair and accurate, if sketchy, portrayal.

(1867)   SAMUEL AUGUSTUS BARNETT   203

Abel, Emily K. "A Victorian Views Reconstruction: The American Diary of Samuel Augustus Barnett." *Civil War History* 20 (June 1974):135–56.

Evaluates Barnett's comments about the South by comparing them with the social assumptions current in England at the time of his trip, April to July, 1867. Barnett readily accepted the ethnic and religious stereotypes in the United States that were popularly applied to the Irish in his own country. In addition, he confused the racial situation in America with the problem of class structure in England. The author says that Barnett's visit to a society in crisis had permanent effects on him. He came as a naive, smug young man, but returned to England to devote his life to social reform.

4

Southeast

GENERAL

(1566–1567)   **JUAN PARDO**   **204**

Folmsbee, Stanley J., and Lewis, Madeline Kneberg, eds.; Wade, Gerald W., tr. "Journals of the Juan Pardo Expeditions 1566–1567." *East Tennessee Historical Society Publications* 37 (1965):106–21.

    Juan Pardo was sent on two expeditions to the interior of the southern United States by the Spanish to counter the French influence. He was to form alliances with and convert the Indians and open a trail that might extend as far as Mexico. Presented here are three accounts written by Pardo and two soldiers, all translated into English for the first time by Gerald W. Wade. The editors hope this translation will assist scholars in reconciling differences between Pardo's expeditions and the DeSoto expedition of 1539–1542.

(1861–1863)   **JOHN C. BUCHANAN**   **205**

Blackburn, George M., ed. "The Negro as Viewed by a Michigan Civil War Soldier: Letters of John C. Buchanan." *Michigan History* 47 (March 1963):75–84.

    Captain Buchanan of the Eighth Michigan Infantry blamed the "peculiar institution" of slavery for the poor economic and intellectual state of the blacks he saw in Maryland, South Carolina, and Louisiana. At first, he objected to using blacks as soldiers because of the divisiveness it would create among Unionists. He later commended the performances of black soldiers in battle. His letters were written between October 10, 1861, and July 30, 1863.

(1861–1864)   **ANGUS MCDERMID**   **206**

Rountree, Benjamin. "Letters from a Confederate Soldier." *Georgia Review* 18 (Fall 1964):267–97.

    Using excerpts from the letters of Angus McDermid (October 8, 1861–November 20, 1864), Rountree follows the development of this Georgia soldier from a callow 17-year-old to a mature, battle-hardened veteran. McDermid's troop (the Twenty-ninth Georgia Infantry?) served in Georgia, Mississippi, Tennessee, South Carolina, and North Carolina. His letters describe the war in which he was fighting and his concern for home. He relates incidents of battles, desertions, low morale, hopes for a leave, his illnesses, and the realization after the fall of Vicksburg (July, 1863) that the Confederacy was finished. He mourns his brother who was killed in battle, and he tries to develop one potential matrimonial relationship by letter, while fending off another. Always he longs for the day he will again taste his mother's cooking. That day never came. Sergeant McDermid was killed around Florence, Alabama, on December 7, 1864.

(1862–1865)   FRANK H. SHIRAS   207

Workmaster, Wallace F., ed. "The Frank H. Shiras Letters, 1862–1865." *Western Pennsylvania Historical Magazine* 40 (Fall 1957):163–90.

Lieutenant Shiras's correspondence (September 3, 1862–January 20, 1865) usually focuses on the fighting, but he occasionally comments on the social conditions. For example, in January, 1865, he wrote that he was surprised to see how large numbers of blacks in Virginia had stayed with their former owners, even though the white families had little food and poor clothing. Shiras served with Hampton's Battery F, Independent Pennsylvania Light Artillery, around the Washington, D.C. area and in Pennsylvania and Virginia.

(1863–1865)   JOSEPH JULIUS WESCOAT   208

Gregorie, Anne King, ed. "Diary of Captain Joseph Julius Wescoat, 1863–1865." (Part I) *South Carolina Historical Magazine* 59 (January 1958):11–23.
———. (Part II) *South Carolina Historical Magazine*, 59 (April 1958):84–95.

Wescoat's entries (September 8, 1863–April 30, 1865) begin during the Union shelling of Charleston, continue through campaigns in Florida, Virginia, and North Carolina, and conclude when Wescoat was a prisoner of war at Fort Delaware. His period of imprisonment, February 20 to April 30, 1865, is perhaps the most interesting portion. Wescoat found incarceration at the hands of the Yankees to be insufferable and interminable. As news of southern defeats poured in, he became sarcastic: "Can we rely on northern newspapers?" (p. 93) And when Lincoln was assassinated: "What a pity. What a pity." (p. 94) He remained unrepentant until the last, refusing to take the oath of loyalty to the United States of America and heaping abuse on those who did. Wescoat served with the Eleventh South Carolina Infantry.

(1864)   ISAIAH CONLEY   209

Harmon, George D., and Hazlehurst, Edith Blackburn, eds. "Captain Isaiah Conley's Escape from a Southern Prison, 1864." (Part I) *Western Pennsylvania Historical Magazine* 47 (April 1964):81–106.
———. (Part II) *Western Pennsylvania Historical Magazine* 47 (July 1964):225–47.

After being captured in North Carolina in April, 1864, Captain Conley and other officers of the 101st Pennsylvania Infantry were sent to several Confederate prisons. In October, while being transferred by train from Charleston, he and others escaped. They followed a course north to Columbia and Spartanburg, through western North Carolina, and finally to Knoxville, Tennessee, where they met Union troops on November 13. All along the way Conley received assistance from slaves and white mountaineers. The editors add that the willingness shown by these two groups of southerners to help the escaped prisoners indicates a major fault of the Confederacy, the inability to command the support of all of its people.

(1864)   OLIVIA DELOACH   210

Holden, John A., ed. "Journey of a Confederate Mother, June 7–Sept. 12, 1864." *West Tennessee Historical Society Papers* 19 (1965):36–57.

The diary of Mrs. Olivia Deloach provides some insights into the disastrous effects of the war on transportation lines in the South. She and her husband left their home in Collierville, Tennessee, and traveled for three months across Mississippi, Alabama, Georgia, South Carolina, and North Carolina before finally catching up with her son at Petersburg, Virginia. In Georgia, Deloach left his wife briefly to visit another son in Atlanta, but the editor says it is improbable that Deloach ever found him. The editor adds a great deal of important background material to Mrs. Deloach's brief entries.

(1865) **RAPHAEL SEMMES** **211**

Hoole, W. Stanley, ed. "Admiral on Horseback: The Diary of Brigadier General Raphael Semmes, February-May, 1865." *Alabama Review* 28 (April 1975):129–50.

During the final months of the Civil War, Semmes was appointed commander of the James River Fleet until he was ordered to destroy his ships. He was then appointed brigadier general and told to defend the new Confederate capital of Danville, Virginia, with his sailors. After ten days in the trenches he fell back to Greensboro, North Carolina, where on May 1, he signed his parole. That same day Semmes, his son, and the remaining officers started their 800-mile trek home to Mobile. Semmes tells of seeing ragged soldiers and congregations of blacks everywhere; he heard stories of marauders, and he describes the effect of the war on the countryside.

(1865) **HARVEY M. WATTERSON** **212**

Abbott, Martin, ed. "A Southerner Views the South, 1865: Letters of Harvey M. Watterson." *Virginia Magazine of History and Biography* 68 (October 1960):478–89.

In June and July, 1865, this Tennesseean reported on sentiment in Richmond, Virginia, and Raleigh, New Bern, and Wilmington, North Carolina, for President Andrew Johnson. Watterson wrote that southerners were contrite, tired of war, and willing to make the transition from slavery to the employment of freedmen. The editor adds that other evidence does not support the same degree of abject contrition by southerners. (See also item 372.)

DELAWARE

(1651) **THOMAS DOXEY** **213**

Butler, Eva L., and Weslager, C. A., eds. "Thomas Doxey's Letter from the Delaware, 1651." *Delaware History* 8 (March 1958):51–53.

Doxey was an English trader from Connecticut who was in Delaware to collect debts. His letter of June 7, 1651, discusses the contest between the Swedish and Dutch populations for preeminence in the region.

(1700–1740) **DELAWARE** **214**

Hancock, Harold B., ed. "Descriptions and Travel Accounts of Delaware, 1700–1740." *Delaware History* 10 (October 1962):115–51.
Contains excerpts from ten accounts.

(1775–1783) **WILLIAM ADAIR** **215**

———. "The Revolutionary War Diary of William Adair." *Delaware History* 13 (October 1968):154–65.

This soldier's diary (May, 1775–October, 1783) provides a glimpse of Sussex County, Maryland, during the American Revolution. Adair reveals that early in the war British vessels off the coast of Lewes, Delaware, provoked Sussex County Tories to create disturbances and to sell cattle and produce at profitable prices. He also mentions local reaction to the Declaration of Independence and the turbulence that surrounded elections. Adair believes that if the Tories had won the 1783 local election, the Whigs were prepared to leave the state.

(1790) THOMAS RODNEY 216

Merwin, M. M., ed. "Thomas Rodney's Diary of a Journey by Carriage from Delaware to New York City." *Delaware History* 17 (Spring/Summer 1977):199–213.

In June, 1790, Rodney traveled from Dover, Delaware, to New York City to settle some family financial affairs. He passed through Wilmington and Darby, Delaware, through New Jersey to Paulus Hook, then across the Hudson River to New York City. He noted the conditions of the road and the traffic, the location of taverns, and kept a record of his expenses. Around Elizabethtown, New Jersey, he reported that the devastation of the recent war was apparent, as was the poverty of the people.

(1830–1831) ALEXANDER RANDALL 217

Randall, Richard, ed. "Travel Extracts from the Journal of Alexander Randall, 1830–1831." *Maryland Historical Magazine* 49 (September 1954):251–56.

Passages that record a trip through the Chesapeake and Delaware Canal en route to Upstate New York. Also includes an excursion from Washington, D.C. to the Great Falls of the Potomac River. The first trip took place in May and June, 1830, and the second in May, 1831.

(1863) JOSEPH TAYLOR 218

Reinders, Robert C., ed. "Two Letters of English Soliders in Louisiana Confederate Regiments." *Louisiana History* 8 (Summer 1967):260–64.

Letters of encouragement to Edward Stuart Wortley, member of the House of Lords, who was raising funds in England to aid Confederate prisoners in Union prison camps. Joseph Taylor (Fifth Louisiana Infantry) relates his poor treatment at Fort Delaware in 1863. Fred Hampson (Gladden Rifles, Thirteenth Louisiana Infantry) describes similar experiences during his capture and incarceration in Union prison camps during the same year.

(1864–1865) FRANCIS ATHERTON BOYLE 219

Thornton, Mary Lindsay, ed. "The Prison Diary of Adjutant Francis Atherton Boyle, C.S.A." *North Carolina Historical Review* 39 (Winter 1962):58–84.

Boyle, who served with the Thirty-second North Carolina Infantry, was captured near Spotsylvania (Virginia) in May, 1864. He was imprisoned at Point Lookout (Maryland) and then Fort Delaware until his release in July, 1865. Boyle's account possesses more cold objectivity than do similar prison diaries. At one point he draws up separate columns of advantages and disadvantages of each Union prison he had seen.

DISTRICT OF COLUMBIA

(1797) FRANÇOIS ALEXANDRE FRÉDÉRIC, 220
DUC DE LA
ROCHEFOUCAULD-LIANCOURT

Brandenburg, David J., and Brandenburg, Millicent H. "The Duc De La Rochefoucauld-Liancourt's Visit to the Federal City in 1797: A New Translation." *Records of the Columbia Historical Society of Washington, D.C.* (1973/1974):35–60.

During his extensive travels in the eastern United States, French exile François Alexandre Frédéric, duc de la Rochefoucauld-Liancourt, visited Washington, D.C. in March, 1797. In his *Voyage dans les États-Unis d'Amérique, fait en 1795, 1796, et 1797* (Paris, 1799), he discusses the location of the city, the financial speculation surrounding its establishment, the population, and the public buildings. In their introduction the authors provide a bibliographic history of Liancourt's eight-volume work and the need for the new translation then in progress. (See also item 11.)

(1804) CHARLES WILLSON PEALE 221

Friis, Herman R. "Baron Alexander von Humboldt's Visit to Washington, D.C., June 1 through June 13, 1804." *Records of the Columbia Historical Society of Washington, D.C.* (1960/1962):1–35.

Upon completion of a five-year geographic exploration of Mexico and South America, the Prussian scientist paused in the nation's capital to visit President Jefferson. Friis points out that although the two men admired each other, Jefferson had a further motive. He wanted to learn more about the unknown regions of the American Southwest where he was preparing to send a series of expeditions. Humboldt shared his knowledge of New Spain with Jefferson and contributed to intelligence about the American West at an extremely important period in our history. Based on the diary of Charles Willson Peale, who traveled with Humboldt in Philadelphia and Washington, D.C., and contemporary accounts.

(1825) HENRY D. GILPIN 222

Gray, Ralph D., ed. "Washington in 1825: Observations by Henry D. Gilpin." *Delaware History* 11 (April 1965):240–50.

Gilpin was in the nation's capital on a business trip and to attend the inauguration of President John Quincy Adams. His letters (March 2-5, 1825) describe his journey from Philadelphia, the inauguration ceremony, and the ball. He mentions the many prominent people he met.

(1825) LUKAS VISCHER 223

Feest, Christian F., ed. and tr. "Lukas Vischer in Washington: A Swiss View of the District of Columbia in 1825." *Records of the Columbia Historical Society of Washington, D.C.* (1973/1974):78–110.

During his five-year stay in the United States, this Swiss businessman visited the capital city twice in 1825. His diary consists of short impressions of Washington. On his first visit he did not like the presidential mansion nor the Capitol building. In the House of Representatives, he felt there was too much milling about and the behavior was too informal. On his second visit the city appealed to him more, although he still found it unpleasant in appearance because of waste lots where trees could have been left to form parks. His opinion of the buildings of the city remained unchanged. Vischer also visited Columbian College (later George Washington University) and dined with former President John Adams.

(1852) HENRY ARTHUR BRIGHT 224

Ehrenpreis, Anne Hanry, ed. "A Victorian Englishman on Tour: Henry Arthur Bright's Southern Journal, 1852." *Virginia Magazine of History and Biography* 84 (July 1976):333–61.

During his tour of the United States, Bright visited the major eastern cities, then went south to Virginia, west to Saint Louis, north to Minnesota, and into Canada. In this article are recorded impressions of his travels to Washington, D.C. and Virginia in June, 1852. The editor says Bright writes with "candor and good humor." (p. 334) Thus, when Bright says that President Fillmore's daughter was "fat and plain," that Mrs. Fillmore was "ordinary," and that the president "is the best of the family as externals go," there is no attempt to be insulting. (p. 337)

Bright became acquainted with many prominent individuals in Washington. In addition to the president, he met Daniel Webster. During his visit to the House of Representatives he saw only a "little spitting and whistling," a jab directed at those English travelers who had reported that such activities characterized congressional sessions. (p. 338) In Richmond, after a stop at Mount Vernon, he attended the First Baptist Church (the African Church) and a slave auction, which he describes as a curious occurrence. Bright observes that the blacks seemed to be happy, and he explores some of the problems with letting the slaves go free. Before leaving the state, he visited Charlottesville, Lexington, the Natural Bridge, and the Virginia Springs.

(1874)   FRIEDRICH RATZEL   225

Stehlin, Stewart A. "The Smithsonian Institution in 1874: A German Visitor's Description." *Records of the Columbia Historical Society of Washington, D.C.* (1970):245–51.

The German geographer and anthropologist Friedrich Ratzel was traveling in the United States during 1873 and 1874 as a correspondent for *Kölnische Zeitung*. In this selection from his *Städte und culturbilder aus Nordamerika* (Leipzig, 1876), Ratzel praises the Smithsonian for its collections and for being an international clearinghouse for the exchange of scientific information. (See also items 64 and 170.)

(1943)   ISAIAH BERLIN   226

Hachey, Thomas E., ed. "American Profiles on Capital Hill: A Confidential Study for the British Foreign Office in 1943." *Wisconsin Magazine of History* 57 (Winter 1973/1974):141–53.

Because the English government was increasingly concerned about the role partisan politics played in shaping official American foreign policy, it instructed Sir Isaiah Berlin of the British Information Service in Washington to report on the Senate Foreign Relations Committee and the Foreign Affairs Committee of the House of Representatives. The memorandum reprinted here describes the activities and composition of each group, and provides sketches of the political inclinations of many of the members, with special attention to their attitudes toward England.

FLORIDA

(1564)   HERNANDO MANRIQUE DE ROJAS   227

Wenhold, Lucy L., tr. "Manrique de Rojas' Report on French Settlement in Florida, 1564." *Florida Historical Quarterly* 38 (July 1959):45–62.

Captain Hernando Manrique de Rojas was assigned the mission of destroying the French fort of Charlesfort at Port Royal, which had been established by Huguenot Jean Ribault in 1562. Here the captain repeats his instructions from the governor of Cuba, gives the official report of his actions in May and June of 1564, and provides some facts about French relations with the Indians.

(1696–1774)   JONATHAN DICKINSON   228

Mattfield, Mary S. "Journey to the Wilderness: Two Travelers in Florida, 1696–1774." *Florida Historical Quarterly* 45 (April 1967):327–51.

Jonathan Dickinson's *Journal* . . . (Philadelphia, 1699) and William Bartram's *Travels through North & South Carolina, Georgia, East and West Florida* . . . (Philadelphia, 1791) are useful for social and physical information about Florida, as well as being dramatic travel accounts. Because both are representative of their own centuries, however, they have different outlooks on nature and the Indians. Dickinson was shipwrecked and captured by Indians before struggling back to civilization. He described his experience as a terrible ordeal and his successful perseverance as proving the workings of the Divine Providence.

Nearly a century later the naturalist Bartram welcomed his travel experience with a scientist's zeal and gave a precise technical account of what he observed. He saw in nature and the Indians the presence of the God omnipotent. Although the two writers are separated by time, personal temperament, and philosophical differences, Mattfield believes that they are united by a spiritual concept. For the romanticist, it was his quest for truth behind the facts. For the Quaker, it was the evidence of Divine Providence. Mattfield uses these works to indicate the development of American literature. (See also items 231 and 232.)

(1757) FRANCISCO MARIA CELI 229

Ware, John D., ed. "Tampa Bay in 1757: Francisco Maria Celi's Journal and Logbook." (Part I) *Florida Historical Quarterly* 50 (October 1971):158–79.
————. (Part II) *Florida Historical Quarterly* 50 (January 1972):262–77.

Celi's survey of Tampa Bay in April and May, 1757, is the first detailed report of this body of water. His journal also describes several peaceful meetings betwen the Spanish and the Indians.

(1764–1765) THOMAS CAMPBELL 230

Fabel, Robin F. A., and Rea, Robert R., eds. "Lieutenant Thomas Campbell's Sojourn Among the Creeks, November, 1764–May, 1765." *Alabama Historical Quarterly* 36 (Summer 1974):97–111.

This English officer was sent to ensure the friendship of the Upper Creeks when the British occupied West Florida following the Seven Years War. His 225-mile trip from Pensacola to Tallapoosa took eleven days. During his stay in the Creek villages he took note of the agriculture and cattle raising of the Indians, and he noted their customs of killing and marriage.

(1773–1776) WILLIAM BARTRAM 231

Lee, Grattan Berta. "William Bartram: Naturalist or 'Poet'?" *Early American Literature* 7 (Fall 1972):124–29.

Between 1773 and 1776, naturalist William Bartram traveled throughout east Florida, west Florida, western Georgia, North Carolina, South Carolina, and southern Alabama and Mississippi. Lee says Bartram's *Travels through North & South Carolina, Georgia, East and West Florida* . . . (Philadelphia, 1791) polarized its readers on the issue of accuracy. Most of the argument concerns Bartram's vivid description of the alligator in Florida. Both admirers and detractors have gathered evidence to prove the objectivity of his report, and Lee summarizes the findings here. While Lee does not deny that Bartram was an important naturalist, he says the scientist filtered his observations through a highly developed literary imagination to make his writings more readable. Lee sees no real problem with awarding Bartram both the titles of "poet" and "naturalist." (See also items 228 and 232.)

(1773–1776) 232

Merritt, J. I., III. "William Bartram in America's Eden." *History Today* 28 (November 1978):712–21.

A biographical sketch and summary of the contributions that resulted from Bartram's *Travels*. Merritt says that Bartram "wedded a romantic vision to a keen descriptive eye." (p. 714) The result was a literature that was to inspire Coleridge and Wordsworth, as well as make a lasting contribution to natural history. (See also items 228 and 231.)

(1791)   FRANÇOIS AUGUSTE RENÉ DE CHATEAUBRIAND   233

Panagopoulos, E. P. "Chateaubriand's Florida and His Journey to America." *Florida Historical Quarterly* 49 (October 1970):140–52.

Vicomte François Auguste René de Chateaubriand arrived in the United States on July 10, 1791, and allegedly traveled throughout the North, the Ohio Valley region, and the South before returning to France on October 10, 1791. Panagopoulos emphasizes the importance of this trip to Chateaubriand's literary efforts and to European perceptions of America. Although Chateaubriand's works contain details about the land and social organizations that were accepted at the time, later historians have shown that he did not travel so widely and that many of his descriptions are taken from other travelers and even transferred geographically. Panagopoulos calls attention to a fanciful meeting with George Washington, as well as some problems with using Chateaubriand's work as a historical source for Florida.

But if Chateaubriand did not write with historical fidelity and exactitude, Panagopoulos points out, his works contain no more historical inaccuracies than do those of his contemporaries. "His romantic disposition and his sensitivity to aesthetic values made dull for him a mere re-creation of reality. He found it more exciting to create history." (p. 150) Consults volume 4 of Chateaubriand's *Oeuvres Complètes . . . Voyage en Amérique* (Paris, 1827). (See also item 9.)

(1794)   JOHN HAMBLY   234

Murdock, Richard K., ed. "Mission to the Creek Nation in 1794." *Florida Historical Quarterly* 34 (January 1956):266–84.

John Hambly was a shopkeeper for an Indian trading firm who accepted commissions from the Spanish governor of east Florida to procure information about relations between the Indians and the Americans. The diary, kept from January 14 to April 7, 1794, records a journey among the Cusseta (a Lower Creek Indian group), who lived along the Chattahoochee and Flint rivers.

(1794)   235

Ross, Daniel J. J., and Chapell, Bruce S., eds. "Visit to the Indian Nations: The Diary of John Hambly." *Florida Historical Quarterly* 55 (July 1976):60–73.

This diary (June 29-August 27, 1794) was kept during a mission to obtain information for the Spanish from the Indians about their boundary negotiations with the United States.

(1800s)   FLORIDA   236

Rogers, Benjamin F. "Florida Seen Through the Eyes of Nineteenth Century Travellers." *Florida Historical Quarterly* 34 (October 1955):177–89.

Before the Civil War poor transportation facilities and the presence of the Seminole Indians discouraged travel to Florida. After 1865, Jacksonville and Orlando became headquarters for visitors, who praised the climate but who were less enthusiastic about the scenery. Economic prospects were thought good for a variety of crops and cattle raising, and the potential for tourism was also acknowledged. The presence of northern emigrants was evident, especially in the architecture of the homes. Travelers viewed Floridians as sociable, but had mixed feelings about the poor whites and were ambivalent about the future of blacks.

(1824–1826)   ALFRED BECKLEY   237

Eby, Cecil D., Jr., ed. "Memoir of a West Pointer in Saint Augustine: 1824–1826." *Florida Historical Quarterly* 42 (April 1964): 307–20.

During these years Lieutenant Alfred Beckley served with the Fourth Artillery, United States Army, at Fort Marion. Some sixty years later he recalls details about the Fort and the social life at Saint Augustine. Annotated by Doris C. Wiles and Eugenia B. Arana. (See also item 238.)

(1825) **238**

————. "Memoir of a West Pointer in Florida: 1825." *Florida Historical Quarterly* 41 (October 1962):154–64.

Lieutenant Alfred Beckley recalls the difficulties he encountered while marching from Fort Marion to reinforce army troops at Fort King in June, 1825. Poor transportation and accommodations and the watery terrain conspired to limit the advance to only twenty-four miles in four days. Beckley's mission was recalled when the incident, which almost brought war with the Seminole Indians, was resolved before his troops reached their destination. (See also item 237.)

(1834) **JOHN DURKEE** **239**

Hoole, W. Stanley, ed. "East Florida in 1834: Letters of Dr. John Durkee." *Florida Historical Quarterly* 52 (January 1974):294–308.

The correspondence of a New Hampshire physician in Jacksonville for his health provides detailed descriptions of many animals he saw. He devotes a lengthy passage to the habits of the alligator and he was curious enough to dissect one he had killed. He relates how the dreaded rattlesnake could be easily disposed of by a blacksnake or the quick hoofs of a deer. Even a grasshopper that exhibited courage in battle with a chicken drew his attention. He does not comment on the people, except to say that they were stupid for burning off the pine barrens, for by destroying the grass and not allowing it to decompose, the soil was robbed of much of its fertility. He mentions the cattle ranchers who followed the practice of letting their cattle graze unmolested in the forests. Dr. Durkee's scientific curiosity led him to poke around in an ancient Indian burial mound of unknown origin. He offers a complimentary description of Jacksonville.

(1835–1840) **JOSEPH R. SMITH** **240**

Mahon, John K., ed. "Letters From the Second Seminole War." *Florida Historical Quarterly* 36 (April 1958):331–52.

The editor admits there is little in the letters (November 9, 1837-March 22, 1840) of Lieutenant Joseph R. Smith that is "important enough to require an interpretation of the Second Seminole War, 1835–1842." (p. 331) They are significant, however, because they bring to life an interesting era. The letters contain battle tactics, troop strength, the hardships of battle conditions, the flies, wading in water waist-deep, the rain, the dysentery, and Smith's constant concern for his family.

(1836) **ALEXANDER BEAUFORT MEEK** **241**

————. "The Journal of A. B. Meek and the Second Seminole War, 1836." *Florida Historical Quarterly* 38 (April 1960):302–18.

Portions of the journal of Alexander Beaufort Meek (February 21-April 19, 1836), an Alabama volunteer in the Florida State Guard, which was attempting to defeat the Seminole Indians. Meek relates troop movement from Tuscaloosa, Alabama, to the Tampa Bay area, the building of a fort, and the poor relations between the regular army soldiers and the volunteers from Alabama, Georgia, and Florida.

(1836–1837) **JOHN PICKELL** **242**

White, Frank L., Jr., ed. "The Journals of Lieutenant John Pickell, 1836–1837." *Florida Historical Quarterly* 38 (October 1959):142–71.

Pickell was in Florida with the Fourth Regiment of Artillery that was attempting to subdue the Seminole Indians. His two diaries (July 16-August, 1836, and November 8-December 16, 1837) provide attitudes about the peace negotiations and describe the flora and fauna he observed on an exploration of the Saint Johns River.

(1837)   HENRY SUMMER   243

Moore, John Hammond, ed. "A South Carolina Lawyer Visits St. Augustine—1837." *Florida Historical Quarterly* 43 (April 1965):361–78.

Henry Summer kept a journal of his trip (February 2-March 25, 1837) from Newberry to Charleston, South Carolina, by rail, and on to Saint Augustine by sea, as well as his return trip. Summer offers his impressions and descriptions of Charleston, Saint Augustine, and nearby Fort Marion. He did not see a bright future for Saint Augustine and thought Charleston would capture any commerce in the region. All in all, Saint Augustine was "an extremely dull place." (p. 377) A popular topic of conversation was the war with Seminole Indians. Summer was present when General Jessup was successful in getting the Indians to sign a peace treaty that temporarily halted the hostilities.

(1839)   JOHN T. SPRAGUE   244

White, Frank F., Jr., ed. "Macomb's Mission to the Seminoles; John T. Sprague's Journal Kept During April and May, 1839." *Florida Historical Quarterly* 35 (October 1956):130–93.

Major General Alexander Macomb left Washington to go to Florida in an unsuccessful attempt to end the four-year war against the Seminole Indians. His aide-de-camp, Lieutenant Sprague, maintained an official diary from March 22 to May 30, 1839. Although a peace agreement called a temporary end to the war, hostilities again broke out after Macomb left. Sprague, whose sympathies were with the Seminole, describes the trips to and from Florida, the country around Fort King, and a trip up the Saint Johns River.

(1852)   W. T. ALLEN   245

Thompson, Arthur W., ed. "A Massachusetts Traveller on the Florida Frontier." *Florida Historical Quarterly* 38 (October 1959):129–41.

A portion of the journal kept on a 49-day tour of the East, Middle West, and Gulf Coast by W. T. Allen in March and April, 1852. The lengthiest passages provide descriptions of Savannah and the region around Saint Augustine. They offer information about the continuing problems with the Seminoles, especially with Chief Billy Bowlegs.

(1855)   GEORGE BANCROFT   246

Clark, Patricia, ed. "'A Tale to Tell from Paradise Itself': George Bancroft's Letters from Florida, March 1855." *Florida Historical Quarterly* 48 (January 1970):264–78.

The historian-diplomat spent March 10 to March 24 traveling between Palatka, Ocala, Orange Springs, Saint Augustine, and Jacksonville. He commented on general social conditions and the hovel in which he spent his time in Ocala, and he observed that the people of Florida were extremely temperate. Although Bancroft saw slaves singing and an absence of cruelty, he believed that the slaves' condition made them stolid. In another place he reported that an adverse feeling toward Massachusetts was very strong in Florida.

(1861)   "BATCHELOR"   247

Rogers, William Warren, ed. "Florida on the Eve of the Civil War as Seen by a Southern Reporter." *Florida Historical Quarterly* 39 (October 1960):145–58.

"Batchelor," a journalist for the *Charleston Daily Courier*, wrote these columns from Jacksonville, Lake City, Tallahassee, Madison, and the Saint Johns River between March and April, 1861. He praises the beauty of the land and efforts at internal improvements, and predicts a rosy future for the state. The only significant mention of the Civil War was of the battalion of Florida volunteers that was being raised in Pensacola.

(1861–1862)   AUGUSTUS HENRY MATHERS   248

Doty, Franklin A., ed. "The Civil War Letters of Augustus Henry Mathers, Assistant Surgeon, Fourth Florida Regiment, C.S.A." *Florida Historical Quarterly* 36 (October 1957):94–124.

Most of these letters (September 12, 1861-February 12, 1862) were written from Camp Fernandina (Florida). Mathers tells of the leisurely attitude of Confederate soldiers, the effect of the Union blockade, the types of diseases he had to treat, and his concern for his family.

(1863)   NOAH BROOKS   249

Staudenraus, P. J., ed. "A War Correspondent's View of St. Augustine and Fernandina: 1863." *Florida Historical Quarterly* 41 (July 1962):60–65.

In this account by reporter Noah Brooks, which was first published in the *Sacramento Daily Union* on July 21, 1863, the writer blends some history with a report on the present condition of the two Union-occupied cities. In Saint Augustine he describes how the war was working a hardship on the inhabitants of the city. Times were especially difficult for those who had relatives in the Confederacy because they were being forced to join their relatives and leave their possessions behind. In Fernandina he observed that most of the original inhabitants had left and the town was filled with blacks from Georgia. Brooks approved of raising black military units and had heard that they were successful in instilling terror in rebel troops.

(1866)   HARRIET A. BARNES   250

Proctor, Samuel, ed. "Yankee 'Schoolmarms' in Post-War Florida." *Journal of Negro History* 44 (July 1959):275–77.

Presents a letter dated March 14, 1866, written by Harriet A. Barnes and Catharine R. Bent, who were assigned to Gainesville by the Freedman's Bureau of Florida. They say the buildings they were given to teach in were crude dwellings. Their pupils were poor but anxious to start a new life and get an education. The blacks' efforts were hampered by the hostility of whites who threw stones at the school buildings and continually challenged the freedmen to fight. Nevertheless, the ladies felt their school was flourishing.

(1866)   A. E. KINNE   251

Richardson, Joe M., ed. "A Northerner Reports on Florida: 1866." *Florida Historical Quarterly* 40 (April 1962):381–90.

While on an inspection tour to ascertain the condition of the former slaves of eastern Florida for the Freedman's Bureau, A. E. Kinne made the following observations in a letter written on October 15, 1866. There were plenty of jobs available, but an unequal distribution of the labor force resulted because the blacks chose to work for those planters with good reputations. Many contracts existed between employers and laborers, some of which were fair, others unfair. The size of the crops was difficult to determine. His figures on schooling indicated many more black children than white children in schools. Kinne mentions violence and the hatred the poor whites felt toward the former slaves.

(1870) **JARED POTTER KIRTLAND** 252

Large, John, Jr. "A Scientist Observes Florida: 1870." *Florida Historical Quarterly* 42 (July 1963):48–54.

At the advanced age of seventy-seven, Ohioan Jared Potter Kirtland launched upon a project to explore the flora and fauna of Florida. Two letters, upon which Large bases this article, show that the doctor sailed the Saint Johns River to the inlet of Lake Harney and collected many specimens. Kirtland relates his impressions of the former Confederates, the poor whites, and the blacks.

(1871) **SOFIA CHARLOTTA SJÖBORG** 253

Sjöborg, Sofia Charlotta. "Journey to Florida, 1871." *Swedish Pioneer History Quarterly* 26 (January 1975):24–45.

A journal (April 18–May ?, 1871) kept by a 66-year-old woman, who, along with about fifty other Swedes, was immigrating to a settlement in central Florida. The first half of the journal relates her sadness at leaving her home and her activities on the voyage from Uppsala to New York City. On board were other Scandinavians, who were joined by many Irish immigrants in Glasgow, Scotland. After they docked New York, another ship took Sofia's group to Charleston (where she got lost while wandering around the city), Savannah, Fernandina, Jacksonville, and the settlement. Sofia describes the flora and fauna of her new home, but chooses to say little about the cramped quarters of their tent or the heat which drove them into the lake for daily baths.

GEORGIA

(1733–1734) **PHILIPP GEORG FRIEDRICH VON RECK** 254

Jones, George Fenwick, ed. and tr. "Commissary Von Reck's Report on Georgia." *Georgia Historical Quarterly* 47 (March 1963):95–110.

In 1733 and 1734, Baron von Reck transported the first group of exiled Lutherans of Salzburg from their temporary home in Holland to Ebenezer, Georgia, where with the help of James Oglethorpe, they established a Protestant colony. This report emphasizes the trying conditions the immigrants faced upon arrival, the physical surroundings of the colony, and includes a long passage about the Creek Indians. The source of this report and items 255–260 comprise the *Urlsperger Reports*, Samuel Urlsperger, *Der aüsfuhrlichen Nachrichten der Königlich-Grossbritannischen Colonie Saltzburgischer Emigranten in America* . . . (Halle, 1735–52.)

(1736) 255

———. "Von Reck's Second Report from Georgia." *William and Mary Quarterly* 22 (April 1965):319–33.

During his second journey with the third transport of Salzburg exiles, von Reck describes the poor condition of the colony, the decision to move to the confluence of the Savannah and Ebenezer rivers, the wildlife and vegetation, the Georgia sea islands, and northern Spanish Florida. He also remarks about his illness that forced him to return home. (See also items 254 and 256–260.)

(1737) **JOHANN MARTIN BOLZIUS** 256

———. "Pastor Bolzius' Letter of June 1737 to a Friend." *Georgia Review* 18 (Winter 1964):457–62.

Johann Martin Bolzius, chief pastor of the Protestant exiles from Salzburg who settled in Georgia in 1734, describes the progress of the colony. He writes that they moved from Old

Ebenezer to New Ebenezer on the Savannah River because it provided improved transportation, greater agricultural possibilities, and better fishing. He relates how the Indians resisted Christian learning, turning instead to places where they could find liquor. Bolzius says the Indians were disorderly and would not work even when starving. He also provides information about a Swiss colony in Georgia and the problems they were having in establishing their colony. (See also items 254–255 and 257–260.)

(1740) 257

———. "John Martin Bolzius Reports on Georgia." *Georgia Historical Quarterly* 47 (June 1963):216–19.

This report, written about 1740, relates religious conditions in the colony. It also includes information about Catholics and Jews of various nationalities in the region. (See also items 254–256 and 258–260.)

(1748) 258

Tresp, Lothar L., ed. and tr. "Pastor Bolzius Reports: Life in Georgia Among the Salzburgers." *American-German Review* 29 (April/May 1963):20–23, 39.

In a general report dated July 31, 1748, Bolzius expressed fear the Indians would attack because they were usually more hostile when the corn was ripe. He reported that many people wished the Indians would be exterminated, but the pastor recognized the Indians' claim to the land. Besides, their absence would remove the buffer zone that existed between the German colony and the French Indians to the northwest. (See also items 254–257 and 259–260)

(1748) 259

———. "August, 1748 in Georgia, from the Diary of John Martin Bolzius." *Georgia Historical Quarterly* 47 (June 1963):204–16.

Bolzius says that the toll placed on East Indian tea by the English forced the colonists to use a kind of tea that grew wild near salt water. Although war with the Indians was feared, Bolzius says that the governing council considered it unlikely. He adds that some members of a colony in South Carolina were moving into Georgia because they could not find adequate salt for their cattle in South Carolina. (See also items 254–258 and 260.)

(1748) 260

———. "September, 1748 in Georgia, from the Diary of John Martin Bolzius." *Georgia Historical Quarterly* 47 (September 1963):320–32.

Although Bolzius was convinced that many European crops could be successfully grown in Georgia, he says that the colonists did not know how to grow according to proper planting cycles. Furthermore, they were stubborn. They preferred to continue patterns they were accustomed to in the Old World, ignoring his suggestions for improvements. He describes the progress of the crops and the damaging effects of the overabundance of rain. (See also items 254–259.)

(1784–1786) **SAMUEL EDWARD BUTLER** 261

Herndon, G. Melvin, ed. "The Diary of Samuel Edward Butler, 1784–1786 and the Inventory and Appraisement of His Estate." *Georgia Historical Quarterly* 52 (June 1968):203–20.

A terse travel diary and expense account by a Virginian who set down the bare details of a month-long trip to investigate lands for purchase in Wilkes County, Georgia, early in 1784. Includes his return trip that same year and a nine-day trip in Georgia once he had moved there in 1786.

(1796)   **BENJAMIN HAWKINS**   262

Hemperley, Marion R., ed. "Benjamin Hawkins' Trip Across Georgia in 1796." *Georgia Historical Quarterly* 55 (Spring 1971):114–37.

On his way to commence his duties as principal Indian agent for all Indians south of the Ohio River, Hawkins traveled across northwestern South Carolina and Georgia and into eastern Alabama between November 24 and December 10, 1796. This is the first portion of Hawkins's diary of his trip. The editor states that Hawkins's diaries are important because he was often the first white man to leave a record of the area in which he traveled. (See also item 375.)

(1811)   **J. B. DUNLOP**   263

Mohl, Raymond A., ed. "A Scotsman Visits Georgia in 1811." *Georgia Historical Quarterly* 55 (Summer 1971):259–74.

During his year-long visit to South Carolina, the northeastern United States, and Canada, J. B. Dunlop visited Georgia in February, 1811. He traveled extensively from Savannah, along the rivers and sea islands of Georgia, and as far south as Saint Marys River on the border between the United States and Spanish east Florida. Dunlop discusses the Yazoo land controversy, the topography, and the crops grown, and offers an interesting account of the rough back-country people.

He saw the "crackers" as barbarous and contrary individuals who were devoted to deciding differences of opinion with the rule of the fist and eye gouging. He admired their independence and their ability to be happy in the midst of poverty. He also relates the effects of smuggling in Spanish-owned Amelia Island during the American embargo against trade with France and England. Finally, Dunlop discusses the rough mode of travel throughout the state, especially on his return to Charleston from Savannah by carriage. (See also items 115 and 306.)

(1826)   **JARED SPARKS**   264

Moore, John Hammond, ed. "Jared Sparks in Georgia, April 1826." *Georgia Historical Quarterly* 47 (December 1963):425–35.

Jared Sparks, editor of the *North American Review*, was in Georgia in search of Revolutionary War records. He crossed Georgia from Savannah to Atlanta, describing the crops, witnessing the whipping of a slave, and exhibiting interest in the current excitement in Georgia over the Creek Treaty and the lottery scheme to dispose of the Indian lands. (See also item 292.)

(1827)   **JOHN R. VINTON**   265

Bonner, James C., ed. "Journal of a Mission to Georgia in 1827." *Georgia Historical Quarterly* 44 (March 1960):74–85.

Lieutenant John R. Vinton was on an official mission to deliver a message to the governor of Georgia regarding the Creek Indians. His journal, kept during the first half of 1827, describes the frontier capital of Milledgeville and includes his travel through southwest Georgia.

(1838–1839)   **FRANCES ANNE KEMBLE**   266

Cate, Margaret Davis. "Mistakes in Fanny Kemble's Georgia Journal." *Georgia Historical Quarterly* 44 (March 1960):1–17.

British actress Fanny Kemble spent four months (December 30, 1838-April 17, 1839) on the Georgia sea islands of Butler and Saint Simons as the wife of the plantation owner. When her experiences were published in 1863, the work became a popular but controversial account of slavery. In this article Cate questions the accuracy of Kemble's *Journal of a Residence on a Georgian Plantation in 1838–1839* (New York, 1863) by locating several errors and suggesting that because they exist "every statement in the *Journal* is open to suspicion." (p. 17) Cate is also suspicious of Kemble's purpose for writing twenty-five years after her visit, which was to counter English sympathy for the South.

Cate criticizes Kemble's literary form, a day-by-day diary which she says Kemble admits in another place in it that she did not have time to keep when she was actually in Georgia. *Note*: For a rebuttal to Cate's article, read John A. Scott, "On the Authenticity of Fanny Kemble's 'Journal of a Residence on a Georgian Plantation, 1838–1839'," *Journal of Negro History* 46 (October 1961):233–42. A popular account of Kemble's stay in Georgia, the circumstances surrounding the publication of the journal, her subsequent life, and the fate of the plantation may be found in Robert Wernick, "Glamorous Actress Found No Glamor in Georgia Slavery," *Smithsonian* 5 (November 1974):74–81. (See also item 277.)

(1843) JOHN NEWLAND 267

Dann, John C., ed. "A Northern Traveler in Georgia, 1843." *Georgia Historical Quarterly* 56 (Summer 1972):282–90.

Reverend John Newland of Albany, New York, came to Georgia to restore his failing health. In addition to offering a vignette of Savannah, Newland's letters describe conditions of his travel. He praises the sea voyage from Charleston to Savannah, but complains about the journey from Savannah to Macon by train and stage, as well as the crude accommodations for rest.

(1862) FELIX GREGORY DE FONTAINE 268

Merrill, James M., ed. "Personne Goes to Georgia: Five Civil War Letters." *Georgia Historical Quarterly* 43 (June 1959):202–11.

"Personne" was Felix Gregory De Fontaine, a war correspondent with the *Charleston Daily Courier*. These letters, written between March 1 and March 18, 1862, describe Savannah's preparation for an anticipated attack that never came. He writes of deserted city streets and empty factories because the men had gone off to war. He praises the patriotic contributions of the civilians and criticizes those men who stayed home to make personal gains out of the situation. He describes similar conditions in Atlanta and stresses the fine hospital facilities there.

(1862–1863) 269

Mahon, John K., ed. "Peter Dekle's Letters." *Civil War History* 4 (December 1958):11–22.

In 1862, while momentous battles raged to the west and north, Private Dekle and the Twenty-ninth Georgia Volunteers were restricted to the dullness of guard duty on the Georgia coast. The editor adds that although these letters contain little about the strategy and tactics of the war, they do represent the "worm's-eye" view of the conflict. They reveal Dekle's thoughts of discharge, as well as the variety of life to be seen in the camp. He admonishes his wife to take care of her teeth, defends himself against someone who has been defaming his character at home, and expresses concern about the destruction of his property. After hearing camp stories about the unfaithfulness of wives, Dekle betrays a gnawing but apparently unfounded fear about his own wife. He tells her, "I want you to be on your guard and not let no one get a holt on you." (p. 16)

By late 1862, Dekle was thoroughly bored with inactivity and longed to engage the enemy. Early in 1862 his unit marched to the Carolinas, and after their return to Georgia, they were transferred to Mississippi, where he was killed in August, 1863. Shortly before his death Dekle wrote that he longed to return home to fight for his wife and child, "as for the Confederacy, that is gone up—there is no use in fighting for that anymore." (p. 22)

(1864)   **ALLEN D. CHANDLER**   270

Chandler, Allen D. "Watch on the Chattahoochee: A Civil War Letter." *Georgia Historical Quarterly* 43 (December 1959):427–28.

During the Atlanta campaign, Colonel Allen D. Chandler wrote this letter (July 7, 1864) in which he contemplates the changed conditions and his personal losses should the Confederacy be defeated. To his wife he writes, "Then my darling what will you do? You have been raised with a servant at your elbow to do your bidding but then there will be no servants." (p. 428)

(1864)   **CHARLES G. LEE**   271

Helmreich, Paul C., ed. "The Diary of Charles G. Lee in the Andersonville and Florence Prison Camps, 1864." *Connecticut Historical Society Bulletin* 41 (January 1976):12–28.

Lee was a color corporal serving with the Sixteenth Connecticut Infantry when he was captured at Plymouth, North Carolina, on April 20, 1864. In these portions of his diary, which cover all of 1864, he records conditions in the prison camps. At Andersonville, Georgia, he describes his constant hunger and rations that were only partly cooked, escape plans, alternating extremes of weather that made the overcrowded "pens" seem worse, and such serious illnesses as diarrhea and scurvy, in addition to the usual headaches and coughs. Lee also relates some of the atrocities Union soldiers inflicted upon their fellow prisoners. As the diary ends, Lee has been transferred to Florence, South Carolina, awaiting exchange in conditions as miserable as they were at Andersonville. In February 18, 1865, he was exchanged, but the following month he died of pneumonia in a Union hospital.

(1864)   **ALBERT HARRY SHATZEL**   272

Danker, Donald F., ed. "Imprisoned at Andersonville: The Diary of Albert Harry Shatzel, May 5, 1864—September 12, 1864." *Nebraska History* 38 (June 1957):81–125.

Private Shatzel (First Vermont Cavalry) was captured at the Battle of the Wilderness (Virginia) on May 5, 1864, and was imprisoned at Andersonville, Georgia, from May 22 to September 12, 1864. He describes the train ride to Andersonville, the oppressive humidity and heat, the lice and maggot-infested earth; the frequent deaths in the prison (thirty or more each day), and rumors about the war. On September 12 he was transferred to a prison at Florence, South Carolina, which, the editor says, Shatzel later compared unfavorably to Andersonville. On December 11, 1864, Shatzel was released.

(1865)   **JAMES W. CHAPIN**   273

Reynolds, Donald E., and Kele, Max H., eds. "A Yank in the Carolinas Campaign: The Diary of James W. Chapin, Eighth Indiana Cavalry." *North Carolina Historical Review* 46 (January 1969):42–57.

Brief diary entries from January 28 to March 25, 1865, by Lieutenant Chapin that describe a 425-mile march, requiring fifty days, from Savannah, Georgia, to Goldsboro, North Carolina, through swamps and creeks at flood stage. Relates rumors of Confederate executions of Union prisoners and hints at how Sherman's officers attempted to curb their soldiers' excesses.

(1865)   **JOHN M. GLIDDEN**   274

Glidden, John M. "A Yankee Views the Agony of Savannah." *Georgia Historical Quarterly* 43 (December 1959):428–31.

A letter from a Boston lawyer, whose ship stopped over at Savannah on January 29, 1865, relates the suffering and destruction he found in that Georgia city.

Smits, A. C. G. "A Comment on Savannah, 1866." *Georgia Historical Quarterly* 50 (December 1966):459–60.

Originally many southerners feared that former slaves would prove unreliable as employees. In this letter of April 25, 1866, however, A. C. G. Smits of Virginia reports that agriculture was being well tended. In his opinion residents of Savannah were adjusting to Reconstruction.

Wagner, George. "A Freedmen's Bureau Diary by George Wagner." (Part I) *Georgia Historical Quarterly* 48 (June 1964):196–214.
————. (Part II) *Georgia Historical Quarterly* 48 (September 1964):333–60.

Lieutenant Wagner recorded the bare details of his travels between Macon, Augusta, and Americus, Georgia, from May 26, 1866, to December 20, 1868. Most of the references to the freedmen were to problems between blacks. There was one complaint from whites that blacks would not work and some excitement at election time of 1868, but Wagner usually reports that freedmen affairs were uneventful.

Wynes, Charles E. "Fanny Kemble's South Revisited: The South as Seen Through the Eyes of Her Daughter, Frances." *Louisiana Studies* 12 (Fall 1973):473–88.

In 1867, Frances Butler Leigh returned to the family rice and cotton plantations on Georgia's Butler and Saint Simons sea islands where she had lived briefly some thirty years earlier as a very small child. From those experiences, her mother, Fanny Kemble, wrote *Journal of a Residence on a Georgia Plantation in 1838–1839*, which became a widely read, controversial description of American slavery. (See item 266.) For most of a decade (1867 to 1877) Frances lived on and managed the plantation from Butler Island, accompanied first by her father and later her husband.

Frances' account of her years (*Ten Years on a Georgia Plantation Since the War* [London, 1833]) describes how the plantation was affected by wage-earning blacks. Frances originally shared most southerners' feelings that blacks would not work unless compelled to by a strong white personality. She believed that to the former slaves, liberty really meant idleness. But Wynes says that Frances quickly changed her mind when the blacks proved to be efficient, wage-earning laborers. In her work, Frances also offers opinions on the adverse effects of Reconstruction and the presence of northerners in the South. Wynes completes this biographical sketch with a few comparisons between the accounts written by the daughter and the mother.

Maryland

Kimber, Edward. "Eighteenth-Century Maryland as Portrayed in the 'Itinerant Observations' of Edward Kimber." *Maryland Historical Magazine* 51 (December 1956):315–36.

This English "hack writer" visited America in 1745 and 1746 and used his experiences as background material for one of his novels. (p. 315) He also published the factual narrative of his adventures in the *London Magazine*, from which this article is taken. Kimber tells of a cold, rough voyage from New York to Sene-Puxon in Maryland and then describes a trip through the colony. He observed that the planters were shifting their crops from tobacco to grain and were raising more livestock.

He found the towns and cities to be sparsely populated because the people preferred to live apart. Kimber saw a large number of militia units among these people who stood ready to defend their lands against the Indians. He believed this was important because there were no regular troops stationed nearby. He disliked slavery, especially the immoral practices involving women, but Kimber thought the blacks were treated well. He also mentions the use of convicts from England, the Roman Catholics he met on his travels, and the different values paper money held from place to place.

(1824)   HORATIO RIDOUT   279

Ridout, Horatio. "Journal of a Voyage Down the Chesapeake Bay on a Fishing Expedition, 1824." *Maryland Historical Magazine* 51 (June 1956):140–53.

The author describes the many activities he encountered in the Chesapeake Bay area: the fishing boats and the kinds of fish caught, the commercial enterprises on the water and in the towns, the agriculture along the shore, and the people he met.

(1827)   HENRY D. GILPIN   280

Gray, Ralph D., and Hartdagen, Gerald E., eds. "A Glimpse of Baltimore Society in 1827: Letters by Henry D. Gilpin." *Maryland Historical Magazine* 69 (Fall 1974):256–70.

Henry D. Gilpin was a young lawyer who traveled to Virginia and Maryland in September, 1827. These letters describe only his social experiences in Baltimore.

(1846–1850)   HENRI HERZ   281

Hill, Henry Bertram, and Gara, Larry, eds. "Henri Herz' Description of Baltimore." *Maryland Historical Magazine* 52 (June 1957):120–23.

During his visits to Baltimore the musician found the city gay and charming, Baltimore women beautiful, and the "spitters club" humorous. From *Mes voyages en Amérique* (Paris, 1866). Herz visited the United States between 1846 and 1850. (See also items 52, 53, 65, and 410.)

(1859)   ANONYMOUS   282

Clark, Ella E., ed. "Life on the C. & O. Canal: 1859." *Maryland Historical Magazine* 55 (June 1960):81–122.

During the period when the anonymous author of this manuscript was made unemployed by the Panic of 1857, he found work on a mule-drawn canal boat. He recalls a trip down the Chesapeake and Ohio Canal from its starting point at Cumberland, Maryland, to its terminus at Georgetown, D.C., in the summer of 1859. Perhaps because it was his first trip, he remembers many aspects of the journey. He describes work and life aboard the barge, the lock system, wildlife along the paths, and the people he met. He provides glimpses of Cumberland and Williamsport, Maryland; Alexandria, Virginia; and Washington, D.C.

(1861–1863)   VALENTIN BECHLER   283

Goodell, Robert C., and Taylor, P.A.M. "A German Immigrant in the Union Army: Selected Letters of Valentin Bechler." *Journal of American Studies* 4 (February 1971):145–62.

This portion of the correspondence between Valentin and Leokadia Bechler reveals the hardships the war placed on an immigrant family. Although Valentin was loyal to his unit, he was hardly patriotic. The editors add that Bechler was isolated because he was not an American and was cut off from his German culture. His lack of fluency in the English language made him suspicious. For example, he writes about his treatment in the hospital. "If a man can't speak well they let him go to hell." (p. 159)

Though Valentin sent most of his pay to his wife in Newark, it was not enough to handle the effect of rising prices on an already poor family. Leokadia writes, "You can imagine how it is, a woman with 5 children and the husband not at home . . . If only the lousy war was over." (p. 157) The letters were written from late 1861 to early 1863 while Bechler was serving in Maryland and Virginia with first the Eighth New York Infantry and then the Sixth Independent Battery, New York Light Artillery.

(1861–1863)   GORHAM COFFIN   284

Wisbey, Herbert A., Jr., ed. "Civil War Letters of Gorham Coffin." *Essex Institute Historical Collections* 93 (January 1957):58–92.

Coffin served with the Nineteenth Massachusetts Infantry and wrote these letters from Maryland and Virginia between August, 1861 and June, 1863. Since his unit was stationed in and near Rockville, Maryland for six months, he had an opportunity to observe the social life of the city. He stressed the intemperate nature of the inhabitants and the religious intensity of the blacks. Coffin also describes action in the Peninsular campaign (March-July, 1862). He was killed at Gettysburg.

NORTH CAROLINA

(1662)   WILLIAM HILTON   285

Wright, J. Leitch, Jr., ed. "William Hilton's Voyage to Carolina in 1662." *Essex Institute Historical Collections* 105 (April 1969):96–102.

A portion of a journal that describes the climate, the wildlife, and the agricultural possibilities of the Cape Fear River (North Carolina) region for the New England Company, which hoped to establish a settlement there.

(1700–1701)   JOHN LAWSON   286

Diket, A. L. "The Noble Savage Convention as Epitomized in John Lawson's 'A New Voyage to Carolina'." *North Carolina Historical Review* 43 (October 1966):413–29.

During 1700 and 1701, Lawson traveled the Carolina frontier and wrote a careful and observant description, *A New Voyage to Carolina* (London, 1709). Diket says that the work was instrumental in the ideas of the wilderness paradise and the "noble savage" in eighteenth-century writings. (See also item 287.)

(1700–1701)   287

Lindgren, W. H., III. "Agricultural Propaganda in Lawson's 'A New Voyage to Carolina'." *North Carolina Historical Review* 49 (October 1972):333–44.

Questions the reliability of the geography, folklore, and especially the agricultural figures presented in John Lawson's *New Voyage to Carolina* (London, 1709). Lindgren says that the agricultural figures were exaggerated just enough to encourage Englishmen to want to settle in North Carolina. (See also item 286.)

(1777–1778)   EBENEZER HAZARD   288

Johnston, Hugh Buckner, ed. "The Journal of Ebenezer Hazard in North Carolina, 1777 and 1778." *North Carolina Historical Review* 36 (July 1959):358–81.

Hazard was surveyor of the post roads, with the duties of regulating the continental postal route between Philadelphia and Savannah. This diary records trips from Suffolk, Virginia, to Edenton, North Carolina (June 12-June 20, 1777), and Williamsburg, Virginia, to Edenton, Bath, New Bern, and Wilmington, North Carolina (December 14, 1777-January 16, 1778). Although he is most interested in the condition of the roads, Hazard also describes the people, the produce of the land, and the organization of towns. (See also items 99 and 301.)

(1783–1860)	NORTH CAROLINA	289

Patton, James W. "Glimpses of North Carolina in the Writings of Northern and Foreign Travelers, 1782–1860." *North Carolina Historical Review* 45 (July 1968):298–323.

Patton summarizes the motives that impelled travelers to come to the South, the route taken on the "Grand Tour," and the impressions of those who passed through North Carolina. Most glimpses resulted in negative comments about the state's backwardness. The travelers described being transported over vast, sandy, pine lands or through cypress swamps by wild stage drivers to inns with primitive accommodations. The population, which was spread thinly over the state, was usually described as slovenly. Patton uses quotations extensively to illustrate these impressions.

(1806)	THOMAS LENOIR	290

————, ed. "Thomas Lenoir's Journey to Tennessee in 1806." *Tennessee Historical Quarterly* 17 (June 1958):156–66.

Lenoir traveled from North Carolina to Bedford County, Tennessee, to collect debts owed to his father and to locate some property he owned on the Duck River. Contains brief comments about the conditions of travel and the land, and an itinerary of the trip from June 1 to July 18, 1806.

(1817–1818)	SAMUEL HUNTINGTON PERKINS	291

McLean, Robert C., ed. "A Yankee Tutor in the Old South." *North Carolina Historical Review* 47 (January 1970):51–85.

Connecticut-born Samuel Huntington Perkins spent one year during 1817 and 1818 on Lake Plantation in Hyde County, North Carolina, educating the daughters of the plantation owner. His journal describes travel to the area; the climate, wildlife, and vegetation of the coastal region; the laziness of the poor whites; the gentility of the southern women and their domination by southern men. Though Perkins opposed slavery, he writes with some apparent ambivalence. He tells of observing a slave being punished for suspicion of stealing. Even after he learned the slave was killed, he explains that this incident was an exception and that most slaveowners tried to make their slaves comfortable. In another place he writes that freeing the slaves without first educating them in the ways of liberty would be a great cruelty.

(1826)	JARED SPARKS	292

Moore, John Hammond, ed. "Jared Sparks in North Carolina." *North Carolina Historical Review* 40 (July 1963):285–94.

During the spring of 1826, the editor of the *North American Review* searched throughout the South for manuscripts, documents, and letters that would preserve America's past. These extracts from the North Carolina portion of Sparks's diary (May 2-May 10) describe people, buildings, food, and roads and include some comments about the records he found. (See also item 264.)

(1854) **WILLIAM REES** 293

Thornburg, Opal, ed. "From Indiana to North Carolina in 1854: The Diary of William Rees." *Quaker History* 59 (Autumn 1970):67–80.

While serving as a delegate from Indiana to the North Carolina Yearly Meeting of Friends in 1854, Rees recorded conditions of his travel by several modes of transportation from Richmond, Indiana, to Raleigh, North Carolina. During the period between October and December, 1854, the delegates visited many meetings in western North Carolina. Rees reports on the state of Quakerism, as well as on the copper and gold mines and agriculture.

(1861–1865) **HENRY W. BARROW** 294

Blair, Marian H., ed. "Civil War Letters of Henry W. Barrow Written to John W. Fries." *North Carolina Historical Review* 34 (January 1957):68–85.

Quartermaster Sergeant Barrow of the Twenty-first North Carolina Infantry saw firsthand in North Carolina and Virginia how inadequate provisions prevented treating the many fevers among the men. His letters, written between July 4, 1861 and February 19, 1865, reflect his discouragement with the war and a growing sense of impending disaster.

(1864–1865) **JAMES W. EBERHART** 295

McLaughlin, Florence C., ed. "Diary of Salisbury Prison by James W. Eberhart." *Western Pennsylvania Historical Magazine* 56 (July 1973):211–51.

The editor believes that the most remarkable thing about Eberhart's stay in two Confederate prisons was his determination to do whatever was necessary to keep himself alive. His diary (August 18, 1864-March 18, 1865) follows his capture at Petersburg, Virginia, his imprisonment at Belle Isle on the James River and at Salisbury, North Carolina, and his eventual release. During the winter Eberhart volunteered for wood and water duty to keep active. Eberhart relates an incident involving a man who stayed huddled around the small fires and became so stiff that he yelled in pain when his friends tried to help him exercise. Eberhart braved the cold to delouse himself by holding his clothes over the fire, listening to the bugs crackle. Poor rations were always a problem, but he made dumplings from flour and bone marrow. Eberhart worked to keep his spirits up, but it must have been difficult when nearly every entry ends with a comment about someone who died that day. Sergeant Eberhart served with the 191st Pennsylvania Infantry.

(1865) **STEPHEN CHAULKER BARTLETT** 296

Murray, Paul, and Bartlett, Stephen Russell, Jr., eds. "The Letters of Stephen Chaulker Bartlett Aboard U.S.S. 'Lenapee', January to August, 1865." *North Carolina Historical Review* 33 (Winter 1956):66–92.

Bartlett was a surgeon aboard a ship in the Cape Fear River during the siege of Wilmington, North Carolina. He found the bombardment exciting but the condition of Wilmington depressing. The city was dirty and filled with refugees, both black and white, and various fevers raged. His impression of the blacks was that they were lazy and would not use their freedom to work. Bartlett's impression of the young ladies from the North who came to begin schools was that they were diligent and dedicated but still had time to flirt with the Yankee officers.

(1874–1880) **CYNTHIA THOMAS** 297

Raper, Horace W., ed. "Accounts of Moravian Mountain Excursions of a Hundred Years Ago." *North Carolina Historical Review* 47 (July 1970):281–316.

These four diaries of recreational trips taken between 1874 and 1880 by prominent families of the North Carolina Moravian community were perhaps written by Cynthia Thomas. They provide historical descriptions of geographic landmarks and traveling conditions in western North Carolina and Virginia.

(1885)   **WILLIAM BREWSTER**   298

Simpson, Marcus B., Jr., ed. "William Brewster's Exploration of the Southern Appalachian Mountains: The Journal of 1885." *North Carolina Historical Review* 57 (January 1980):43–77.

Because the Appalachians extend from Canada to the Carolinas the flora and fauna of the whole range has a common evolutionary history. While this fact was recognized about the botany of the region early in the nineteenth century, it was not established to be true about the zoology of the range until much later. In the 1880s biologists speculated that birds thought to have been lost to the northern climate might be found in a familiar environment to the south. Between May 22 and June 2, 1885, Boston ornithologist William Brewster searched the mountains around Asheville, North Carolina, in quest of species of northern birds that might be found in cold upper reaches of this mountain chain. In addition to reprinting the journal with drawings of some of the northern birds Brewster found in the region, the editor summarizes the value of Brewster's short trip in stimulating scientific interest.

South Carolina

(1700–1740)   **SOUTH CAROLINA**   299

Smyth, William D. "Travelers in South Carolina in the Early Eighteenth Century." *South Carolina Historical Magazine* 79 (April 1978):113–25.

During the first four decades of the eighteenth century, most travelers included in their accounts a description of Charleston harbor, the fortification of the city, the flora and fauna, the agriculture, the Indians, and the great number of slaves. One traveler estimated the ratio of blacks to whites was five to one. Near the end of this period, the effects two religious travelers, George Whitefield and John Wesley, were having on South Carolina society was widely reported.

(1764)   **MOSES LOPEZ**   300

Tobias, Thomas J., ed. "Charles Town in 1764." *South Carolina Historical Magazine* 67 (April 1966):64–74.

New England merchant Moses Lopez was in Charles Town to sell his goods, and his letters (April 13-May 23) concern commercial matters. Of particular interest is the fashion in which Lopez says planters and merchants traded. The planters seldom came to town and would do business only with "their" merchant even though they might have been able to obtain goods cheaper elsewhere. The two parties settled all accounts the first of each year. For the merchant, this arrangement sometimes meant bad debts or delayed payments. Lopez also describes the city and compares it with the way it looked during his previous visit in 1742.

(1778)   **EBENEZER HAZARD**   301

Merrens, H. Roy, ed. "A View of Coastal South Carolina in 1778: The Journal of Ebenezer Hazard." *South Carolina Historical Magazine* 73 (October 1972):177–93.

Hazard was in South Carolina in his capacity as surveyor of post roads to improve postal communications. The editor thinks Hazard was an excellent early geographer. In his journal he recorded topographical details, as well as providing an itinerary. He also made notes on a variety of topics: towns and taverns, agriculture and farming methods, matters of social importance, and current events. He kept abreast of the debate in the South Carolina General Assembly over the proposed constitution for the Confederation. Hazard understood that the Carolina lawmakers, whom he believed were "very jealous of the northern, especially the New England states," were going to make a number of alterations in the draft copy. (p. 184)

Hazard noticed the dialect of the common whites and compared it to that of the blacks. He commented on the relationships between the whites and the blacks, and described "black balls" hosted by black men and mulatto women to which they invited white gentlemen, "so called." (p. 190) Hazard disliked slavery and thought it a sorry state of affairs where fear ruled. He said the slaves were afraid of the masters and the masters were afraid of insurrection. He dismissed southern arguments that blacks were needed for labor because of their adaptability to the climate. Hazard believed slaves were kept because of the indolence and pride of the white people, "which are great beyond description." (p. 193) The editor lists other publications from Hazard's journal. (See also items 99 and 288.)

(1779–1780) JAMES SIMPSON 302

Brown, Alan S., ed. "James Simpson's Reports on the Carolina Loyalists, 1779–1780." *Journal of Southern History* 21 (November 1955):513–19.

Simpson's letters to his British commanders stated that it was practicable to reestablish the King's government in South Carolina and Georgia.

(1780) HENRY CLINTON 303

Bulger, William T., ed. "Sir Henry Clinton's 'Journal of the Siege of Charleston, 1780'." *South Carolina Historical Magazine* 66 (July 1965):147–82.

In addition to relating the progress of the siege, Clinton criticizes his second in command, Charles, Lord Cornwallis, and Admiral Marriott Arbuthnot, commander in chief of the Royal Navy. Journal kept between early April and May 31, 1780.

(1780) JOHN WILSON 304

Waring, Joseph Ioor, ed. "Lieutenant John Wilson's 'Journal of the Siege of Charleston'." *South Carolina Historical Magazine* 66 (July 1965):175–82.

Journal kept by Lieutenant Wilson of the Seventy-first British Infantry, February 29 to May 12, 1780.

(1785) JOSEPH SALVADOR 305

Roth, Cecil, ed. "A Description of America, 1785." *American Jewish Archives* 17 (April 1965):27–33.

An account of Charleston, South Carolina, is given in a letter written in January, 1785, by Joseph Salvador. The recent immigrant from England thought the people were ignorant, drunken descendants of the wild Irish. Furthermore, they had all the bad Spanish customs ("poor as rats, proud as dons . . . lazy . . . no morals"), but possessed none of the good qualities of that race. (p. 29) They cared more about their horses than their wives and families. Salvador knew that there were better people in South Carolina, but he believed that they were too docile and unimproved to do anything, even about government. As for the face of the land, Salvador thought the woods were strange and dangerous, as were the animals that inhabited them; that the climate was unhealthy; and, though the soil was fertile, it was not adequately cultivated by the inhabitants.

(1810–1811)   **J. B. DUNLOP**   **306**

Mohl, Raymond A., ed. "The Grand Fabric of Republicanism: A Scotsman Describes South Carolina—1810–1811." *South Carolina Historical Magazine* 71 (July 1970):170–88.

After arriving in Charleston on October 11, 1810, J. B. Dunlop spent most of his time in South Carolina, except for a short trip to Georgia. In June, 1811, he ventured into the northeastern United States and Canada, then back to New York City. In November, 1811, he departed New York City for Cuba before returning home. In the portion of his journal devoted to South Carolina, he describes the streets and buildings, institutions, shops, and geographical setting of Charleston, and the rice and cotton grown throughout the countryside. Dunlop explains how the planters deserted their plantations for the city in the summer to avoid the effects of yellow fever. He says those who stayed in the country, as well as those who came to the city, looked unhealthy during this period. He saw an absence of industry and blamed it on the "sloth and Indolence" of the whites. (p. 179)

Dunlop writes despairingly about the system of elections: too much noise, confusion and disagreement that often led to duels, a practice he condemns. Generally, he found the people to be hospitable and the women beautiful. He agreed with the women when they complained that the men spent too much time gambling. Dunlop says in any society there are bound to be different levels of social distinction, and this is also true in any of "the states united by the grand fabric of republicanism." (p. 184) In this scheme of things he thought South Carolinians were the aristocracy. Dunlop discusses their chief amusements, horse races in Charleston during February and deer hunting in the country.

In the city the religious principles of the Church of England prevailed, but in the country the "ridiculous fanaticism" of Methodism was strong. (p. 184) Dunlop believed whites were kind to their slaves, which was why the slaves were so subordinate despite their greater numbers. (See also items 115 and 263.)

(1818–1827)   **ABIEL ABBOT**   **307**

Moore, John Hammond, ed. "The Abiel Abbot Journals: A Yankee Preacher in Charleston Society, 1818–1827." (Part I) *South Carolina Historical Magazine* 68 (April 1967):51–73.

————. (Part II) *South Carolina Historical Magazine* 68 (July 1967):115–39.

————. (Part III) *South Carolina Historical Magazine* 68 (October 1967):232–54.

Reverend Abbot was a Unitarian minister who kept a journal of two visits to South Carolina taken for his health. The first covers November 9 to December 9, 1818, and the second, November 2 to 14, 1827, with several letters added that are dated February, 1828. Most of the writing tells of the people he met and the places he went. His descriptions of the city hospital for the insane and the Sugar House, a jail for black prisoners, are particularly informative.

(1821–1822)   **SAMUEL SITGREAVES, JR.**   **308**

Staudenraus, P. J., ed. "Letters from South Carolina, 1821–1822." *South Carolina Historical Magazine* 58 (October 1957):209–17.

Episcopal clergyman Samuel Sitgreaves, Jr., of Easton, Pennsylvania, came to South Carolina in two successive years seeking to improve his health and to serve in several parishes. His letters (January 4, 1821–February 9, 1822) tell of the ravages of yellow fever in the Savannah, Georgia, area where the disease was becoming epidemic as more lands were cleared of timber and the marshy lands exposed. While Sitgreaves thought the pleasures of the table and refined society to be of high quality, he felt they were the only enjoyments the region offered. Although his parish was considered uncivilized, Sitgreaves believed the women were devout. On his second visit, he made a tour of the sea islands and went to the remote parishes, which many residents were vacating because of the yellow fever. He judged that the vacant parishes had deteriorated too greatly to be reorganized.

(1825) CAROLINE OLIVIA LAURENS 309

King, Louise C., ed. "Journal of a Visit to Greenville from Charleston in the Summer of 1825: Caroline Olivia Laurens, May 1825." (Part I) *South Carolina Historical Magazine* 72 (July 1971):164–73.
————. (Part II) *South Carolina Historical Magazine* 72 (October 1971):220–33.

A diary relating conditions of travel and mundane comments about the people she met, the food she ate, and so forth, and kept May 23 to November 11, 1825.

(1850s) CHARLESTON 310

Steen, Ivan D. "Charleston in the 1850s: As Described by British Travelers." *South Carolina Historical Magazine* 71 (January 1970):36–45.

British travelers described Charleston as visually pleasing, with good hotels, wide, well-paved streets, attractive homes (for the rich), and a good harbor with a beautiful promenade along the water's edge. The police force and fire department were reported to be well organized. Public buildings were not acclaimed, there was a noticeable absence of benevolent institutions, and entertainment was limited to some theater and a gala horseracing season in February. The British thought society was divided into two classes, the rich and the poor. The blacks, of whom so many were seen in the streets that some travelers thought they outnumbered the whites, were felt to be obedient. They were always off the streets by the nine o'clock curfew. The Jewish population was also observed to be numerous. Despite Charleston's commercial importance, the city seemed to lack the bustle of the northeastern cities or even New Orleans.

(1851–1853) ROSALIE ULRIKA ROOS 311

Olsson, Nils William, ed. and tr. "Rosalie Ulrika Roos in South Carolina: Excerpts from a Recently Discovered Collection of Her American Letters." *Swedish Pioneer Historical Quarterly* 10 (October 1959):117–40.

These letters, written between 1851 and 1853, describe Roos's trip from Sweden to Limestone Spring, South Carolina, where she taught music and French at a girls' college. Later she worked as a governess on a plantation. In addition to revealing incidents of her personal life, she provides some information about the activities of Swedish settlers in South Carolina.

(1861–1862) MICHIGAN SOLDIERS 312

Blackburn, George M. "A Michigan Regiment in the Palmetto State." *South Carolina Historical Magazine* 68 (July 1967):154–64.

Using reminiscences and letters published in Michigan newspapers, Blackburn summarizes the comments of the Eighth Michigan Infantry during its occupation of the Port Royal-Hilton Head area in South Carolina between November, 1861 and June, 1862. The climate and food were very different from that to which the soldiers were accustomed, and they usually welcomed the change. The houses at Beaufort, which had been vacated by the owners and ransacked by both the slaves and Union soldiers, were regarded as impressive. Although the soldiers were sympathetic to the slaves, not many approved of abolition and certainly were not in favor of using the blacks as soldiers.

(1863) NOAH BROOKS 313

Staudenraus, P. J., ed. "Occupied Beaufort, 1863: A War Correspondent's View." *South Carolina Historical Magazine* 64 (July 1963):136–45.

In a letter that first appeared in the *Sacramento Daily Union* (July 16, 1863), reporter Noah Brooks compared the South Carolina sea island of that time with the way it looked in the past. He wrote of the charm of the old houses of Beaufort, although they were presently occupied by blacks or Union officers. He explains that in November, 1861, when the northern forces captured Hilton Head, the cry "the Yankees are coming" created a "Grand Skedaddle." (p. 138) First the blacks and then the Union soldiers ransacked what was left behind. He wrote about the "contrabands" (former slaves) who were being moved from place to place by circumstances beyond their control. Brooks also explains the management of the plantations and the operations of the military government.

(1864)   **JOHN STORTZ**   314

Stortz, John. "Experiences of a Prisoner During the Civil War In and Out of the Hands of the Rebels." *Annals of Iowa* 37 (Winter 1964):167–94.

Stortz describes his capture on July 23, 1864, at the Battle of Atlanta, his imprisonment, and his escapes while serving with the Second Battalion, Sixteenth U.S. Infantry. Much of this portion of his journal is concerned with tramping around South Carolina trying to avoid Confederate troops until he could obtain reliable directions to Union lines. He eventually made contact with Union forces just before Christmas, 1864.

(1864–1865)   **ANNA HASELL THOMAS**   315

Thomas, Charles E., ed. "The Diary of Anna Hasell Thomas." *South Carolina Historical Magazine* 74 (July 1973):128–43.

The apprehension of the people and the devastation created by Sherman's march through South Carolina is revealed in Mrs. Thomas's diary (December 27, 1864-May, 1865). During this time she traveled from New York City to Ridgeway, South Carolina, to visit her mother. Throughout South Carolina rumors of the impending crisis and of atrocities committed by the Yankees were rampant. Before the Union troops entered the mother's estate, the family had the slaves bury the eatables and silverware. The ransacking troops found nearly everything of value, however, and enticed some black girls and all the men to desert, leaving Thomas and the remaining blacks with few provisions. After about a week (February 20-26), the soldiers moved on. As the Thomas family traveled back to Charleston to return to New York, the pillaging by the Yankees and the Confederate scouts was apparent.

(1865)   **CHARLES C. SOULE**   316

Abbott, Martin, ed. "A New Englander in the South, 1865: A Letter." *New England Quarterly* 32 (September 1959):388–93.

A letter written June 12, 1865, to the Freedman's Bureau by Captain Charles C. Soule, Fifty-fifth Massachusetts Infantry Regiment (Colored) relating the difficulties of teaching former slaves and their former masters in South Carolina to adapt to their new relationship. After describing the chaotic conditions present when his troops of occupation arrived, Soule tells how his command went into the countryside and assembled the planters and former slaves to explain the new contracts of employment. After his arrival many contracts were signed and conditions quieted. Soule was more critical of the freedmen than of the plantation owners, although he knew that the blacks had been led to believe that the plantation lands would be theirs. He wrote that the former slaves acted as though freedom meant life without restraint. Soule concludes by describing the contracts that had been drawn up and expressing his thoughts about the future of the South.

(1865)   **EDWARD L. STEVENS**   317

Moore, John Hammond, ed. "The Last Officer—April, 1865." *South Carolina Historical Magazine* 67 (January 1966):1–14.

On April 5, 1865, Lt. Edward L. Stevens and the Fifty-fourth Massachusetts Infantry (Colored) set out from Georgetown, South Carolina, to destroy rail communications between Camden and Florence. His diary (April 5-16), together with the official report of commanding officer Colonel E. N. Hallowell, describes those last moments of the Civil War. They were joyous moments for the Union troops and the former slaves, but bitter ones for the residents of South Carolina. As the soldiers marched they confiscated mules, horses, and chickens in the country and store goods in Sumter; they burned cotton; and they destroyed rail lines and engines. Throughout the destruction of their homeland, Stevens said, the civilians looked on with woeful expressions. He thought it was a terrible sight. The number of "contrabands" (former slaves) that followed the army increased daily up to a total of 3,200. Stevens thought the variety of humanity so curious that it deserved the attention of an artist. He could not help wondering what would "become of this Race of uneducated, hopeful, anxious people." (p. 5) In his official report, Colonel Hallowell wrote, "During the whole march the troops were in perfectly good spirits and both officers and enlisted men carried out instructions with energy and cheerfulness." But when the twenty-day mission was over, Stevens did not return. He had been killed on April 18, nine days after the surrender at Appomattox.

(1869-1871)　　　　　BENJAMIN HODGES　　　　　318

Marchione, William P., Jr., ed. "Go South, Young Man! Reconstructionist Letters of a Massachusetts Yankee." *South Carolina Historical Magazine* 80 (January 1979):18–35.

Benjamin Hodges was attracted to South Carolina in hopes of becoming a successful cotton planter. These letters from his first years (December 21, 1869-April 15, 1871) indicate frustration, however. His farm near Owen's Place was distant from any other whites; the land was low-lying and mosquito infested; the blacks stole liberally and would not work until they were starving; and finally, cotton prices fell. His letters tell about a carpetbagging politician, the Ku Klux Klan, and the fate of formerly aristocratic plantation owners. As these letters end, Hodges has decided to leave his farm and rent a plantation near Sumter. The editor says Hodges eventually became a successful planter.

VIRGINIA

(1684-1686)　　　　　JOHN CLAYTON　　　　　319

Berkeley, Edmund, and Berkeley, Dorothy S., eds. "Another 'Account of Virginia' By the Reverend John Clayton." *Virginia Magazine of History and Biography* 76 (October 1968):415–36.

While in the American colonies Clayton served as rector of James Town Parish from 1684 until 1686. This account describes fish, insects, agricultural methods, Indian customs, and the bad influence some of the settlers were having on the natives. Pagination irregular; p. 436 end of article (?).

(1732-1733)　　　　　WILLIAM HUGH GROVE　　　　　320

Stiverson, Gregory A., and Butler III, Patrick H., eds. "Virginia in 1732: The Travel Journal of William Hugh Grove." *Virginia Magazine of History and Biography* 85 (January 1977):18–44.

The editors believe that Grove's journal is one of the few accounts of the colony in the first half of the eighteenth century. They point out that because this Englishman was an experienced traveler and deeply interested in natural history, he was well qualified to describe what he observed. Grove's interest was directed toward the flora and fauna of the countryside where he spent his time, rather than buildings and towns. He offers a systematic comparison of different groups of Virginia society—the gentry, the blacks, and the Indians—at a time when no other such comparisons were being made. The dates of his visit are uncertain since the journal is arranged topically rather than chronologically, but it began on April 1, 1732, and perhaps extended to March of 1733.

(1776–1780)   ANDREAS WIEDERHOLD   321

Walker, Ralph S., ed. "Trenton, I Shall Never Forget." *American History Illustrated* 11 (December 1976):43–49.

Presents portions of Hessian officer Andreas Wiederhold's diary written between December 14, 1776 and December 7, 1780. The editor focuses on Wiederhold's capture at the Battle of Trenton (December, 1776), and the next year and a half he spent as a prisoner. The Hessian officers were shuttled from Philadelphia, to Dumfries, Virginia, then to the Valley of Virginia, and to Fredericksburg before their exchange in April, 1779. Wiederhold liked most Americans wherever he met them, but especially the ones in Fredericksburg. He found the German-Americans of Pennsylvania and the Valley of Virginia to be unfriendly, however.

(1789)   FRANÇOIS XAVIER DUPONT   322

Nall, Charles T., ed. "A Letter From Petersburg, Virginia, January 10, 1789." *Virginia Magazine of History and Biography* 82 (April 1974):144–49.

François Xavier Dupont was interested in America in terms of its possibilities for speculation on Revolutionary War debts and commerce. Therefore, he took note of the high prices of the inns and of items in the marketplaces, the quality of goods imported, and the possibilities for better agricultural techniques. As a place for investment he much preferred Virginia to France. He says the reputation of Virginians was poor, and from what he had seen it was an accurate appraisal. They were "indolent, unindustrious, poor credit risks" and "spoiled by the abundance of Negroes." (p. 146) The blacks fared no better; they seemed to "prefer idleness to work." (p. 146) Dupont comments on the effect of the new Federal Constitution and the strength of the Anti-Federalist party and its eloquent leader, Patrick Henry.

(1801–1802)   RUTH HENSHAW BASCOM   323

Roeber, A. G., ed. "A New England Woman's Perspective on Norfolk, Virginia, 1801–1802: Excerpts from the Diary of Ruth Henshaw Bascom." *Proceedings of the American Antiquarian Society* 88 (October 1978):277–325.

While these entries are filled with reports of daily activities—sewing, cooking, reading, going on drives, and card games—the editors point out that the diary also contains some criticism the cultured New England lady felt toward Virginia society. For example, she believed Sundays were not properly observed by churchgoers, and she was glad to get back to a familiar New England cuisine. Ruth did like the mild climate, especially when New England was buried under fifteen feet of February snow and Virginia luxuriated in warm weather. At Christmas she saw the streets filled with blacks and explained that for five days during the holidays their time was their own. Nevertheless, "on the first day of January is a kind of market day for slavery on which they are hired and let, bought and sold like the horses in the stalls." (p. 289) She also mentioned the executions in the aftermath of the Easter, 1802, slave rebellion in Norfolk.

(1801–1823)   JOHN PINTARD   324

Vail, R. W. G. "Two Early Visitors to Mount Vernon." *New York Historical Society Quarterly* 42 (October 1958):349–65.

The first visitor was John Pintard, who described a dinner with Martha Washington on June 29, 1801. The second was an unidentified Scottish traveler who came to Virginia on March

9, 1823. Though Pintard was impressed by the mansion, he complained that George Washington's burial place was not dignified enough for so great a man. He described it as a simple, unornamented vault grown over with tall grass and despoiled by sightseers' names on the door.

(1807–1808)　　　　　　**ANONYMOUS**　　　　　　**325**

Beeman, Richard R., ed. "Trade and Travel in Post-Revolutionary Virginia: A Diary of an Itinerant Peddler, 1807–1808." *Virginia Magazine of History and Biography* 84 (April 1976):174–88.

The editor says that this unknown Irish peddler adds to our knowledge of economic life in the Old Dominion in several ways. He reveals that most others of this important class of merchants were also Irish; the county seats were the most attractive to peddlers; buyers were short of ready cash; and fines for peddling without a license were high. The diary relates the hardships of illnesses these men suffered because of the hazards of bad roads, poor weather conditions, and indifferent innkeepers.

(1814)　　　　　　**THOMAS H. PALMER**　　　　　　**326**

Wyllie, John Cook, ed. "'Observations Made During a Short Residence in Virginia': In a Letter from Thomas H. Palmer, May 30, 1814." *Virginia Magazine of History and Biography* 76 (October 1968):387–414.

During a trip over the mail route from Alexandria to Petersburg, this Scot from Philadelphia noticed many aspects of Virginia society: Virginians' hospitality, the peculiarities of their speech, their propensity for gambling, houses with chimneys on the outside, and the superior appearance of the towns, especially Richmond and Petersburg. Palmer offers long passages on the system of banks, taxation, and the elections; the conditions of the slaves; and the state of religious instruction, which he considers deplorable; and he concludes with a list of the manufacturers of Virginia for the year of 1810. This letter, which the editor indicates was one of the few accounts of travel in Virginia during the War of 1812, was first published in *The Historical Register of the United States* (vol. 3, part 1; 1814).

(1825–1826)　　　　　　**CARLO VIDUA**　　　　　　**327**

Cometti, Elizabeth, and Gennaro-Lerda, Valeria. "The Presidential Tour of Carlo Vidua with Letters on Virginia." *Virginia Magazine of History and Biography* 77 (October 1969):387–406.

Count Carlo Vidua of the Piedmont intended to write a history of the world, and he managed to visit a great deal of it before death halted his undertaking. He toured the United States between 1825 and 1826 and visited all five living presidents. He described his meetings with John Quincy Adams in Washington; James Monroe, Thomas Jefferson, and James Madison in Virginia; and John Adams in Boston. He also related incidents of his travels to the Shenandoah Valley, Richmond, Pennsylvania, and Massachusetts. These experiences are taken from his *Lettere del Conte Carlo Vidua* (Turin, 1835).

(1827)　　　　　　**HENRY D. GILPIN**　　　　　　**328**

Gray, Ralph D., ed. "A Tour of Virginia in 1827: Letters of Henry D. Gilpin to his Father." *Virginia Magazine of History and Biography* 76 (October 1968):444–71.

On this part of his journey through Maryland and Virginia, Gilpin visited Harpers Ferry, Lexington, Weylers Cave, Charlottesville, Natural Bridge, and Fredericksburg in September, 1827. Pagination irregular.

(1847)   **JOHN S. SKINNER**   **329**

Bishko, Lucretia Ramsey, ed. "John S. Skinner Visits the Virginia Springs, 1847."
Virginia Magazine of History and Biography 80 (April 1972):158–92.

Excerpts from articles that appeared in *The Farmers Library and Monthly Journal of Agri-culture* which describe Skinner's travel in the summer and fall of 1847. His writings mention his acquaintances and include matters of farming and agricultural importance.

(1851)   **MARY JANE BOGGS**   **330**

Buni, Andrew, ed. "'Rambles Among the Virginia Mountains': The Journal of Mary Jane Boggs, June 1851." *Virginia Magazine of History and Biography* 77 (January 1969):78–111.

A highly personal diary written for "no eyes except my own" which focuses on Miss Boggs's own activities and reactions. (p. 80) She does include some description of the natural beauty of the Shenandoah Valley and the Blue Ridge Mountains, and of the people who lived in those areas.

(1861)   **HARRY INNES THORNTON, JR.**   **331**

Thornton, Harry Innes, Jr. "Recollection of the War by a Confederate Officer from California." *Southern California Quarterly* 45 (September 1963):195–218.

Focuses on the period from July, 1861, to about November of that year. Thornton reveals his patriotic reasons for leaving California to join the Confederacy and tells of his arrival in New York, where he characterizes the northern and southern sentiment he found there. He writes of his early service in Virginia as an officer with the Thirty-seventh Alabama Infantry. Thornton provides his impressions of several southern officers, including Stonewall Jackson.

(1861–1863)   **WILLIAM DORSEY PENDER**   **332**

Hassler, William W., Jr. "The Civil War Letters of General William Dorsey Pender to His Wife." *Georgia Review* 17 (Spring 1964):57–75.

Follows Pender's career from the time he resigned his commission in the U.S. Army and joined the Confederacy, to just before Gettysburg (March 4, 1861-June 28, 1863). Pender's letters tell of the action he saw in Virginia, especially at Second Manassas, but they are also concerned with the strain the war put on his relationship with his wife. His depiction of north-erners and federal soldiers is interesting. Pender writes that Pennsylvanians were coarse and dirty, and there were no attractive women. On the march to Gettysburg, he says, the soldiers of the Confederacy paid for property and crops taken, and did not plunder like the Union troops. Pender reached the rank of brigadier general in command of a division of light artillery, Army of Northern Virginia, before being killed at Gettysburg.

(1861–1863)   **LEONIDAS TORRENCE**   **333**

Monroe, Haskell, ed. "The Road to Gettysburg: The Diary and Letters of Leonidas Torrence of the Gaston Guards." *North Carolina Historical Review* 36 (October 1959):476–517.

Torrence's first writings describe his initiation into army life (Thirteenth North Carolina, later Twenty-third) and the illnesses that confined him to hospitals in Richmond and Charlottes-ville. Many of his letters to his parents during this period reveal the shortage of clothes among Confederate troops, as well as the high prices of food. His later writings, from the summer of 1862 until his death at Gettysburg, tell of battle incidents. His letters were written between July 20, 1861, and June 13, 1863.

(1861–1865) **JAMES S. PEERY** 334

Hilldrup, Robert Leroy, ed. "The Romance of a Man in Gray Including the Love Letters of Captain James S. Peery, Forty-Fifth Virginia Infantry Regiment, C.S.A." (Part I) *West Virginia History* 22 (January 1961):83–116.

———. (Part II) *West Virginia History* 22 (April 1961):166–83.

———. (Part III) *West Virginia History* 22 (July 1961):217–39.

In Parts I and II the editor summarizes Peery's service and his lengthy romance with a girl who lived for most of the time only about thirty miles from where he was posted. Part III consists of the surviving eighteen letters written between June 26, 1861, and February 22, 1865. They describe Peery's participation in the war in southwest Virginia and West Virginia, as well as conditions at the federal prison on Johnson's Island, Ohio, where he was incarcerated for six months. The editor reminds us that the restrained expressions of affection by both parties was characteristic of their social class and generation.

(1861–1865) **HERMAN LORENZO WHITE** 335

Kroll, Kathleen, and Moran, Charles, eds. "The White Papers: Letters (1861–1865) of Pvt. Herman Lorenzo White, 22nd Regiment Massachusetts Volunteers." *Massachusetts Review*, 18 (Summer 1976):248–70.

Traces White's changing attitude about the war from the time he was an enthusiastic 16-year-old recruit to a disillusioned veteran. In addition to describing the fighting in Virginia, where he was captured at Gaines's Mill on June 27, 1863, and exchanged a month later, White reveals the mood of his fellow soldiers and his own feelings about the war. He tells how demoralized the Army of the Potomac was during the winter of 1862–63, when he observed drunken Union officers threatening to pit their units against one another. White was opposed to President Lincoln's conduct of the war, and especially the Emancipation Proclamation, which White believed made the conflict a "nigger war." (p. 249) These letters make it clear that White often disagreed with his parents with regard to the slavery issue and Abraham Lincoln.

(1862) **HARRIET DOUGLAS WHETTEN** 336

Hass, Paul, ed. "A Volunteer Nurse in the Civil War: The Letters of Harriet Douglas Whetten." *Wisconsin Magazine of History* 48 (Winter 1964/1965):131–51.

———. "A Volunteer Nurse in the Civil War: The Diary of Harriet Douglas Whetten." *Wisconsin Magazine of History* 48 (Spring 1965):205–21.

Records one episode of a war-long service to wounded Union soldiers. During this period (May 8-August 23, 1862) Whetten served as a nurse with the civilian U.S. Sanitary Commission providing assistance to the casualties of the Peninsular Campaign. She was stationed aboard a ship giving temporary comfort to the ill and wounded who were awaiting transportation to a permanent hospital. She describes the conditions under which she lived and worked—men lying on the deck only six inches apart, in filth and blood—and her own reactions to what she was doing. She never before thought she would be able to serve in the war and she thanked God for the opportunity. She would rather have treated the wounded than the sick, especially the typhoid patients, because the latter needed constant observation.

Whetten relates incidents with other nurses and the aid societies, her fear of treating wounded southern soldiers, and her prejudice against southerners in general. During the summer, the fighting ceased temporarily, and everyone waited for the hostilities to resume. When a battle provided fresh casualties, or when Union prisoners were released from Richmond's Libby Prison, the nurses sprang into action. In August, 1862, the government took over the hospital transport ships and Whetten was released. The editor says that Whetten continued to work in various hospitals from Rhode Island to New Orleans until the war's end.

(1863)   **ANONYMOUS**   **337**

Bandy, William T., ed. and tr. "Civil War Notes of a French Volunteer." *Wisconsin Magazine of History* 45 (Summer 1962):239–50.

In 1863 an unidentified Frenchman described action with the Union forces in Virginia and West Virginia for the French periodical *La Vie Parisienne*. The author stressed the undignified nature of the war to his readers, who would "wax enthusiastic about its glory, while you sit before a fire, a cigar in your mouth. . . ." (p. 210) He reported the poor condition of the soldiers and the bedraggled blacks that flocked to the army for sustenance and protection. All walked through mud and the difficult, rocky passes of the Blue Ridge Mountains and the Shenandoah Valley. On the march the troops came upon a camp of Confederate bushwhackers and the writer described the ambush in detail. When they reached Madison, Virginia, the townspeople were pleasantly accommodating until several of their slaves elected to go with the soldiers, angering the town's matrons. He describes the chaos of human suffering and carnage at Chancellorsville in May, 1863.

(1863–1865)   **DANVILLE PRISON**   **338**

Robertson, James I., Jr. "Houses of Horror: Danville's Civil War Prisons." *Virginia Magazine of History and Biography* 69 (July 1961):329–45.

Utilizes the diaries of federal prisoners confined at the Danville, Virginia, Prison from November, 1863, until February, 1865, to describe conditions there. The prisoners were moved from Richmond and Belle Isle because Richmond was a prime Union target. The men were placed in six tobacco warehouses that were filthy and infested with vermin. During the first winter the stoves for heating were inadequate, personal hygiene was impossible, and smallpox began to spread. Complaints about the poor conditions from Danville citizens went unheeded and escapes further aroused the countryside. After some escapes, the prisoners were confined to the top two floors of the buildings. They were allowed only brief periods in the courtyard to cook or to relieve themselves, a particular hardship for the many diarrhea sufferers. When the summer found more prisoners being placed in the already overcrowded prison, suffocation became a serious problem. Approaching the windows for air was dangerous because the guards, who were regarded as rejects from the front, frequently shot at the prisoners. The winter of 1864–65 was even colder than the previous winter. Diarists wrote that the prisoners were resigned to their condition and morale hit a new low after the failure of a large-scale escape attempt in December, 1864. In February, 1865, the remaining three thousand federal troops were exchanged from a total of seven thousand who had been confined to Danville during its fifteen-month history.

(1864)   **MARIA SMITH**   **339**

Smith, Maria. "It Was a Very Serious Undertaking." *Civil War Times Illustrated* 13 (August 1974):18–22.

Mrs. Smith recorded her harrowing experiences encountered when she traveled between Virginia and Maryland en route to Cooperstown, New York, in November, 1864, to visit her ailing father. She and her three small children were forced to cross the Potomac River in a Confederate Signal Corps boat at night to avoid federal gunboats. They stayed with strangers and acquaintances, fearing that they would be revealed as Confederates. Once she arrived home, she learned her father was not really ill. Mrs. Smith had been tricked by her family into returning to her former home in the North, where they felt she would be safer.

(1864–1865)   **ALBERT ROGALL**   **340**

Levstik, Frank, ed. "The Civil War Diary of Colonel Albert Rogall." *Polish-American Studies* 27 (Spring/Autumn 1970):33–79.

Rogall, a member of Polish nobility, came to America in 1851 as Florien Albert Rogall de Salmonski. During the period of this diary (March 27, 1864-April 5, 1865), he served in Virginia, first with the Twenty-seventh Regiment of United States Colored Troops, and then with the 118th Regiment, United States Colored Troops, which he commanded. He fought in the Wilderness Campaign (May 5-7, 1864), and at the siege of Petersburg (June 15-18, 1864).

Rogall's comments are wide-ranging. He tells his reactions to the noise and the carnage of the battlefield, as well as the physical discomforts of camp life. Thoughts of home are always on Rogall's mind and they become an obsession as the diary progresses. He is quite certain about the cause of the war, the "scoundrely preachers." (p. 36) Rogall is critical of the conduct of the war, other officers, and his own troops. He is angered about the absence of the Thanksgiving dinner that was promised: "Some rascality of the commisary and the quartermaster." (p. 63) Ill with dysentery, he directs his wrath at the medical department's treatment of his soldiers. "They are [a] set of thieves and whoremasters, especially in the colored division." (p. 43) Then, "all this war is a humbug—money affair—especially surgeons." (p. 44) In other places he adds more about war profiteering.

Rogall apparently did not hold his colored soldiers in high regard. He deplored their foraging and depredation, "all niggers are thieves" (p. 36), but felt helpless to prevent it. In Pittsburgh, he says, the colored troops were stoned and in Washington they were spit upon. Rogall regretted his decision to serve with the colored troops and believed these regiments were an unnecessary expense to the government. When he accepted command of the 118th U.S. Colored Troops, it was apparently from a sense of duty.

(1865)   ABNER R. COX   341

Shingleton, Royce Gordon, ed. "South from Appomattox: The Diary of Abner R. Cox." *South Carolina Historical Magazine* 75 (October 1974):238–44.

Lieutenant Cox's diary (April 11-27, 1865) records the march home by the Palmetto Sharpshooters after surrendering their arms in Virginia. Cox reveals some of the confusion that existed immediately following the war's conclusion. He relates continued hostilities by Confederate troops and makes reference to marauding civilians. On their way home his troops were well treated by the people of Virginia and North Carolina.

(1865)   EDWARD JOHN HAMILTON   342

Mooney, Chase C., ed. "A Union Chaplain's Diary." *Proceedings of the New Jersey Historical Society* 75 (January 1957):1–17.

Edward John Hamilton served as chaplain for the Seventh New Jersey Infantry. This portion of his diary (March 29-July 7, 1865) describes the last days of fighting in Virginia, his dazed reaction to Lee's surrender, the slaves' jubilation over being freed, the southern civilians' relief that the war was over, and his own feelings of distress at the excessive foraging and desecration by federal troops.

(1865)   ANTOINE AUGUSTE LAUGEL   343

Joyaux, Georges J., ed. "Auguste Laugel Visits the Army of the Potomac." *Virginia Magazine of History and Biography* 69 (October 1961):469–88.

Antoine Auguste Laugel was a French engineer who wrote historical and biographical works, as well as many articles about the United States. He spent six months touring the North and Middle West between September, 1864, and February, 1865. During January, 1865, Laugel visited the Army of the Potomac in Virginia. One of the things he noticed about the Union army was the variety of social classes and the lack of hierarchy within the army officer corps. As he sailed along the Virginia coast, Laugel saw the effects of the war, which was negligible in some places. After seeing a Negro military unit, he was dissuaded from believing that all blacks looked alike. He described the camps and living quarters; he had dinner with General Grant and remarked that the General refused to let whiskey be served at the meal or on the campground; and he visited the front-line positions. Because a kind of truce was in effect at the time, he was able to visit some enemy encampments. Laugel reported that an average of a hundred southern soldiers were deserting each day. This article is an excerpt from *Les États-Unis pendant la guerre Civil 1861–1865* (Paris, 1866.) (See also item 532.)

(1865)   EDWARD MOSELEY   344

Robertson, James I., Jr., ed. "English Views of the Civil War: A Unique Excursion to Virginia, April 2–8, 1865." *Virginia Magazine of History and Biography* 77 (April 1969):201–12.

Combines Edward Moseley's text with eight sketches by Edward Kennard to tell the story of how a party of Englishmen made an unauthorized trip up the James River. As their yacht passed through federal blockades, they were confronted by Admiral David D. Porter, who initially ordered their arrest but relented after a conversation with T. W. Kennard, the yacht captain. Moseley says, "Luck and the British flag had carried us through." (p. 206) He describes the ruins of Petersburg, the privation suffered by the people, and the high price of goods there. He also describes the devastation in Richmond, but he judged that neither Petersburg nor Richmond had been pillaged by federal soldiers. Moseley said he had heard of no complaints by the white inhabitants of Richmond about their treatment by the troops of occupation. The editor compares Moseley's account of the trip with that of Edward Kennard.

(1865)   ALFRED PAUL   345

Spencer, Warren F., ed. "A French View of the Fall of Richmond: Alfred Paul's Report to Drouyn de Lhuys, April 11, 1865." *Virginia Magazine of History and Biography* 73 (April 1965):178–88.

Paul, who was the French consul in Richmond throughout the Civil War, recorded the Confederate evacuation of that city in this letter to the French foreign minister. While Paul's letter confirms reports of the chaotic conditions that existed at first and then quickly subsided as federal troops took charge, his depiction of Secretary of State Judah P. Benjamin's demeanor contrasts with other accounts. The editor says that Benjamin is usually credited with exhibiting calm on April 2 and 3, 1865, but Paul says Benjamin was extremely nervous during their meeting.

(1865)   CHRISTOPHER Q. TOMPKINS   346

Rachal, William M. E., ed. "The Occupation of Richmond, April 1865: The Memorandum of Events of Colonel Christopher Q. Tompkins." *Virginia Magazine of History and Biography* 73 (April 1965):189–98.

Colonel Tompkins, who was a mining engineer operating the Dover coal pits for the Confederacy on the James River, made a trip to Richmond between April 6 and May 4, 1865. He contrasts the unsettled conditions in the countryside with the quiet that existed in Richmond because of martial law. Tompkins reports that during the final days of the Confederacy, Virginia troops were deserting in great numbers. While the majority of the slaves utilized in the coal pits were slow to realize they were free, once they became aware they quickly left for Richmond. Tompkins thinks the blacks will be the real sufferers in the conflict and predicts their extermination after the war. One benefit of the war that he could foresee was that when slave labor ceased to exist, the plantations would be divided.

(1866)   FREDERICK W. A. BRUCE   347

Jones, Wilbur Devereaux, ed. "A British Report on Postwar Virginia." *Virginia Magazine of History and Biography* 69 (July 1961):346–52.

An official memorandum from British representative Sir Frederick W. A. Bruce, who was sent to ascertain the public mood in Virginia in January, 1866. Although Virginians were proud of the sacrifices they had made, Bruce says they were glad the struggle was over. They refused to admit they were defeated, however, except in the face of overwhelming odds, and expressed a universal feeling of hatred for the Yankees.

(1866–1869) MARGARET NEWBOLD THORPE 348

Morton, Richard L., ed. "Life in Virginia, by a 'Yankee Teacher', Margaret Newbold Thorpe." *Virginia Magazine of History and Biography* 64 (April 1956):180–207.

Thorpe was sent by the Friends Association of Philadelphia to run a school for freedmen at Fort Magruder, Virginia, in 1866. In addition to teaching both day and night classes, Thorpe and a friend also conducted sewing classes and charities. In a letter of July, 1866, she writes that she thought highly of the blacks' ability to learn in all branches of study and commended those who worked hard all day on the plantations and came to school at night. Her notebook describes visits to the black settlement, which revealed poor homes and much illness. Despite the blacks' suffering and their desire to learn, she did not believe they were prepared for suffrage. When Thorpe told some freedmen that they were not qualified to run for office, they became angry with her and accused her of "trying to keep them down." (p. 202) She describes the attitudes of the local white people and their fear of the Ku Klux Klan. Thorpe returned to Philadelphia in June, 1869.

WEST VIRGINIA

(1819) JARED SPARKS 349

Moore, John Hammond, ed. "Jared Sparks Visits Harpers Ferry, 1819." *West Virginia History* 25 (January 1964):81–91.

An account of a five-week tour (August 6-September 10, 1819) of Harpers Ferry, western Maryland, and the springs of southern Pennsylvania. Sparks was a Unitarian minister, then editor of the *North American Review*; later, he was a historian at Harvard University and became president of Harvard.

(1829) BENJAMIN L. C. WAILES 350

Moore, John Hebron, ed. "A Glimpse of Industrial Wheeling in 1829: A Selection from the Journal of B. L. C. Wailes of Natchez." *West Virginia History* 20 (January 1959):126–29.

En route to Baltimore, Benjamin L. C. Wailes spent three days in Wheeling (December 14-17, 1829). During his stay he visited glass, cotton, and woolen factories. He thought the scenery beautiful but "deformed by the buildings which are ordinary and blackened by coal, the atmosphere being constantly obscured by it." (p. 129)

(1861) WILLIAM B. FLETCHER 351

Brigham, Loriman S., ed. "The Civil War Journal of William B. Fletcher." *Indiana Magazine of History* 57 (March 1961):39–76.

Presents the existing fragment of a larger document that reveals Dr. Fletcher's activities with the Sixth Regiment of Indiana Infantry from April to June, 1861. It tells of patriotic sentiment in Indiana after the fall of Fort Sumter and the favorable reception the Union troops received in western Virginia. Fletcher also describes activities as a Union spy in western Virginia.

(1861)   **ISAAC NOYES SMITH**   352

Childers, William, ed. "A Virginian's Dilemma." *West Virginia History* 27 (April 1966):173–200.

Major Isaac Noyes Smith's dilemma was whether he should pursue his own personal convictions about the legitimacy of the Confederate cause, or follow those of his father, a Unionist. Between September 15 and November 30, 1861, Smith fought with the Twenty-second Virginia Infantry in western Virginia. His diary tells of the muddy roads, the bad food, the demoralized state of the troops, and the political quarrel between two Virginia generals, which caused his unit to be shuttled back and forth and to receive increased picket duty. About the time Smith had a disagreement with another officer and resigned his commission, he learned that his father was a leading participant in a move to keep western Virginia in the Union. The editor wonders whether Smith's decision to resign was caused by the conflict with the other officer, his disillusionment with the war, or his divided loyalties to his Unionist father and the Confederacy.

(1862–1863)   **JOEL C. BLAKE**   353

Reaver, J. Russell, ed. "Letters of Joel C. Blake." *Apalachee* 5 (1957/1962):5–25.

Lieutenant Blake (Fifth Florida Infantry) wrote these letters between June 22, 1862, and June 5, 1863. He describes the beauty and fertile soil of West Virginia, his own illness, and his joy at receiving news from home. His remarks about his family's fortunes are most poignant. He offers advice and encouragement to his wife on how to handle their misbehaving son, expresses concern over Yankee attacks on Florida, and fears that the taxes the Confederate government was imposing would be too high for anyone to pay. Later Blake tells of the prelude to and his participation in the Chancellorsville Campaign (April-May 1863). Blake was killed at Gettysburg.

5

South Central and Gulf

(*including the Lower Mississippi River and Old Southwest*)

GENERAL

(1738–1740)   **PIERRE VITRY**   **354**

Delanglez, Jean, ed. and tr. "The Journal of Pierre Vitry, S. J., 1738–1740." *Louisiana Studies* 3 (Fall 1964):247–313.

    Father Vitry was chaplain in the second French expedition up the Mississippi River to engage the Chickasaw Indians in their Tennessee stronghold. The expedition, led by Governor Jean-Baptiste Le Moyne, Sieur de Bienville, was a failure for reasons that Delanglez summarizes. Father Vitry's journal is the only complete record of the entire eighteen-month campaign (September 6, 1738-April 1, 1740). An introduction is provided by Katherine Bridges.

(1764)   **ARTHUR LOFTUS**   **355**

Haffner, Gerald O., ed. "Major Arthur Loftus' Journal of the Proceedings of His Majesty's Twenty-Second Regiment up the River Mississippi in 1764." *Louisiana History* 20 (Summer 1979):325–34.

    Records an aborted attempt to effect the transfer of Ford de Chartres in Illinois country from French to British ownership in accordance with the Treaty of Paris. Loftus left New Orleans with four hundred men, but 240 miles up the Mississippi he was forced to retreat after being attacked by Indians.

(1836)   **EDWARD FONTAINE**   **356**

Halsell, Willie D., ed. "A Stranger Indeed in a Strange Land." *Alabama Historical Quarterly* 30 (Summer 1968):61–75.

    A travel journal (November 6-November 23, 1836) kept by Edward Fontaine, who undertook a horseback journey from Cumberland County, Kentucky, to Nashville, into Alabama, and on to Pontotoc in northeastern Mississippi. Most of the entries concern conditions of the roads, the storms, wildlife, vegetation, taverns, fellow travelers, and some brief portraits of the towns, especially Bowling Green, Nashville, and Pontotoc.

(1837)   **GEORGE WILLIAM FEATHERSTONHAUGH**   **357**

Foreman, Carolyn Thomas, ed. "An Early Account of the Cherokees." *Chronicles of Oklahoma* 34 (Summer 1956):141–58.

    In *A Canoe Voyage up the Minnay Sotor* (London, 1847), the English traveler George William Featherstonhaugh tells of the time he spent with the Cherokee Indians in Alabama, Tennessee, and Georgia during July and August, 1837. Featherstonhaugh deeply sympathizes with the Indians. He relates how they had been driven off the land of their nativity by those who falsely represented themselves as leaders and by the people of Georgia. He describes the Cherokee as handsome, well-dressed, religious people who were not to be confused with the savages of the West. Among those with whom he talked was the Indian leader John Ross.

(1841–1842)   GUERDON GATES   358

Guthrie, Blaine A., Jr., and Guthrie, Mitchell R., eds. "Catfish, Cornmeal and the Broad Canopy of Heaven: The Journal of the Reverend Guerdon Gates Describing His Trip on the Red River of Louisiana and Texas, 1841–1842." *Register of the Kentucky Historical Society* 66 (January 1968):3–34.

Gates and about three hundred emigrants bound for homesteading land near the Dallas-Fort Worth region had left Nashville by steamboat and made their way to Shreveport when the journal begins. Gates describes the trip by keelboat up the Red River through the "raft" (the log-jammed portion of the river), through bayous, into Arkansas, and finally to Texas, after which he returned to Nashville. Predominant in Gates's descriptions are hazards to navigation, the procurement of food by hunting and once catching a 70-pound catfish, desertions by those unwilling to endure the hardships, and a debate over who rendered the greatest public service, George Washington or Napoleon. Still, in the midst of all the travails, or the "varieties of life" as Gates called them, he could fall asleep looking at the wide expanse of sky and wonder at God's glory. Journal kept from December of 1841 to late March of 1842.

(1849–1851)   GEORGE FOREMAN   359

Davis, William E., and McKiernan, F. Mark, eds. "The Mighty Mississippi: Two 19th Century Accounts." *Louisiana History* 18 (Summer 1977):338–48.

Combines excerpts from a biographical sketch of George Foreman and watercolors from Henry Lewis's *Das Illustrite Mississippithal* (Dusseldorf, 1854). Foreman traveled the Mississippi River between 1849 and 1851, boating and logging.

(1855–1857)   GAIL BORDEN   360

Frantz, Joe B., ed. "Trips Up the River: 1855 and 1857." *Louisiana History* 1 (Spring 1960):147–52.

Gail Borden, who discovered the process for condensed milk, made several trips for business reasons from his Texas home up the Mississippi, departing from New Orleans. The first of these two letters tells of a river trip to Saint Louis and then on to Albany by train. The second took him by boat to Louisville, en route to Washington, D.C.

(1856)   THOMAS JEFFERSON EATON   361

Morrow, Sara Sprott. "Thomas Jefferson Eaton: The Traveling Surgeon." *Tennessee Historical Quarterly* 29 (Summer 1970):160–65.

Presents quotations from an itinerant surgeon's diary that provide a brief look at the activities of an important figure in rural areas. During 1856, Eaton traveled to Kentucky, Tennessee, and Georgia, specializing in operations for harelip, clubfoot, and cross-eyes.

(1857)   JESSE MILTON EMERSON   362

Kemp, Susan, ed. "Up the Mississippi." *Louisiana History* 12 (Fall 1971):335–54.

An anonymous account of a trip up the lower Mississippi from New Orleans to Vicksburg that was published in the October, 1857 issue of *Emerson's Magazine and Putnam's Monthly*. The author, perhaps editor-publisher Jesse Milton Emerson, concentrated on the mouth of the Mississippi and New Orleans. Includes drawings.

(1861–1864)   HIRAM TALBERT HOLT   363

Partin, Robert, ed. "'The Momentous Events' of the Civil War as Reported by a Confederate Private-Sergeant." *Tennessee Historical Quarterly* 18 (March 1959):69–86.

The editor believes the many letters (dated April 11, 1861 to February 17, 1864) written by Hiram Talbert Holt (Alabama Greys, then Second Alabama Infantry, and then Thirty-eighth Alabama Infantry) contain a variety of interesting material. Holt wrote about his personal life, the earthy side of soldiering, the officers, and the battles. He grasped some of the international effects of the war. The editor uses quotations to reveal how Holt reported the great events, both those battles he heard about and the ones he witnessed. Partin says that Holt's letters reveal his initial optimism about the southern cause and his increasing pessimism about the war's outcome. After his service in Alabama and Tennessee, Holt was killed near Dalton, Georgia, in February, 1864. (See also item 364.)

(1861–1864)   364

———. "The 'Money Matters' of a Confederate Soldier." *Alabama Historical Quarterly* 25 (Spring/Summer 1963):49–69.

The letters Hiram Talbert Holt wrote between April, 1861, and February, 1864, indicate the problems enlisted men encountered because of the inadequate Confederate financial system. The editor uses excerpts from Holt's letters to reveal that he needed money to travel home, for his wife and baby's upkeep, to purchase his own food and necessities, to pay his debts, and to pay for letters. (See also item 363.)

(1861–1864)   OLOF LILJEGREN   365

Swanson, Alan, ed. and tr. "The Civil War Letters of Olof Liljegren." *Swedish Pioneer Historical Quarterly* 31 (April 1980):86–121

The editor believes that these letters (December 1, 1861-May 1, 1864) are unique because there is little documentation about Swedish participants in the Civil War. Although typical of many other Civil War letters, they perhaps provide some insights about why some were willing to fight. Liljegren writes that in the United States fighting for one's country was considered the highest duty. Because he was writing to relatives in Sweden who knew little about the conflict, Liljegren expresses himself in detailed prose that shows traces of Union war propaganda. The rebels were devil-like, filled with barbarism and tyranny, and neither women nor property were safe from their ravages. Liljegren relates incidents of military action and service in Kentucky, Mississippi, Missouri, and Arkansas. He includes information about the Sioux massacres in 1862 and the following conflict in which the Third Minnesota Infantry was called back home to participate. He also reveals something of his relationship with his father, who wanted him to return to Sweden and farm. Liljegren died of illness in Arkansas in September of 1864.

(1861–1865)   HENRY CLINTON FORBES   366

Kaiser, Leo M., ed. "Wild Eagle Flight: A Union Soldier's View of the Civil War and the South, 1861–1865." *Louisiana Studies* 14 (Winter 1975):395–412.

Henry Clinton Forbes of the Seventh Illinois Cavalry rose from the rank of captain to lieutenant colonel during the period covered by this correspondence (February 8, 1861-March 17, 1865). His unit served in Missouri, Mississippi, Tennessee, and Louisiana. These letters contain little detail of the fighting, with some about Grierson's Raid in the Vicksburg Campaign (April 17-May 2, 1863) and a cavalry ride from Memphis to West Point, Mississippi. The editor selected these letters to illuminate Forbes's character, rather than to describe battles. Forbes disliked war, but he enjoyed the flair of wearing the uniform and was sincerely patriotic. He hated the killing, but he could see the necessity for waging total war if the South was ever to be subdued.

He admired the serenity of plantation life, but believed peace depended on the removal of the aristocracy. His remarks about the blacks are intriguing as he struggles to overcome his "educational prejudices." (p. 399) Forbes considered blacks reliable sources of information and enjoyed having the "contrabands" (former slaves) around. He describes blacks in extremely unflattering ways, however. He did not consider them fit for freedom at that time, but perhaps in the future. Other passages reveal the shifting moods of a sensitive man whose style, the editor suggests, indicates that he may have been writing these letters for posterity.

(1862–1865)   **JOHN F. BROBST**   **367**

Taylor, A. Reed. "The War History of Two Soldiers: A Two-Sided View of the Civil War." *Alabama Review* 23 (April 1970):83–109.

Focuses on three aspects of the letters written by a Union soldier, John F. Brobst (Twenty-fifth Wisconsin Infantry), and a Confederate soldier, William Anderson Stephens (Forty-sixth Alabama Infantry). Taylor compares the men's reactions to camp life, their feelings about the war, and their personal characteristics. While Taylor discovers both differences and similarities in these letters, he finds enough common ground to emphasize the underlying universality of men's experiences in war. Brobst served at Vicksburg (October, 1862-July, 1863) and in the Atlanta Campaign (May-September, 1864). His correspondence begins in 1862 and ends in 1865. The letters written by Stephens, who also served at Vicksburg and in the Atlanta Campaign, where he was captured, run from mid-1862 to early 1865 when he died at the Johnson's Island, Ohio, prison camp.

(1862–1865)   **JAMES GREENALCH**   **368**

Melon, Knox, Jr., ed. "Letters of James Greenalch." *Michigan History* 44 (June 1960):188–240.

A record of service with the First Michigan Engineers and Mechanics from September 28, 1862, to April 28, 1865, in Kentucky, Tennessee, Georgia, and the Carolinas. In an early letter, Greenalch tells of how an orderly sergeant with the Seventy-fourth Ohio Infantry, who had already served twenty months, was revealed to be a woman. Later, Corporal Greenalch describes the inability of Georgia civilians to stop the Union soldiers from pillaging. As sad as the soldiers' actions were, he believed they were only fitting retribution for what the Confederates did on their raid into Pennsylvania in 1863. Greenalch writes that most of the women of the South were convinced that Yankee soldiers had horns on their heads. After observing acts of indecency by his fellow soldiers, he believed the women's fears were justified. He also describes the destructive march through the Carolinas (December, 1864-March, 1865) and more activities of Union forages. In a final letter he relates the demoralizing effect that Lincoln's assassination had on him and the rest of the troops.

(1861–1865)   **CLAUDE LEE HADAWAY**   **369**

Shingleton, Royce, ed. "'With Loyalty and Honor as a Patriot': Recollections of a Confederate Soldier." *Alabama Historical Quarterly* 33 (Fall/Winter 1971):240–63.

Claude Lee Hadaway (Twenty-second Alabama Regiment) saw action in Tennessee, Mississippi, Kentucky, Georgia, and Alabama between August 10, 1861, and April 26, 1865. Most of this document is filled with incidents of battles, evaluations of superior officers, hardships of camp life, and poor provisions. Although he was never captured or wounded, Hadaway found that sickness in the camp could be as hazardous as combat. Between battles he contracted mumps and pneumonia and was provided with poor medical treatment. These recollections, which were recorded in 1913, reveal Hadaway's pride in his service for the Confederacy.

(1861–1865)   JOHN SHARP   370

Mills, George, ed. "The Sharp Family Civil War Letters." *Annals of Iowa* 34 (January 1959):481–532.

Correspondence between John Sharp and his wife Helen Maria. The first letters from John begin December 31, 1861, when he was serving with the Second Iowa Infantry, and end with a letter from Helen in October, 1862. John was discharged in October, 1862, but he reenlisted in the Tenth Iowa Infantry and several more letters follow until August, 1865. John's letters tell of his participation at Shiloh (April 6–7, 1862, Tennessee) and later of his march with Sherman through the Carolinas (December, 1864-March, 1865). Helen's letters poignantly describe her fears at being unable to provide for her family without her husband's support.

(1863–1864)   DANIEL O'LEARY   371

O'Leary, Jenny, and Jackson, Harvey H., eds. "The Civil War Letters of Captain Daniel O'Leary, U.S.A." *Register of the Kentucky Historical Society* 77 (Summer 1979):157–85.

O'Leary served with the Fifteenth Kentucky Infantry in Tennessee, Alabama, and Georgia during the period of these letters (April 7, 1863-November 29, 1864). Except for the Atlanta Campaign (May-September, 1864), O'Leary writes more about incidents he observed or feelings he held than about the fighting. Because his wife's loyalties lay with the South, O'Leary advised her to keep her attitudes to herself. He was afraid that she might suffer once Kentucky was occupied by Union troops. He shows great compassion for the civilians he saw suffering in Alabama, as well as for the Confederate troops at Atlanta who came across the Union lines to exchange tobacco and newspapers. He wrote contemptuously about the "Southern Rights" and referred to Charleston as a "hot bed of traitors" who instigated the hostilities. (p. 162) In Atlanta he saw how the civilians had dug themselves into cisterns and holes in the ground to avoid bombardment. In Chattanooga he observed how the Union army began to reform the city's morals by sending the "frail fair ones" (the prostitutes) to Nashville.

(1865)   HARVEY M. WATTERSON   372

Abbott, Martin, ed. "The South as Seen by a Tennessee Unionist in 1865: Letters of H. M. Watterson." *Tennessee Historical Quarterly* 18 (June 1959):148–61.

President Andrew Johnson dispatched four observers to the South in 1865 to survey the conditions and gather information about southern sentiment that would help him shape postwar policy. These letters, written from Alabama, Louisiana, Georgia, and Mississippi between September 26 and October 28, 1865, are from an old friend of Johnson's. Watterson portrayed the mood of southerners to be one of contrition with a willingness to repay debts and amend errors, which the editor says was not the case. His attitude toward the activities of the Freedman's Bureau in Louisiana is that they were acting as an intermediary court of justice for the blacks and were impeding the progress of civilian courts in matters between whites and former slaves. Watterson assures the President that he can remove the military from Georgia and leave the legislature to provide justice for the freedmen. (See also item 212.)

(1868)   SALLIE D. SMITH   373

Jensen, Mrs. Dana O., ed. "The Journal of Sallie D. Smith." *Bulletin of the Missouri Historical Society* 20 (January 1964):124–45.

Portions of a manuscript diary (June 3-October 18, 1868) that cover Sallie's trip from Missouri to Howard County, Kentucky. Provides a glimpse of river travel on the Missouri, Mississippi, and Ohio rivers, and some of her everyday activities while in Kentucky.

(1875–1884)   **MISSISSIPPI RIVER**   **374**

Parsons, Coleman O. "Steamboating as Seen by Passengers and River Men: 1875–1884." *Mississippi Quarterly* 24 (Winter 1970/1971):19–34.

Parsons consults the accounts of three who traveled on the Ohio and Mississippi rivers between 1875 and 1884 to describe the food and accommodations, the work required aboard the boat, such landing places as Natchez and New Orleans, and the panoramic view of the shore. He uses the unpublished manuscripts of James Newell Swift and Thomas Jennings Hand, and Lafcadio Hearn's *Letters from the Raven. . . .* (London, 1908).

Alabama

(1796)   **BENJAMIN HAWKINS**   **375**

Hemperley, Marion R., ed. "Benjamin Hawkins' Trip Through Alabama, 1796." *Alabama Historical Quarterly* 31 (Fall/Winter 1969):207–36.

This second portion of Hawkins's diary kept while en route to assume his duties as principal Indian agent for all Indians south of the Ohio River describes travel in central Alabama and in the Creek Nation in east-central Alabama. (See also item 262.)

(1798)   **376**

———. "Benjamin Hawkins' Trip from New York to Coweta Tallahassee, 1798." *Alabama Historical Quarterly* 33 (Fall/Winter 1971):218–26.

A diary kept by the principal Indian agent for all Indians south of the Ohio River during a journey in east-central Alabama from the Creek Indian town of New York to Coweta Tallahassee, another Creek village in today's Russell County, Alabama.

(1799)   **BARTHOLOMEW SCHAUMBURGH**   **377**

Holmes, Jack D. L., ed. "Fort Stoddard in 1799: Seven Letters of Captain Bartholomew Schaumburgh." *Alabama Historical Quarterly* 26 (Fall/Winter 1964):231–52.

The editor says these letters of Captain Schaumburgh (Second U.S. Infantry) are the earliest documents relating to the Alabama installation located on the Mobile River, three (or four) miles below the confluence of the Alabama and Tombigbee rivers. He records daily activities of the fort and news of relations with the Creek Indians and the Spanish.

(1807–1808)   **EDMUND PENDLETON GAINES**   **378**

Stone, James H., ed. "Surveying the Gaines Trace, 1807-1808." (Part I) *Alabama Historical Quarterly* 33 (Summer 1971):135–52.

———. "Edmund Pendleton Gaines' Description of the Upper Tombigbee River, January, 1808." (Part II) *Alabama Historical Quarterly* 33 (Fall/Winter 1971):227–39.

A survey by Captain Gaines to record the feasibility of a wagon road from Muscle Shoals on the Tennessee River to Cotton Gin Port on the Tombigbee River. The purpose was to establish a means to supply American settlements in south Alabama. The diary describes the topography, the richness of the soil, and the vegetation.

(1836)   **RICHARD WYLLY HABERSHAM**   **379**

Collins, Donald E., ed. "A Georgian's View of Alabama in 1836." *Alabama Review* 25 (July 1972):218–26.

Richard Wylly Habersham provides a look at the towns of Montgomery and Selma while in Alabama on business. He observed a slave being sold in a fashion that was unfamiliar to him. He was shocked by the high price of slaves and attributed it to the production of cotton. His two letters are written from Cahaba, and his description of the rustic condition of his cabin reflect the frontier conditions of east-central Alabama.

(1862) SAMUEL COULTER BALDRIDGE 380

Temple, Wayne C., ed. "A Chaplain in the 11th Missouri Infantry." *Lincoln Herald* 64 (Summer 1962):81–88.

These letters of Samuel Coulter Baldridge, written between August and December, 1862, from Alabama and Mississippi, reveal the frustrations of attempting to do the Lord's work amid the chaos of war. He writes of the gambling and vulgarities that flourished among rowdy men. Baldridge blames part of the situation on the idleness that existed between battles, the lack of reading materials, and the absence of financial support from his Indiana church. Although it was difficult to find an occasion to preach, he says the men were always ready to talk about home. He also writes of social conditions in the South and the progress of the war.

(1862–1863) JOE T. SCOTT 381

Jones, Allen W., ed. "A Georgia Confederate Soldier Visits Montgomery, Alabama, 1862–1863." *Alabama Historical Quarterly* 25 (Spring/Summer 1963):99–113.

Lieutenant Joe T. Scott of the Twentieth Georgia Infantry was a soldier correspondent for two Columbus, Georgia, newspapers. This collection of articles describes conditions in Montgomery between September 18, 1862, and December 15, 1863. In his early letters Scott writes that Montgomery was no longer a gay and fashionable city. The men had gone off to war and the women, exhibiting a "kind of heroism equal to female Spartans," had laid aside their fancy wardrobes to satisfy the demands of the occasion. (p. 103) He describes the fine hospital in the city and tells how a manufacturing company gave all of its cloth to families of soldiers. In January, 1863, he saw a trainload of Union soldiers and favored housing them in Vicksburg to discourage bombardment of that city.

Nearly a year later, December 31, 1863, Scott writes that he hoped the upcoming year would be happier than the previous one. With the winter upon the South, Scott saw much suffering from want on the battlefield as well as at home. He believes the drafting of those who had been able to avoid service up to that time by hiring substitutes offered a source of new enthusiasm in the army. Even though the Confederate government had passed legislation authorizing their induction, Scott wonders if it will really happen.

(1865) HOLIDAY AMES 382

Filler, Louis, ed. "Waiting for the War's End: The Letter of an Ohio Soldier in Alabama After Learning of Lincoln's Death." *Ohio History* 74 (Winter 1965):55–62.

Lieutenant Holiday Ames's immediate reaction to the assassination was a feeling of wanting revenge and a fear that no other person in government was capable of replacing Lincoln. Ames served with the 102nd Ohio Infantry and wrote this letter April 23 and 24, 1865.

(1866–1887) MARY GORDON DUFFEE 383

Brown, Virginia Pounds, and Nabers, Jane Porter, eds. "Mary Gordon Duffee's 'Sketches of Alabama'." (Part I) *Alabama Review* 9 (April 1956):135–51.

———— and ————. (Part II) *Alabama Review* 9 (July 1956):224–36.

———— and ————. (Part III) *Alabama Review* 9 (October 1956):263–88.

———— and ————. (Part IV) *Alabama Review* 10 (January 1957):52–69.

Edited portions of Duffee's articles that appeared in the *Birmingham Weekly Iron Age* between 1866 and 1887. Using her annual journeys as a framework for her writings, she included details about Alabama families, folklore, history, Indians, and so forth.

ARKANSAS

(1804–1805)   WILLIAM DUNBAR   384

DeRosier, Arthur H., Jr. "William Dunbar, Explorer." *Journal of Mississippi History* 25 (July 1963):165–85.

Emphasizes the importance of Dunbar's Hot Springs expedition (1804–1805), the second exploration of the Louisiana Purchase after Lewis and Clark. His 103-day expedition left from Saint Catherine's Landing, below Natchez, and journeyed up the Ouachita River to the Hot Springs in present-day Arkansas. Because Dunbar included detailed reports about the river, animals, and vegetation, his writings greatly assisted later travelers. Based on Dunbar's "Journal of a Voyage," in *Life, Letters and Papers of William Dunbar* (Jackson, 1930).

(1804–1805)   GEORGE HUNTER   385

McDermott, John Francis. "The Western Journals of George Hunter, 1796–1805." *Proceedings of the American Philosophical Society* 103 (December 1959):770–73.

Hunter's diaries include description of trips from Philadelphia to Kentucky and to Illinois country in 1796, and again to Kentucky in 1802. The most important was the account of an expedition charting the course of the Ouachita River to Hot Springs on the Ozark Plateau in 1804 and 1805, a portion of which is reprinted here. Hunter had originally been chosen by President Jefferson to lead a larger expedition that would explore the Red River, but it was called off because of expected hostility from the Osage Indians. McDermott believes that the importance of Hunter's diaries is that they reveal something of Thomas Jefferson's extensive plan of exploration.

(1815–1854)   MIGRATION TO ARKANSAS   386

Swint, Henry L. "Ho for Arkansas." *Arkansas Historical Quarterly* 24 (Autumn 1965):195–207.

Reviews comments written by travelers to Arkansas during the first half of the nineteenth century that inspired the dream of the West and encouraged immigration. Swint focuses on the attractive qualities of Arkansas that were presented to German readers. He also explores the travelers' explanations for why pioneers were continually on the move. Uses primarily the accounts of Timothy Flint, Gottfried Duden, Frederich Wilhelm Christian Gerstaecker, Henry R. Schoolcraft, and Thomas Nuttall.

(1817–1818)   JOHN FOWLER   387

Magnaghi, Russell M., ed. "The Red River Valley North of Natchitoches, 1817–1818: The Letters of John Fowler." *Louisiana Studies* 15 (Fall 1976):287–93.

As chief trader for the government trading post at Natchitoches (Louisiana), Fowler was responsible for locating a new site when it was decided to relocate the trading post. In these three letters, written between April 8, 1817, and June 25, 1818, Fowler reports that a location at the confluence of the Sulphur and Red rivers in southwestern Arkansas was ideal. He stresses the advantages of the site for trading, describes the location of Indians in the region, and emphasizes the impetus the post would serve to settlement of the frontier. In his journey to the region he passed over long, flat sections of the Red River known as "the raft." Fowler recommended that the timber lodged there be cleared away to improve navigation.

(1838–1842)   FREDERICH WILHELM   388
CHRISTIAN GERSTAECKER

Bukey, Evan Burr. "Frederick Gerstaecker and Arkansas." *Arkansas Historical Quarterly* 31 (Spring 1972):3–14.

Gerstaecker was a nineteenth-century German writer of popular travel and adventure stories who lived in Arkansas as a backwoodsman and hunter between 1838 and 1842. Bukey says that Gerstaecker's writings about this period provide a glimpse of Arkansas pioneer life that is an accurate source for the historian. Bukey reviews previous writings about Gerstaecker, and the themes, characterizations, and social criticism found in his works. (See also item 386.)

(1858)   DAVID FRENCH BOYD   389

Reed, Germaine M., ed. "Journey Through Southwest Arkansas, 1858." *Arkansas Historical Quarterly* 30 (Summer 1971):161–69.

In need of a vacation, schoolteacher David French Boyd traveled by horseback from Homer, Louisiana, through southwestern Arkansas and into Indian Territory. In his "Notes of Travel," from July 27 to August 1, 1858, he comments on the trees, the soil, the swamps, and the people he met, and includes a list of expenses incurred through August 4.

(1862–1863)   WILLIAM ELISHA STOKER   390

Glover, Robert W., ed. "The War Letters of a Texas Conscript in Arkansas." *Arkansas Historical Quarterly* 20 (Winter 1961):355–87.

The editor believes the correspondence of Private William Elisha Stoker (Eighteenth Texas Infantry) to be interesting because it relates his opinion of the Civil War and unique because Stoker represented the small slaveowner class. This selection of letters was written between July 27, 1862, and April 12, 1863, while Stoker served in Arkansas. Besides comments about the hard life of a soldier and his constant hope for a furlough, Stoker reveals his worries about his farm with its two slaves. Stoker also expresses concern for his wife's well-being. He says he has seen how badly some soldiers treated women whose husbands have gone off to war, as well as how husbandless Arkansas women have acted without virtue.

(1863–1864)   ROBERT C. GILLIAM   391

Hudson, James J., ed. "From Paraclifta to Marks's Mill: The Civil War Correspondence of Lieutenant Robert C. Gilliam." *Arkansas Historical Quarterly* 17 (Autumn 1958):272–302.

Gilliam records how the Arkansas battalion of state militia helped thwart the Union thrust into Arkansas between October, 1863, and May, 1864. His letters also reveal how he attempted to run his plantation while in the field of battle. His unit served as a part of Cabell's Cavalry Brigade in battles at Poison Springs (April 18, 1864) and at Marks's Mill (April 25, 1864), where Gilliam was killed. The letters date from October 22, 1863, to April 18, 1864, and include a letter to Gilliam from his wife and another to his wife from a friend after the lieutenant's death.

(1867)   FREDERICH WILHELM   392
CHRISTIAN GERSTAECKER

Bukey, Anita, and Bukey, Evan Burr, eds. "Arkansas After the War: From the Journal of Frederick Gerstaecker." *Arkansas Historical Quarterly* 32 (Autumn 1973):255–73.

In 1867 the German writer returned to the state where he lived between 1838 and 1842, "the best years of my youth." (p. 256) A sense of sadness mixed with frustration pervades this portion of Gerstaecker's journal. He found that the region was no longer the virgin forest in which he had once felt free and independent. It had changed in ways that were not to his liking. "A railroad in Arkansas! I didn't want to think about it." (p. 257) Little Rock had gas lights and strange signs. Worst of all, some of his friends had been treated badly during the Civil War because of their Unionist sympathies, and others he had known had died. Taken from volume one of *Neue reisen durch die Vereinigten Staaten, Mexico, Ecuador Westindien und Venezuela* (Jena, 1868–69).

(1870)   **ANONYMOUS**   393

Anonymous. "An Excursion Over the Unfinished Little Rock Railroad." *Arkansas Historical Quarterly* 15 (Autumn 1956):220–27.

   A day-long train ride over the almost seventy miles of completed track west from Memphis. The unidentified author was concerned with enjoying himself and tells little about the Memphis and Little Rock Railroad. He does provide brief pictures of Madison and Forest City, Arkansas. Taken from the *Memphis Public Ledger* (July 25, 1870).

(1887)   **ANONYMOUS**   394

Westermeier, Therese S. "'Die Grande Prairie von Arkansas'." *Arkansas Historical Quarterly* 15 (Spring 1956):76–84.

   After summarizing German interest in the frontier, the author reprints an unidentified traveler's account of Arkansas that first appeared in *Der Deutsche Pioneer* (vol. 18, no. 4; 1887. Westermeier believes it contains several elements of German interest in Arkansas: a pride in livestock, a preference for wooded land with meadows, and love for the family.

KENTUCKY

(1779–1780)   **JAMES NOURSE, JR.**   395

Hammon, Neal O., ed. "The Journal of James Nourse, Jr., 1779–1780." *Filson Club Historical Quarterly* 47 (July 1973):258–66.

   This brief journal (December 27, 1779-February 16, 1780) covers a trip from Virginia to Kentucky for the purpose of acquiring a land grant. Although it was a hard winter, Nourse and his brothers found plenty of buffalo and other game. Includes a brief entry about a stop at Boonesboro.

(1810)   **ALEXANDER WILSON**   396

Wilson, Gordon. "An Ornithologist Visits Kentucky." (Part I) *Register of the Kentucky Historical Society* 55 (October 1957):338–44.
———. (Part II) *Register of the Kentucky Historical Society* 56 (July 1958):233–40.

   Using primarily Alexander Wilson's letters, the author traces the ornithologist's fifty-day visit to Kentucky in 1810. Wilson was in Kentucky to collect new species and to solicit subscriptions for his own *American Ornithologist* and *The New American Cyclopedia*

(1810–1835)   **LEXINGTON**   397

Coleman, J. Winston, Jr. "Lexington As Seen by Travellers, 1810–1835." *Filson Club Historical Quarterly* 29 (July 1955):267–81.

   Early in the nineteenth century travelers were eager to visit Lexington because it was a cultural center and the wealthiest city west of the Alleghenies, with the exception of New Orleans. Most visitors believed the city deserved its nickname, "Athens of the West." They praised its educational institutions, its churches, and its society, as well as the quantity of European goods available and the variety of agriculture and manufacturing. Scattered among the positive opinions was criticism of the public flogging of blacks, of buildings in need of repair, and problems with paper currency, incessant swearing, and constant talk of horses.

(1839–1842) CHARLES FENTON MERCER NOLAND 398

Williams, Leonard, ed. "Lingering in Louisville: Impressions of an Early Visitor." *Filson Club Historical Quarterly* 52 (April 1978):191–205.

Six columns that Charles Fenton Mercer Noland, a frequent visitor of Louisville, published in the *Spirit of the Times* (New York) between 1839 and 1842. He covered a range of topics that include fictional tales the editor thinks are an important forerunner of early southwestern humor.

(1870s) JAMES MCDONALD 399

Harrison, Lowell H., ed. "A British View of Kentucky Agriculture in the 1870's." *Register of the Kentucky Historical Society* 63 (January 1965):24–29.

James McDonald wrote a series of letters from the United States that described Kentucky agriculture favorably for the purpose of luring British investment. They were first published in a newspaper, *The Scotsman*, and later a book, *Food from the Far West* (London, 1878), from which this article is extracted.

(1879) CLAIRE REED 400

———. "Kentucky's Agriculture, 1879: A British Report." *Filson Club Historical Quarterly* 44 (July 1970):273–81.

In the 1870s, when British agriculture was encountering a series of bad crops, American agriculture experienced rapid improvements in farming techniques and transportation facilities. Two members of Parliament, Claire Reed and Albert Pell, along with an authority on cattle, John Clay, Jr., were dispatched to see if American agricultural methods could provide a solution to the British problems. The group visited Kentucky in November, 1879. The report, which is devoted to stock raising, praises the Kentucky short-horn herds as the best in the nation, and describes practices on several farms. One portion of the report tells of a charity hospital and an orphan asylum in Lexington. (See also item 470.)

(1885) HEINRICH LEMCKE 401

Weisert, John J., ed. "Lemcke Visits Kentucky's German Colonies in 1885." *Register of the Kentucky Historical Society* 75 (July 1977):222–32.

Heinrich Lemcke was hired by the Kentucky Bureau of Immigration to come to Kentucky and study its advantages for foreign immigration. He visited Louisville, Frankfort, Eddyville, Bowling Green, and the German colonies. Lemcke presented an extremely attractive portrait of life in Kentucky for prospective German and Swiss immigrants in the January and February, 1886, issues of the *Louisville Anzeiger*.

(1888) HERMANN ZAGEL 402

Zagel, Hermann. "An Excursion to Mammoth Cave in Kentucky." *Register of the Kentucky Historical Society* 71 (July 1973):272–95.

A detailed description of the cave by an American teacher and a popular travel writer. This article originally appeared in a German-language Lutheran family magazine, *Die Abendschule* (vol. 34; 1888). Translated with introduction and notes by Richard A. Weiss.

LOUISIANA

(1718)   FATHER LEMAIRE   403

Lyon, Zoë. "Louisiana Seen Through the Eyes of an Eighteenth Century Missionary."
Revue de Louisiane/Louisiana Review 3 (Summer 1974):19–23.

Lyon paraphrases and quotes from the memoire to the court of France written in 1718 by
Father Lemaire, a Parisian priest. Lemaire believes in the future of northern Louisiana because
of its many ports and favorable prospects for growing wheat. He feels the whole region would
be easy to govern because the rivers would provide excellent communication and transportation.
Lemaire deplores the tardiness of the French crown in failing to explore the region to the west.

(1727)   MARIE TRANCHEPAIN DE ST. AUGUSTINE   404

Ware, Marion, ed. "An Adventurous Voyage to French Colonial Louisiana: The Narrative of Mother Tranchepain, 1727." *Louisiana History* 1 (Summer 1960):212–29.

Mother Superior Marie Tranchepain de St. Augustine led a small group of Ursuline nuns
from France to establish the Ursuline Academy in New Orleans. Most of the narrative describes
the sea voyage, but several pages are devoted to their reception in New Orleans.

(1800–1860)   ANTEBELLUM LOUISIANA   405

Conrad, Glenn R. "Should We Take Another Look at Antebellum Louisiana?" *Revue
de Louisiane/Louisiana Review* 7 (Summer 1978):35–48.

Conrad uses travelers' accounts to take another look at the stereotyped picture of prewar
Louisiana developed by novelists and film makers over the past 150 years. Was the "Creole
myth" authentic? Conrad finds enough disagreement over such points as Creole chivalry, charm,
and elegance, and the beauty and gracefulness of Creole women to question the stereotype that
has emerged.

(1820–1860)   LAKE PONTCHARTRAIN   406

Baughman, James P. "A Southern Spa: Antebellum Lake Pontchartrain." *Louisiana
History* 3 (Winter 1962):5–32.

Despite New Orleans' reputation for heat and epidemic disease, healthy recreational facilities developed on the shores of Lake Pontchartrain beginning in the 1820s. The author discusses
the patrons, the accommodations, and the activities available at these "watering places." Taken
from newspapers and travelers' accounts written before the Civil War.

(1822–1825)   TIMOTHY FLINT   407

Cavanaugh, Georgia Johnson. "Northwest Louisiana As Seen By Timothy Flint." *Louisiana Studies* 3 (Winter 1964):385–92.

A biography of the Reverend Flint and a summary of his activities in Louisiana between
1822 and 1825 that later appeared in his *Recollections of the Last Ten Years Passed in Occasional
Residences and Journeyings in the Valley of the Mississippi* (Boston, 1826).

(1830–1860)   NEW ORLEANS   408

Martin, John M. "The People of New Orleans as Seen By Her Visitors, 1830–1860."
Louisiana Studies 6 (Winter 1967):361–75.

Martin finds that travelers to New Orleans divided the population into three categories.
First, by national or racial origins, which included Creoles, Anglo-Americans, Irish, German,

and a blend of many other groups. The Creoles were a subject for much discussion as the visitors described their physical beauty and social life. The influx of Anglo-Americans and their conflict with the Creoles was noted as the newcomers further changed the population of the city. The presence of people of mixed blood and the existence of free blacks were also frequently written about. Second, by the amount of time people spent in the city: New Orleans had a large transient population that included gamblers and boatmen, as well as northerners getting away from the cold weather. Third, by occupation. In this category, Martin points out the competition between the Irish and the blacks for menial jobs.

(1831) PRUDENT FOREST 409

Joyaux, Georges J., ed. "Forest's 'Voyage aux États-Unis de l'Amérique en 1831'." *Louisiana Historical Quarterly* 39 (October 1956):457–72.

Pages from Prudent Forest's *Voyage aux États-Unis de l'Amérique in 1831* (Lyon, 1834), which relate his observations about life in and around New Orleans. He discusses the people's eating and drinking habits, the social life of the slaves, the treatment, and living conditions of the blacks, cock-fights, the disease epidemics in New Orleans, and the Indians who lived on the east bank of the Mississippi River.

(1846–1850) HENRI HERZ 410

Hill, Henry Bertram, and Gara, Larry, eds. "A French Traveler's View of Antebellum New Orleans." *Louisiana History* 1 (Fall 1960):335–41.

Between 1846 and 1850, French composer and pianist Henri Herz toured American cities. The editors say New Orleans was Herz's favorite southern city, and they excerpt portions of his *Mes voyages en Amérique* (Paris, 1866) that are mostly descriptive. (See also items 52, 53, 165, and 281.)

(1850) FREDRIKA BREMER 411

Viccars, Marion. "A Swedish Writer Visits the Deep South in 1851." *Alabama Historical Quarterly* 38 (Spring 1976):30–43.

Fredrika Bremer spent portions of 1849 through 1851 in the United States. Late in 1850 she visited New Orleans and Mobile. Except for a slave auction in New Orleans, she found both cities to her liking. Viccars draws attention to Bremer's visit with Choctaw Indians in Mobile and her social life there. More of Bremer's descriptions and attitudes may be found in *The Homes of the New World* (London, 1853). (See also items 465 and 557.)

(1857) EMMA LAY LANE 412

Anderson, John Q., ed. "A Letter from a Yankee Bride in Antebellum Louisiana." *Louisiana History* 1 (Summer 1960):245–50.

Emma Lay Lane arrived at her father-in-law's plantation near Clinton, Louisiana, shortly after her marriage to James Tyson Lane. Her letter of October 6, 1857, reveals Mrs. Lane's first reactions to customs strange to one from the North. Everything she describes—the church service, the food, and the servants—is written about in glowing terms. She also relates the details of picking and ginning cotton, the layout of the plantation, and a slave funeral.

(1860–1861) ANONYMOUS 413

Schultz, Charles R., ed. "New Orleans in December 1860." *Louisiana History* 9 (Winter 1968):53–61.

A portion of a journal by the 17-year-old son of a Maine shipowner who took a sea voyage from Bristol, Maine, to New Orleans for his health. The youth's name is unknown. Most of this selection of entries (December 7, 1860-January 2, 1861) describes the approach to New Orleans' waterfront, matters of commercial interest, and the French Quarter. During his stay there was great unrest over the election of Abraham Lincoln and talk of secession was rampant.

(1861–1865)   SLAVES AND FREEDOM   414

Taylor, Joe Gray. "Slavery in Louisiana During the Civil War." *Louisiana History* 8 (Winter 1967):27–33.

Using primarily the documents of travelers, Taylor investigates the reaction of Louisiana's slaves to anticipated and realized freedom. He finds that slaves became restive as Union troops neared and that once free, the blacks exhibited no high degree of loyalty to their former masters. Most left the plantations, never to return. No widespread insurrection by slaves occurred. Although violence was inflicted on some whites by some freedmen, it was not the rule. Taylor offers several possible explanations for why slave revolts did not occur, but he stresses that such action would not be looked upon favorably by the Union troops. The slave realized "that the attitude of the Northern soldier toward the Negro differed only in degree from the attitude of the master and the master's neighbors." (p. 33)

(1862)   FRANK D. HARDING   415

Reinders, Robert C., ed. "A Wisconsin Soldier Reports from New Orleans." *Louisiana History* 3 (Fall 1962):360–65.

A single letter (May 3, 1862) in which Frank D. Harding (Fourth Wisconsin Infantry) relates the Union bombardment and seizure of New Orleans. He describes how joyful the slaves in the fields were upon seeing Union troops during the trip down the Mississippi River. Needless to say, the residents of the Crescent City offered the Union troops a less than warm reception.

(1862)   GEORGE C. HARDING   416

Bergeron, Arthur W., Jr., ed. "Prison Life at Camp Pratt." *Louisiana History* 14 (Fall 1973):386–91.

Lieutenant George C. Harding, Twenty-first Indiana Infantry, was captured while serving in Louisiana. During his six weeks of imprisonment at Camp Pratt, Louisiana (September and October, 1862), Harding says he suffered terribly. He was incarcerated with a group of Yankees who annoyed and disgusted him. They turned all the beef rations into boiled beef, "the meanest thing on earth, except half-cooked, yellow mush." (p. 389) After eating cornmeal mush his stomach revolted, and "the ghost of every good dinner ever I ate in my life haunted my weary slumbers." (p. 389) Harding's other cellmates, Cajun conscripts, irritated him even more. Perhaps worst of all, Harding rated the camp's library resources as meager. There was a Dutch dictionary, a Catholic prayer book (in French), and *Robinson Crusoe*, which, he says, grew a little stale after thirty or forty readings. Harding was a newspaperman and his acerbic anecdotes are from *The Miscellaneous Writings of George C. Harding* (Indianapolis, 1882).

(1862)   GEORGE W. BOOTH   417

Booth, George W. "We've Played Cards and Lost." *Civil War Times Illustrated* 11 (January 1973):16–24.

The New Jersey hatter, who had just arrived from Newark, describes life in New Orleans between April 19 and 30, 1862, as the city was assaulted and captured by the Union forces. (See also item 198.)

(1862–1863)   AMBERT O. REMINGTON   418

Simms, L. Moody, Jr., ed. "The Occupation of Southeastern Louisiana: Impressions of a New York Volunteer, 1862–1863." *Louisiana Studies* 7 (Spring 1968):83–91.

Ambert O. Remington (Seventy-fifth New York Infantry) reveals the boredom of the troops assigned the occupation of New Orleans. His letters (September 7, 1862-January 30, 1863) show impatience with the leadership of a war he thought would be over soon after his enlistment. He complains about war profiteering, expresses fears of what might happen to the Union if the Confederacy captured Washington and Philadelphia, and relates an incident that reveals how much the people of New Orleans disliked the occupation.

(1862-1864)   HENRY R. GARDNER   419

Shewmaker, Kenneth E., and Prinz, Andrew K., eds. "A Yankee in Louisiana: Selections from the Diary and Correspondence of Henry R. Gardner, 1862–1866." *Louisiana History* 5 (Summer 1964):271–95.

The editors have arranged Gardner's highly literate comments about his service into several topics: "Army life; Mail; Rumors; Military operations; People, places and things; Negro soldiers; Southern women; Grant; Lincoln; Southern attitudes toward occupation; and Reconstruction." Henry Rufus Gardner served as a private in the Eighteenth New York Independent Light Artillery from August, 1862, until April, 1864. From May to October, 1864, he was employed by the Quartermaster's Department in New Orleans. He was commissioned First Lieutenant, Company G of the Tenth U.S. Colored Artillery (Heavy) on November 11, 1864, and served in that capacity until his discharge on September 13, 1866.

(1863)   THOMAS FREMANTLE   420

Peoples, Morgan, ed. "An Excursion Across North Louisiana: Excerpts From the Diary of British Lieutenant Colonel Thomas Fremantle (May 8 to May 15, 1863)." *North Louisiana Historical Association Journal* 8 (Summer 1977):159–69.

During this week Fremantle traveled from Shreveport to Monroe, then down the Mississippi River to Vidalia, and then crossed over to Natchez. He tells about the soldiers and civilians he traveled with and about conversations with southerners, as well as with Yankee deserters from Vicksburg. His talks with Louisianans reveal southern attitudes toward the British role in the war. Fremantle also describes the fortifications he observed and relates how he nearly stumbled into a battle at Harrisonburg, Louisiana.

(1867)   WILLIAM WALLACE LEE   421

———. "A Mississippian Moves to Franklin Parish: The Journal of Dr. William Wallace Lee, 1867." *North Louisiana Historical Association Journal* 6 (Summer 1975):154–63.

Upon his arrival in Louisiana, Lee exclaimed: "So at last I am in the land of pecans, catfish, dumplings, kangaroo fritters, elephant potfries, and ugly women." (p. 157) He did, however, really like the state in which he had chosen to practice medicine. He praised the fertility of the land and the comfort and luxury in which the citizens lived, but he also observed how close houses were built to the water and how easily they could slip into the river in rainy seasons. He saw how much damage the Yankees had caused in the war, but predicted Louisiana will rise "Phoenix like, from its degradation." (p. 157) The travel portion of the journal covers September 12 to 21, 1867, but the entries include his first days of adjustment in Gilbert, Louisiana.

MISSISSIPPI

(1799-1800)   JOSEPH BULLEN   422

Phelps, Dawson A., ed. "Excerpts from the Journal of the Reverend Joseph Bullen, 1799–1800." *Journal of Mississippi History* 17 (October 1955):254–81.

Bullen was a representative of the New York Missionary Society of the Presbyterian Church who served four years in the Chickasaw Nation attempting to convert the Indians. In an issue of the *New York Missionary Magazine and Repository of Religious Intelligence*, published in 1800, he describes his efforts and his travels in the Mississippi counties of Lee, Pontotoc, and Chickasaw. The editor speculates on why Bullen was unsuccessful in his mission.

(1800–1860)   ANTEBELLUM MISSISSIPPI   423

Box, Mrs. Eugene. "Ante-Bellum Travelers in Mississippi." *Journal of Mississippi History* 17 (April 1955):110–26.

While most visitors between 1800 and 1860 appreciated the landscape and wild vegetation of Mississippi, they underestimated the commercial value of the trees and mineral resources, and the value of the soil, which had been severely eroded. Most agreed, however, that the area was unhealthy. Discussion of the population was of three categories: Europeans and their descendants, Africans and their descendants, and the Indians. The travelers usually described the social life of each group, emphasizing the blacks, religion, and the great amount of vice found in Vicksburg and Natchez.

(1852)   BENJAMIN L. C. WAILES   424

Moore, John Hebron, ed. "South Mississippi in 1852: Some Selections from the Journal of Benjamin L. C. Wailes." *Journal of Mississippi History* 18 (January 1956):18–32.

While engaged in an agricultural and geological survey of Mississippi, Professor Wailes made a journey through the piney woods region. In these excerpts from his journal (August 9-September 5, 1852), Wailes discusses the economy and agriculture of the area and mentions the towns he passed through, including an ancient Indian fortification and mounds. The editor emphasizes that Wailes's observations show how the area was changing from a cattle-based economy to one derived from the forests.

(1862–1864)   GEORGE HOVEY CADMAN   425

Quenzel, Carrol H. "Johnny Bull-Billy Yank." *Tennessee Historical Quarterly* 14 (June 1955):120–41.

Using excerpts from the 105 letters written by George Hovey Cadman (August 22, 1863-September, 1864), Quenzel summarizes the Civil War as seen by Cadman. A recent arrival from England (see item 551), Cadman quickly developed a sense of loyalty to his Thirty-ninth Ohio Infantry Regiment. He worried about his family, especially the delays in being paid and the dangers involved in getting the money home safely. He described the devastation in the South; he deplored the debauchery of men too long away from liquor and women; and he complained that being in the front line put the troops in more danger of being shot from behind by their own side than from enemy fire. Cadman detested "Copperheads" (antiwar Democrats) and composed an insulting poem as proof. Cadman served in Mississippi and Georgia and was killed in the Atlanta Campaign.

(1863)   CHRISTIAN WILHELM HANDER   426

Plummer, Leonard B., ed. and tr. "Excerpts From the Hander Diary." *Journal of Mississippi History* 26 (May 1964):141–49.

Christian Wilhelm Hander, a Confederate soldier from Denmark, kept an account of the battle for Vicksburg from May 13, 1863, to July 18, 1863. Even though the city was treated well by Union soldiers after its surrender, Hander says that tensions persisted. He describes the conditions under which he and other Confederate soldiers were paroled. On his way back to

Texas, Hander passed by ruined Louisiana plantations that had been flourishing the first time he saw them. He comments that he saw no whites and only a few blacks in the area. He relates that Union money was the only accepted currency.

TENNESSEE

(1788–1815)   FRANCIS ASBURY   427

Posey, Walter B., ed. "Bishop Asbury Visits Tennessee, 1788–1815: Extracts from his Journal." *Tennessee Historical Quarterly* 15 (September 1956):253–68.

  Francis Asbury, a Methodist circuit rider, visited Tennessee in seventeen different years. Through the period he observed the growth of towns and churches and the development of roads and travel accommodations. He recorded the poor living conditions in the mountains, the vast consumption of whiskey, and the generosity of Tennessee people. He belived it was difficult to bring religion to the people of the West because there were too many distractions, among them "good" air and cheap land. Taken from *The Journal of the Rev. Francis Asbury, Bishop of the Methodist Episcopal Church, from August 7, 1771 to December 7, 1815* (New York, 1821).

(1818)   DANIEL BERRY   428

Newcomer, Lee Nathaniel, ed. "Two New England Teachers in Nashville, 1818." *Tennessee Historical Quarterly* 19 (March 1960):74–79.

  Dr. Daniel Berry and his wife "S" came to Nashville, he as principal and she as teacher of the first classes in the Nashville Female Academy, in 1817 and stayed until 1819. These two letters relate some of the activities of the school and privide some information about the population and agriculture of the Nashville area.

(1818)   EBENEZER NEWTON   429

Newton, Charlotte, ed. "Ebenezer Newton's 1818 Diary." *Georgia Historical Quarterly* 53 (June 1969):205–19.

  In the fall of 1818, Newton, who was an instructor at the Athens, Georgia, Grammar School, traveled on horseback to his home in Tennessee. Most of the diary relates conditions of travel, especially the uneven quality of the lodging that his party found. He also describes the Cherokee lands he crossed, the Indians and the missionary he met, and conversations and incidents along the way.

(1820–1823)   CALVIN JONES   430

Owsley, Harriet C. "Westward to Tennessee." *Tennessee Historical Quarterly* 24 (Spring 1965):31–38.

  Calvin Jones made two trips (1820 and 1823) from Ashe County, North Carolina, to Tennessee to take up some land warrants he had received for outstanding service in the War of 1812. His letters, which are paraphrased and quoted, describe the landscape and the travel, and include a lengthy passage about Nashville in 1823.

(1821)   J. D. STEEL   431

Remini, Robert V., ed. "A New York 'Yankee' in Tennessee, 1821." *Tennessee Historical Quarterly* 37 (Fall 1978):278–92.

The bad January weather may have made J. D. Steel irritable, at least he seemed to have had many unpleasant experiences. He argued with a woman over the relative worth of northern and southern women, as well as whether marriage was more advantageous for the husband or the wife. Nights were particularly bad for him. He was forced to lodge in a smoky cabin and a dirty tavern, and one night he fell in with a drunk who harangued him until dawn. He does reveal some interesting experiences, such as watching the boring of limestone for salt, where he observed a divining rod in action.

Steel also comments on the local reaction to the Missouri Compromise Bill of 1820. He says that although the planters in Tennessee did not want slavery, they were opposed to the easterners who the planters felt wanted to split the Union. Steel spent an evening at Andrew Jackson's plantation and found the General to be a very profane man, a horse racer, and a great duelist. Since Steel was opposed to all these habits and activities, and perhaps to Jackson's social class, the conversation became heated.

(1852)   ROSINE PARMENTIER   432

McClary, Ben H., and Graf, LeRoy P., eds. "'Vineland' in Tennessee: The Journal of Rosine Parmentier." *East Tennessee Historical Society Publications* 31 (1959):95–111.

Describes a journey from New York to the Sylco Mountains of east Tennessee to visit a colony of European Catholics the Parmentier family had helped to establish as wine growers. After a four-day voyage Rosine arrived at Savannah. To her the city looked old and abandoned, and blacks were almost the only people she saw in the streets. She describes the colony, the mountains, and especially the vegetation of Tennessee. Journal kept October 2 to October 30, 1852.

(1862)   FELIX GREGORY DE FONTAINE   433

Merrill, James M. "'Nothing to Eat But Raw Bacon': Letters from a War Correspondent, 1862." *Tennessee Historical Quarterly* 17 (June 1958):141–55.

An article written by "Personne" (Felix Gregory De Fontaine) about the Battle of Shiloh (Tennessee) for the *Charleston Daily Courier* on April 22, 1862. He relates the tactics of fighting, the losses, the valor shown by "western" men on both sides, capturing Union camps, ransacking and eating from Union stores that were better provisioned than their own, and some interviews with Union prisoners. He also describes the destruction of the battle and its effect on the civilians who were forced to leave Corinth, Mississippi.

(1862)   JOSEPH DIMMIT THOMPSON   434

Biel, John G., ed. "The Battle of Shiloh: From the Letters and Diary of Joseph Dimmit Thompson." *Tennessee Historical Quarterly* 17 (September 1958):250–74.

Excerpts from the writings of a young southern soldier (Thirty-eighth Tennessee Infantry) during the war in Tennessee between April 5 and 10, 1862. Perhaps to reassure himself, Thompson writes that the Yankees could not withstand the cold steel of the Confederate bayonet. He describes the kind of loot the southern troops took from the encampments hastily vacated by better-equipped Union soldiers. Thompson also reveals some of the problems Confederate soldiers had with the credibility of the money they were issued.

(1862–1864)   JOSEPH J. PITTS   435

Martin, John M., ed. "A Methodist Circuit Rider Between the Lines: The Private Journal of Joseph J. Pitts, 1862–1864." *Tennessee Historical Quarterly* 19 (September 1960):252–69.

Pitts was a rider on the Smith's Fork circuit east of Nashville. He relates some of the problems of conducting his church work during the war. Military operations kept him from appointments and caused members to stay away from the church; his horse was impressed by military authorities, he had to secure passes and submit to questioning, and he endured shortages of food and clothing. Journal kept from December 1, 1862, through December 31, 1864.

(1862–1865)   JACOB W. BARTMESS   436

Carmony, Donald F., ed. "Jacob W. Bartmess Civil War Letters." (Part I) *Indiana Magazine of History* 52 (March 1956):49–74.

————. (Part II) *Indiana Magazine of History* 53 (June 1956): 157–86.

Presents the diary of a patriotic, God-fearing man who disliked his military service from the beginning. Bartmess volunteered in the fall of 1862 (to escape being drafted) for nine months, but he was later chagrined to find that his enlistment had fraudulently been changed to three years. Bartmess appears to have hated the immorality, the profanity, and the drinking more than he feared the battles. Most of all, he disliked being away from his wife and son. Money problems loomed large for the family, especially after Bartmess learned his wife was destitute. At various times he was torn between asking her for money for supplies and a desire to send her as much of his pay as possible. He was determined not to accumulate personal debts. He tried unsuccessfully to sell his blacksmith shop, and later became angry when someone attempted to take the chimney for debts.

Bartmess also wrote about the war, camp life, rebel desertions, executions, the low quality of civilian life in Tennessee, the unrest in North Carolina following the war, Indiana and national politics, and Lincoln's death. Most of the letters were written between 1862 and 1865 from Tennessee and Georgia where he served with the Eighth Indiana Cavalry.

(1863–1864)   NADINE TURCHIN   437

McElligott, Mary Ellen, ed. "'A Monotony Full of Sadness': The Diary of Nadine Turchin, May, 1863–April 1864." *Journal of the Illinois State Historical Society* 70 (February 1977):27–89.

The wife of Brigadier General John Basil Turchin (first commander of the Nineteenth Illinois Infantry, then of a cavalry division with the Army of the Cumberland) followed her husband to the front during the Civil War. In this surviving section of her diary (May 26, 1863-April 26, 1864), she recorded experiences mostly from Tennessee. Because of her military background, Nadine was able to offer informed descriptions of the Battle of Missionary Ridge (November 25, 1863) and the campaigns of Chattanooga (October-November, 1863) and Chickamauga (August-September, 1863). Her comments about the progress of the war and its participants are perhaps the most interesting portions.

Because she and her husband were immigrants from Russia, her perceptive critique of American society gives the viewpoint of a foreign observer. Nadine was bitter toward the men who were in charge of the war, from the officials in Washington to the generals in charge of the Army of the Potomac, down to corps commanders. She praises the citizen-soldier for his endurance and patience, but is more ambivalent about Americans in general. For example, in several places she exhibits empathy for laborers and common people who were supporting the war effort, but she particularly opposes the sacrifices they were making for the benefit of a "detestable" aristocracy, the "enriched industrialists." (p. 30)

Nadine refers to the lack of dignity in American society, as well as to other traits she found deplorable. She also addresses such topics as religion, war aims, camp rumors, the press, and the character of the people of the South. Though she obviously meant for her diary to be read, at the time she wrote it, she regarded it as her "safety valve" to help relieve her frustration with the long periods of inactivity and with the inefficient conduct of the war. (p. 32)

(1863–1865)   RICHARD CALVIN MCCALLA   438

Partin, Robert, ed. "The Civil War in East Tennessee as Reported By a Confederate Railroad Bridge Builder." *Tennessee Historical Quarterly* 22 (September 1963):238–58.

These letters of Richard Calvin McCalla (August 17, 1863-February 10, 1865) present a picture of building and rebuilding bridges in east Tennessee and southwest Virginia. He offers his opinion on military policy and leaders, describes the ravaging effects of Yankee occupation in eastern Tennessee, and provides advice for his wife. McCalla served first with Presstman's battalion of engineer troops between the fall of 1861 and the spring of 1863. The battalion later became the Third Regiment Engineer Troops and McCalla became the captain of Company B.

(1869–1874)   CALVIN HENDERSON WILEY   439

Wiley, Mary M., ed. "With Calvin H. Wiley in Tennessee Through Unpublished Letters." *North Carolina Historical Review* 36 (January 1959):72–95.

Calvin Henderson Wiley went to Tennessee from Raleigh, North Carolina, in 1869 to undertake the work of the American Bible Society. He tells of travel by horseback, of the desolation and discord all over Tennessee, and of the poor people to whom he ministered. His diary and letters date from May 31, 1869, to March 18, 1874.

6

North Central

(including the Old Northwest, Ohio River, and Upper Mississippi)

GENERAL

(1720–1850)   MIDWEST TRAVEL NARRATIVES   440

Hubach, Robert R. "Unpublished Travel Narratives on the Early Midwest, 1720–1850: A Preliminary Bibliography." *Mississippi Valley Historical Review* 42 (December 1955):525–48.

Lists 199 travel accounts gathered from thirty libraries and historical societies. These were later included in the author's more expansive *Early Midwestern Travel Narratives: An Annotated Bibliography, 1634–1850* (Detroit, 1961).

(1750–1800)   OHIO VALLEY LOCALISMS   441

Finnie, W. Bruce. "Ohio Valley Localisms: Topographical Terms, 1750–1800." *American Speech* 38 (October 1963):178–87.

From the writings of travelers to the Ohio Valley the author culled descriptions of topographic features that were apparently unique to this region. A glossary of terms is included.

(1775–1811)   RIVERS OF OLD NORTHWEST   442

McDermott, John Francis. "Travelers on the Western Waters." *Proceedings of the American Antiquarian Society* 77 (October 1977):255–80.

Accounts of those who traveled by flatboat and keelboat on the Mississippi, Ohio, and other rivers in late eighteenth century. Many of these military men, government appointees, missionaries, fur traders, scientists, and spies have left detailed records in the form of diaries, memoranda, and accounts of business.

(1788–1792)   FRENCH TRAVELERS   443

Galvin, Martin. "French Travelers in the Ohio Valley, 1788–1792." *Western Pennsylvania Historical Magazine* 59 (October 1976):463–72.

Galvin points out that although the French contributed to the development of the West, documents of their activities are rare. The author surveys the writings of three French travelers to the Pittsburgh area: Jean Pierre Brissot de Warville, Antoine Saugrain, and Claude Lezay-Marnézia. Galvin discusses the purposes of their visits and their impressions of the frontiersmen, the Indians, and the land.

(1793–1796)   JAMES ELLIOT   444

Huddleston, Eugene L. "James Elliot and 'The Garden of North America': A New Englander's Impressions of the Old Northwest." *Northwest Ohio Quarterly* 42 (Summer 1970):64–75.

After spending three years in western Pennsylvania and the Ohio Valley (1793 to 1796), Elliot penned his impressions of the region in a series of prose and poetic works. As a child in New England he was enamored with the West. Even though personal experience had shown him that travel was difficult and that the region could be both uncomfortable and unhealthy, he still described its natural wonders in idealistic terms. Huddleston says Elliot had ambivalent feelings about the inhabitants of the West, the frontiersmen and the Indians.

(1805–1806)   ZEBULON MONTGOMERY PIKE   445

Petersen, William J., ed. "Pike's Mississippi Expedition." *Palimpsest* 36 (May 1955):171–204.

Between August 9, 1805, and April 30, 1806, Lieutenant Zebulon Montgomery Pike traveled from Saint Louis to the source of the Mississippi River in northern Minnesota. His assignment was to explore the region, to locate sites for military posts, to treat with the Indians, to make peace between the Sioux and Ojibway tribes, and to learn how many British traders still occupied trading posts in the Louisiana Purchase. These extracts from Pike's *An Account of Expeditions to the Sources of the Mississippi and Through the Western Parts of Louisiana* (Baltimore, 1810) are accompanied by a fold-out map. A brief biography precedes this article.

(1812–1813)   WILLIAM B. NORTHCUTT   446

Clift, G. Glenn, ed. "War of 1812: Diary of William B. Northcutt." (Part I) *Register of the Kentucky Historical Society* 56 (April 1958):165–80.

————. (Part II) *Register of the Kentucky Historical Society* 56 (July 1958):253–69.

————. (Part III) *Register of the Kentucky Historical Society* 56 (October 1958):325–43.

Reminiscences of a member of the Kentucky militia unit, the "Bourbon Blues." In August, 1812, the troops departed Georgetown and marched to Fort Wayne (Indiana) to relieve that beseiged military post, after which they moved on to Fort Defiance (Ohio). In November and December, 1812, they fought against the Miami Indian villages on the Mississinewa River in Indiana. After a brief leave, Northcutt returned to duty in Ohio, where he spent the remainder of 1813 in skirmishes and on guard duty. Northcutt relates some incidents of the fighting against the British and Indians. He says that frequently the men would fire their weapons prematurely out of fear.

He tells of tending the wounded, and once he observed doctors hastening the inevitable by giving a man who had been shot in the head "something to finish him so we would bury the rest of the poor fellows." (p. 262) He refers to problems between the regulars and the militia, insubordination by enlisted men, and punishment for sleeping on duty. He describes the drudgery of marching, sometimes at half rations. Northcutt includes a final muster role of the "Bourbon Blues."

(1816–1818)   NATHANIEL DIKE   447

Smith, Dwight L., ed. "Nine Letters of Nathaniel Dike On the Western Country, 1816–1818." *Ohio Historical Quarterly* 67 (July 1958):189–220.

Dike was a young lawyer from Haverhill, Massachusetts, who set out to establish himself in Ohio. His earlier letters describe his journey across Massachusetts, Connecticut, New York, and Pennsylvania. Dike addresses himself to a wide range of topics. He comments on Newgate Prison in Simsbury, Connecticut; the Pennsylvania Dutch between Carlisle and Easton, Pennsylvania; wagons of people returning from the western country, "Sick almost to death of Ohio" (p. 196); and Pittsburgh, which Dike disliked because of the bad water and snakes. He saw the society of Pittsburgh as "a great gathering together of the scum of humanity from every part of creation." (p. 200)

Dike often compared what he saw with New England. For example, as he evaluated religion and education, he judged the society of the West to be immensely inferior to that of New England. He also wrote about the availability of land and land speculation, the court system and legal practice, and the distressed economic situation in the West caused, he believed, by the overabundance of paper money.

In his last letter Dike noted a change in travel writing. Where earlier books for travelers were designed "to gratify a laudable curiosity, and to extend geographical knowledge and historical intelligence," Dike thought travel writings were becoming more of an inducement for emigration. (p. 219)

(1835)   ELIZABETH VENILEA TROWBRIDGE GREENE   448

Greene, Elizabeth Venilea Trowbridge. "Going West: A Journey to Illinois in 1835." *Vermont History* 41 (Spring 1973):95–100.

The author and her husband were among a party of New Yorkers who caught western fever and emigrated to Illinois. The trip from Rochester took them across Ontario, Canada, to Detroit, along Lake Michigan, and then west of Chicago between February 12 and March 14, 1835. Extracted from a family genealogy by William Bertram Greene, *The Greenes on the East Branch of the DuPage* . . . (Aurora, 1966).

(1835–1837)   EZRA KELLER   449

Rehmer, R. F., ed. "Letters of Lutheran Traveling Missionaries Keller and Heyer, 1835–1837." *Concordia Historical Institute Quarterly* 47 (Summer 1974):70–89.

Rehmer reprints two letters each from Ezra Keller and John Christian Frederick Heyer, who were sent on separate six-month journeys to report on Lutheran communities in the West. Heyer visited Illinois and Indiana, and Keller traveled in Indiana and Ohio. Their letters provide insights into problems the church was encountering during this period, as well as locations of Lutheran settlements and accounts of what the two men judged to be moral laxity. (See also item 450.)

(1835–1837)   450

———. "Sheep Without Shepherds: Letters of Two Lutheran Traveling Missionaries, 1835–1837." *Indiana Magazine of History* 71 (March 1975):21–84.

More letters written by Ezra Keller and John Christian Frederick Heyer. (See also item 449.)

(1836–1839)   JOSEPH N. NICOLLET   451

Bray, Martha Coleman. "Joseph N. Nicollet: Parisian in Washington." *Smithsonian Journal of History* 3 (Winter 1968/1969):45–62.

Between 1836 and 1839 this French cartographer and astronomer led a series of explorations into Minnesota and North Dakota. His purpose was to investigate the drainage system of the Mississippi River and to explore the Saint Croix River and the plains region as far west as Devil's Lake. In 1843 the United States Senate published his *A Map of the Hydrographic Basin of the Upper Mississippi* and an accompanying report. Although his work was a highly significant contribution to American geography, Bray believes Nicollet has not been awarded the fame that is his due. She describes the years in America between his arrival in 1832 and his death in 1843.

Note: Another article of interest is Bray's "Joseph Nicholas Nicollet, Geologist," *Proceedings of the American Philosophical Society* 114 (February 1970):37–59.

(1839)   ANNE POPE VAILE   452

Thurman, Helen, ed. "Anne Pope Vaile's Wedding Trip Letter." *Western Pennsylvania Historical Magazine* 42 (December 1959):335–47.

The trip was from Newark, New Jersey, to Richmond, Indiana, in April, 1839. The bride describes her reactions to traveling from Newark to Philadelphia, through New Jersey, and across Pennsylvania by rail (too speedy to see very much); from Harrisburg to Pittsburgh by canal boat (too slow); down the Ohio River to Cincinnati by steamboat (a splendid trip); and overland to Richmond from Cincinnati by coach (crowded and unpleasant trip; they had to get out and walk too often).

(1852)   A. J. BRUNER   453

Britton, Nancy Moore, ed. "From Greene County, Tennessee, to Illinois: A Perilous Trip." *East Tennessee Historical Society Publications* 44 (1972):126–29.

In November, 1852, A. J. Bruner and his family traveled to Adams County, Illinois, on the Tennessee, Ohio, and Mississippi rivers. On the way his mother-in-law and one of his two daughters died. In this letter of April 17, 1853, he advises his father to tell anyone wishing to come to Illinois not to come in the winter and certainly not by water.

(1853)   HIRAM MILLS   454

Mills, Hiram. "Steamboat Experiences From the Journal of Dr. Hiram Mills: The Romantic Past?" *Bulletin of the Missouri Historical Society* 13 (July 1957):384–92.

From what he observed on his travels between May and late November of 1853, Dr. Mills would have concluded that riverboat travel on the Ohio and Missouri rivers was very unromantic. He tells of disgruntled passengers who had been promised better berths and food and who encountered long delays in disembarkation and crooked gamblers' tables that fleeced the unsuspecting.

(1853)   ANDRES WIBERG   455

Norton, John, ed. and tr. "Anders Wiberg's Account of a Trip to the United States in 1852–1853." (Part I) *Swedish Pioneer History Quarterly* 29 (April 1978):91–116.

———. (Part II) *Swedish Pioneer History Quarterly* 29 (July 1978):162–79.

The editor says that Wiberg's account of his trip to the Middle West (April 14-June 22, 1853), which appeared in the Stockholm newspaper *Aftonbladet*, may have exerted a profound positive influence on immigration because Wiberg describes religious affairs and conditions in Swedish communities in appealing terms. Wiberg, a recent convert from the Swedish Lutheran Church to the more liberal Swedish Baptist movement, points out the sense of religious freedom in America. He relates a discussion with General Lewis Cass in Detroit on the topic of freedom of religion, and he praises the interdenominational Sunday school movement he found there. In Chicago, Wiberg observed that there were six active religions, each with its own newspaper. But also in Chicago, he saw a depressing side of immigration: the high mortality rates among the Swedish from eating bad pork, drinking excessively, and crowding together in hovels. He says the Swedes' bad reputation was second only to that of the "otherwise despised Irish." (p. 94)

Wiberg provides more glowing pictures of Swedish settlements throughout the northern half of Illinois, eastern Iowa, and southwestern Wisconsin. He describes in detail the Swedish Erik-Janssonist Colony near Galesburg, Illinois. As he returned east through Saint Louis (a long passage about the potential of the Mississippi Valley), and up the Ohio River to Cincinnati, then by rail to Columbus, Cleveland, Buffalo, Niagara Falls, Rochester, and Albany, then down the

Hudson River to New York City, the same theme continues in his writing: America is a good place for Swedes to live.

(1855) ISAIAH MORRIS HARRIS 456

Brodhead, Michael J., and Unruh, Jr., John D., eds. "Isaiah Harris' 'Minutes of a trip to Kansas Territory' in 1855." *Kansas Historical Quarterly* 35 (Winter 1969):373–85.

Most of his diary describes a two-week (October 29-November 15 or 16, 1855) trip from Cincinnati down the Ohio River, then up the Mississippi and Missouri rivers to Westport, Missouri. Harris includes incidents of his river journey, as well as comments about his fellow travelers. As the editors point out, Harris is more interested in the physical details of the land for the purposes of emigration than he is about the controversial issue of slavery. He does, however, mention that on the trip down the Ohio, passengers seemed reluctant to talk about slavery. At a church meeting in Westport, the sentiment was in favor of making Kansas a free state. Harris also comments on the efforts of Quaker missionaries with the Indians in Westport.

(1859) THEODORE L. PUTNAM 457

Miller, Ernest C., ed. "Down the Rivers: A Rafting Journal of 1859—from Warren, Pa., to Louisville, Ky." *Western Pennsylvania Historical Magazine* 40 (Fall 1957):149–62.

During March and April, 1859, Theodore L. Putnam floated the largest raft ever to go down the Allegheny and the Ohio rivers. In this account Putnam relates problems with the rivers, the snags, and the winds, and he comments on the steamboats they passed during the 32-day trip.

ILLINOIS

(1770) GEORGE MORGAN 458

Oaks, Robert F., ed. "George Morgan's 'Memorandums': A Journey to the Illinois Country, 1770." *Journal of the Illinois State Historical Society* 69 (August 1976):185–200.

In the mid-1760s the Philadelphia firm of Baynton, Wharton and Morgan was one of the most successful frontier trading companies in Illinois Country. During the next few years, however, a series of reverses—overextended resources, a decline in furs, politics, and trouble between the partners—caused George Morgan to return to Illinois in the spring of 1770 to salvage what he could from an accumulated inventory of supplies. Morgan's Memorandums (March 9-December 1770) describe the flotilla trip down the Ohio River from Fort Pitt (Pennsylvania), and up the Mississippi to Kaskaskia and Fort de Chartres. They also contain documents by Morgan and others regarding his dispute with the British later in the year.

(1820–1850) ILLINOIS 459

Spahn, Raymond Jürgen. "German Accounts of Early Nineteenth-Century Life in Illinois." *Papers on Language and Literature* 14 (Fall 1978):473–88.

Reviews the many books published in Germany about the United States between 1820 and 1850, with particular attention to those accounts that evaluated cultural life in Illinois. German travelers usually praised the existence of newspapers, libraries, and public support of schools. Spahn also comments on the effect of these travel books on immigration from Germany.

(1829–1831)   **ADOLF VON AMAN**   **460**

Tonsor, Stephen J., ed. "'I Am My Own Boss'—A German Immigrant Writes from Illinois." *Journal of the Illinois State Historical Society* 54 (Winter 1961):392–404.

These letters from Adolf von Aman were originally published in *Eos* (Munich, Germany) between 1829 and 1831. Once he settled on his farm in White County, he never regretted coming to America. His letters are filled with the details of his life: descriptions of Illinois and of his land, the crops he grew and how he supplemented his needs by making and laying bricks, the grapes and wine that the region produced, his proximity to his neighbors, the prices of food, and the fact that he had never yet spoken German to his children because he was waiting until they had mastered English.

(1830–1831)   **ASA FITCH**   **461**

Rezneck, Samuel. "Diary of a New York Doctor in Illinois—1830–1831." *Journal of Illinois State Historical Society* 54 (Spring 1961):25–50.

When Asa Fitch left his New York home he was in high spirits, but his winter in Greenville (Bond County), Illinois, proved to be an unhappy episode in his life. The town already had a doctor and because Fitch did not get along with his peer, he found cases only occasionally. In addition, his plans to start a school were shattered by a teaching rival. His living quarters were poor. The cracks between the boards permitted cold air and the exceptionally heavy snow of that winter to pour through.

Rezneck says there is a tone of self-pitying discontent in Fitch's diary. Fitch was so concerned with his health and with trying to stay warm that Rezneck suggests he was a hypochondriac. Fitch perked up during the Christmas festivities, however. He felt he had returned to his "old tricks of gallanting the girls," but his "bold push" gave way to reality as he realized there were "too small and too few materials for such a thing in Greenville." (p. 44) After the Christmas parties, Rezneck says, Fitch returned to his familiar conditions of ill health and ill humor. Except for Saturday nights with "stewed whiskey" at the town store and his participation in the Greenville Polemical Society, Fitch simply waited out the winter. By March he had returned to New York.

(1830–1834)   **JOSEPH CRESS**   **462**

Patton, James W., ed. "Letters from North Carolina Emigrants in the Old Northwest, 1830–1834." *Mississippi Valley Historical Review* 47 (September 1960):263–77.

During the first third of the nineteenth century North Carolina lost many of its inhabitants to Indiana and Illinois. These two sets of letters generally compare North Carolina unfavorably to the emigrants' new homes in the West. Joseph Cress describes his farm in Montgomery County, Illinois, and writes back to North Carolina: "I ame realy sorrow for you that you work them old red filds and git nothing and hear it is as black and rich as you wold want it." (p. 267) Daniel F. Ludewick also describes his farm in the same county, relates events of the Black Hawk War of 1832, and tells of his illness.

(1835–1836)   **FREDERICK JULIUS GUSTORF**   **463**

Gustorf, Fred, ed. "Frontier Perils Told By an Early Illinois Visitor." (Part I) *Journal of the Illinois State Historical Society* 55 (Summer 1962):136–56.
————. (Part II) *Journal of the Illinois State Historical Society* 55 (Autumn 1962):255–70.

Frederick Julius Gustorf visited Illinois and Missouri between July 13, 1835 and July 23, 1836. The editor says that Gustorf's journal reveals the disillusionment of a German who had viewed the frontier romantically. Gustorf did not merely complain, though. His criticism is based on personal observation and written so articulately that the journal is a valuable and interesting critique of the harsh realities of frontier life. Travel was arduous, and three times Gustorf had coach accidents, causing him to remark that anyone who wanted to get any place in the West should walk.

After working as a hired laborer he wrote, "a farmer's life is neither romantic or idyllic— just hard work with small rewards." (p. 143) He followed a doctor on his rounds to observe the illnesses and medicine available to frontier families. Gustorf attributed the widespread sickness to the wretched living conditions.

He also wrote of frontier violence, excessive drinking, land speculation, and the tragedy of people who had moved to the frontier expecting a better life. He visited the English colonies of New Albion and Wanborough founded by George Flower and Morris Birbeck, respectively, and he traveled to Saint Louis and Belleville, where he visited Gottfried Duden's German settlement.

Gustorf perhaps summarized his impressions of the West when he wrote about Peoria: "Europeans think that the West is the newest of the New World and expect to find here the best manners, morals, and customs, but, to the contrary, these new frontier towns attract the excrement from the older cities of the East." (p. 261)

(1836)   GEORGE W. BROCKWAY   464

Cornet, Florence Doll, ed. "The Experiences of a Midwest Salesman in 1836." *Bulletin of the Missouri Historical Society* 29 (July 1973):227–35.

George W. Brockway, a Vermont agent for a scale company, traveled north from Saint Louis on the Mississippi River and overland through the Illinois River Valley in April, 1836. He refers to Peoria, Pekin, and Springfield, and tells of the beauty of the prairie over which he rode. Among his descriptions are those of a pioneer family, a cave containing many skeletal remains near Grafton, Illinois, and the mob action that led to the lynching of a black in Saint Louis.

(1850)   FREDRIKA BREMER   465

Ekman, Ernst, ed. and tr. "Fredrika Bremer in Chicago in 1850." *Swedish Pioneer Historical Quarterly* 19 (October 1968):234–44.

During her three-year stay in America (1849 to 1851), the Swedish writer visited Chicago in September, 1850. Her first visit was to the prairie near the city. Although Fredrika described the land in somewhat romantic terms, when she asked a pioneer wife what she thought of her life, the woman replied more realistically: "It was so monotonous." (p. 237) While Fredrika liked the people of Chicago, she thought it was a shabby and ugly city. Her account provides information about Swedish and German settlements in Chicago. These excerpts are from her book, *The Homes of the New World* (London, 1853). (See also items 411 and 557.)

(1867)   HEINRICH SCHLIEMANN   466

Zochert, Donald, ed. "Heinrich Schliemann's Chicago Journal." *Chicago History, New Series* 2 (Spring/Summer 1973):173–81.

The future discoverer of the ancient city of Troy spent four days in Chicago in November, 1867. Since Schliemann had made his fortune in a variety of businesses, perhaps it was natural that he reported on the stockyards, the breweries, the waterworks, and the grain elevators, and on the land sales of the Illinois Central Railroad.

(1889)   RUDYARD KIPLING   467

Peterson, William S. "Kipling's First Visit to Chicago." *Journal of the Illinois State Historical Society* 63 (Autumn 1970):290–301.

Proceeding from India to England in the summer of 1889, Rudyard Kipling wrote a series of letters for publication in newspapers that portrayed American society in an irreverent light. Chicago was a microcosm of all he disliked in America. The Palmer House was a symbol of vulgar opulence, the city's streets were dirty, church worship was a circus, and the commercial enterprises were greedy. When his "American letters" were serialized, Chicago, like the rest of America, reacted with indignation. (See also item 824.)

(1892–1893)   MME. LEON GRANDIN   468

Grandin, Mme. Leon "The Gay Nineties in Chicago: a French View." *Chicago History* 7 (Spring 1966):341–48.

Comments about middle-class life in Chicago from *Impressions d'une Parisienne à Chicago* (Paris, 1894). Mme. Grandin came to Chicago with her husband, who was setting up a sculpture for the World's Columbian Exposition, in July, 1892; they remained until May, 1893. She relates the difficulties of finding a boarding house to provide all the amenities to which they were accustomed. She and her husband were used to having more food to eat than they were served and to having their shoes shined when they were set in the hall at night. She disliked men removing their jackets in hot weather and their chewing tobacco and gum. She did like Lake Michigan, the Gunther Candy Store, popcorn and peanuts, and she approved of the way men helped their wives with housework. She especially liked the freedom America gave her as a woman.

As she contemplated her return to France she wrote: "I revolted at returning to the passive and inferior role that awaited me. I enjoyed the consideration and respect accorded to women, and I would return to the scorn, the disdainful pity, which masculine superiority heaps on women in France." (p. 347) Later, as she steamed out of New York Harbor, she vowed, "I WILL RETURN." (p. 348)

INDIANA

(1862)   JAMES E. PATON   469

Paton, James E. "Civil War Journal of James E. Paton." *Register of the Kentucky Historical Society* 61 (July 1963):220–31.

Paton's entries (July 1-August 4, 1862) are written from the Union prison at Camp Morton (Indiana), "that hell on earth." (p. 228) They describe the Confederate defeat at Fort Donelson (Tennessee) and his capture and imprisonment. Paton tells of prisoners trying to escape but being betrayed by their own comrades. He says the shooting of inoffensive Confederates by prison guards was an everyday occurrence. In his last entry, however, he was still in high spirits and promises the eventual victory of the C.S.A., "free from the clanking chains of northern despotism." (p. 231) Paton served with the Second Kentucky Infantry.

(1879)   CLAIRE READ   470

Harrison, Lowell H., ed. "A British View of Indiana's Agriculture, 1879." *Indiana Magazine of History* 68 (December 1972):307–14.

A portion of the official report to the British Parliament, which had sent Claire Read and Albert Pell to study the nature of increased agricultural competition from the United States and Canada. Only a few days were spent in Indiana. (See also item 400.)

Iowa

(1834) REVEREND MARSH 471

Nichols, Roger L. "A Missionary Journey to the Sac-Fox Indians, 1834." *Annals of Iowa*, 36 (Spring 1962):301–15.

Reveals an unsuccessful effort by a Reverend Marsh of the American Board of Commissioners for Foreign Missions to get the Sac and Fox Indians along the eastern Iowa rivers to accept Christianity.

(1840) LEWIS SCHOFIELD 472

Schofield, Lewis. "An Emigrant's Letter in 1840." *Annals of Iowa* 34 (October 1958):460–64.

Schofield's letter was written to a prospective emigrant to provide advice concerning conditions in Iowa. He says steamboat travel was the cheapest and quickest but advises overland travel. Although grains were the most popular crops, Schofield believes tobacco could be grown profitably in Iowa. He describes the availability and the price of land and believes investment in land to be a wise choice. Although sickness was rampant in Iowa and Illinois, Schofield simply accepts it as a fact of frontier life.

(1843–1847) EBENEZER ALDEN, JR. 473

Alden, Ebenezer, Jr. "The Ebenezer Alden Jr., Letters From Iowa Territory." (Part I) *Annuals of Iowa* 33 (January 1957):473–509.
———. (Part II) *Annals of Iowa* 33 (April 1957):572–611.

Letters by a Congregationalist minister at Solon and Tipton, Iowa, between October 9, 1843, and February 12, 1847. In addition to revealing Alden's role in the establishment of Grinnell College and the struggles of an early Iowa church, these letters provide bits of information about many small communities, the disastrous effects of a tornado, and the caves near Dubuque. There is some reference to other religions in Iowa.

(1847) SJOERD AUKES SIPMA 474

Swierenga, Robert P., ed. "A Dutch Immigrant's View of Frontier Iowa." *Annals of Iowa* 38 (Fall 1965):81–118.

A letter from Sjoerd Aukes Sipma from the province of Friesland, who was one of the Netherlanders that immigrated to Iowa and established a colony at Pella in August, 1847. The editor says that in addition to giving an excellent picture of pioneer life in Iowa, the letter also "reveals various facets of cultural conflict between native and foreign-born and even among the foreign-born themselves. . . ." (p. 86)

(1856) ARCHER WALTERS 475

Petersen, William J., ed. "The Handcart Expeditions: 1856." *Palimpsest* 36 (November 1956):528–44.

In the summer of 1856, thirteen hundred European Mormons were deposited in Iowa City, the terminus of the Mississippi and Missouri Railroad. Their destination was Salt Lake City, but because of the cost of wagons, Brigham Young decreed that they could walk and pull their belongings in handcarts. These recent converts to Mormonism were working-class people totally unsuited to travel on the open prairie. The Iowa press made many unfavorable comments about their rag-tag appearance, but the people whose lands they crossed were friendly and sometimes provided them with food. By the time they reached Nebraska, the handcarts were in need of frequent repair, and the wind and storms, stampeding buffalo, and a constant shortage of food had taken a heavy toll. Petersen focuses on the Iowa portion of the arduous trek, using the diary of a Welsh convert, Archer Walters, who died of dysentery five weeks after reaching the "land of Zion."

(1858)   MARY ST. JOHN   476

Riley, Glenda, ed. "A Prairie Diary." *Annals of Iowa* 44 (Fall 1977):103–17.

Describes a New York family's first year of life on a farm near Saratoga, Iowa. These portions of the diary (March 31-December 31, 1858) were kept by Mary St. John, with contributions by her sister. As she records the daily activities, Mary illuminates the endless domestic duties performed by frontier women and frontier men.

(1859–1872)   TRAVELS IN IOWA   477

Petersen, William J., ed. "Letters to Iowa Editors." *Palimpsest* 40 (March 1959):81–128.

These seven letters are a sampling of the many written by travelers and published in Iowa newspapers between 1859 and 1872. Most letters had been commissioned by editors to acquaint their readers with existing conditions around the state.

(1862)   MARY ALICE SHUTES   478

Riley, Glenda, ed. "Pioneer Migration: The Diary of Mary Alice Shutes." (Part I) *Annals of Iowa* 43 (Winter 1977):487–514.

————.(Part II) *Annals of Iowa* 43 (Spring 1977):567–92.

Thirteen-year-old Mary Alice kept this record of her family's journey from Wyandott County, Ohio, to their new home in Carroll County, Iowa. They covered the eight hundred miles in a covered wagon between May 4 and June 12, 1862. *Note*: An interesting summary of the diary and its relevance to a descendant is found in Lida L. Greene, "To Ioway for Keeps," *Annals of Iowa* 39 (Summer 1968):393–97.

(1862–1863)   ELLEN STRANG   479

Greene, Lida L., ed. "Diary of a Young Girl: Grundy County to Correctionville, 1862." *Annals of Iowa* 36 (Fall 1962):437–57.

Ellen Strang had previously accompanied her Quaker family from New York to Iowa in 1853. This portion of her diary, which describes a trip to visit her sister and the stay at Correctionville, covers November 7, 1862, to April 14, 1863. It reveals the kinds of work women were expected to perform on the recently settled frontier, as well as the effects of the "spotted fever," or meningitis, epidemic that plagued the community that winter.

(1871)   JOHN FOUNDERS DIXON   480

Erickson, Charlotte, ed. "An Emigrant's Letter From Iowa, 1871." *British Association for American Studies Bulletin, New Series* 12/13 (1966):5–41.

In his letter of June 17, 1871, John Founders Dixon describes his journey from England to Dallas County, Iowa, and his impressions of farming there. He first tells of the ocean voyage by steerage class—board beds, poor food, people from many parts of the world, ship officials disinfecting the rooms regularly to avoid diseases—and the delay at being allowed to enter the country in New York City. He traveled west by immigrant train, stopping at immigrant houses, where he believed the owners were out to make an exorbitant profit. He describes the Iowa farmers, their houses, their eating habits, the price of land, and the employment possibilities in the state.

(1876)   **JAMES LONSDALE BRODERICK**   **481**

Horton, Loren N., ed. "The Character of the Country: Excerpts." *Palimpsest* 57 (September/October 1976):157–60.

    James Lonsdale Broderick came from England to Dubuque, Iowa, to spend six months in 1876. In these portions of his diary (December-March) he tells of visiting a pig-killing and pork-packing plant—an interesting and instructive experience, but he had no desire to return. He felt the American press to be poor in reporting politics because they chose to pamper the tastes of the multitudes. He also visited the New Melleray Monastery, where he evaluated their stock-raising efforts.

(1881)   **WILLARD GLAZIER**   **482**

Glazier, Willard. "Captain Willard Glazier." *Palimpsest* 51 (September 1970):353–416.

    During the last two weeks of September, 1881, Glazier passed along Iowa on a canoe trip down the Mississippi that had begun at Lake Itasca, Minnesota. In this excerpt from his travel book, *Down the Great River* (Philadelphia, 1888), he blends his experiences with a little history and description of the Mississippi River and eastern Iowa. Dubuque, Davenport, Rock Island, Burlington, and Keokuk all receive special mention.

(1885)   **GEORGE C. DUFFIELD**   **483**

Duffield, George C. "An 1885 Excursion from Keosauqua to Storm Lake." *Annals of Iowa* 41 (Winter 1972):867–74.

    Duffield's diary records only bare details of a journey on horseback from southeastern Iowa to western Iowa, which occurred between October 17 and November 24, 1885. Mostly concerned with hunting and camping experiences.

(1894)   **JACK LONDON**   **484**

London, Jack. "Tramping with Kelly through Iowa: A Jack London Diary." *Palimpsest* 52 (June 1971):316–46.

    In the spring of 1894, "General" Charles T. Kelly led a mob of fifteen hundred unemployed workers from San Francisco across the United States to Washington, D.C. Reproduced here is writer Jack London's diary of the trek from Oakland, California, to southeastern Iowa (April 6-May 18, 1894). This issue is devoted to the dilemma that Kelly's army posed for the state of Iowa.

(1899)   **CARRIE MCKINLEY CARSON**   **485**

Carson, Clifford M., ed. "A Summer at Lake Okoboji: Excerpts from a Vacation Diary, 1899." *Palimpsest* 57 (May/June 1976):86–95.

    Carrie McKinley Carson's diary of a family vacation records recreational activities she found available at the famous Iowa resort area. She wrote of the dancing pavilion, rowing, swimming in a store-bought suit, fishing, and sailing around the lakes on a steamship. She relates the fate of a lavish hotel that was unable to meet its expenses as a regular hotel because it was forced to stop selling liquor.

(1914)   **HELENE DEAN OLSON**   **486**

Olson, Helene Dean. "My First Auto Trip." *Kansas Quarterly* 8 (Spring 1976):21–24.

Reminiscences of a 400-mile car trip, when as a young girl Olson traveled from north-western Iowa to near Janesville, Wisconsin, sometime in 1914. She had a fear of traveling over muddy, single-lane roads that sloped to the middle. On this trip they never encountered rain, but they did face axle-deep sand that had been dumped as a road improvement. She describes preparation for the trip (including protection of her fashionably white chin from sunburn) and her first views of broad expanses of water at Clear Lake (Iowa) and at the Mississippi River. She remembers that in her hometown she was treated as an important figure for having made such a long trip.

MICHIGAN

(1675)   HENRY NOUVEL   487

Moll, Harold W., ed. "A Canoe Trip to Midland in 1675." *Michigan History* 46 (September 1962):255–74.

An extract from a letter by Father Henry Nouvel, a Jesuit missionary, who traveled the Saginaw-Tittabawassee rivers of central Michigan. From this document the editor places the establishment of an early Catholic mission near Midland, Michigan.

(1763–1764)   ALEXANDER HENRY   488

Quimby, George I. "Alexander Henry in Central Michigan, 1763–64." *Michigan History* 46 (September 1962):193–200.

Analyzes Henry's *Travels and Adventures in Canada and the Indian Territories Between the Years 1760 and 1776* (Toronto, 1901) to determine precisely what places the fur trader was describing during the winter of 1763–64, which he spent with a Chippewa Indian family. (See also item 489.)

(1763–1764)   489

———. "A Year With a Chippewa Family, 1763–1764." *Ethnohistory* 9 (Summer 1962):217–39.

After surviving the Indian attack on the British Fort Michilimackinac in June, 1763, fur trader Alexander Henry spent the next year as an adopted relative of the Chippewas. Using Henry's journal, *Travels and Adventures in Canada and the Indian Territories Between the Years 1760 and 1776* (Toronto, 1901), the author reconstructs Indian life as it existed in this northern lower-peninsular Michigan tribe. (See also item 488.)

(1827)   SALMON KEENEY   490

Everett, Helen, ed. "Salmon Keeney's Visit to Michigan in 1827." *Michigan History* 40 (December 1956):433–46.

Keeney came to Monroe County, Michigan, by traveling from Braintrim, Pennsylvania, through New York, across Lake Erie to Detroit, to Ann Arbor, and then back home. Includes many brief references to the people, the commerce, the climate, and especially the land of Michigan, where Keeney returned a year later to settle. Diary kept June 16 to August 10, 1827.

(1830)   HENRY PARKER SMITH   491

Peters, Bernard C., ed. "Henry Parker Smith's Reminiscences of a Young Pioneer." *Michigan History* 59 (Winter 1975):255–74.

Henry Parker Smith was only four years old when his family came to Prairie Ronde in Kalamazoo County, Michigan, in the spring of 1830. He remembers the plowing, the serenade of the wolves, the town of Schoolcraft, his father's store, and the Indians, one of whom offered two squaws for Henry's mother.

(1831) **DOUGLASS HOUGHTON** **492**

Mason, Philip P., ed. "Trip to Sault Ste Marie, 1831." *Michigan History* 39 (December 1955):474–80.

After briefly mentioning his rough trip across Lake Erie to Detroit from Fredonia, New York, Douglass Houghton relates the events of his journey from Green Bay to the Sault in more detail. He provides a description of the British fortifications on Drummond and Saint Joseph's Island, as well as the Sault. Houghton was en route to join Indian agent Henry Rowe Schoolcraft on an expedition to visit the warring Chippewa tribes in the Lake Superior–Mississippi River region.

(1831–1838) **JOHN FISHER** **493**

Tucker, Louis Leonard, ed. "The Correspondence of John Fisher." *Michigan History* 45 (September 1961):219–36.

Records a pioneer's immigration from England and his settlement in Lenawee County, Michigan. The letters, which date from February 12, 1831, to May 29, 1838, focus on Fisher's successful struggle to improve his farm. The editor adds that "forest land gave way to cultivated fields, oxen were replaced by horses, wells were dug and new buildings erected." (p. 219) Fisher mentions the fate of the Indians who were living on the lands that were rapidly becoming farms, the great advantages of living in America over England, the progress of his farm, and his constant wish to see his mother again, although he could not because he needed to put his money back into the farm. He is interested in getting married, but does not like Yankee girls. He eventually met a woman from Yorkshire and advised his mother: "It is very likely that the next letter you receive from me will inform you that I am married as I find it difficult to hire a woman to do my work in the house." (p. 228)

(1836) **JOHN MONTGOMERY GORDON** **494**

Gordon, Douglas H., and May, George S., eds. "The Michigan Land Rush in 1836." (Part I) *Michigan History* 43 (March 1959):1–42.

———. (Part II) *Michigan History* 43 (June 1959):129–49.

———. (Part III) *Michigan History* 43 (September 1959):257–93.

———. (Part IV) *Michigan History* 43 (December 1959):433–78.

John Montgomery Gordon of Baltimore came to Michigan in August, 1836, invested in large amounts of land, and stayed until the following December. His journal records the trip from Baltimore to New York, up the Hudson River to Albany, westward to Buffalo, across Lake Erie to Detroit, and down to southern Michigan near Saint Joseph and Ionia. In addition to describing his preparations for the trip, conditions of travel, and other travelers, Gordon sheds some light on the tremendous volume of Michigan land sales. During his extensive travels throughout Michigan, he observed factors that might affect the future value of land. Gordon recorded land prices, the availability of water, the quality of the soil, the timber supply, the transportation facilities, the climate, and the healthfulness of the region.

He also wrote about the settlers and others, especially the people of Detroit. He offers a lengthy description of the Michigan Indians at Grand Rapids as they were receiving payment for their lands. This extant portion of Gordon's diary runs from July 15 to October 30, 1836. The entries for the remainder of the trip are missing.

(1838) **OLIVER HAZARD PERRY** **495**

Burroughs, Raymond Darwin, ed. "Hunting Expeditions of Oliver H. Perry." *Michigan History* 40 (September 1956):291–96.

An account of a hunting trip north of Port Huron in the Black River Valley in December, 1838. (See also item 496.)

(1838–1855)   496

————. "Perry's Deer Hunting in Michigan, 1838–1855." *Michigan History* 42 (March 1958):35–58.

During these years Oliver Hazard Perry made twenty-four hunting trips into northern Ohio and Michigan. His diary tells a great deal about the wildlife he saw and, the editor says, Perry corrects modern impressions that Michigan's wilderness was a hunters' paradise during that period. (See also item 495.)

(1840–1842)   JOHN C. PEMBERTON   497

May, George S. "The Adventures of John C. Pemberton on Mackinac Island." *Michigan History* 49 (June 1965):108–22.

When this young second lieutenant first arrived at his northern Michigan station in May, 1840, he was unhappy at being posted so far from civilization. Instead of finding himself in the company of young ladies, he was among "Indians and half breeds." (p. 110) Life was uneventful during his two years on the island. Nevertheless, Pemberton occasionally found young ladies to participate in his adventures. May traces several such episodes through Pemberton's letters.

(1846)   WILLIAM IVES   498

Gilchrist, Marie E., ed. "William Ives' Huron Mountain Survey, 1846." *Michigan History* 50 (December 1966):323–40.

The purpose of the survey was to divide the townships of the heavily wooded mountain area into sections for sale to mineral prospectors. Ives's journal (May 12-November 16, 1846) briefly records each day's activities but does not mention any copper or iron in the mountains.

(1846)   WILLIAM CULLEN BRYANT   499

Ringe, Donald A. "William Cullen Bryant's Account of Michigan in 1846." *Michigan History* 40 (September 1956):317–27.

En route to visit his mother in Illinois, Bryant wrote letters describing his one-week stop-over in northern Michigan. He treated Sault Sainte Marie and Mackinac Island in detail. First published in the *New York Evening Post* and then in *Letters of a Traveller* (New York, 1850).

(1854)   ALANSON FORMAN LYON   500

Beeson, Lewis, ed. "A Trip Up the Menominee River in 1854." *Michigan History* 47 (December 1963):301–11.

Because sawmill owner Alanson Forman Lyon was investigating lumbering possibilities, he kept track of the kinds of trees, the rapids, and the width and depth of the river at various locations. His diary covers September 4 to 28, 1854.

(1856)   JOHN WESLEY   501

————. "From England to the United States in 1856: The Diary of John Wesley." *Michigan History* 48 (March 1964):47–65.

John Wesley and his family immigrated to the United States in August and September, 1856. He describes the rough, six-weeks-long ocean passage and train trip to Adrian, Michigan, with a brief stay in Toledo, Ohio. Appended to the diary is a list of the Methodist churches in Michigan in which Wesley served.

(1861–1862)   GEORGE MERRYWEATHER   502

Merryweather, George. "George Merryweather's United States 1861–1862." *Chicago History* 7 (Summer 1965):245–53.

Excerpts from the letters of a 14-year-old boy who originally came to Michigan to live with an uncle. Merryweather's travels eventually took him to Canada, to New York, and back to Michigan in an unsuccessful search for work before he enlisted in the United States Army in 1862. He liked Americans and sought to refute criticism of such English travelers as Frances (Milton) Trollope and Charles Dickens. His letters contain descriptions of Michigan farm life, Niagara Falls, and American eating habits.

(1865)   BERNHARD SIEVERS   503

Hattstaedt, Otto, tr. "A Missionary Journal to Michigan." *Concordia Historical Institute Quarterly* 39 (January 1967):159–68.

The Reverend Bernhard Sievers reminisces about a journey in July, 1856. As an 11-year-old boy, he went with his father to bring the gospel to scattered Lutherans of the Big Rapids and Traverse City region. The trip was exhausting and much of it was made on foot through wilderness in which they were occasionally lost.

(1870)   G. M. STEELE   504

McCann, William, ed. "A Trip to the Mining Country of Lake Superior." *Michigan History* 40 (June 1956):225–35.

G. M. Steele inspected the central mine of Keweenaw Peninsula in 1870. First appeared as "Down in a Cooper Mine" in *The Ladies Repository* (August 1871).

(1879)   ANSELL JUDD NORTHRUP   505

Petersen, Eugene T., ed. "Vacationing in Northern Michigan, 1879." *Michigan History* 42 (June 1958):154–74.

Ansell Judd Northrup spent a week in northern Michigan in the summer of 1879 and provides a description of sport fishing for the grayling, which, the editor says, had disappeared from Michigan waters by 1900.

(1898)   ABRAHAM KUYPER   506

Jellema, Dirk. "Kuyper's Visit to America in 1898." *Michigan History* 42 (June 1958):227–36.

Abraham Kuyper was both a political figure and a theologian from Holland who observed with interest life in the United States, especially the Dutch settlements in western Michigan. Jellema summarizes Kuyper's impressions of the United States from *Varia Americania* (Amsterdam, 1899). Kuyper thought the American working class was much better off than the Dutch workers and that there was less class consciousness here than in Europe. He thought the condition of blacks was a blight on society. He observed the vitality of Americans and the degree of material progress, and he believed family ties to be strong because of the Calvinist influence. Kuyper observed that women and men were nearly equal and that congregations in America mingled more than they did in Europe.

After tracing the reason for Dutch immigration to Michigan (religious freedom), Kuyper assessed the strength of the Calvinist Church in that state. He thought the use of the Dutch language in Michigan was decreasing and thought it fruitless to try to stop the trend. Kuyper believed the Dutch heritage should be retained by teaching Dutch history and literature at all levels of education, but the teaching should be in English.

(1913)   **JENNIE WATERMAN ARNOLD**   **507**

Beeson, Lewis, ed. "East Jordan to York in 1913." *Michigan History* 47 (March 1963):29–40.

The family of Jennie Waterman Arnold traveled 2,018 miles by automobile from East Jordan, Michigan, to LeRoy, New York, and back home again in August, 1913. The twenty-one day trip was unusual for a period when broken springs and punctured tires were frequent casualties of uneven roads. As Jennie Arnold soon learned, one quickly became an expert at putting up and taking down the collapsible car top at the first sign of threatening weather.

(1943)   **CYRIL CANE**   **508**

Hachey, Thomas E., ed. "The Wages of War: A British Commentary on Life in Detroit in July, 1943." *Michigan History* 59 (Winter 1975):227–38.

A part of Cyril H. Cane's assignment as the British consul-general in Detroit during World War II was to monitor and analyze the impact of the war on America for the Foreign Office. Cane focuses on rising prices and wages, as well as the ways in which money was spent; the changes in family life resulting from the greater numbers of working women, along with higher rates of divorce and juvenile delinquency; the crowding in public and in housing; the changes in styles of dress, with women wearing slacks and men wearing "zoot suits"; the boomtown atmosphere of Detroit; and the possible impact returning soldiers would have on the city. In his introduction to Cane's report, the editor points out that while Cane is a perceptive viewer of the Detroit scene from 1941 to 1943, he also reveals something of his own personality in his unconscious elitism and condescension toward minorities and working-class people.

MINNESOTA

(1823)   **WILLIAM HYPOLITUS KEATING**   **509**

Miles, Wyndham D. "A Versatile Explorer: A Sketch of William H. Keating." *Minnesota History* 36 (December 1959):294–99.

Keating was a mineralogist and geologist who served as historian for the Stephen H. Long expedition into the valley of the Red and Minnesota rivers during the summer of 1823. Miles says that from Keating's *Narrative of an Expedition to the Source of the St. Peter River, Lake Winnipeek, Lake of the Woods . . . in the Year 1823 . . .* (Philadelphia, 1824), the American public gained its early impressions of Minnesota.

(1839)   **HENRY H. SIBLEY**   **510**

Flanagan, John T. "Big Game Hunter, Henry H. Sibley." *Minnesota History* 41 (Spring 1969):217–28.

In 1839, Sibley took the first of several hunting expeditions into southern and central Minnesota, which he described in William T. Porter's weekly, *Spirit of the Times* (New York). Sibley's accounts tell of hunting techniques of the Indians and the diminishing wildlife population.

(1846)   **"RAMBLER"**   **511**

Flanagan, John R., ed. "From La Pointe to the Falls of St. Anthony in 1846." *Minnesota History* 41 (Fall 1968):137–44.

Three pseudonymous letters by "Rambler" describe a hunting safari from Sault Sainte Marie to the Missouri River.

(1847–1848) **HENRY LEWIS** **512**

Heilbron, Bertha L., ed. "Where to Settle? A Brother's Advice." *Minnesota History* 39 (Fall 1965):286–89.

In giving his advice, artist Henry Lewis, who had spent parts of 1847 and 1848 in southeastern Minnesota, describes the area in a letter and suggests that his brother was too old to farm. He recommends that his brother should buy land and rent it to settlers.

(1852) **JOHN P. OWENS** **513**

Owens, John P. "A Winter's Journey to Minnesota in 1852." *Minnesota History* 40 (Winter 1967):387–90.

Reminiscences of a 233-mile trip from Prairie du Chien, Wisconsin, to Saint Paul, Minnesota. The road was only partially completed and homes along the way provided food and lodging.

(1856–1858) **JOSEF KAPLAN** **514**

Jerabek, Esther, ed. and tr. "Letters to Bohemia: A Czech Settler Writes From Owatonna, 1856–1858." *Minnesota History* 43 (Winter 1972):136–41.

The letters of a recent immigrant, Josef Kaplan, provide a picture of life in territorial Minnesota before the railroad was available for travel and before the Civil War. After describing his ocean voyage from Hamburg and his first stop at Freeport, Illinois, Kaplan tells of his wagon trip with other Czech families to Minnesota. His letters relate the details of obtaining land, the work involved in establishing a farm and building houses, and his hopes for a railroad to come to Owatonna. Kaplan writes that the work was so hard that he believed anyone who immigrated to America sacrificed his life for the betterment of his descendants.

(1857) **JAMES SHIELDS** **515**

Shields, James. "Thrilling Adventures Among the Sioux and Chippewas." *Bulletin of the Missouri Historical Society* 13 (April 1957):275–82.

During the summer of 1857 when the Sioux were waging war against the Chippewas, the author traveled into the Big Woods region about forty miles south of Saint Paul. Shields presents enough bloody details of scalping and torture and titillating hints of savage, half-dressed Sioux women to excite the readers of the *Ware's Valley Monthly* (vol. 2; May, 1876), from which this account is reprinted.

(1857) **"VIATOR"** **516**

Giddens, Paul H., ed. "Impressions of Minnesota Territory by a Pennsylvania Visitor of 1857." *Minnesota History* 46 (Summer 1979):211–27.

Reprints letters to the *Venango Spectator* (Franklin, Pennsylvania) that appeared July through September, 1857, and were written pseudonymously by "Viator." Among the places he visited in Minnesota and Wisconsin were Prairie du Chien, La Crosse, Winona, Red Wing, Hastings, Fairbualt, Saint Paul, Fort Snelling, and the Falls of Saint Anthony. He describes the preemption of Indian land and a visit to the Winnebago Reservation just after the Indians had received a payment from the government. As he observed the Indians gambling into the night, it confirmed his low opinion of their character. He also described their physical appearance in uncomplimentary terms.

On a steamboat trip down the Saint Peter's (or Minnesota) River from Mankato to Saint Paul, he traveled in the company of gamblers and French voyageurs who created noise and chaos throughout the night. In his final letter, Viator summarized the soil, the climate, the inhabitants, and the area's prospects, along with his thoughts about Minnesota's future. Although he believed the region to be favorable for settlement, he left it to the readers to make their own decisions.

MISSOURI

(1766–1859)   **SAINT LOUIS**   **517**

Lass, William E. "Tourists' Impressions of St. Louis, 1766–1859." (Part I) *Missouri Historical Review* 52 (July 1958):325–38.

————. (Part II) *Missouri Historical Review* 53 (October 1958):10–21.

Lass treats individual visitors to Saint Louis chronologically and includes brief summaries of their comments. Most were impressed with the city's commercial growth and the consensus was that the city's progress was due to Anglo-Saxon influences. Lass adds that few had any precise ideas about Saint Louis history.

(1819)   **FELIX RENICK**   **518**

Henlein, Paul C., ed. "Journal of F. and W. Renick on an Exploring Tour to the Mississippi and Missouri Rivers in the Year 1819." *Agricultural History* 30 (October 1956):174–86.

Cattlemen Felix and William Renick rode horseback from Chillicothe, Ohio, to central Missouri to investigate "Missouri fever." The editor believes the document is of geographical importance because it describes the north and central parts of Missouri in great detail.

(1831)   **ANONYMOUS**   **519**

Anonymous. "Views of Missouri by an Anglo-American." *Bulletin of the Missouri Historical Society* 28 (October 1971):47–51.

An unidentified Englishman evidently wrote this article for an English newspaper, and it was simply pirated for publication in the *Missouri Republic* on November 1, 1831. Written from Boonville, Missouri, the letter reported that the agriculture of Missouri was abundant, that a sense of equality existed among the social classes (perhaps in too great a degree for the writer's comfort), and that public sentiment prevailed in law. He thought the inhabitants of the frontier to be shrewd in their business dealings and hospitable to travelers.

(1839)   **ANONYMOUS**   **520**

Nelson, Frank G., ed. "A Danish Account of Missouri in 1839." *Bulletin of the Missouri Historical Society* 33 (July 1977):265–68.

Translation of a letter published in a Norwegian newspaper that describes an immigrant's travels from Florida to New Orleans and finally to Missouri (perhaps Saint Genevieve County), where he took up farming.

(1846–1848)   **ELIZABETH COOLEY MCCLURE**   **521**

Jervey, Edward D., and Moss, James E., eds. "From Virginia to Missouri in 1846: The Journal of Elizabeth Ann Cooley." *Missouri Historical Review* 60 (January 1966):162–206.

Immediately following her marriage, Elizabeth Cooley McClure traveled from Virginia to Texas, where she and her husband stayed only a short time before moving to Jackson County, Missouri. Her diary (March 15, 1846-March 18, 1848) describes many incidents of her travels, as well as revealing a young woman's anguish at being away from her childhood home.

During most of 1846, while they were in transit, she hated everything and longed to be back home. Once they settled in Missouri and she and her husband became teachers, Elizabeth seemed happier. Throughout her diary she complains of various illnesses, and on March 28, 1848, Elizabeth died of typhoid fever.

(1847)   GERT GÖBEL   522

Heinrichsmeyer, M., tr. "Dangerous Highways." *Bulletin of the Missouri Historical Society* 13 (October 1956):66–70.

    Gert Göbel's *Länger als ein menschenleben in Missouri* (Saint Louis, 1877) describes his life in Missouri to 1877 beginning with his arrival from Germany in 1834. In this chapter he relates a horseback trip of fifty-four miles from Washington, Missouri, to Saint Louis in February, 1847, over roads that were nearly impassable because of the mud. After the ground froze, the trip home was easier.

(1848)   PETER NELSON   523

Nelson, Frank G., ed. "Following the Pathfinder: A Norwegian's Account of Western Missouri in 1848." *Bulletin of the Missouri Historical Society* 32 (January 1976):110–16.

    A letter from Peter Nelson (Peder Nielsen Kalvehaven), who came to Buchanan County, Missouri, in 1846. He describes his journey with a group of other immigrants, their search for land, and their fortunes and misfortunes as farmers. Nelson encourages others from Norway to come to America, but warns that they must be willing to work hard.

(1848)   CARL EDWARD NORSTRÖM   524

Celsing, Mrs. Fredrik, ed. "A Swedish View of St. Louis: 1848." *Bulletin of the Missouri Historical Society* 27 (January 1971):147–50.

    Carl Edward Norström, who was in the United States to study railway construction, describes his trip from Chicago to Saint Louis by way of LaSalle and Peoria. He complains about several customs he found. In Saint Louis he did not like the way Americans put their feet up on railings or anything else handy. On the boat trip, he was not enamored of freedom and independence when it meant having to share his cabin with uninvited guests.

(1849)   MARGARET MARSTON LAWRENCE   525

Norton, Henry L., ed. "The Travels of the Marstons." *Journal of the Illinois State Historical Society* 58 (Autumn 1965):279–300.

    In 1849 this middle-class English family, accompanied by its servants, came to Boonville, Missouri, having been convinced it would be a highly desirable place to live. The slavery in Missouri and the crudeness of the town was not to their liking, however. They soon moved on to a permanent residence in the older, more settled city of Quincy, Illinois. From the recollections of the daughter, Margaret Marston Lawrence.

(1849)   JAMES A. PRITCHARD   526

Williamson, Hugh P., ed. "An Overland Journey in 1849." *Register of the Kentucky Historical Society* 66 (April 1968):147–58.

    A section of *The Overland Diary of James A. Pritchard from Kentucky to California in 1849* (Denver, 1959) that describes the formation of the Kentucky gold seekers' company and its trip from Saint Louis to Independence, Missouri, between April 10 and May 2, 1849. Includes biographical information about Pritchard.

(1849)   **CHARLES ROBINSON**   **527**

Barry, Louise, ed. "Charles Robinson—Yankee '49er: His Journey to California."
Kansas Historical Quarterly 34 (Summer 1968):179–88.

Excerpts from several editions of Dr. Charles Robinson's narrative about his overland
journey from Massachusetts to California. This portion of his writing is concerned with the
period he spent in Missouri in April and May, 1849. Robinson came to Kansas City with a party
of gold seekers known as the Congress and California Mutual Protection Association, but dissension split the group near the Missouri border. Before his small group proceeded westward,
Robinson visited Independence, Westport, and the Indian city of Wyandott. Robinson offers his
impressions of the Wyandot Indians in Missouri and the Potawatomi Indians as his train passed
through northeastern Kansas. He also mentions problems with abolitionists near the Missouri-
Kansas border.

(1849)   **JAMES A. TATE**   **528**

Williamson, Hugh P., ed. "One Who Went West." *Missouri Historical Review* 57
(July 1963):369–78.

A portion of the diary of James A. Tate, who journeyed from Callaway County, Missouri,
to the California goldfields with a party of sixty during the summer of 1849. Most of the
description is of travel in Missouri, although the editor follows Tate's travels with brief quotations from his diary.

(1854)   **ADELBERT BAUDISSIN**   **529**

Gregory, Ralph, ed. "Count Baudissin on Missouri Towns." *Bulletin of the Missouri
Historical Society* 27 (January 1971):111–24.

In 1852, Count Adelbert Baudissin immigrated from Germany to Callaway County, Missouri. Two years later he published a book in German with the purpose of providing practical
advice on all phases of life in Missouri for prospective immigrants. The editor says *The Settlers
in Missouri (Der Ansiedler im Missouri-Staate* [Iserdohn, Germany, 1854]) ranks among the best
of the many books for German immigrants published in the mid-nineteenth century. Reproduced
here is the chapter on Portland, Missouri

(1861)   **ALBERT TRACY**   **530**

Irwin, Ray W., ed. "Missouri in Crisis: The Journal of Captain Albert Tracy, 1861."
(Part I) *Missouri Historical Review* 51 (October 1956):8–21.
———. (Part II) *Missouri Historical Review* 51 (January 1957):151–64.
———. (Part III) *Missouri Historical Review* 51 (April 1957):271–83.

These letters, dated February 4 to November 26, 1861, describe the tensions that existed
in Missouri between pro–Union and pro–Confederate forces before the fall of Fort Sumter and
during the first year of the Civil War. Tracy was stationed at the Saint Louis arsenal when
federals took over the Confederate encampment at Camp Jackson in May, 1861. Later that year
he served with General John C. Frémont as he pursued the Confederate forces under Sterling
Price in southwest Missouri.

(1864)   **ANTOINE AUGUSTE LAUGEL**   **531**

Joyaux, Georges J., ed. and tr. "Auguste Laugel Visits St. Louis, 1864." *Bulletin of the
Missouri Historical Society* 14 (October 1957):33–45.

French writer Antoine Auguste Laugel visited the United States during 1864 and 1865.
He wrote *Les États-Unis pendant la guerre Civil 1861–1865* (Paris, 1866), from which this
article is taken. Laugel found it painful that the French population was without influence in
public affairs in Saint Louis. He described this population as favoring slavery and being colo-

nial-minded. He saw the Catholic clergy as being interested only in keeping Catholic children away from public schools. He contrasted the French with the Germans, who were against slavery. The Germans were energetic and exhibited a deep devotion to their new country. He described the Civil War in Missouri, the guerrilla activities, the hospitals, and Camp Benton, as well as discussing sentiment surrounding the 1864 presidential campaign. (See also item 343.)

(1874) **BEATRICE RENGGLI** **532**

Renggli, Beatrice. "From Rickenbach to Maryville: An Account of the Journey [1874]." *American Benedictine Review* 27 (September 1976):247–69.

Mother Renggli and four other Benedictine sisters traveled from Maria Rickenbach Convent in Switzerland to Maryville, Missouri, in 1874. She relates the ocean voyage and her experiences in New York City, which reminded her of Paris because of the hustle and bustle. Mother Renggli offers a long description of Saint Louis and Maryville, where she intended to open a school. Translated by Sister M. Agnes Voth.

(1874–1889) **SAINT LOUIS** **533**

Holt, Glen E. "St. Louis Observed 'from Two Different Worlds': An Exploration of the City through French and English Travelers' Accounts, 1874–1889." *Bulletin of the Missouri Historical Society* 29 (January 1973):63–87.

By the time the eleven French and eight British visitors in this study had reached Saint Louis, they had already seen the other major American cities. Holt says that this travel left them experienced in urban American patterns, but somewhat jaded.

The French described a narrower range of topics, as they appear to have traveled a prescribed route. Commercial and economic aspects of the city that attracted their attention were the Mississippi River trade, the recently completed Eads Bridge that spanned the river, the city's water works, and the outlying mineral industries. They looked for French beginnings of the town and paid particular attention to conditions of the Catholics. For some, the city contained the worst aspects of American living and the meaner attributes of American life. In general, the French found the city pleasant but not outstanding.

Perhaps because they were facile with the language and attuned to an industrialized society, the British offered more detailed descriptions of the same things the French saw. The British poked around in factories and businesses and commented on slums and benevolent societies that the French did not mention. Holt believes the French accounts are useful, however. Not only did they compare American society to high culture, where the British were inclined to take society the way they found it, but the French described cultural and religious topics more fully.

(1916) **LILBURN A. KINGSBURY** **534**

Kingsbury, Lilburn A. "Loath to Leave: An Account of a Visit to St. Louis." *Bulletin of the Missouri Historical Society* 25 (April 1969):207–12.

Relates two days of fun in Saint Louis in 1916. Kingsbury offers a tongue-in-cheek description of the Russian ballet's performance of "Scheherazade." Then he returned to the Jefferson Hotel, where he found the antics of late-night diners and dancers amusing. The next day he saw "Birth of a Nation," took three showers, saw another play, ate, and returned home by train, tired, but "loath to leave." (p. 212)

OHIO

(1764) **HENRY BOUQUET** **535**

Williams, Edward G., ed. "The Orderly Book of Henry Bouquet's Expedition Against the Ohio Indians, 1764." (Part I) *Western Pennsylvania Historical Magazine* 42 (March 1959):9–33.

————. (Part II) *Western Pennsylvania Historical Magazine* 42 (June 1959):179–200.
————. (Part III) *Western Pennsylvania Historical Magazine* 42 (September 1959):283–302.

This second orderly book is an account of the march from Fort Pitt (Pennsylvania) to the Muskingum River in Ohio against the Indians who disputed British dominance and resented the spread of settlers following the French and Indian Wars. This phase of the march took place October 2 to November 9, 1764. (See also item 146.)

(1775)   **RICHARD BUTLER**   **536**

————. "The Journal of Richard Butler, 1775: Continental Congress Envoy to the Western Indians." (Part I) *Western Pennsylvania Historical Magazine* 46 (October 1963):381–95.
————. (Part II) *Western Pennsylvania Historical Magazine* 47 (January 1964):31–46.
————. (Part III) *Western Pennsylvania Historical Magazine* 47 (April 1964):141–56.

Indian trader Richard Butler was the agent responsible for informing the Indians of the Middle Department for Indian Affairs, located in Pittsburgh, that war existed between the colonies and the mother country. His task was to convince the Indians that they should remain neutral. Between August 22 and September 20, 1775, Butler visited every important Indian town and prominent chief in the Ohio Valley. The editor provides a lengthy introduction and extensive notes explaining the political forces at work to undermine the success of Butler's mission.

(1778)   **LACHLAN MCINTOSH**   **537**

————. "A Revolutionary Journal and Orderly Book of General Lachlan McIntosh's Expedition, 1778." (Part I) *Western Pennsylvania Historical Magazine* 43 (March 1960):1–17.
————. (Part II) *Western Pennsylvania Historical Magazine* 43 (June 1960):157–77.
————. (Part III) *Western Pennsylvania Historical Magazine* 43 (September 1960):267–88.

General McIntosh commanded this expedition from Fort Pitt (Pennsylvania) to the Ohio region to fight the Indians who supported the British. They marched along the road opened by Colonel Bouquet in 1764. (See items 146 and 536.) Reproduced here are two documents of that trip kept by a regimental adjutant. The journal is dated November 8 to 20 and the orderly book October 17 to December 8, 1778.

(1788)   **ISRAEL ANGELL**   **538**

Smith, Dwight L., ed. "Israel Angell and the West in 1788." (Part I) *Rhode Island History* 22 (January 1963):1–15.
————. (Part II) *Rhode Island History* 22 (April 1963):39–50.

Angell's trip west and back east again took him from Johnston, Rhode Island, to Marietta, Ohio, to visit friends and investigate his business investments. The slowness of travel by horseback and his own inquisitiveness allowed him to record many details. For example, he paused at a cemetery where a body was being exhumed to determine cause of death. He took time to measure trees, to examine wildlife, to note streams flooded out by beavers, and crops along the way. He describes a catfish, apparently the first he had seen. The 1,548-mile journey took sixty-seven days (August 4-October 9, 1788).

(1790)   **"D'ALLEMANGE"**   **539**

Yeager, Henry J., ed. "Nouvelles du Scioto: The Story of a Fraud." *Ohio History* 78 (Autumn 1969):261–72.

Settlement in America seemed especially attractive to "D'Allemange" and many other Frenchmen who suffered from Rousseauian illusions about the New World and sought refuge from their country's revolutionary turmoil. Such eager French immigrants bought land from the Scioto Land Company of Paris, which had purchased large sections in southern Ohio for speculation. Once D'Allemange and the other potential settlers arrived in 1790, they found that the company had misled them about the present capabilities of the land: it still needed clearing and was extremely vulnerable to Indian attacks. The company also failed to provide the promised assistance when the Frenchmen arrived in Alexandria, Virginia. All Monsieur D'Allemange could do was return to France and pseudonymously tell of his experiences in what is now an extremely rare booklet.

(1810) MARGARET VAN HORN DWIGHT 540

Anderson, David D. "The Beginnings of Ohio Literature: 'A Journey to Ohio in 1810'." *Great Lakes Review* 3 (Winter 1977):35–40.

Has excerpts from a journal written by Margaret Van Horn Dwight to describe the young Connecticut woman's reaction to Ohio, where she hoped to find a husband. Miss Dwight learned something about men from the Pennsylvania Dutchmen, the "waggoners," and those she saw at the inns. Anderson adds that her search for a husband was ultimately successful and she became the mother of thirteen children.

(1830–1832) THOMAS K. WHARTON 541

Rodabaugh, James H., ed. "From England to Ohio, 1830–1832: The Journal of Thomas K. Wharton." (Part I) *Ohio Historical Quarterly* 65 (January 1956):1–27.
———. (Part II) *Ohio Historical Quarterly* 65 (April 1956):111–51.

Sixteen-year-old Thomas traveled from Hull, England, to New York City, up the Hudson River to Albany on a packet towed by a steamer, along the Erie Canal to Buffalo by canal boat, across Lake Erie to Sandusky, Ohio, by steamboat, and then on to his father's farm in Piqua. Wharton comments on the cities and towns he passed through—New York City, Albany, Schenectady, Utica, Syracuse, and Buffalo—and the vegetation of New York State. He describes life on the farm and subsequent moves by the family in Ohio to Dayton, Springfield, Columbus, and Zanesville. Shortly after the family's last move, Thomas went to New York to study architecture. Includes Wharton's drawings of New York City and Ohio.

(1835) JAMES MCELROY 542

Eustis, Alvin, ed. "On the Road in 1835: A Journey of the Reverend James McElroy." *Ohio History* 81 (Summer 1972):221–27.

Letters from July 7 to September 17, 1835, that tell of McElroy's journey from Delaware, Ohio, to Lexington, Kentucky, as an agent for the American Bible Society. He describes the countryside in western Ohio and northern Kentucky and comments on a Fourth of July celebration in Troy, Ohio. He mentions a cholera outbreak near Cincinnati and a conversation with a Kentucky mountaineer.

(1835) HARRIET MARTINEAU 543

Seat, William R., Jr. "A Rebuttal to Mrs. Trollope: Harriet Martineau in Cincinnati." *Ohio Historical Quarterly* 68 (July 1959):276–89.

Harriet Martineau visited Cincinnati for ten days in June, 1835. Although there is no direct reference to the negative remarks about the city made by Frances Trollope in *Domestic Manners of the Americans* (London, 1832), Seat believes the praise for Cincinnati found in Martineau's *Retrospect of Western Travel* (London, 1838) serves to refute Trollope's criticism. (See also item 46.)

(1837)   **CLARK GUERNSEY**   544

Dillon, Merton L., ed. "A Visit to the Ohio State Prison in 1837." *Ohio Historical Quarterly* 69 (January 1960):69–72.

As Clark Guernsey was touring the Ohio River Valley he became curious about Ohio's state prison because Ohio was one of a number of states that had adopted New York's innovative prison plan. Prisoners were kept in small cells at night, brought together in workshops during the day, and kept in silence at all times. Although he felt mankind's disgrace at needing such institutions, Guernsey believed the prison was well run.

(1837)   **JOHN ELLIS MARSHALL**   545

Synder, Charles M. "Dr. Marshall's Ohio Journey: Travel, 1837 Style." *Old Northwest* 5 (Fall 1979):221–35.

John Ellis Marshall's trip to Ohio took him from Buffalo, New York, to Cleveland, as far south and west as Columbus, then east to Wheeling, West Virginia, and north to Lake Erie along the Ohio-Pennsylvania border. The purpose of the trip (June 19-July 12, 1837) was to visit family and his in-laws' graves, and to conduct some business. Since the majority of his comments are about conditions of travel, his journal serves to remind us that travel in Ohio was a tiring undertaking in 1837. The editor has traced on a map the five conveyances Marshall employed: lake steamer, canal boat, wagon, stage, and riverboat. Marshall includes brief descriptions of Columbus, Zanesville, and Wheeling, as well as an account of travel expenses, which totaled $57.15.

(1850s)   **CINCINNATI**   546

Steen, Ivan D. "Cincinnati in the 1850's As Described By British Travelers." *Cincinnati Historical Society Bulletin* 26 (July 1968):255–75.

British travelers praised the comforts of Cincinnati's large hotels, but universally detested the spitting of tobacco, which usually ended up outside the spittoons. The streets were poorly lit and attitudes about the cleanliness of the streets varied. Some who said they were clean attributed the condition to the hilly streets. Others believed the cleanliness was because the hogs that ran wild in the streets ate the debris. The pork industry was one of the city's major attractions.

The houses were believed to be handsome, but opinions differed about the variety of goods available in the retail shops. Cincinnati's entertainment facilities were thought to be meager, but the libraries and schools were judged good. The number of Germans and German institutions were always noted. In many ways, Steen concludes, Cincinnati bore many of the qualities of a large, cosmopolitan eastern city, rather than a raw, growing city of the West.

(1853–1854)   **CHARLES B. MOORE**   547

Bowman, Larry G., and Scroggs, Jack B., eds. "A Tennessean Visits Cincinnati in 1853–1854." *Cincinnati Historical Society Bulletin* 36 (Fall 1978):151–73.

Charles B. Moore apparently spent a great deal of time exploring the city while he was in Cincinnati to supervise the manufacture of a mill during December, 1853, and January, 1854. He attended lectures at the Eclectic Medical College, went to a Quaker church, saw a performance of "Uncle Tom's Cabin," and went to a concert of Negro "varieties." He frequently refers to the Bedini riots that occurred while he was in the city.

(1857)   **ALEXANDER LAKIER**   548

Schrier, Arnold, ed. "A Russian Observer's Visit to 'Porkopolis', 1857." *Cincinnati Historical Society Bulletin* 29 (Spring 1971):28–51.

Because he believed that no serious book about the New World existed in his country, Russian lawyer Alexander Lakier sought to gather information in his travels and disseminate it through various writings. In the summer of 1857 he came to Cincinnati. Writing in a manner that would not be lost on his own people, he stressed many attributes of a progressive, technological society. He explored such themes as why Americans wanted to move west when there appeared to be plenty of land behind them. He related his visit to a slaughterhouse, a firehouse with its new engine, and schools, and he told of the planning for the bridge over the river. He also discusses the presence of the Germans in Cincinnati.

(1857)   ALEXANDER ZIMMERMAN   549

Starr, S. Frederick, ed. and tr. "The Ohio Valley Through Russian Eyes, 1857." *Cincinnati Historical Society Bulletin* 24 (July 1966):211–20.

While touring Cincinnati, Russian industrialist Alexander Zimmerman found much to praise in American progress, the intellectual interests of the people, and the resourcefulness of their character. The editor indicates, however, that Zimmerman had a purpose for stressing those qualities. He was among those who were trying to convince the Russian people that their humiliating loss in the Crimean War was the result of serfdom and an ignorance of the benefits that modern technology can bring to a nation. These articles originally appeared in a liberal Moscow journal, *Russkii Vestnik (The Russian Messenger)* in 1859.

(1857–1858)   GEORGE HOVEY CADMAN   550

Quenzel, Carrol H., ed. "Life Was Rugged a Century Ago: Experiences of an English Immigrant." *Ohio Historical Quarterly* 65 (July 1956):297–301.

George Hovey Cadman tells of trans-Atlantic travel in 1857 aboard a packet ship ("floating hells") and of work on a farm in Hamilton County, Ohio. (p. 291) He thought America was a great, free country and assured his wife in England that women in America were treated better than women back home because few worked in the fields with their husbands. Letters written in 1857 and 1858. (See also item 425.)

(1859–1860)   MARY SEARS   551

Jones, Daryl E., and Pickering, James H., eds. "A Young Woman in the Midwest: The Journal of Mary Sears, 1859–1860." *Ohio History* 82 (Summer/Autumn 1973):215–34.

Mary's diary, dated January 1, 1859 to August 26, 1860, reveals the tribulations of a young Massachusetts woman seeking happiness in Ohio and Illinois. As a first-time schoolteacher near Rochester, Ohio, she was constantly upset by the students, and she lamented the absence of regular religious services. After a brief period in Columbus, which was pleasant, she went to Amboy, Illinois, to be with her sister. Her sister soon died and shortly thereafter her brother-in-law also succumbed, leaving Mary as guardian of their baby.

In her last entries Mary had moved on to Pana, Illinois, a town she did not think was pretty. Its streets were muddy and filled with stagnant pools of water, and hogs ran free. The editors suggest that Mary Sears was a highly sensitive woman, ill-prepared to cope with the harsh realities of a still crude frontier. They add that two and one-half years later Mary died.

(1862–1865)   THOMAS J. TAYLOR   552

Wall, Lillian Taylor, and McBride, Robert M., eds. "'An Extraordinary Perseverance': The Journal of Capt. Thomas J. Taylor, C.S.A." *Tennessee Historical Quarterly* 31 (Winter 1972):328–59.

Thomas Taylor (Forty-ninth Alabama Infantry) was captured at Port Hudson, Louisiana in July, 1862, and spent the next three years imprisoned on Johnson's Island in Lake Erie.

During the trip north he described his reactions to the land and the conditions he observed. Throughout his long imprisonment Taylor remained philosophical about the circumstances that isolated him from his family and the cause to which he had dedicated his life. He writes that one may approach prison with a resolve to make the best of the situation by using it for reflection and personal improvement. But, he said, because of the crowd, one usually finds that goal impossible to accomplish. Although he admits that living conditions are not bad, especially when compared to those of Confederate prisons, he laments the loss of freedom and youthful spirit.

Taylor describes life behind bars—the food, the societies established by prisoners, the appearance of Lake Erie and Canada, the approaching seasons, the rumors of freedom, the precious letters, and his perception of the war. Taylor thought about the continuing bloodshed, those individuals who had vested interests in keeping the war going, how impressed he was at the South's ability to resist the North, and northern politics. The extant portion of the journal begins February, 1862, and ends January 1, 1865.

(1945)   ARTHUR TANDY   553

Hachey, Thomas E., ed. "Cincinnati Through English Spectacles: A British Diplomat's Confidential View in 1945." *Ohio History* 81 (Autumn 1972):279–91.

In an attempt to assess public opinion in the United States at the end of World War II, the British Foreign Office required its consuls in major cities to prepare memoranda that would blend experienced opinion with factual information. This report on Cincinnati was written by Arthur Tandy, who had held his post in the "Queen City of the West" for two years. Underlying the range of economic, historical, social, and intellectual topics that Tandy covers is an estimation of how Americans might be expected to act toward England in the postwar world.

WISCONSIN

(1838–1845)   EDWARD MATHEWS   554

Haygood, William C., ed. "An Abolitionist in Territorial Wisconsin: The Journal of Reverend Edward Mathews." (Part I) *Wisconsin Magazine of History* 52 (Autumn 1968):3–18.

———. (Part II) *Wisconsin Magazine of History* 52 (Winter 1968/1969):117–31.

———. (Part III) *Wisconsin Magazine of History* 52 (Spring 1969):248–62.

———. (Part IV) *Wisconsin Magazine of History* 52 (Summer 1969):330–43.

When Edward Mathews arrived in Wisconsin in 1838, twenty-seven of the ninety-one blacks in the territory were listed in the 1836 Census as being slaves. By 1840 the number was reduced to eleven. Nevertheless, Mathews, who first came to Wisconsin as a member of the American Baptist Home Mission, found these figures appalling. He rode throughout the territory organizing Baptist churches with rules requiring the members to be temperate and not hold slaves. Although he soon broke with the Baptist Society because it allowed members to be slaveholders, he continued to speak against slavery. His travels were filled with hazards, ranging from getting lost for three days in the dense woods near Sheboygan to facing violent mobs in Iowa and Grant counties. The editor says Mathews may have had something of a martyr complex because he spent so much time in those two southwestern countries, which were populated by southern slaveholders attracted there by the lead mining activity.

(1847)   GEORGE ADAM FROMADER   555

Detzler, Jack J. "'I Live Here Happily': A German Immigrant in Territorial Wisconsin." *Wisconsin Magazine of History* 50 (Spring 1967):254–59.

A letter written by George Adam Fromader in January, 1847, telling of his passage to America and stressing that living conditions in America were better than in Germany. He praises the farmland in Wisconsin, the food, the homes, the liberty, the law, the high state of art and science, and the passive character of Americans. He also provides advice on how to travel and what to bring.

(1848)   **ALFRED COPE**   **556**

Haygood, William C., ed. "A Mission to the Menominee: Alfred Cope's Green Bay Diary." (Part I) *Wisconsin Magazine of History* 49 (Summer 1966):302–23.
————. (Part II) *Wisconsin Magazine of History* 50 (Autumn 1966):18–42.
————. (Part III) *Wisconsin Magazine of History* 50 (Winter 1967):120–46.
————. (Part IV) *Wisconsin Magazine of History* 50 (Spring 1967):211–41.

The Menominee Indians were the last Indian tribe to retain portions of their ancestral lands in Wisconsin. In 1848 they were forced to relinquish their land and to accept $350,000 and 600,000 acres of land in Minnesota. Forty thousand dollars of that sum was designated for their brothers of mixed blood. Alfred Cope was a Quaker who came to Wisconsin at the request of President Zachary Taylor to ensure that the $40,000 was distributed equitably.

Cope records his trip across the Great Lakes and provides lengthy descriptions of Mackinac Island and Green Bay. He relates the initial problems of getting the Indian delegates to come to Fort Howard (Wisconsin) and of keeping the whiskey salesmen away from the traditionally intemperate Menominee. Cope describes the negotiations and the subsequent problems that arose; he provides descriptions of the chiefs and offers comments on Indian customs. During his stay Cope also visited the Stockbridge, Brotherton, and Oneida Indians, all of whom had been removed from New York State. The editor adds that because the Menominee later objected to being placed so near the warlike Sioux, they were never removed from Wisconsin.

(1850)   **FREDRIKA BREMER**   **557**

Brown, George C., ed. "A Swedish Traveler in Early Wisconsin: The Observations of Fredrika Bremer." (Part I) *Wisconsin Magazine of History* 61 (Summer 1978):300–18.
————. (Part II) *Wisconsin Magazine of History* 62 (Autumn 1978):41–56.

Extracts from novelist and feminist Fredrika Bremer's *The Homes in the New World* (London, 1853), which describe the Wisconsin portion of her travels made during October, 1850. In Milwaukee she noted the German immigrants who banded together. She wrote that their enjoyment of amusements "distinguish them from the Anglo-American people who, particularly in the West, have no other pleasure than 'business'." (p. 308) She was so impressed with the buildings, the people, and the farms around Milwaukee that she felt that it, not Chicago, deserved the title "Queen of the West." Bremer visited the Swedish settlement at Pine Lake, which she praised for its fine appearance. After a second visit to Watertown, where she stayed with some Danes, she was "shook onward to Madison," a reference to the poor roads and crowded and uncomfortable conveyances. (p. 41) She offers a lengthy passage about Madison, the Blue Mounds, and Galena, Illinois, from where she traveled the Mississippi to Saint Paul. (See also items 411 and 465.)

7

Plains

(including Missouri River)

GENERAL

(1714) ÉTIENNE VÉNIARD DE BOURGMONT 558

Giraud, Marcel, ed., and Myer, Mrs. Max, tr. "Étienne Véniard De Bourgmont's 'Exact Description of Louisiana'." *Bulletin of the Missouri Historical Society* 15 (October 1958):3–19.

Reproduces the document Bourgmont wrote of his trip to the lower Missouri River area in 1714. Giraud places great value on the ethnological and geographical data included in the report. "The text fixes the location of indigenous populations which were settled along the river and its principal tributaries, describes for the first time the regions it traverses, and lastly, it particularizes the extent of the French penetration." (p. 3)

(1809) DR. THOMAS 559

Jackson, Donald, ed. "Journey to the Mandans, 1809: The Lost Narrative of Dr. Thomas." *Bulletin of the Missouri Historical Society* 20 (April 1964):179–92.

Little is known about Dr. Thomas except that he accompanied the recently formed Saint Louis Missouri Fur Company on its first trip up the Missouri River. This narrative was published in November and December, 1809, in the *Missouri Gazette* (Saint Louis). The second installment then disappeared until it was found reprinted in an 1810 issue of the *Pittsburgh Gazette*. The editor says this account is of interest to historians because it was the first published account of the region above the Platte following the early Lewis and Clark reports. The Company also returned a Mandan chief whom Lewis and Clark had brought back east.

(1811) GEORGE CHAMPLIN SIBLEY 560

Brooks, George, ed. "George C. Sibley's Journal of a Trip to the Salines in 1811." *Bulletin of the Missouri Historical Society* 21 (April 1965):167–207.

George Champlin Sibley was chief factor at Fort Osage (Missouri) on the Missouri River when he undertook this trip that spanned portions of Nebraska, Kansas, and Oklahoma between May 11 and July 11, 1811. His purpose was to make peace between warring Indian tribes and to solidify good relations between the Indians and the United States in the event of war with England. All along the way he took notes about the vegetation, the wildlife, and the topography, and was the first white man to record a description of the salt deposits, the Great Salines, south of the Arkansas River in Oklahoma. His descriptions of the Kansa, Pawnee, and Osage Indians are considered accurate.

Sibley also provides information about Zebulon Pike's earlier expedition and his confrontation with the Pawnee in Nebraska, which was told to Sibley by the Indians. This account of Sibley's exploits is contained in a letter to his father dated August 11, 1811. *Note*: Another slightly different account, in a letter dated September 4, 1811, to General William Clark, superintendent for Indian Affairs for Missouri Territory, is Thomas D. Isern, ed., "Exploration and Diplomacy: George Champlin Sibley's Report to William Clark, 1811," *Missouri Historical Review*, 73 (October 1978):85–102.

(1820)   **EDWIN JAMES**   **561**

Tucker, John M. "Major Long's Route from the Arkansas to the Canadian River, 1820." *New Mexico Historical Review* 38 (July 1963):185–219.

Major Stephen H. Long was an engineer and explorer who led an expedition to locate the headwaters of the Arkansas, Platte, and Red rivers. Although the mission failed in its primary purpose, its report gave credence to the idea that the area east of the Rockies was a "Great American Desert" and not fit for cultivation. Using primarily the journal of Edwin James, the physician, geologist, and botanist for the expedition (*An Account of An Expedition from Pittsburgh to the Rocky Mountains Performed in the Years 1819, 1820*. Philadelphia, 1823), Tucker attempts to clarify portions of the route in Colorado and New Mexico. *Note*: Other articles that also utilize James's account are Roger L. Nichols, "Stephen Long and Scientific Exploration on the Plains," *Nebraska History* 52 (Spring 1971):51–64, and Richard H. Dillon, "Stephen Long's Great American Desert," *Proceedings of the American Philosophical Society* 111 (April 1967):93–108.

(1822)   **ANONYMOUS**   **562**

Myer, Mrs. Max W., ed. and tr. "To Fort Lisa by Keelboat." *Bulletin of the Missouri Historical Society* 16 (October 1959):14–19.

A fragment of an anonymous manuscript kept by one of a party of French fur traders up the Missouri River between May 17 and June 13, 1822. Although the complete trip was presumably from Saint Louis to Fort Lisa (Nebraska), this surviving portion of the journal covers travel only as far as Clay County, Missouri. The author is concerned with hazards of river travel, the contrary winds, and rising waters. He also tells about his cargo and contracts with other boatmen.

(1825)   **HENRY ATKINSON**   **563**

Nichols, Roger L., ed. "General Henry Atkinson's Report of the Yellowstone Expedition of 1825." *Nebraska History* 44 (June 1963):65–82.

In 1825, Atkinson and Indian agent Benjamin O'Fallon were appointed government commissioners to conclude treaties of peace and friendship with the tribes living along the Missouri as far as the Yellowstone River in North Dakota. Atkinson's report relates the success of the mission and provides descriptions of the Indian tribes and the country above Fort Atkinson, Nebraska. The editor says that General Atkinson was unaware of the historical importance of the trek and presents only a minimum of detail in somewhat dull prose.

(1827)   **JOHN CORCORAN**   **564**

Van Ravenswaay, Charles, ed. "The Diary of John Corcoran: Voyage from the Red River in Hudson's Bay Territory to St. Louis, Missouri in the Year 1827." *Bulletin of the Missouri Historical Society* 13 (April 1957):264–74.

Corcoran was with one group of disenchanted refugees who deserted Lord Selkirk's social community at the junction of the Red and the Assiniboine rivers near Winnipeg, Canada. They traveled to Pembina, North Dakota, across Minnesota, and down to Galena, Illinois, between

June 25 and September 12, 1827. The diary is mostly concerned with the difficult task of transporting 243 men, women, and children to Saint Louis. They had to cross open prairie, ford rivers, hunt for food, and trade for rations with the forts and Indian encampments they passed.

(1831–1832)   **ALBERT PIKE**   **565**

Haley, J. Evetts, ed. "Albert Pike's 'Journeys in the Prairie, 1831–1832'." *Panhandle-Plains Historical Review* 41 (1968):1–91.

   Consists of two sections of Pike's *Narrative of a Journey in the Prairie* (Boston, 1834). The first part, "Narrative of a Journey in the Prairie," relates Aaron B. Lewis's trip from Arkansas to New Mexico in 1831. The second part, "Narrative of a Second Journey in the Prairie," tells of Pike's trek from Taos, New Mexico, to Fort Smith (Arkansas) in 1832. Haley believes Pike's work is not only the first published work about the frontier between Fort Smith and Santa Fe, but is still one of the most descriptive, with fine literary and typographic qualities. Haley has written a lengthy introduction, "Albert Pike, Man and Author," as well as adding notes and compiling an index to the works.

(1833–1834)   **MAXIMILIAN ALEXANDER PHILLIP**   **566**
                                VON WIED-NEUWIED

Thomas, David, and Ronnefeldt, Karin, eds. "Winter at Fort Clark." *American West* 14 (January/February 1977):36–47.

   During 1833 and 1834, German Prince Maximilian and his artist friend Karl Bodmer traveled with the American Fur Company up the Missouri River to the company's most advanced outpost near the headwaters of the Missouri. During each stop they sketched and studied the natural settings and Indian life. The winter's stay at Fort Clark (North Dakota) resulted in a unique study of the Mandan Indians, an advanced tribe that had recently adopted a settled culture. The Mandans were decimated by smallpox three years later. Based on Maximilian's account, first published in English as *Travels in the Interior of North America in the Years 1832–1834* (London, 1843).

(1838)   **"JACQUES"**   **567**

"Jacques." "Notes of a Tourist Through the Upper Missouri Region." *Bulletin of the Missouri Historical Society* 22 (July 1966):393–409.

   Published serially in the *Missouri Saturday News* (Saint Louis) between August 25 and September 15, 1838, were the activities of a party whose identity and purposes for travel are unknown. "Jacques" reserved most of his comments for describing the character and the customs of the Indians. He believed they had ignored all attempts by the white man to teach them to farm. He reported they neglected their old people by allowing them to starve. Nevertheless, he observed that Indians were affectionate parents and could be gracious hosts. When Jacques contrasted the sexes, he had particular praise for the Sioux women, who he felt were beautiful and kind but mistreated by their society. The Indian males possessed a "braggadocio character" that was evidence of their "constitutional cowardice." (p. 406)

(1839–1844)   **ANONYMOUS**   **568**

Anonymous. "Reminiscences of Some Incidents in the Career of an United States Dragoon Between the Years 1839 and 1844." *Texas Quarterly* 9 (Autumn 1966):7–20.

   Although the author kept both his identity and his reasons for enlisting a mystery—some "previous troubles" are alluded to—he looked back on his adventures with pleasure. Since the dragoons were responsible for keeping peace on the plains, his service took him from Missouri to New Mexico along the Santa Fe Trail as a guard for a wagon train, across Oklahoma to record the exact location of Salt Rock, and into Texas to meet the Comanche Indians, who never appeared. Of the dangers and irritations of life in the open, wood ticks were among the most troublesome. Storms and flooding, buffalo stampedes, prairie dog holes, rattlesnakes, and finding grass for the animals presented additional problems.

(1843)   **JOHN JAMES AUDUBON**   **569**

Petersen, William J. "Audubon on the Missouri in 1843." *Palimpsest* 52 (November 1971):545–84.

This issue is devoted to ornithologist John James Audubon's 1843 trip up the Missouri River to record animal and bird life. It includes two extracts from Maria R. Audubon's *Audubon and His Journals* (New York, 1897). "Birds Along the Missouri" (pp. 550–70) records the trip up the river along the Iowa border by steamboat. "Barging Down from Fort Union" (pp. 571–82) relates the barge trip from the North Dakota post to Saint Louis.

(1846)   **ROBERT CLOUSTON**   **570**

Mitchell, Elaine Allan, ed. "International Buying Trip: Fort Garry to St. Louis in 1846." *Minnesota History* 36 (June 1958):37–53.

In the summer of 1846, when it became apparent that the annual shipment of goods from the Hudson's Bay Company would not be sufficient for the Red River Settlement (near Fort Garry and Winnipeg), Company clerk Robert Clouston was sent to Saint Louis to procure supplies. His three-month (July-October) return trip took his small party over the Red River trails to Saint Paul and by water to Prairie du Chien, Galena, Peoria, and Saint Louis. The difficulties of travel, especially getting the supply carts back to Canada, and his observations of trading posts and traders are contained in his unpublished journal, from which the editor extracts these passages.

(1846)   **JOHN D. LEE**   **571**

Brooks, Juanita, ed. "Diary of the Mormon Battalion Mission: John D. Lee." (Part I) *New Mexico Historical Review* 42 (July 1967):165–209.
———. (Part II) *New Mexico Historical Review* 42 (October 1967): 281–332.

Raising the Mormon Battalion was designed to benefit both the United States government and the Mormons. For the government it provided troops for the war against Mexico, as well as an opportunity to help move the beleaguered religious group from Missouri to the West at a time the Mormons were preparing to settle in Utah. For the Mormons it meant they could move a part of their people at the government's expense. The church could also recover a portion of the soldiers' pay for the common good of all Mormons.

The battalion of about five hundred marched from Council Bluffs, Iowa, to Fort Leavenworth (Kansas), then to Santa Fe, where it was placed under the command of Lieutenant Colonel Philip St. George Cooke. From Santa Fe it continued a grueling march across the desert to San Diego along routes that were later used by forty-niners and the railroads. The portion of the trip from Iowa to Santa Fe and back again is described in the diary of John D. Lee, who was a Mormon official asigned to follow the battalion and return with the soldiers' pay. Lee's diary (August 30-November 19, 1846) describes the march across Kansas, the Oklahoma Panhandle, and New Mexico. His entries focus on the terrain and the wild animals, problems of travel, Mormon Church internal affairs, and fear of Indian attacks. Lee offers a description of Santa Fe and comments on conditions in New Mexico shortly after the region was taken over by the United States. (See also item 572.)

(1846–1857)   **ROBERT W. WHITWORTH**   **572**

Gracy, David B., II, and Rugeley, Helen J. H., eds. "From the Mississippi to the Pacific: An Englishman in the Mormon Battalion." *Arizona and the West* 7 (Summer 1965): 127–60.

Although not a Mormon, Robert W. Whitworth enlisted in the Mormon Battalion that was raised to fight in the Mexican War. His diary (August 13, 1846-July 16, 1847) tells of an earlier journey up the Mississippi River and includes a description of the march from Fort Leavenworth (Kansas) to San Diego. During the march to Santa Fe, nothing significant happened. Whitworth arrived healthy but with sore feet.

After one week's rest the new commander, Lieutenant Colonel Philip St. George Cooke, ordered the men to march with shortened rations to ensure that their provisions would last out the trek. "This caused a great deal of growling." (p. 144) By the time they had reached some Mexican settlements in Sonora, Whitworth says, the men were so hungry they were willing to fight for food, "but our Colonel, not being half starved or else wanting courage, altered our course." (p. 417) Cooke did raise the flour ration by one ounce; Whitworth says the men had a jubilee. The march continued across terrain that offered little water, but a lot of prickly pears and sagebrush. Some ravines were so steep and rocky that the men were forced to carry the wagons across. They met many Apache Indians and Mexicans, and Whitworth describes their adaptation to desert life.

After an uneventful few months of soldiering around San Diego, Whitworth left the army, but first he had to listen to a reenlistment speech by the commanding officer that was "more patriotic than sensible." (p. 159) (See also item 571.)

(1849)   **A. SCARBOROUGH**   **573**

Wright, Bessie L., ed. "Diary of a Member of the First Mule Pack Train to Leave Fort Smith for California in 1849." *Panhandle-Plains Historical Review* 42 (1969):61–119.

Although A. Scarborough's company of gold seekers was warned by the commandant of Fort Smith (Arkansas) against traveling in such small numbers, the party departed on February 20, 1849. The first part of the trip was uneventful and descriptions of the terrain, the weather, and hunting fill the diary. Somewhere in western Texas dissension set in. The commander became a commander in name only when, against his wishes, the men searched for two lost members. In New Mexico the group split and Scarborough was elected as commander. As his party passed into southern Colorado, though, the strife continued. Along the way Scarborough observed the Indian custom of dog sacrifice and a prairie dog village. He describes the touching experience of escorting a white woman away from her Indian (or Mexican) husband at her request. Diary ends abruptly in Colorado on May 26, 1849.

(1853)   **AMIEL WEEKS WHIPPLE**   **574**

Conrad, David E. "The Whipple Expedition on the Great Plains." *Great Plains Journal* 2 (Spring 1963):42–66.

The purpose of the survey by Lieutenant Amiel Weeks Whipple from Fort Smith (Arkansas) to Los Angeles between July, 1853, and March, 1854, was to investigate a feasible route for a transcontinental railroad. This article traces Whipple's route from Fort Smith to eastern New Mexico, along the Canadian River Valley, and across the Staked Plains in the summer and fall of 1853. Consults Whipple's unpublished journal. (See also items 842 and 893.)

(1855)   **JOHN B. S. TODD**   **575**

Mattison, Ray H., ed. "The Harney Expedition Against the Sioux: The Journal of Capt. John B. S. Todd." *Nebraska History* 43 (June 1962):89–130.

Provides an account of General William S. Harney's expedition to chastise the Sioux for wiping out a detachment of soldiers in Wyoming. Todd's journal (May 28-December 2, 1855) relates the march from Fort Leavenworth (Kansas) to Fort Laramie (Wyoming) via Fort Kearny (Nebraska), and the journey from Fort Laramie to Fort Pierre (South Dakota). The early part of the journal tells of the vast herds of buffalo and the great sport of hunting them. No Indians were sighted, except for some friendly Cheyenne, until they left Fort Kearny when they met and defeated a large band of Sioux at Ash Hollow (Nebraska) on September 3. The remainder of the march was relatively uneventful, and Todd devotes himself to describing the landscape and fossils he found in Wyoming and the difficulty of travel as winter approached.

(1855–1856)   ELIZA JOHNSTON   576

Roland, Charles P., and Robbins, Richard C., eds. "The Diary of Eliza (Mrs. Albert Sidney) Johnston." *Southwestern Historical Quarterly* 60 (April 1957):463−500.

Between October 29, 1855, and January 14, 1856, General Albert Sidney Johnston marched from Jefferson Barracks, Missouri, to Fort Mason in western Texas to assume command of the Second U.S. Cavalry Regiment. Mrs. Johnston's personal reactions to incidents encountered along the 700-mile march reveal a range of emotions. She was shocked at seeing troops being drummed out of the service after first being whipped and having their heads shaved. She thought that surely some less degrading form of punishment could be devised. She was sorry for the young soldiers who died on the march and had to be buried in lonely graves far from home. She tells of hearing the tapping of the coffin maker's hammer throughout the night.

In addition, she was highly indignant upon learning that an officer had taken a Missouri man's wife on the trip. The woman was the officer's mistress and the couple had a child. Mrs. Johnston relates many amusing anecdotes, as well as vivid descriptions of the land and inhabitants of Missouri, Oklahoma, and Texas. The diary, which continues to May 7, 1856, also includes a trip from Fort Mason to San Antonio.

(1862)   JOHN O'FALLON DELANY   577

Sunder, John E., ed. "Up the Missouri to the Montana Mines: John O'Fallon Delany's 'Pocket Diary for 1862'." (Part I) *Bulletin of the Missouri Historical Society* 19 (October 1962):3−22.
—————. (Part II) *Bulletin of the Missouri Historical Society* 19 (January 1963):127−49.

Delany accompanied missionary Father Pierre Jean De Smet on this trip to the gold strikes in Montana. The first portion of the diary covers the journey from Saint Joseph, Missouri, up the Missouri River as far as Fort Benton, Montana, in the company of fur traders and miners lured by the discovery of gold. He comments on the Indian agent at Yankton who got the Indians to perform a war dance for the passengers' benefit, passengers setting the prairie on fire for a lark, and passengers killing the buffalo that came near the river. The second part of the diary is concerned with the trip from Fort Benton to the mines and the problems encountered—ferrying the wagons across the streams, broken axles, an accidental shooting, his toothache, and unpredictable weather—and prospecting in Montana. Delany returned to Saint Louis in the fall. The trip took from May 15 to October 5, 1862.

(1864)   WILLIAM L. LARNED   578

Mattison, Ray H., ed. "The Fisk Expedition of 1864: The Diary of William L. Larned." *North Dakota History* 36 (Summer 1969):209−74.

In 1864, James Fisk was commissioned by the United States government to lead an emigrant train along the 45th parallel and the Yellowstone Valley to Bannack City and Virginia City, Montana, for the purpose of opening up a shorter route from Minnesota to the gold fields of

Montana and Idaho. William L. Larned accompanied the train across Minnesota and North Dakota with a wagonload of goods to trade with the prospectors. His diary (June 29-December 31, 1864) is concerned with conditions that affected travel and with Indian attacks in western North Dakota. Larned is critical of the protection and leadership that Fisk provided. (See also item 579.)

(1864)   HORATIO H. LARNED   579

Paulson, Norman, ed. "A Letter From Horatio H. Larned to Kate Larned Alexander." *North Dakota History* 36 (Summer 1969):275–78.

A brief letter from the son of William L. Larned, who accompanied his father on the Fisk expedition in 1864. (See item 578.)

(1864–1866)   JOSEPH WARREN ARNOLD   580

Martin, Charles W., ed. "Joseph Warren Arnold's Journal of His Trip to and from Montana, 1864–66." *Nebraska History* 55 (Winter 1974):463–552.

In March, 1864, Arnold left Galena, Illinois, for the West. The early part of this journal describes the overland crossing from Council Bluffs, Iowa, to Nevada City, Montana. Arnold first got a job as a hotel clerk, then tried prospecting for a while, and later worked for a ranch. Eventually he returned to the hotel to work. In July, 1865, Arnold decided to go back to his family in Kentucky, and the last part of the journal is devoted to the steamboat trip down the Missouri River from Fort Benton, Montana. The journal is dated from March 2, 1864, to July 28, 1866.

(1865)   WILLIAM H. GALLAHER   581

Moss, James E., ed. "Ho! For the Gold Mines of Montana. Up the Missouri in 1865: The Journal of William H. Gallaher." (Part I) *Missouri Historical Review* 57 (January 1963):156–83.

———. (Part II) *Missouri Historical Review* 57 (April 1963):261–84.

During the ten-week trip from Saint Joseph, Missouri, to Fort Benton, Montana, Gallaher's diary reveals that some of the passengers' duties were to chop wood, to help pull the boat over difficult sections of the river, to hunt for food, and to guard against hostile Indians. He describes the river, other boats, searching for firewood along the shore, the wildlife, and disagreements among the passengers. Although he staked a claim around Gallatin, Montana, Gallaher does not mention that he prospected, but only that he worked cutting hay for farmers.

(1865–1866)   ABEL J. VANMETER   582

Hamilton, Jean Tyree, ed. "Abel J. Vanmeter, His Park and His Diary." *Bulletin of the Missouri Historical Society* 28 (October 1971):3–37.

Brief diary entries (March 17, 1865-May 8, 1866) are supplemented by other materials to describe Vanmeter's trip up the Missouri River to the Montana goldfields and his commercial activities there.

(1866)   LEONARD W. GILCHRIST   583

Potter, James E., ed. "The Missouri River Journal of Leonard W. Gilchrist, 1866." *Nebraska History* 58 (Fall 1977):267–300.

Gilchrist's journal (May 13-June 26, 1866) began at Nebraska City and ended two days before the boat reached its destination at Fort Benton, Montana. Because there were few delays and no accidents to write about during the trip, Gilchrist devoted himself to describing the obvious: the appearance of the water and the land along the shore, other passengers, boats sighted, and the Indians who came to trade when the boat docked. The pauses in the trip were always welcome because they provided the opportunity for fresh meat and diversion. The editor says it is somewhat surprising that the passengers roamed around so nonchalantly because the danger of Indian attack was always present. Even on board the boat there was danger. Gilchrist mentions an instance in the previous year when men were killed by Sioux Indians shooting from the shore.

(1866)   **GURDON P. LESTER**   584

Martin, Charles W., ed. "A Round Trip to the Montana Mines: The 1866 Travel Journal of Gurdon P. Lester." *Nebraska History* 46 (December 1965):272–313.

    Lester traveled from Lodomillo, Iowa, to Helena, Montana, overland on the Platte River Trail and back on the Missouri River. He frequently mentions prices, locations of historic importance, people he met, and incidents of travel. Lester says that the trip from Omaha cost $350, and the streets of the city were thronged with emigrants. He relates the joy of sleeping in a bed after riding for forty-eight hours and more than two hundred miles on a stagecoach. The bedbugs, fleas, and cockroaches, and rain and rough muddy roads contributed to his discomfort. The account of the return trip tells of the hazards of river travel, of hearing stories of Indian depredations, and of a visit to a Cree village near Fort Berthold (North Dakota). The entries run from May 31 to October 5, 1866.

(1866)   **C. M. S. MILLARD**   585

White, Lonnie J., ed. "Hugh Kirkendall's Wagon Train on the Bozeman Trail, 1866: Letters of C. M. S. Millard." *Annals of Wyoming* 47 (Spring 1975):45–58.

    Millard was a newspaperman whose adventures with a wagon train of supplies for the gold miners of Helena, Montana, were published in the *Leavenworth (Kansas) Daily Times* between June and October, 1866. His letters provide eyewitness testimony to the chaotic conditions that existed in the Powder River region and his criticism of the army's failure to provide adequate protection. The trip across Nebraska was uneventful, but by the time the party reached Fort Phil Kearny (Wyoming), Millard says, they had changed from a peaceable citizen train to Indian fighters in the fullest sense of the term. He describes several attacks by the Sioux. In his final letter, Millard says there were seventy-nine scalpings on the trip. The editor believes that although there were a great many casualties on the Bozeman Trail in 1866, that figure is an exaggeration.

(1866)   **JOHN POPE**   586

Ellis, Richard N., ed. "General Pope's Report on the West, 1866." *Kansas Historical Quarterly* 35 (Winter 1969):345–72.

    Major General John Pope was commander of the Division of the Missouri, which included most of the Great Plains country. Included in this report is a discussion of the value of the land and the role Pope believed the army should play in the protection of those who either traveled across or settled on the plains. His recommendations for Indian policy are discussed by the editor.

(1866)   **DANIEL WESTON**   587

Silliman, Lee. "'Up This Great River'; Daniel Weston's Missouri Steamboat Diary." *Montana: The Magazine of Western History* 30 (July 1980):32–41.

    Silliman uses this diary to describe a typical trip up the Missouri River in 1866. Weston, who was returning to Montana with goods for his shoe business, was amazed at how much fuel was required for the sidewheeler *Lillie Martin*. Wood was plentiful in the beginning but less available in Dakota and Montana. On a good day, and sometimes on a moonlit night, as much as seventy miles travel was possible, but because of snags and sandbars, six or seven miles was also a frequent advance. Winds and fires threatened to destroy the steamboats. The monotony of travel was enlivened by races with other boats, sighting Indians, wildlife hunts, and the beauty of the plains. The journey in May and June, 1866, took fifty-eight days.

(1866–1868)   WILSON BARBER HARLAN   588

Harlan, Gilbert Drake, ed. "The Diary of Wilson Barber Harlan." (Part I) "A Walk with a Wagon Train: A Teenage Civil War Veteran Strolls into the West." *Journal of the West* 3 (April 1964):141–62.

―――. (Part II) "A Minnesota Farm Boy in the Montana Mines." *Journal of the West* 3 (July 1964):291–312.

Following his two years of service in the Civil War, 18-year-old Harlan joined the wagon train of Captain Robert Fisk, bound for the gold mines of Montana. He paid the wagon master $100 for the privilege of walking with the train. Between June 6 and June 20, 1866, Harlan walked 1,035 miles from Saint Cloud, Minnesota, across North Dakota to Fort Benton, Montana, and finally to Helena, Montana. In the second portion of the diary, October 1, 1866-July 21, 1868, he relates his two years as a prospector in the general vicinity of Helena. The editor adds that Harlan became a prosperous farmer in the Bitterroot Valley.

(1867)   CHARLES W. HOWELL   589

Johnson, Leland R., ed. "An Army Engineer on the Missouri in 1867." *Nebraska History* 53 (Summer 1972):253–91.

Because of the rush of miners into the gold rush regions of Montana in the 1860s, demands for improved transportation on the upper Missouri River increased. In 1867, Major Charles W. Howell was assigned by the Corps of Engineers to inspect the river from Saint Louis to North Dakota. Howell recommends that dangerous snags and boulders be removed from the river, and that channels be excavated and deepened. In addition to recording the physical features of the river in his journal (June 28-September 27, 1867), Howell takes note of the cities and forts near the water, and the agricultural and commercial potential of the region, and he comments on Indian affairs.

(1867)   MRS. WILBUR FISH SANDERS   590

Johnson, Dorothy M., ed. "Slow Boat to Benton." *Montana: The Magazine of Western History* 11 (January 1961):2–11.

An episode from the diary of Mrs. Wilbur Fish Sanders in which she relates the occurrences of an 80-day steamboat trip up the Missouri River from Saint Louis to Fort Benton, Montana, between April and July, 1867. Fog, fire, broken paddle wheels, and the falling river all prevented the long journey from being predictable.

(1869)   FRANK J. NORTH   591

Danker, Donald F., ed. "The Journal of an Indian Fighter: The 1869 Diary of Major Frank J. North." *Nebraska History* 39 (June 1968):87–177.

Major North commanded a battalion of Indian warriors known as the Pawnee Scouts. His diary for the complete year is a tersely written record of day-to-day events in the field in Kansas, Nebraska, and Colorado. In the summer of 1869 the Pawnee Scouts participated in the Republican River Expedition, fought several skirmishes, and destroyed the Cheyenne village at Summit Springs, Colorado, on July 11.

(1889) **J. H. BOND** 592

Bond, I. W., ed. "Old Trails in Reverse." *Colorado Magazine* 32 (July 1955):225–31.

After nearly two years of homesteading, the I. W. Bond family decided to move back to Missouri. The diary of young J. H. Bond records his family's six-week journey (August 26–October 8, 1889) from near Monte Vista, Colorado, across Kansas, to northern Missouri.

(1905–1917) **ARTHUR HARRISON PERRY** 593

Perry, Arthur Harrison. "Alma, Kansas, Boy Goes West." *Kansas Quarterly* 8 (Spring 1976):15–19.

Between 1905 and 1917 the author and his family followed his father's fortunes in moves that took them from Alma, Kansas, to Gates, Oklahoma; to Des Moines, New Mexico; and finally to Wichita, Kansas.

(1917) **BERNARD GRIMES** 594

Grimes, Bernard. "By Boxcar to Idaho." *Idaho Yesterdays* 14 (Fall 1970):2–9.

In the spring of 1917 the author loaded all his belongings (including a pig, which gave him preferred handling) into a boxcar in Illinois and rode a train to a farm near Nampa, Idaho. He relates the events of his trip, which was delayed by an illness and snow on the tracks, and how he settled into his farm to await his family.

Kansas

(1719) **CLAUDE-CHARLES DUTISNÉ** 595

Wedel, Mildred Mott. "Claude-Charles Dutisné: A Review of His 1719 Journeys." (Part I) *Great Plains Journal* 12 (Fall 1972):4–25.

———. (Part II) *Great Plains Journal* 12 (Spring 1973):147–73.

Lieutenant Dutisné made two journeys from Kaskaskia (Illinois) in 1719 as a representative of the French Company of the West. His mission was to look for valuable minerals and possibilities for trade. On the first trip he went up the Missouri River until he was halted by a village of Missouri Indians in Vernon County, Missouri. Later that same year, he traveled across Missouri on foot and visited a Wichita village near Neodesha in southeastern Kansas. Wedel summarizes the valuable documentation of early Wichita life that Dutisné provides.

(1724) **ÉTIENNE VÉNIARD DE BOURGMONT** 596

Reichart, Milton. "Bourgmont's Route to Central Kansas: A Reexamination." *Kansas History* 2 (Summer 1979):96–120.

In 1724, Étienne Véniard de Bourgmont led a French expedition from Fort Orleans, a post he established near Atchison, Kansas, to central Kansas to make peace with the Indians and to establish a trade route to New Mexico. In the 1970s the author retraced the route from descriptions in Bourgmont's journal. Reichart comments on how the landscape changed in the intervening period.

(1828) **ISAAC MCCOY** 597

Wilmeth, Roscoe. "Kansa Village Locations in the Light of McCoy's 1828 Journal." *Kansas Historical Quarterly* 26 (Summer 1960):152–57.

Isaac McCoy was a Baptist missionary who surveyed and explored Indian lands in eastern Kansas for the purpose of removing Indians to this region. Wilmeth consults Lela Barnes, "Journal of Isaac McCoy for the Exploring Expedition of 1828," *The Kansas Historical Quarterly* 5 (August 1936).

(1835–1836) LOUIS RICHARD CORTAMBERT 598

Chapman, Carl H., ed., and Myer, Mrs. Max W., tr. "Journey to the Land of the Osages, 1835–1836." *Bulletin of the Missouri Historical Society* 19 (April 1963):199–229.

Cortambert frankly admits that his journal is one of generalization, rather than filled with details. He thinks this is the only kind of writing one can be expected to produce during rapid travel. After his arrival in New York, the French immigrant traversed Pennsylvania, descended the Ohio River, sailed up the Missouri to Saint Louis, and then went to Independence, Missouri, where he observed the Mormon troubles in Jackson County. His journey then took him overland into Indian country just west of Missouri and as far south as Fort Gibson (Oklahoma) before following the Mississippi River to New Orleans. Along the way he faced the hazards of traveling and camping in the winter along rivers swollen by rain and snow.

He met many Americans on the frontier whom he characterized as being inquisitive and living in a semicivilized state. His most detailed descriptions are of the Osage and the Cherokee Indians. Cortambert ends the essay with some observations on American society, the temperance movement, literature, slavery, and the American experiment in democracy. An extremely rare booklet.

(1854) WILLIAM H. HUTTER 599

Barry, Louise, ed. "Scenes In (And En Route To) Kansas Territory, Autumn, 1854: Five Letters by William H. Hutter." *Kansas Historical Quarterly* 35 (Autumn 1969):312–36.

Reprints the letters that this Pennsylvania newspaper editor published in *Easton Argus*. He first describes the discomforts of a three-day train ride from New York to Chicago and then to Saint Louis, where he embarked on a boat ride up the Missouri River to Leavenworth, Kansas. While in Leavenworth, which he praises, he visited the nearby Munsee Indians at their Moravian mission. The picture he gives of the Kansas landscape is favorable, but as he journeyed west to Fort Riley (Kansas) he was less pleased with the living conditions of the people he met. He saw Indian farmers living in squalid surroundings and frustrated settlers who had moved west in hope of a better life. He criticized the emigrant societies for not fulfilling their promises. Hutter predicted: "The vexed question of slavery will cause some trouble before Kansas becomes a state." (p. 366) The letters run from October 27 to November 29, 1854.

(1859–1861) ANONYMOUS 600

———. "With the First U.S. Cavalry in Indian Country, 1859–1861." (Part I) *Kansas Historical Quarterly* 24 (Autumn 1958):257–84.
———. (Part II) *Kansas Historical Quarterly* 24 (Winter 1958):399–425.

This series of letters from an unknown source (or sources?) to the *Leavenworth Daily Times* describes Indian fighting and life on the plains. Includes involvement in the Kiowa-Comanche Expedition of 1860.

(1859–1861) JOHN S. KIRWAN 601

Mattes, Merrill J., ed. "Patrolling the Santa Fe Trail: Reminiscences of John S. Kirwan." *Kansas Historical Quarterly* 21 (Winter 1955):569–87.

Private Kirwan of the Fourth U.S. Cavalry based at Fort Riley (Kansas) helped to protect communications and transportation lines along the Santa Fe Trail from Indian attacks between 1859 and 1861. One of his experiences was in the Kiowa-Comanche Expedition of 1860.

(1860)   JAMES EWELL BROWN STUART   602

Robinson, W. Stitt, ed. "The Kiowa and Comanche Campaign of 1860 as Recorded in the Personal Diary of Lt. J. E. B. Stuart." *Kansas Historical Quarterly* 23 (Winter 1957):382–400.

The Kiowa-Comanche Expedition of 1860 was undertaken by the U.S. Army to punish the Indians for a series of murders on the Santa Fe Trail in the fall and winter of the previous year. James ("Jeb") Stuart, the future Confederate cavalry leader, was official journalist for the expedition. The diary is mostly devoted to the marches and descriptions of the terrain, with no mention of hostilities. The editor writes that a small skirmish involving Stuart took place on July 11. Diary kept between May 15 and August 15, 1860.

(1863)   HERVEY JOHNSON   603

Unrau, William E., ed. "In Pursuit of Quantrill: An Enlisted Man's Response." *Kansas Historical Quarterly* 39 (Autumn 1973):379–91.

Hervey Johnson tells of the Eleventh Ohio Cavalry's attempt to capture the "bushwhacking" Confederates of William Quantrill, who had just devastated Lawrence, Kansas, on August 21, 1863. Johnson thought the confused, abortive forced march of 150 miles in Kansas and Missouri without food for men or animals accomplished nothing. One man died of sun stroke, several horses were lost, and the Eleventh Ohio's journey to Wyoming was delayed several weeks. Also included in these three letters (August 18-September 1, 1863) is a description of Fort Leavenworth (Kansas).

(1863–1873)   CHARLES MONROE CHASE   604

Barnes, Lela, ed. "An Editor Looks at Early-Day Kansas: The Letters of Charles Monroe Chase." (Part I) *Kansas Historical Quarterly* 26 (Summer 1960):113–51.

———. (Part II) *Kansas Historical Quarterly* 26 (Autumn 1960):267–301.

The author of these letters, who was the editor of the *Vermont Union* newspaper, visited eastern Kansas in 1863 and 1864, and again in 1873. Letters from the first period reflect the civic rivalry between Leavenworth and Kansas City and the violence created by pro-Confederate "Bushwhackers" and the Unionist "Jayhawkers." Chase was in Lawrence the day after Quantrill's raid. Ten years later Chase observed that Kansas City was then the leading city, that there was a large influx of emigrants, and that the railroad and street cars had arrived. During both trips he detailed the beauty and the commercial possibilities of the region.

(1865–1866)   FRIEDRICH VON HOLSTEIN   605

Pickett, Ralph H., ed. "Friedrich von Holstein's Hunting Trips, 1865–1866." *Kansas Historical Quarterly* 32 (Autumn 1966): 314–24.

Letters by a Prussian diplomat who enjoyed two buffalo hunting trips near the Republican and Smoky Hill rivers of Kansas. In describing the details of the hunt, he includes some of its hazards. A companion accidentally shot his own horse and was injured in the fall. Also, there was the ever present danger of the Sioux, Cheyenne, and Arapaho Indians who were attacking settlers and travelers during the fall of 1866.

(1866)   ELIZABETH CUSTER   606

Millbrook, Minnie Dubbs, ed. "Mrs. General Custer at Fort Riley, 1866." *Kansas Historical Quarterly* 40 (Spring 1974):63–71.

A letter from Elizabeth Custer describing life at Fort Riley shortly after Custer's arrival with the Seventh U.S. Cavalry.

(1867)   HENRY MORTON STANLEY   607

Wheeler, Douglas L., ed. "Henry M. Stanley's Letters to the Missouri Democrat." *Bulletin of the Missouri Historical Society* 17 (April 1961):269–86.

Henry Morton Stanley, who later became a famous explorer in Africa, was a special correspondent for the *Saint Louis Missouri Democrat* between March and November, 1867. During this period he accompanied General W. S. Hancock on his military expedition through Kansas and Nebraska, and was present at the peace treaty conferences at Medicine Lodge Creek, Kansas. While Stanley often wrote polemics against the "uncivilized savages" and thought they must not be allowed to stop the flow of emigration, he also found fault with government policies and the general mistreatment of the Indians. When the supply of buffalo ran out, Stanley believed, the Indians could successfully become civilized farmers. (See also item 608.)

(1867)   608

Stanley, Henry Morton. "A British Journalist Reports the Medicine Lodge Peace Councils of 1867." *Kansas Historical Quarterly* 33 (Autumn 1967):249–320.

Letters by Henry Morton Stanley that describe the peace commissions, the Indian chiefs, the meeting place, the behavior of the press corps, and the dialogue of the councils. Published in the *Saint Louis Missouri Democrat* between October 19 and November 2, 1867. (See also item 607.)

(1868–1869)   WINFIELD SCOTT HARVEY   609

Shirk, George H., ed. "Campaigning with Sheridan: A Farrier's Diary." *Chronicles of Oklahoma* 37 (Spring 1959):68–105.

This portion of the diary of Private Winfield Scott Harvey (September 1, 1868-April 4, 1869) deals with the Seventh U.S. Cavalry's participation in General Philip Henry Sheridan's winter campaign in southwestern Kansas and western Oklahoma. He tells of frequent skirmishes around Fort Dodge, the arrival of General George A. Custer to take command of the operations, and the charge into the sleeping Cheyenne village at the Battle of the Washita (Oklahoma) on November 27, 1868.

(1868–1870)   REBECCA RICHMOND   610

Millbrook, Minnie Dubbs, ed. "Rebecca Visits Kansas and the Custers: The Diary of Rebecca Richmond." *Kansas Historical Quarterly* 42 (Winter 1976):366–402.

Rebecca Richmond twice visited her cousin Elizabeth Custer at Fort Leavenworth—once between January and April, 1868, and again in February through March, 1870. Her diary focuses on social activities at the Kansas fort.

(1870–1871)   ABBIE BRIGHT   611

Snell, Joseph W., ed. "Roughing It on Her Kansas Claim: The Diary of Abbie Bright, 1870–1871." (Part I) *Kansas Historical Quarterly* 37 (Autumn 1971):233–68.
———. (Part II) *Kansas Historical Quarterly* 37 (Winter 1971):394–428.

In September, 1870, Abbie Bright traveled to Indiana, where she taught school until the following April. The first part of her diary relates her teaching experiences and life on an Indiana farm. She says that she went to Kansas to visit her brother and for the fun of traveling, but once she arrived others convinced her that she should take up a homestead claim because it was the fashion. With considerable help from her brother, who was also a homesteader, she laid claim to 160 acres in Sedgwick County by living on the land for six months, making improvements, and paying $1.25 an acre.

Throughout the diary Abbie remains cheerful. She was often teased about her good nature and her unmarried state. She was happier during the early part of her stay than she was later on when the hot, dry, windless summer and frequent attacks of ague took their toll on her spirits. By November she was glad her mandatory six months had passed and she could return home.

Much of the diary describes daily life common to everyone who lived on the prairie. Abbie relates how beautiful the vegetation looked in the spring and enjoys such small pleasures as filling her mattress with prairie hay. She describes what her cabin looked like inside, both when it was newly cleaned and after the roof leaked during heavy rains. Everyday problems included the cat dragging a half-eaten rabbit under her bed, having to shoot a rat, a skunk getting inside the cabin, ticks in the bedding, and the illnesses of nearly all her acquaintances.

(1870–1871)   **LAWSON COOKE**   612

Riley, Paul D. ed. "A Winter on the Plains, 1870–1871: The Memoirs of Lawson Cooke." *Kansas Historical Quarterly* 37 (Spring 1971):33–40.

The region between the Smoky Hill River in Kansas and the Platte River in Nebraska was one of the major buffalo ranges of the Great Plains. The editor says Cooke's diary represents one of the few accounts left by professional buffalo hunters of the "Republican herd." The hunt described here took place along Prairie Dog and Sappa creeks in Norton and Decatur counties, Kansas.

(1871)   **GEORGE C. ANDERSON**   613

Anderson, George C. "Touring Kansas and Colorado in 1871: The Journal of George C. Anderson." (Part I) *Kansas Historical Quarterly* 22 (Autumn 1956):193–219.
———. (Part II) *Kansas Historical Quarterly* 22 (Winter 1956):358–84.

Anderson was with a committee of Ohioans searching for suitable lands for colonization. Between May and July, 1871, the group inspected Kansas, Colorado, Wyoming, and Oklahoma, but found no sites to their liking. Among the places Anderson visited and commented on were Saint Louis, Kansas City, Topeka, Wichita, and Emporia. In Colorado they stopped in Denver, Greeley (where they visited the agricultural colony), and Pueblo. After returning to Kansas they went south to Big Cabin in Oklahoma Territory, then back north across Kansas, and finally home to Cincinnati. The whirlwind tour took from May 16 to July 6. The diary describes the agricultural possibilities of every place they visited, as well as some buffalo hunting episodes.

(1871–1874)   **LUNA E. WARNER**   614

Bivans, Venola Lewis, ed. "The Diary of Luna E. Warner, a Kansas Teenager of the Early 1870's." (Part I) *Kansas Historical Quarterly* 35 (Autumn 1969):276–311.
———. (Part II) *Kansas Historical Quarterly* 35 (Winter 1969):345–411.

These excerpts relate events in the lives of a family of homesteaders during their first years (February 23, 1871-December 24, 1874) of a long residency on the Solomon River, south of Downs, Kansas. Luna and her party traveled by train from Jersey City, New Jersey, to Solomon, Kansas, where they bought a wagon and searched for suitable land. Her descriptions of minor events are brief but vivid. For example, after an overnight stop, she says that in the morning "the men had a jaw and the women a cry, and then we started on a-foot as usual." (p. 279) Later, simply, "The cabin is full of mice." (p. 282) During the early period, as they worked to establish their claim and plant gardens, the weather was most unpredictable. Between April 2 and 10, 1871, the temperature rose to 98°, but this was soon followed by hail and then snow. The whole diary continues in the same vein, recording the important and the trivial, the hardships and the joys of a Massachusetts family's adaptation to the prairie.

(1875)   LYDIA E. ENGLISH   615

Snell, Joseph W., ed. "By Wagon From Kansas to Arizona in 1875: The Travel Diary of Lydia E. English." *Kansas Historical Quarterly* 36 (Winter 1970):369–89.

In September, 1875, the William English family emigrated from a prosperous farm in the Republican River valley of Kansas, a region which was then attracting migrants in search of a better life. While the action may have seemed unexplainable to most, William's son simply attributed it to his father's insatiable wanderlust. Judging from her diary of the journey (September 20-December 6, 1875), Lydia did not share her husband's attraction to other lands. From the outset she expressed homesickness.

Most of the way from Concordia, Kansas through southwestern Colorado and northern New Mexico to Prescott, Arizona, she describes the poor quality of the land and the difficulty of travel. Although she describes Prescott as a beautiful mountain town and admits that she saw some attractive country in New Mexico, to Lydia the Republican River Valley was still the most beautiful place. Most of the writing is necessarily devoted to the landscape because they met few people until they reached New Mexico. Included are Lydia's impressions of Dodge City and Albuquerque.

(1876–1877)   PROSPER JACOTOT   616

Thogmartin, Clyde. "Prosper Jacotot: A French Worker Looks at Kansas in 1876–1877." *Kansas Historical Quarterly* 41 (Spring 1976):14–21.

Jacotot operated a two-man coal mine near Williamsburg, Kansas, for almost a year. After the mine failed and he was unable to find employment in Saint Louis and New Orleans, he left America. Several years later he wrote of his experiences in two articles published in France. The aspects of Kansas life that Jacotot seemed to remember most were the cold winters, the religious nature of the people, and the Temperance Society, which was backed by women. Jacotot commented that the only job of the American woman was "to make a home and to make little Americans," but not to work beside her husband as in France. (p. 19)

(1876–1878)   CHARLES D. COWLES   617

Jordan, Weymouth T., ed. "A Soldier's Life on the Indian Frontier, 1876–1878: Letters of 2Lt. C. D. Cowles." *Kansas Historical Quarterly* 38 (Summer 1972):144–55.

Charles D. Cowles spent the first ten years of his long military career in the West. Between 1876 and 1878 he was stationed at Fort Dodge and Fort Hays, Kansas. One of his experiences was to intercept three hundred Cheyennes who had left the reservation in Oklahoma and were raiding in Kansas. Cowles understood that the Indians were starving and had reason to leave the reservation, but he felt it was his soldier's duty to punish them.

(1878)   DAVIS H. WAITE   618

Hurt, R. Douglas, ed. "Davis H. Waite: Travels in Kansas, 1878." *Kansas Historical Quarterly* 42 (Spring 1976):66–74.

Notes of a horseback trip in April, 1878, through Barton, Ellsworth, Saline, and Dickinson counties. Waite describes the terrain, the availability of land, the crop prospects, the settlements, and the commercial prospects of western Kansas.

(1881) **STEPHEN STONE** **619**

Gaither, Gerald, and Finger, John R., eds. "A Journey of Stephen Stone: Observations on Kansas in 1881." *Kansas Historical Quarterly* 37 (Summer 1971):148–54.

During his two-week trip through Kansas in March, 1881, Stephen Stone noticed the commercial, agricultural, and mining potential of south-central Kansas. He also took note of the urban deficiencies of Kansas City.

(1896) **THOMAS BUTCHER** **620**

Littleton, Betty, ed. "Touring the Southeast Kansas Area in 1896: From the Diary of Thomas Butcher." *Kansas Historical Quarterly* 35 (Summer 1969):143–54.

Because Butcher's farm near Sun City, Kansas, was one of the many that failed in the early 1890s, he went in search of new opportunities in southeastern Kansas, northeastern Oklahoma, and southwestern Missouri during June, 1896. His diary is filled with information on the conditions of the crops and the area's farming potential.

NEBRASKA

(1796) **JAMES MACKAY** **621**

Diller, Aubrey. "James Mackay's Journal in Nebraska in 1796." *Nebraska History* 36 (June 1955):123–28.

Mackay was the first white man to visit Nebraska and leave an accurate historical record, but his journal has not survived. Diller traces Mackay's route from a copy of his map.

(1806) **ZEBULON MONTGOMERY PIKE** **622**

Jackson, Donald. "Zebulon Pike and Nebraska." *Nebraska History* 47 (December 1966):355–69.

Discusses the importance of Pike's 1806 expedition to the Great Plains and the Rocky Mountains in terms of future immigration. Although Pike did not think the region was habitable, reports of his expedition stirred desire for westward expansion. The precise location of Pike's confrontation with the Pawnee chiefs, when he lowered the Spanish flag, raised the American flag, and marched south in defiance of a larger group of Indians, has long been a matter of dispute. Was it in Republic County, Kansas, as has been thought? Or was it, as Jackson believes, in Webster County, Nebraska? Quotes extensively from *The Journals of Zebulon Montgomery Pike, with Letters and Related Documents*, edited by Donald Jackson (Norman, 1966).

(1819) **GABRIEL FIELD** **623**

Nichols, Roger L., ed. "The Camp Missouri-Chariton Road, 1819: The Journal of Lt. Gabriel Field." *Bulletin of the Missouri Historical Society* 24 (January 1968):139–52.

Lieutenant Field's mission was to survey a road from Camp Missouri (Nebraska) through to Council Bluffs, Iowa, then south to the army post at Chariton, Missouri, on the Missouri River. While the immediate purpose of the road was as a line of communication for the 1819 Yellowstone Expedition, which had halted its march in Nebraska, for several years the road served as a major overland route. The editor believes the journal is important because it provides an infrequent look at land travel through a region that was usually described by travelers on the Missouri River. Journal kept October 31 to November 27, 1819.

(1830–1863)   **CHIMNEY ROCK**   **624**

Mattes, Merrill J. "Chimney Rock on the Oregon Trail." *Nebraska History* 36 (March 1955):1–26.

    Presents selections from the writings of many who traveled along the central overland route, or Platte River Trail, and who described the natural phenomenon known as Chimney Rock in western Nebraska. There are drawings, a select bibliography, and a tabulation of contemporary references to the eight major Platte River Trail landmarks: Ash Hollow, Courthouse Rock, Chimney Rock, Scott's Bluff, Laramie Peak, Independence Rock, Devil's Gate, and South Pass.

(1834–1864)   **ASH HOLLOW**   **625**

Munkres, Robert L. "Ash Hollow: Gateway to the High Plains." *Annals of Wyoming* 42 (April 1970):5–43.

    The first part of the overland trail through Kansas and Nebraska was relatively easy, but beyond Ash Hollow in western Nebraska travel became increasingly difficult. Munkres summarizes the written experiences of emigrants who crossed the tableland between the South and North forks of the Platte River to reach Ash Hollow. Travel across the fifteen to twenty-five miles of tableland was uncomfortable and frequently dangerous because of deep sand and little grass for the animals. The trail into Ash Hollow was steep. Although some emigrants complained about the lack of good grass, they praised the timber, the water, and the abundance of wildlife.

    In Ash Hollow the emigrants rested and fed their animals. Because it was a preferred resting place, Indians also used Ash Hollow as a temporary campground. Meetings with Sioux and Pawnee Indians were frequent, and there were many reports of trading with the Indians and of Indian thievery. After the 1850s the area became known as a dangerous place for Indian attacks. Munkres says Ash Hollow was considered one of the best stops along the Platte River Trail partly because the trail beyond, up the North Platte and Sweetwater rivers toward the South Pass in Wyoming, was dreary and difficult. The author consulted travel accounts written between 1834 and 1864.

(1857)   **HENRY JAMES HUDSON**   **626**

Burke, Marguerette R., ed. "Henry James Hudson and the Genoa Settlement." *Nebraska History* 41 (September 1960):201–35.

    Hudson's journal of a trip from Saint Louis to Genoa, Nebraska, in April and May, 1857, constitutes most of this article. He was escorting a group of two hundred Mormon colonists to the new and short-lived settlement of Genoa that was established as a way station on the Mormon Trail. The trip was made on a sidewheel steamer and each Mormon paid only four dollars instead of the usual eight. Hudson mentions the prices of goods, including the high price the Mormons were forced to pay for food, the sandbars and indifferent weather that affected travel, and sicknesses and other problems of the passengers. The article includes a letter to *The Mormon* (Salt Lake City) describing Genoa and a speech by Hudson on the same topic.

(1859)   **JOSEPH CAMP**   **627**

Camp, Truman, ed. "The Journal of Joseph Camp, 1859." *Nebraska History* 46 (March 1965):29–38.

    Camp was a Connecticut farmer who traveled to Iowa and to Saint Joseph, Missouri, then on to Omaha to visit friends and relatives. In this portion of his journal, which is supplemented by newspaper articles from the *Hartford Daily Courant*, he describes his distaste for Saint Joseph—"the muddiest, nastiest ruffian border town on earth. It offended the ear, eye and nose"—but he found Omaha much more to his liking. (p. 31) He thought the Pawnee Indians looked degraded but friendly. Camp reported on the so-called Pawnee War of 1859 for the *Daily Courant*. The entries here run from June 21 through September 23, 1859.

(1868)   JOSEPH BARKER   628

Martin, Charles W., ed. "Joseph Barker and the 1868 Union Pacific Railroad Excursion from Omaha." *Nebraska History* 58 (Summer 1977):123–48.

Between September 28 and October 4, 1867, Barker traveled from Omaha to the end of the Union Pacific line near Green River, Wyoming, on a promotional tour and to observe construction work. In this letter Barker concluded that Nebraska was not a desert, but was capable of sustaining cattle and agriculture with irrigation. He believed that Wyoming held great mineral wealth, with manufacturing potential around Laramie. He judged railroad construction to be excellent. Barker also described the flurry of commercial activity that occurred in Omaha during the summer of 1868.

(1869–1871)   MARY CARR   629

King, James T., ed. "Fort McPherson in 1870: A Note by an Army Wife." *Nebraska History* 45 (March 1964):99–107.

Mary Carr, the wife of Brevet Major General Eugene A. Carr of the Fifth U.S. Cavalry, recalls the social life and the celebrities who visited the Nebraska fort, and tells about hunting with greyhounds, foods eaten, Indian scares, and land transactions. The editor adds that although she did not realize it, Mrs. Carr's account provides a description of a frontier that was rapidly changing. Between 1869 and 1871, the years covered here, buffalo were vanishing, cattlemen were moving in, and Indian attacks were less frequent.

(1872)   CHARLES WOOSTER   630

Schmidt, William F., ed. "The Letters of Charles and Helen Wooster: The Problems of Settlement." *Nebraska History* 46 (June 1965):121–37.

Charles originally intended to settle in Minnesota, but while in Chicago he was persuaded that Nebraska offered the best opportunities to establish a farm. These letters to his wife in Michigan describe the land and the people in Silver Glen (Merrick County), Nebraska. The most interesting parts are those in which he tries to convince his wife to leave her familiar surroundings and join him on the frontier. In early letters he tells her that she should not be homesick for Michigan, for "if we find peace and happiness on earth, I suppose 99 percent of it will be within our own home." (p. 123)

To allay her fears of the frontier, he describes the Indians as friendly. He relates his acquaintance with a lovable papoose and sends her some Indian ear decorations. He is determined to keep his land and build a nice wooden house (not a sod house) for his family. In later letters he tells her how lonely it is without her, how foolish it is for them to maintain two households, and how demoralized he has become.

Finally, she agrees to join him. Her letters show enthusiasm for the new house he is building, and she tells him to plant flowers near the front bedroom. Still, hesitancy and money problems delay the trip until mid-December when, perhaps as a final bit of encouragement, he writes: "Charley's little love is coming to stay with him and all her troubles will be at an end." (p. 37) Written between March 12 and December 13, 1872.

(1872–1873)   ROYAL BUCK   631

Riley, Paul D., ed. "Red Willow County Letters of Royal Buck, 1872–1873." *Nebraska History* 47 (December 1966):371–97.

The beginning and the end of a frontier community are revealed in these letters by an early member of the southwestern Nebraska settlement of Red Willow Creek. Since it was Buck's desire to attract settlers, these letters to editors of newspapers usually praise the farming conditions and the abundance of buffalo and beaver. They tell how good the area would be for cattle or sheep raising and how civilized the region was, without Indian attacks or wolves and with elections held.

Still, he could not conceal the plagues of grasshoppers and worms that severely cut crop production, nor the establishment of a rival town, Indianola, which became the county seat of Red Willow County. Buck had unfavorable comments about the Pawnee Indians. He showed little pity when a group was killed by the Sioux at nearby Massacre Canyon on August 5, 1873. Buck visited three days after the event. The editor reveals that Red Willow Creek never developed as a town.

(1872–1874) WILHELM DINESEN 632

Watkins, Donald K., tr. "A Dane's View on Frontier Culture: 'Notes on a Stay in the United States, 1872–1874, by Wilhelm Dinesen'." *Nebraska History* 55 (Summer 1974):264–89.

Dinesen spent a portion of these years in Platte County, Nebraska, regaining his health. After stopping briefly in Chicago, he moved to Columbus, Nebraska, where he worked in a post office and as a real estate agent. He tells a little about the settlers, land sales, farming, and the cattle business. Dinesen stresses some of the negative aspects of the American contact with the unspoiled. He says that wherever the white man went he wiped out the game, and Dinesen relates his participation in a buffalo hunt where only the hides were taken. Dinesen was pessimistic about the Indians' future. He writes that they were doomed to extinction along a predictable historical pattern whenever they came into contact with the white man. His subjects for study were the Pawnee.

(1875) THEODORE E. TRUE 633

Olson, Gary D., ed. "Relief for Nebraska Grasshopper Victims: The Official Journal of Lieutenant Theodore E. True." *Nebraska History* 48 (Summer 1967):119–40.

Lieutenant True was stationed at Fort Fetterman (Wyoming) when he was called to distribute clothing and food to families in Dawson County, Nebraska, who had been left destitute as the result of grasshoppers ravaging crops during the summer of 1874. His journal (January 28-March 7, 1875) documents his work and the number and pitiful condition of families needing help.

(1901) MARY MAHONEY 634

Mahoney, Donald, ed. "End of an Era: The Travel Journal of Mary Mahoney." *Nebraska History* 47 (September 1966):329–38.

By 1901 most travel west was by rail, but this account of a wagon trip from western Nebraska to Colorado indicates that some still traveled the traditional way. The 220-mile trek took twenty days and included all of the discomforts and pleasures of the earlier overland migration. Wagon wheels kept sinking in sand; high rivers and streams were perilous to ford; a daily water supply for the animals had to be located; and food had to be bought from communities along the way. Mary's oil stove was unsuitable for cooking because the wind kept blowing the flame out. There was strife between the families; toothache pain could only be relieved, not cured; the children cried constantly because of the cold May weather. Still, the land was often beautiful, and Mary's only real complaint was that next time she traveled it would be earlier in the year. The editor points out that when the family returned to Nebraska for permanent settlement two years later, they traveled by train.

(1906–1907) **SAMUEL B. MCPHEETERS** 635

Wight, Willard E., ed. "A Young Medical Officer's Letters from Fort Robinson and Fort Leavenworth, 1906–1907." *Nebraska History* 37 (June 1956):135–47.

Dr. Samuel B. McPheeters tells of his adjustment to being in the army as a contract surgeon. He signed on to get experience and to travel abroad. As he describes the forts in Nebraska and Kansas, the climate, the recreational activities, and his medical assignment, it is apparent he did not travel far and received no great variety of medical experience.

NORTH DAKOTA

(1797–1798) **CHARLES JEAN BAPTISTE CHABOILLEZ** 636

Hickerson, Harold, ed. "Journal of Charles Jean Baptiste Chaboillez, 1797–1798." (Part I) *Ethnohistory* 6 (Summer 1959):265–316.
———. (Part II) *Ethnohistory* 6 (Fall 1959):363–427.

Provides the first written account of a fur trader wintering among the Chippewa Indians at the junction of the Red and Pembina rivers in the extreme northeastern corner of North Dakota. *Note*: See also Roy P. Johnson, "Fur Trader at Pembina," *North Dakota History* 32 (April 1965):83–99, which describes Chaboillez's activities and uses Hickerson's translation of the journal.

(1797–1798) **DAVID THOMPSON** 637

Wood, W. Raymond, ed. "David Thompson at the Mandan-Hidatsa Villages, 1797–1798: The Original Journals." *Ethnohistory* 24 (Fall 1977):329–42.

"David Thompson's visit to these villages marks the beginning of serious documentation for these two northern Plains, Siouan-speaking tribes." (p. 329) Thompson was an explorer, geographer, and fur trader for the Canadian North West Company who spent this winter in what are now McLean and Mercer counties of west-central North Dakota. The editor says these accounts, not included in Thompson's other published journals, provide data on the ethnic composition of the Mandan-Hidatsa. They indicate that the villages were more heterogeneous than was previously thought.

(1833) **ROBERT CAMPBELL** 638

Brooks, George R., ed. "The Private Journal of Robert Campbell." (Part I) *Bulletin of the Missouri Historical Society* 20 (October 1963):3–24.
———. (Part II) *Bulletin of the Missouri Historical Society* 20 (January 1964):107–18.

This Saint Louis businessman and fur trader provides a day-to-day account of the establishment of the Fort William trading post at the confluence of the Yellowstone and Missouri rivers in North Dakota. His firm, Sublette and Campbell, was attempting to challenge the powerful American Fur Company post at nearby Fort Union (North Dakota). In the journal, which runs from September 31 to December 31, 1833, Campbell describes the difficulties of trying to lure the Indians' allegiance from the rival company in the cut-throat fur trade.

(1845) **GEORGE ANTOINE BELCOURT** 639

Belcourt, George Antoine. "Hunting Buffalo on the Northern Plains: A Letter From Father Belcourt." *North Dakota History* 38 (Summer 1971):334–48.

For six weeks during the summer of 1845, Father Belcourt accompanied a band of Chippewa Indians and métis (half-bloods) from Manitoba into central North Dakota on their annual buffalo hunt. His letter provides information about the methods of the hunt, dressing the animal, the edible parts, the size of the herd, the number of buffalo killed (1,776), and details of how the kill was divided to be traded. Father Belcourt also discusses relations between the hunters and the role of a priest in these activities.

(1855–1875)   BLACK HILLS EXPEDITIONS   640

McLaird, James D., and Turchen, Lesta V., eds. "Exploring the Black Hills, 1855–1875: Reports of the Government Expeditions. (Part I) The Dacota Explorations of Lieutenant Gouverneur Kemble Warren, 1855–1856–1857." *South Dakota History* 3 (Fall 1973):359–89.

————. (Part II) "The Explorations of Captain William Franklin Raynolds, 1859–1860." *South Dakota History* 4 (Winter 1973):18–62.

————. (Part III) "The Scientist in Western Exploration: Ferdinand Vandiveer Hayden." *South Dakota History* 4 (Spring 1974):161–97.

————. (Part IV) "Colonel William Ludlow and the Custer Expedition." *South Dakota History* 4 (Summer 1974):281–319.

————. (Part V) "The Scientists' Search for Gold, 1875: Walter P. Jenney and Henry Newton." *South Dakota History* 4 (Fall 1974):404–38.

A series on government explorations into the Black Hills preceding the gold rush of 1876. Reprints significant excerpts from the reports, with biographical data about the explorers.

(1857)   HENRY A. BOLLER   641

Mattison, R. H., ed. "Journal of a Trip To, and Residence In, the Indian Country." *North Dakota History* 33 (Summer 1966): 260–315.

More of the activities of fur trader Henry A. Boller while he was stationed at Look-a-Fishhook village near Fort Atkinson (North Dakota). Kept between September 1 and December 31, 1857. (See also item 642.)

(1857–1860)   642

————. "Henry A. Boller: Upper Missouri River Fur Trader." *North Dakota History* 33 (Spring 1966):106–219.

Contains the letters of Henry A. Boller written between March 3, 1857, and June 18, 1860, when he competed unsuccessfully with the American Fur Company in the dwindling fur trade. Boller tells about how and why he first came west on the Ohio River to Saint Louis. He discusses his partners, details of the fur traders' lives around Fort Atkinson (North Dakota), and the contacts between the traders and the Indians, as well as offering many comments about the "opposition," the American Fur Company. Boller wrote of his adventures in *Among the Indians: Eight Years in the Far West, 1858–1866* (Philadelphia, 1868), but these letters describe events not included in the book. (See also item 641.)

(1862–1865)   MILTON SPENCER   643

Goodwin, Carol G. "The Letters of Private Milton Spencer, 1862–1865: A Soldier's View of Military Life on the Northern Plains." *North Dakota History* 37 (Fall 1970):233–69.

These excerpts from Spencer's letters shed some light on Indian fighting in the Dakotas during the Civil War. Private Spencer served as a member of General Alfred Sully's forces with the Sixth Iowa Cavalry and was a participant in several skirmishes and in the battles of Whitestone Hill (1863) and Killdeer Mountain (1864), both in North Dakota. Spencer comments on everyday events and includes some details about the soil, the vegetation, and the weather. Despite that the Indians were the army's adversaries, Spencer was unwilling to make a blanket condemnation of them. On more than one occasion he showed sympathy toward the Indians and once he defended the slaying of a soldier on the grounds that the Indians had been treated shamefully by the white man.

(1863) ROBERT W. FURNAS 644

Rowen, Richard D., ed. "The Second Nebraska's Campaign Against the Sioux." *Nebraska History* 44 (March 1963):3–53.

Presents three documents written by men who served with the Second Nebraska Regiment, which participated in the campaign General Alfred Sully led against the Sioux in Dakota Territory. They are the journal kept by the regimental commander, Colonel Robert W. Furnas (June 16-September 12, 1863), the diary of Corporal Henry W. Pierce (June 23-September 20, 1863), and drawings by Private George P. Belden. The march culminated in the defeat of the Sioux at the Battle of Whitestone Hill (North Dakota) on September 3, 1863.

(1874) CUSTER'S BLACK HILLS EXPEDITION 645

Although in violation of the terms of the Treaty of Fort Laramie (1868), which had guaranteed the area to the Sioux, General Philip Sheridan received permission to dispatch Lieutenant Colonel George A. Custer on an exploring-military reconnaissance of the Black Hills in the summer of 1874. Custer's report provided proof that passage into the region was possible and that the land was rich in farming and stock-raising potential. Custer's statement that there was gold in the Black Hills is credited with causing American miners to flock there, precipitating war with the Sioux in 1876. *Note*: In addition to the two eyewitness accounts that follow in items 646 and 647, a general history of the expedition is Jerry Keenan, "Exploring the Black Hills: An Account of the Custer Expedition," *Journal of the West* 6 (April 1967):248–61. An account that questions the degree of blame that should be placed on the expedition's instigation of hostilities is Max E. Gerber, "The Custer Expedition: A New Look," *North Dakota History* 40 (Winter 1973):4–23.

(1874) WILLIAM LUDLOW 646

McAndrews, Eugene V., ed. "An Army Engineer's Journal of Custer's Black Hills Expedition, July 2, 1874-August 23, 1874." *Journal of the West* 13 (January 1974):78–85.

Captain William Ludlow was chief engineer of the Black Hills Expedition. After recording the routes taken and describing the wildlife and the terrain, Ludlow summarizes his views on the future of the Black Hills. He thought the Indians would not give up the region because it was valuable to them as a hunting ground and as a final asylum. He foresaw hostilities when the white man attempted to move into the area. Ludlow writes that the Indians would have to make a stand because they "have no country farther West to which they can migrate." (p. 85) During the expedition Captain Ludlow saw nothing to substantiate the claim of large amounts of gold in the Black Hills.

(1874) FRED SNOW 647

Moyne, Ernest J., ed. "Fred Snow's Account of the Custer Expedition of 1874." *North Dakota History* 27 (Summer/Fall 1960):145–51.

Reminiscences of "Antelope Fred" Snow, the civilian ambulance driver for Custer's Black Hills expedition during July and August, 1874. Besides describing the terrain and vegetation, Snow tells how the party was constantly on the alert for Indians. They sighted only a village that was on the move, however, and the ever present scavengers who ransacked the expedition's deserted campsites. The only incident occurred when one of Custer's Indian scouts killed a Sioux that he was escorting away from the troops. Snow tells how Custer would rush off across streams in search of game, forcing the wagons to search for a suitable crossing and then catch up with the rest of the expedition as best they could. Snow also says that he and J. R. Rice discovered the first specimen of gold on July 27, 1874.

(1874–1875)   **WILMOT P. SANFORD**   648

Innis, Ben, ed. "The Fort Buford Diary of Pvt. Sanford." *North Dakota History* 33 (Fall 1966):335–78.

Wilmot P. Sanford served with the Sixth Regiment, U.S. Infantry, at Fort Buford, in western North Dakota near the confluence of the Missouri and Yellowstone rivers. In the extant portion of his diary (September 26, 1874-May 23, 1875), the editor believes Sanford reveals the attitude of every common soldier, a "let's get it over with" attitude. (p. 337) Sanford describes everyday activities of frontier post life, the absence of relaxing activities, the drudgery of duty, dull food, bad weather, illness, and some curious financial arrangements with other soldiers.

(1876)   **JAMES M. DEWOLF**   649

Luce, Edward S., ed. "The Diary and Letters of Dr. James M. DeWolf, Acting Assistant Surgeon, U.S. Army: His Record of the Sioux Expedition of 1876 as Kept Until His Death." *North Dakota History* 25 (April/June 1958):33–81.

During the period covered by this diary (March 10-June 21, 1876), DeWolf describes the medical problems incurred on the difficult march that began at Fort Totten (North Dakota). The troops were beseiged with frozen hands and feet, rattlesnake bites, boils, headaches, and chills. As late as June 8 they still had seen no Indians. He wrote that it was generally believed that the Indians had returned to the reservation, but DeWolf predicted if they were found they would not be in a fighting mood. On June 25, 1876, Dr. DeWolf was killed at the Battle of the Little Bighorn (Montana).

(1876)   **LEANDER P. RICHARDSON**   650

McFarling, Lloyd, ed. "A Trip to the Black Hills in 1876." *Annals of Wyoming* 27 (April 1955):35–42.

Reprints portions of an article by Leander P. Richardson that was published in *Scribners Magazine* (April 1877). His travel experiences from Fort Laramie (Wyoming) to Deadwood, South Dakota, in late July, 1876, were disappointing, with it being too wet, and there were sand flies and dull meals. McFarling says these conditions may have caused Richardson to offer negative and incorrect conclusions about the Black Hills' economic prospects. Richardson was in Deadwood when Wild Bill Hickok was murdered.

(1878)   **GEORGE WATSON SMITH**   651

Parker, Watson, ed. "An Illinois Greenhorn in Bismarck, D.T." *North Dakota History* 35 (Winter 1968):20–27.

George Watson Smith's purpose for coming to Bismarck, North Dakota, was to explore the possibilities of extending mortgage loans on farmlands. He spent about a week on this trip, during which he bought some land and later learned he had been swindled. His brief diary

(May 16–31, 1878) tells how the people and the lands of the prairie looked to a Yale-educated man from Chicago.

(1884–1886) **WILLIAM W. SEWALL** **652**

Mattison, Ray H., ed. "Life at Roosevelt's Elkhorn Ranch—The Letters of William W. and Mary Sewall." *North Dakota History* 27 (Summer/Fall 1960):105–41.

Sewall spent two years in North Dakota as manager of Theodore Roosevelt's expanding cattle business. These letters (August 17, 1884-August 7, 1886) shed light not only on Roosevelt's ranching operations but on the whole range cattle industry. They also show the impact of rattlesnakes, flies, and grasshoppers, the threat of Indian war, the cold winters and dry summers, and cattle thieves on a Maine family transported to the frontier.

(1889–1890) **JOSIAH JANNEY BEST** **653**

Brown, Stuart E., Jr., ed. "Letters from Dakota, or Life and Scenes Among the Indians: Fort Berthold Agency, 1889–1890." *North Dakota History* 43 (Winter 1976):5–31.

Josiah Janney Best was a doctor at the Fort Berthold Indian Reservation in North Dakota. He describes the isolation of the agency and trips to visit the Indian settlements, where he observed customs of burial, marriage, council, and farming practices of the Mandan, Hidatsa, and Arikara Indians. Best had a negative attitude about official government policy toward the Indians.

(1909–1911) **ANNA ERICKSON** **654**

Bern, Enid, ed. "They had a Wonderful Time: The Homesteading Letters of Anna and Ethel Erickson." *North Dakota History* 45 (Fall 1978):4–31.

Two sisters from Marshalltown, Iowa, homesteaded in Hettinger County, North Dakota, long enough to lay claim to their land. Their letters (September 21, 1909-August 9, 1911) describe many aspects of their experiences—guarding chickens against coyotes, rain, and Ethel's teaching at the local school. They also reveal something of the development of Bentley, a nearby town.

Oklahoma

(1718–1719) **JEAN-BAPTISTE BÉNARD DE LA HARPE** **655**

Smith, Ralph A., ed. and tr. "Account of the Journey of Bénard de la Harpe: Discovery Made By Him of Several Nations Situated in the West." (Part I) *Southwestern Historical Quarterly* 62 (July 1958):75–86.

———. (Part II) *Southwestern Historical Quarterly* 62 (January 1959):371–85.

———. (Part III) *Southwestern Historical Quarterly* 62 (April 1959):525–41.

On this mission for the Council of Louisiana, Jean-Baptiste Bénard, Sieur de la Harpe, was to attempt to enter into trade with the Spanish in Texas and make discoveries in the western part of Louisiana. Between December, 1718, and December, 1719, he ascended the Mississippi, the Red, and the Arkansas rivers, and journeyed overland into central Oklahoma. His report mentions many Indian tribes and describes in detail a Wichita village. Because of hostilities between France and Spain, the Indians were discouraged from entering into alliances with the French at that time. The Council of Louisiana advised him not to pursue his expedition into New Mexico. *Note*: Another article that stresses La Harpe's importance as an explorer in providing information about Louisiana and the southern Plains Indians between 1718 and 1723 is

Mildred Mott Wedel, "J. B. Bénard, Sieur de la Harpe: Visitor to the Wichitas in 1719," *Great Plains Journal* 10 (Spring 1971):37–70.

(1831–1836)   CEPHAS WASHBURN   656

Ross, Margaret Smith, ed. "Three Letters of Cephas Washburn." *Arkansas Historical Quarterly* 16 (Summer 1957):174–91.

Reverend Washburn wrote these letters between February 17, 1831, and March 29, 1836, relating his activities and a great deal of soul-searching while at the Dwight Mission in Oklahoma. For example, he fears a general loss of religious spirit among the Cherokee Indians and places the blame on himself. Washburn says that cholera took a heavy toll among the Cherokees and Choctaws during these years.

(1832)   WASHINGTON IRVING   657

Short, Julee. "Irving's Eden: Oklahoma, 1832." *Journal of the West* 10 (October 1971):700–12.

In 1832, Charles Joseph Latrobe, Count Albert-Alexandre Pourtalès, Henry Leavitt Ellsworth, and Washington Irving traveled together to eastern Oklahoma. All wrote books relating their experiences. Short discusses the similarities of their accounts briefly, but treats Irving's *Tour on the Prairies* (Norman, 1956) in detail. Although literary critics and historians have traditionally denounced this account, Short agrees with more recent writers who see merit in the work. She believes that Irving not only wrote the earliest social and cultural history of the West, but that in so doing he "cut the literary reins which bound America to Europe." (p. 712)

(1833–1835)   CASSANDRA SAWYER LOCKWOOD   658

Lockwood, Cassandra Sawyer. "Letters of Cassandra Sawyer Lockwood: Dwight Mission, 1834." *Chronicles of Oklahoma* 33 (Summer 1955):202–37.

For a little over a year Mrs. Lockwood, from Massachusetts, was a missionary for the American Board of Commissioners for Foreign Missions. In these letters, addressed to the Ipswich Female Seminary after her return, she describes her extremely difficult passage down the Ohio, the Mississippi, and the White rivers into Arkansas, and then to the Dwight Mission in Oklahoma late in 1833. She relates her daily duties at the mission and the religious exercises with the Cherokee Indians, whom she held in high regard. She thought less of the Osage Indians because of their poor living conditions and their love for whiskey. She ends her letters with an account of her exhausting return trip back East with her sick baby in the spring of 1835.

(1845)   WILLIAM GRAHAM   659

Graham, William. "Lost Among the Choctaws During a Tour in the Indian Territory, 1845." *Chronicles of Oklahoma* 50 (Summer 1972):226–33.

While traveling to Texas, this Methodist missionary became lost in Choctaw country where he was harassed by several intoxicated Indians. Nevertheless, Graham expresses sympathy toward the Choctaws because of their removal from Mississippi and an appreciation of their natural beauty and "native mode of living." (p. 228) Reprinted from *The Ladies Repository* (1863).

(1846–1848)   AUGUSTUS W. LOOMIS   660

Loomis, Augustus W. "Scenes in the Indian Territory: Kowetah Mission." *Chronicles of Oklahoma* 46 (Spring 1968):64–72.

Sometime between 1846 and 1848, Colonel Loomis, who was in command of Fort Gibson (Oklahoma), made this trip up the Arkansas River to visit the Kowetah Mission. He describes the physical layout, the history of the establishment, the Christian education administered by the missionaries, the teaching of farming to the boys and domestic chores to the girls, the recreational activities, and the use of black interpreters. Loomis praises the work done by the women missionaries. From his *Scenes in the Indian Country* (Philadelphia, 1859).

(1849)   **JAMES HERVEY SIMPSON**   **661**

Dott, Robert H. "Lieutenant Simpson's California Road Across Oklahoma." *Chronicles of Oklahoma* 38 (Summer 1960):154–79.

James H. Simpson was a member of Captain Randolph B. Marcy's troop that marched across Oklahoma from Fort Smith (Arkansas) to Santa Fe in April and June, 1849, to establish a road to California. Dott uses a report and a letter written by Simpson and other documents to describe the Oklahoma landscape.

(1860)   **WILLIAM TALLACK**   **662**

Franks, Kenny A., ed. "The California Overland Express Through Indian Territory and Western Arkansas." *Arkansas Historical Quarterly* 33 (Spring 1974):70–81.

Presents William Tallack's account of the last five days of his 23-day ride that began at San Francisco. The Butterfield Stage took him across the Southwest to the railroad's terminus, 170 miles west of Saint Louis. In this article he describes his travel across Oklahoma, Arkansas, and western Missouri in 1860. Reprinted from an 1865 issue of the London periodical *Leisure Hour*.

(1861)   **WILLIAM W. AVERELL**   **663**

Wright, Muriel H., ed. "Lieutenant Averell's Ride at the Outbreak of the Civil War." *Chronicles of Oklahoma* 39 (Spring 1961):2–14.

Four days after Fort Sumter was fired upon, Lieutenant William W. Averell (First Regiment of Mounted Riflemen, Third U.S. Cavalry) was given the assignment of reaching Lieutenant Colonel William H. Emory with the War Department order to withdraw federal troops from Oklahoma Territory. Because his trip took him through the secessionist hotbeds of Missouri and Arkansas, Averell was forced to assume disguises before reaching Emory near Fort Arbuckle (Oklahoma) on May 2, 1861. Includes Averell's account of his ride and Emory's report of his immediate removal to Fort Leavenworth (Kansas).

(1866)   **THOMAS A. MUZZALL**   **664**

Shirk, George H., ed. "The Lost Colonel." *Chronicles of Oklahoma* 35 (Summer 1957):180–93.

Thomas A. Muzzall kept this diary (June 8-October 29, 1866) of a march with the third U.S. Cavalry from Fort Smith (Arkansas) to Fort Union (New Mexico), then on to Fort Stanton (New Mexico). Among his experiences were hunting a solitary buffalo in a rather timid fashion, capturing a prairie dog for a pet, and witnessing the remains of a family that had been murdered by the Indians. During the march Colonel Paul Harwood, the commanding officer of an accompanying unit, became lost and was feared killed by the Indians. On August 21, however, he walked into camp unharmed. *Note:* An unedited version of Muzzall's diary was published as "Across the Plains," *New Mexico Historical Review* 32 (July 1957):246–58.

(1874)   **CLAIRBORNE ADDISON YOUNG**   **665**

Young, Clairborne Addison. "A Walking Tour in the Indian Territory, 1874." *Chronicles of Oklahoma* 36 (Summer 1958):167–80.

Clairborne Addison Young rode from southeastern Kansas to Tahlequah in northeastern Oklahoma to visit the capital of the Cherokee Nation. Along the way he learned that "sectioniz-

ing," or placing the territory under territorial government, was a controversial idea. (p. 169)
He traveled through the Quapaw Agency, the temporary home of the Modocs who had been
transferred from California after staging a resistance in 1873. During the year the Modocs had
been in Oklahoma, Young says, the government still had not issued food or clothing.

He stopped by the cabin of Mrs. Stand Watie, the wife of the famous Cherokee Indian
who had been a Confederate general. After observing operations at the National School of Teachers for the Cherokee Nations in Tahlequah, he judged the institution to be subject to political
influence. Young believed that the "civilized" clothes the Cherokees wore were simply a veneer.
Originally published in the *Cherokee Advocate* (Tahlequah), July 25, 1874.

(1880s)   **FREDERIC REMINGTON**   666

Franks, Kenny A., ed. "Among the Plains Tribes in Oklahoma with Frederic Remington." *Chronicles of Oklahoma* 52 (Winter 1974/1975):419–38.

The western artist made his observations of Indians at three Indian forts. He saw the
Comanches at Fort Sill, the Apaches at the Indian Agency at Anadarko, and the Arapahos and
Cheyennes near Fort Reno. Remington liked all Indians (except perhaps the Apaches) and thought
it would be a sad day when they were forced to become farmers. He did believe they would be
proficient at raising stock.

Remington criticized the government's Indian policy and felt that it was destined to reduce
the Indians to begging for scraps from western villages. He was somewhat repelled at the method
of distributing beef to the Indians at Fort Reno. When the official called the recipient's name the
Indian came forward and marked the steer with his knife by cutting off an ear or the tail. When
all of the cattle were allotted, they were released and the Indians gave chase. Remington says the
Indians had to shoot the cattle many times because of their lack of skill with the revolver. Written
sometime during the 1880s and published in *The Century* in July and August, 1889.

(1885)   **HILARY CASSAL**   667

Cassal, Hilary. "Missionary Tour in the Chickasaw Nation and Western Indian Territory." *Chronicles of Oklahoma* 34 (Winter 1956–1957):397–416.

The Reverend Father Hilary Cassal, O.S.B., served at the Sacred Heart Monastery (near
Asher), the first permanent Catholic institution in Oklahoma. He relates a tour of the outlying
settlements and the army posts of Fort Sill and Fort Reno. Cassal lists the communities he visited
and comments on his reception by Catholic whites and Indians. Contrary to what he had been
told, he found no hostile Indians. On his trip (October 1–31, 1885), Cassal talked with Quanah
Parker, chief of the Comanches.

(1889)   **CHARLES W. WHIPPLE**   668

Wright, Muriel H., ed. "Captain Charles W. Whipple's Notebook: The Week of the
Run Into Oklahoma in 1889." *Chronicles of Oklahoma* 48 (Summer 1970):146–54.

The editor believes that Whipple's notebook (April 18–29, 1889) is one of the few firsthand
accounts written by a member of the army in command of the opening of Indian Territory.

(1893)   **ANNA S. WOOD**   669

Ragland, H. D., ed. "The Diary of Mrs. Anna S. Wood: Trip to the Opening of the
Cherokee Outlet in 1893." *Chronicles of Oklahoma* 50 (Autumn 1972):307–25.

Mrs. Wood and her son traveled by covered wagon from Denver and across Kansas to Pond
Creek, Oklahoma, where they secured a land claim in present-day Alfalfa County. Diary kept
from September 1 to November 12, 1893.

(1900)   **E. L. JACOBS**   **670**

Jacobs, E. L. "A Magic Journey." *American West* 4 (August 1967):50–51, 75–77.
Boyhood reminiscences of a wagon trip from Oklahoma Territory to Kansas about 1900.

(1901)   **WILLIAM E. BAKER**   **671**

Baker, William E. "Pioneering on the Great Plains." *Chronicles of Oklahoma* 35 (Autumn 1957):288–94.

In August of 1901, while the Baker family traveled from Guthrie, Oklahoma, to their homestead eighty miles to the west, their wagon, containing all the family possessions, became stuck in the quicksand of the raging Canadian River. Although several nearby men saved him, Baker says years later that incidents such as that one never made him long for "the good old days."

(1905–1906)   **ALEXANDER POSEY**   **672**

Posey, Alexander. "Journal of Creek Enrollment Field Party 1905." *Chronicles of Oklahoma* 46 (Spring 1966):2–19.

Posey was clerk in charge and interpreter with the Creek Enrollment Party of the Five Civilized Tribes. It was his job to search for and placate those Creek Indians deserving of a portion of the tribal lands about to be distributed. He was searching for "lost Creeks," those whose names appeared on tribal rolls but who could not be located, and "Snakes," a faction who opposed land distribution. His journal (August 29, 1905-March 30, 1906) tells of his travels, some of the people he met, and the interviews he conducted. It includes his "notes afield" written in 1902 from his farm near Checotah.

South Dakota

(1839–1840)   **JOSEPH N. NICOLLET**   **673**

De Mallie, Raymond J., Jr. "Joseph N. Nicollet's Account of the Sioux and Assiniboin in 1839." *South Dakota History* 5 (Fall 1975):343–59.

Between June, 1839, and early 1840 this French scientist and explorer traveled the elevated plains that separate the Upper Mississippi River from the Missouri River. The author says that Nicollet's still unpublished manuscript provides the best listing of Indian band names, territories, and Indian chiefs.

(1865–1866)   **NOAH M. GLATFELTER**   **674**

Glatfelter, Noah M. "Letters from Dakota Territory, 1865." *Bulletin of the Missouri Historical Society* 18 (January 1962):104–34.

Written between June 28, 1865, and September 5, 1866, from the Crow and Creek Indian Agency where Dr. Glatfelter served as an army surgeon. The letters describe the land, the conditions of travel, and his fellow travelers from Dubuque, Iowa to Fort Randall (South Dakota). Glatfelter tried unsuccessfully to coax his wife to come west by favorably depicting frontier life. He tells her of everyday life and about other wives at the agency. He mentions some Indian customs and tells of activities with which he busied himself. Only occasionally does he mention his medical work.

(1874)   **WILLIAM J. HURLBUT**   **675**

Hurlbut, William J. "Beyond the Border: A Thousand Mile Tramp in Dakota on a Government Survey, 1874." *South Dakota History* 1 (Winter 1970):1–32.

A reminiscence of a survey made between the James and Missouri rivers north of Yankton between July and September, 1874. Among Hurlbut's experiences was a 30-mile march over ground infested with hatching grasshoppers. He also tells of encountering an intensely hot windstorm known as a "simoon." Hurlbut provides detailed suggestions for the clothing and provisions needed on such a trip.

(1884)   WILBURN JEFFRIES   676

Burmester, Ruth Seymour, ed. "Jeffries Letters." *South Dakota History* 6 (Summer 1976):316–23.

Wilburn Jeffries left his wife and family at home while he established his homestead near Ree Heights, South Dakota. In these letters written in 1884, Jeffries tells of his struggle to live on his new land and of his loneliness. He comments on the development of a community and the prospects for schoolteachers. Jeffries gave up the farm and returned home to Baraboo, Wisconsin, in 1885.

(1892)   WALBORG STROM HOLTH   677

Herseth, Lorna B., ed. "A Pioneer's Letter." *South Dakota History* 6 (Summer 1976):306–15.

Walborg Strom Holth, a homesteader recently arrived from Norway, writes about her trip across the Atlantic, her unfavorable impressions of Chicago, and her life in Brown County, South Dakota, in a letter of October 29, 1892.

(1909–1910)   ADA BLAYNEY CLARKE   678

Billington, Monroe, ed. "Pothook Pioneer, a Reminiscence by Ada Blayney Clarke." *Nebraska History* 39 (March 1958):41–56.

Miss Blayney interrupted her stenographic career in Chicago to join family members on a fourteen-month homesteading venture in near Oelrichs, South Dakota, during 1909 and 1910. She recalls their building a home to establish the required occupancy and furnishing it from a mail order catalog. Some problems they encountered were an inadequate water supply, stray cattle that once nearly brought the house down by rubbing themselves against the loose boards, prairie dogs that chewed the tops from potato crops, and rattlesnakes, which necessitated being constantly armed with a garden hoe. Although she liked the prairie, the farm was a losing proposition, and the family members returned to their homes in Minnesota and Chicago in 1910.

8

West

(general, including Lewis and Clark and overland travel)

GENERAL

(1803–1806)   LEWIS AND CLARK EXPEDITION   679

Meriwether Lewis and William Clark were authorized by President Thomas Jefferson to head an expedition to explore up the Missouri River to its source in the Rocky Mountains, then down the nearest westward-flowing stream to the Pacific. The purpose of the expedition was to prepare for expansion of the American fur trade to the tribes throughout the area and to advance geographical knowledge of the continent.

Lewis spent the spring of 1803 making initial preparations for the trek. In the summer he and Clark traveled to a camp on the Wood River (Illinois) opposite the mouth of the Missouri River, where they spent the final months selecting and training their men and gathering information and supplies for the trip. On May 14, 1804, the expedition started up the Missouri River. The group reached North Dakota by October, where they wintered at the Mandan Indian villages.

On April 7, 1805, the journey was resumed and the expedition was at the limits of the Missouri on August 17. Lewis and Clark then crossed the Rockies at the Continental Divide through Lemhi Pass. They turned north along the Lemhi and Salmon rivers, traveled up the Lost Trail Pass and down the Bitterroot valley. At the mouth of Lolo Creek, Montana, the expedition crossed the Bitterroot Range on the Lolo Trail. By September they had crossed the mountains and descended the Clearwater, the Snake, and the Columbia rivers, reaching the Pacific on November 7, 1805.

After wintering on the Columbia River at Fort Clatsop, the expedition began retracing its route homeward on March 23, 1806. In early July the party split at the mouth of Lolo Creek. Lewis and one party headed cross-country to the Falls of the Missouri, then explored the Marias River in northern Montana before descending the Missouri. Clark and the rest of the party returned to the Three Forks of the Missouri, crossed over to the Yellowstone River and went down that river to the Missouri, where the two parties were reunited. The expedition continued homeward, pausing only at the Mandan villages, and reached Saint Louis on September 23, 1806.

Interest in the expedition between 1955 and 1980 is reflected in the quantity of material and in the variety of themes that have inspired popular and scholarly articles. The following items are by no means a complete list of articles dealing with the expedition, but these were selected because they illustrate five areas of interest that are not mutually exclusive:

(1) The importance of the expedition and the expedition in general;
(2) Preparation for the journey;
(3) The members of the party;
(4) The various aspects of the trip; and
(5) Documents relating to the expedition.

The authors of these articles have consulted a variety of source material about the expedition. The standard is the *Original Journals of the Lewis and Clark Expedition, 1804–1806*, edited by Reuben Gold Thwaites (New York, 1904–1905). Other publications cited are *History of the Expedition under the Command of Lewis and Clark*, edited by Elliott Coues (New York, 1893); *The Journals of Lewis and Clark*, by Bernard DeVoto (Boston, 1955); *Letters and Documents of the Lewis and Clark Expedition with Related Documents*, edited by Donald Jackson (Urbana, Illinois, 1962); *The Field Notes of Captain William Clark, 1803–1805*, edited by Ernest S. Osgood (New Haven, 1964); *History of the Expedition under the Command of Captains Lewis and Clark . . .*, prepared for press by Paul Allen, [by Nicholas Biddle] (Philadelphia, 1814); *A Journal of the Voyages and Travels of a Corps of Discovery, under the Command of Captain Lewis and Captain Clarke*, by Patrick Gass (Pittsburgh, 1807); and, *The Journals of Captain Meriwether Lewis and Sergeant John Ordway*, edited by Milo M. Quaife (Madison, 1916).

(1803–1806)   **680**

Abrams, Mrs. Rochonne. "A Song of the Promise of the Land: The Style of the Lewis and Clark Journals." *Bulletin of the Missouri Historical Society* 32 (April 1976):141–57.

    Points out romantic imagery in the *Journals*.

(1803–1806)   **681**

Allen, John L. "An Analysis of the Exploratory Process: The Lewis and Clark Expedition of 1804–1806." *Geographical Review* 62 (January 1972):13–39.

    Although every expedition seeks to establish a goal based on the best available knowledge, it usually becomes necessary to alter the goal in relation to the existing conditions found in exploration. The information available to Lewis and Clark told them that they could locate the long-coveted northwest passage by following the Missouri River to its source, where they would pass over a narrow band of mountains and then descend to the Pacific Ocean. When they found their immediate goal was not attainable, they submitted their geographic findings to the "exploratory process," which the author defines as zones of real and perceived knowledge.

(1803–1806)   **682**

———. "Lewis and Clark on the Upper Missouri: Decision at the Marias." *Montana: The Magazine of Western History* 21 (July 1971):2–17.

    A discussion of the importance of the correct decision to follow the real Missouri River rather than its tributary, the Marias, when confronted by a junction of the two rivers in June of 1805.

(1803–1806)   **683**

Anderson, Irving W. "Probing the Riddle of the Bird Woman." *Montana: The Magazine of Western History* 23 (October 1973):2–17.

Anderson says that two well-meaning women authors, who were both ardent leaders in the suffrage movement, magnified Sacajawea's role and virtues beyond credibility and awarded her seven additional decades beyond her actual life. The two works are Eva Emery Dye, *The Conquest* (Chicago, 1902) and Grace Raymond Hebard, *Sacajawea, Guide of the Lewis and Clark Expedition* (Glendale, California, 1932). Anderson reviews the evidence that proves the Indian woman died at Fort Manuel (South Dakota) in 1812.

(1803–1806) 684

Appleman, Roy E. "The Lost Site of Camp Wood: The Lewis and Clark Winter Camp, 1803–04." *Journal of the West* 7 (April 1968):270–74.

The precise location of the campsite at which the party wintered before proceeding into the Louisiana Territory has been obscured by an absence of latitude and longitude measurements, and by changes in the channels of the Mississippi, Missouri, and Wood rivers. The discovery of William Clark's Field Notes in 1953 helped Appleman place the camp on the west bank of the Mississippi River in Missouri.

(1803–1806) 685

Cappon, Lester J. "Who Is the Author of 'History of the Expedition under the Command of Captains Lewis and Clark' (1814)?." *William and Mary Quarterly. Third Series* 19 (April 1962):257–68.

Criticizes the recent publication of the *History* . . . under the new title *The Lewis and Clark Expedition* by Meriwether Lewis (Philadelphia, 1961). Cappon says the *History* is known by historians and bibliographers as "Biddle's *History*." Therefore, Nicholas Biddle's authorship should be acknowledged because the writing was primarily done by him from notes provided by Lewis. In Cappon's bibliographic history of the work he includes the contribution of Paul Allen to Biddle's 1814 edition, the edition by Elliott Coues in 1893, and the publication of the *Original Journals* . . . by Reuben Gold Thwaites in 1904–05.

(1803–1806) 686

Chuinard, E. G. "The Actual Role of the Bird Woman." *Montana: The Magazine of Western History* 26 (July 1976):18–29.

Reviews the controversy over Sacajawea's value to the Lewis and Clark Expedition. Concludes that her function as a contact agent with the Shoshone was far more important to the captains than her help as a guide or interpreter.

(1803–1806) 687

———. "Thomas Jefferson and the Corps of Discovery: Could He Have Done More?" *American West* 12 (November 1975):4–13.

Exonerates Jefferson of blame by those who believed he could have done more to ensure the success of the Lewis and Clark Expedition and to preserve its findings for posterity. The criticisms discussed are that Jefferson should have sent a medical doctor and a naturalist along to treat the men and to make adequate scientific observations; that Jefferson should have assured William Clark's captaincy; that Jefferson should have sent a ship to the Columbia River to bring the expedition home; that Jefferson should have taken greater precautions to preserve the items collected; and that Jefferson should not have allowed the journals to remain in private hands.

(1803–1806) 688

Cutright, Paul Russell. "Jefferson's Instructions to Lewis and Clark." *Bulletin of the Missouri Historical Society* 22 (April 1966):302–20.

Examines the scope of the instructions for the expedition, which the two explorers followed to the letter. Cutright thinks this document provides insight into Thomas Jefferson's thoughts about the expedition.

(1803–1806)   689

————. "The Journal of Private Joseph Whitehouse, A Soldier with Lewis and Clark." *Bulletin of the Missouri Historical Society* 28 (April 1972):143–61.

After reviewing the circumstances surrounding the discovery of a previously unknown paraphrased version of Whitehouse's journal in 1966, Cutright summarizes the importance of the document and compares it with existing knowledge of the expedition. Although Cutright admits that it presents little new information, he believes it contains "many items of interest and a few of intrinsic worth."

(1803–1806)   690

————. "Lewis and Clark and Cottonwood." *Bulletin of the Missouri Historical Society* 22 (October 1965):35–44.

Focuses on the many uses the expedition found for the cottonwood tree.

(1803–1806)   691

————. "Lewis and Clark Begin a Journey." *Bulletin of the Missouri Historical Society* 24 (October 1967):20–25.

Examines the early days of the expedition, then between the Mississippi and the Kansas rivers, when the explorers established practices they were to continue throughout the trek. They regarded Jefferson's instructions as articles of faith. Cutright examines the instructions and the procedures established with regard to geography, meteorology, mineralogy, botany, zoology, and ethnology.

(1803–1806)   692

————. "Lewis and Clark Indian Peace Medals." *Bulletin of the Missouri Historical Society* 24 (January 1968):160–67

Discusses the presentation of medals to prominent chiefs, the continuation of a practice begun in colonial times. The Indians accepted the medals as tokens of peace and friendship and regarded them highly. At least eighty-six medals were taken on the expedition and six survive today.

(1803–1806)   693

————. "Lewis on the Marias, 1806." *Montana: The Magazine of Western History* 18 (July 1968):30–43.

Describes Meriwether Lewis's adventures on the Marias River after the party had divided July 3, 1806, on the eastward journey at the mouth of Travellers' Rest Creek near present-day Missoula, Montana.

(1803–1806)   694

————. "Meriwether Lewis: Botanist." *Oregon Historical Quarterly* 69 (June 1968):148–70.

Because Lewis kept notes of the flora seen across the continent, he expanded knowledge of the geographical range of many plants heretofore known only in the East. Cutright praises

Lewis's ability to describe flora utilizing botanical terminology. Of the specimens Lewis collected, seventy or more were new to the science. Cutright traces the history of the collection and discusses the number and condition of those that presently exist.

(1803–1806) 695

———. "Meriwether Lewis Prepares for a Trip West." *Bulletin of the Missouri Historical Society* 23 (October 1966):3–20.

Discusses the way Lewis spent his time in Philadelphia early in 1803. In preparation for the expedition, he assembled necessary supplies and equipment and consulted with five members of the American Philosophical Society. Jefferson had previously written letters to the five asking them to lend their expertise.

(1803–1806) 696

———. "Meriwether Lewis: Zoologist." *Oregon Historical Quarterly* 69 (June 1968):5–28.

Although Lewis is not usually thought of as a zoologist or botanist, Cutright believes he possessed the qualities to make him a patient and accurate observer of faunal information. *The Original Journals* contain references to some 250 species. Twenty-six descriptions run more than five hundred words each with the grizzly bear, the buffalo, and the beaver drawing the most attention. Lewis discovered more than a hundred animals that were unknown at the time and returned many specimens to the East. Jefferson has been criticized for not sending a trained zoologist on the expedition, but Cutright maintains faith in Jefferson's decision to entrust this work to Lewis. The author does think, however, that the President should have had a ship present at the Columbia River to receive the specimens and ensure that more would be returned in good condition.

(1803–1806) 697

———. "The Odyssey of the Magpie and the Prairie Dog." *Bulletin of the Missouri Historical Society* 23 (April 1967):215–28.

President Jefferson had instructed Lewis and Clark to pay close attention to the animals of the country they crossed. On April 7, 1805, Meriwether Lewis attempted to ship six live amimals back to Washington, D.C., by way of New Orleans, along with a collection of bones and skins. When the cargo reached Jefferson in August, a prairie dog and a magpie remained alive.

(1803–1806) 698

DeVoto, Bernard. "An Inference Regarding the Expedition of Lewis and Clark." *Proceedings of the American Philosophical Society* 99 (August 1955):185–94.

After speculating on the importance of recently discovered but yet unevaluated documents written by William Clark, DeVoto laments how little historians have read, understood, or probed the Lewis and Clark Expedition. He believes the expedition to be especially valuable to students of westward expansion. Often the importance of the trek has been thought of as crossing of Louisiana Territory. For DeVoto, the importance of the expedition lies in Thomas Jefferson's desire not only to enhance the United States' claim to Oregon but to promote a more tenable claim to lands above the 49th parallel. For this grand design, DeVoto believes, Jefferson should be recognized as our first geopolitician.

(1803–1806) 699

Ewers, John C. "Plains Indian Reactions to the Lewis and Clark Expedition." *Montana: The Magazine of Western History* 16 (January 1966):2–12.

The Lewis and Clark Expedition initiated official government relations with eleven of the fourteen tribes that inhabited the Upper Missouri River region. The author believes that diplomacy was the least successful aspect of the expedition, especially in the case of the Blackfeet and Arikara, whose later hostility toward fur traders was the direct result of unpleasant incidents with the Lewis and Clark Expedition.

(1803–1806)   700

Heilbron, Bertha L., Bahmer, Robert H., and Angle, Paul M. "The Case of the Clark Papers." *Minnesota History* 36 (June 1959):216–29.

Discusses the discovery of the William Clark papers in a Saint Paul attic in 1953 by a curator of the Minnesota Historical Society. After a lengthy court case the papers were awarded to the heirs, the Hammond family, with the stipulation that they be made available to researchers. But were they rightfully public documents? Robert Bahmer argues "The Case for Government Ownership," (pp. 219–27) and Paul Angle argues "The Case for Private Ownership." (pp. 227–29)

(1803–1806)   701

Jackson, Donald. "Lewis and Clark Among the Oto." *Nebraska History* 41 (September 1960):237–48.

One important assignment of the expedition was to win the allegiance of the western tribes. Jackson summarizes how their diplomacy fared with the Otoe, the first tribe they encountered about ten weeks into their journey. The meetings were held at what is presently known as Council Bluffs, Nebraska, in the summer of 1804.

(1803–1806)   702

———. "A New Lewis and Clark Map." *Bulletin of the Missouri Historical Society* 17 (October 1960):117–32.

Announces the recent identification of the first cartographic product of the Lewis and Clark Expedition, a map drawn in the spring of 1804 while the party was still in preparation for the trip. This map presents a portion of the Mississippi River, the lower Missouri River, the Osage River, and a crude portrayal of waterways to the Northwest. A copy of the map is included as Part II of the January, 1961, issue.

(1803–1806)   703

———. "On Reading Lewis and Clark." *Montana: The Magazine of Western History* 18 (July 1968):2–7.

A brief summary that focuses on the many aspects of publication on the Lewis and Clark theme.

(1803–1806)   704

———. "The Race to Publish Lewis and Clark." *Pennsylvania Magazine of History and Biography* 85 (April 1961):163–77.

When the Lewis and Clark Expedition was completed in 1806, both the public and many publishers were anxious to obtain details of the journey. Jackson relates how the two explorers attempted to squelch other accounts until Lewis could undertake an accurate, detailed narrative. Jackson suggests that Lewis's inability to publish the journals may have added to his sense of failure and perhaps to his death (suicide?) in 1809. Although Biddle's brief version was published in 1814, the complete journals, through which Thomas Jefferson and the two explorers had hoped to reveal the full potential of the Louisiana Territory, were not published until 1904 by Reuben Gold Thwaites.

(1803–1806) **705**

———. "Some Advice for the Next Editor of Lewis and Clark." *Bulletin of the Missouri Historical Society* 24 (October 1967):52–62.

Reviews the bibliographic history of documents relating to the expedition and calls for a new edition that would employ standards for editorial scholarship presently in acceptance. The problems that face the "next editor" are the incompleteness of the record, the duplication of information, and the question of how the journals were produced.

(1803–1806) **706**

———. "Some Books Carried by Lewis and Clark." *Bulletin of the Missouri Historical Society* 16 (October 1959):3–13.

Jackson stresses that books were vital to Lewis and Clark, even though there are few specific references in their accounts. From these few direct citations and from his own conjectures, the author has pieced together a list of materials that probably were helpful. He groups them under the categories of natural history, geography, medicine, and the practical arts.

(1803–1806) **707**

Larsell, O. "Medical Aspects of the Lewis and Clark Expedition." *Oregon Historical Quarterly* 56 (September 1955):211–25.

Larsell focuses on the medical problems encountered during the journey. They included gastrointestinal disorders, rheumatism, boils, and venereal diseases contracted from the Mandan, Shoshone, Chinook, and Clatsop squaws. Meriwether Lewis doctored these ailments with hot packs, barks, opium, mercury, and laudanum, but some problems simply went away when better food became available. Larsell also discusses ailments suffered by the Indians that those in the expedition observed and treated.

(1803–1806) **708**

Nichols, William. "Lewis and Clark Probe the Heart of Darkness." *American Scholar* 49 (Winter 1979/1980):94–101.

Nichols discusses the change in the explorers' relations with the Indians encountered on the journey west and on the return trip. On the way west the explorers were able to transcend contemporary ethnocentric views about the Indians and approach the tribes with a desire to understand. For some reason, the tone of Lewis's writings during the long, wet winter at Fort Clatsop on the Pacific and the return trip changed from one of patient understanding of Indian peculiarities to a reliance on stereotype. Simple thievery became villainy. "Good Indians" and "bad Indians" were terms of reference. Nichols believes this attitude was partly responsible for the expedition's confrontation with the Blackfeet.

Why the change in attitude? Nichols believes it was caused by the expedition's extended dealings with the Clatsop and Chinook during the winter of 1805–06. He explains that when the Corps of Discovery reached the Pacific Coast, the men were ragged, nearly starved, and in need of help. Unfortunately, they found Indians who were willing to trade only at prices the explorers could not afford. Moreover, the Indians appeared physically ugly and they stole liberally. At this point Lewis began to stress the value of suspicion in dealing with Indians and the ever-present danger of treachery. Nichols points out that the change in mood did not come about because of the whites' disgust with any single "bad" quality, for a great deal of sexual intercourse between the two cultures occurred.

In addition, the explorers admired some aspects of the coastal Indians' civilization. What

Nichols thinks the explorers were disturbed by was their inability to understand these Indians; they were deemed inscrutable. To the explorers they were subhuman and beneath contempt, but at the same time they were also highly capable and admirable. Nichols says their inability to understand the Indian culture caused Lewis and Clark to view the Indians through "irrationally conceived, rigid stereotypes." (p. 100) Nichols comments on the occurrence of this phenomena in other anthropologists studying primitive societies. He also discusses similarities between Lewis's and Clark's scientific approach as men of the Enlightenment and the scientific techniques of today.

(1803–1806)   **709**

Osgood, Ernest S. "Clark on the Yellowstone 1806." *Montana: The Magazine of Western History* 18 (July 1968):8–29.

Describes Clark's adventures in the Yellowstone Valley on the return journey after the expedition divided on July 3, 1806, at the mouth of Travellers' Rest Creek near present-day Missoula, Montana.

(1803–1806)   **710**

———. "Our Dog Scannon: Partner in Discovery." *Montana: The Magazine of Western History* 26 (July 1976):8–17.

Reviews the contribution of a Newfoundland dog named Scannon, who was considered an important member of the party. Although Scannon was not mentioned after July, 1806, Osgood says that we cannot conclude that this means the dog died on the journey.

(1803–1806)   **711**

Overland, Helen Howard. "Fabled Friendship—Lewis and Clark." *Montana: The Magazine of Western History* 5 (July 1955):2–18.

Biographical sketch assessing the two explorers' association during and after the expedition.

(1803–1806)   **712**

Petersen, William J. "The Lewis and Clark Expedition." *Palimpsest* 45 (March 1964):97–144.

This issue is devoted to the expedition. "Sergeant Floyd's Journal" (pp. 130–44) presents the sections Charles Floyd wrote about the southwestern Iowa portion of the trip in July and August, 1804. He died on August 20 and was buried near Sioux City, Iowa.

(1803–1806)   **713**

Rees, John E. "The Shoshoni Contribution to Lewis and Clark." *Idaho Yesterdays* 2 (Summer 1958):3–13.

Stresses Sacajawea's importance in helping the expedition to achieve friendship with the Shoshone in Idaho. Rees believes the Indian woman's role as a guide has been vastly exaggerated. He does, however, believe her role as a go-between, as well as her very presence with her child, probably prevented the party from being destroyed by any one of several savage tribes.

(1803–1806)   **714**

Russell, Carl P. "The Guns of the Lewis and Clark Expedition." *North Dakota History* 27 (Winter 1960):25–34.

Provides some details about the guns, the ammunition, and the use of arms against the wildlife and the Indians.

(1803–1806) **715**

Schroer, Blanche. "Boat-pusher or Bird Woman? Sacagawea or Sacajawea?" *Annals of Wyoming* 52 (Spring 1980):46–54.

Takes to task two authors who have asserted that the lone female member of the Lewis and Clark Expedition lived long past December 20, 1812, and is buried in Wind River, Wyoming, rather than Fort Manuel (South Dakota). Schroer says that there are simply no substantiated historical facts to support Grace Raymond Hebard's *Sacajawea, Guide of the Lewis and Clark Expedition* (Glendale, California, 1932). Schroer is not sure whether Anna Lee Waldo's *Sacajawea* (New York, 1979) is poor history or a historical novel. Schroer's criticism is not directed at the contribution the Indian woman made to the expedition, although she points out in several places that it was not precisely as myth would have it to be.

(1803–1806) **716**

Smith, James, S., and Smith, Kathryn. "Sedulous Sergeant, Patrick Gass." *Montana: The Magazine of Western History* 5 (July 1955):20–27.

Biographical sketch of the frontiersman who accompanied Lewis and Clark and published the first account of the expedition in 1807.

(1803–1806) **717**

Steffen, Jerome O. "William Clark: A Reappraisal." *Montana: The Magazine of Western History* 25 (Spring 1975):52–61.

Challenges the idea that William Clark was the less intelligent of the two leaders of the Lewis and Clark Expedition. In examining his early interests and his life following the journey, Steffen finds that Clark had deep scientific interests. He postulates that Clark's ungrammatical writing style may have led Thwaites and DeVoto to project this image.

(1830–1900) **THE WEST AND HEALTHFULNESS** **718**

Baur, John E. "The Health Seeker in the Westward Movement, 1830–1900." *Mississippi Valley Historical Review* 46 (June 1959):91–110.

Contends that although the search for renewed health was a significant factor in populating the West, its importance has been generally neglected by historians. Among the reasons it has been ignored are that health seekers did not form specific groups and that the search for better health was often not the only reason for migrating. Nevertheless, after examining the writings of travelers, Baur concludes that improved health was prominent in their thoughts. He also reviews contemporary medical opinions that often exaggerated the beneficial effects of the western climate on health. Putting aside the question of whether the climate of the West was actually healthy for some, Baur asserts that the West certainly benefited from the health seekers' talents, manpower, and money.

(1832–1869) **CHOLERA ON THE OVERLAND TRAILS** **719**

Powers, Ramon, and Younger, Gene. "Cholera on the Overland Trails, 1832–1869." *Kansas Quarterly* 5 (Spring 1973):32–49.

Travelers' diaries and journals are a primary source for information about where cholera spread and its toll on emigrants' lives and emotional reserves. The disease struck quickly. It was transmitted by human contact, thrived in unsanitary conditions along the crowded trails, and there was no effective remedy. Death from cholera was a significant hazard of the overland trails. Powers suggests that perhaps of even greater importance was that cholera decimated the prairie-plains Indians, leaving them in a weakened position for their battle to retain possession of their western lands.

(1834–1858)   INDIANS ON THE OVERLAND TRAILS   720

Munkres, Robert L. "The Plains Indian Threat Before 1860." *Annals of Wyoming* 40 (October 1968):193–221.

Nearly every fictionalized overland wagon train story includes a battle with Indians. Was this actually the case? After examining sixty-six diaries written by those who traveled the Oregon-California Trail as far as Fort Bridger (Wyoming) between 1834 and 1858, the author determines that few emigrants experienced trouble with the Indians. Much more frequent than attacks were such harassments as stealing cattle and extracting presents as toll to cross the Indians' territory. Some attacks came about when individuals wandered from their wagons alone or in small parties, but Indians did not normally confront large groups. Nevertheless, since those who were passing through Indian lands did not know that attacks were few, but had frequently heard rumors of Indian depredations, the emigrants' fear was great.

(1838–1860)   WOMEN ON THE OVERLAND TRAILS   721

————. "Wives, Mothers, Daughters: Women's Life on the Road West." *Annals of Wyoming* 42 (October 1970):191–224.

Uses diaries written mostly by women between 1838 and 1860 to document their experiences during overland travel. They emphasize the illnesses and deaths brought about by the tremendous drain on physical reserves and trail accidents; the continuation of the usual domestic arts, along with the need to adapt to new foods and dirty living conditions; marital strife; and the constant fear of Indian attack.

(1840–1860)   EASTWARD ON THE OVERLAND TRAILS   722

Unruh, John D., Jr. "Against the Grain: West to East on the Overland Trail." *Kansas Quarterly* 5 (Spring 1973):172–84.

Uses travel accounts to describe the "go-backs," those who returned home because of discouragement, disease, or loss of members of their company, or who were going home to bring their families back to the West. The eastbound traffic had some distinctive features: there were fewer women and children, the parties were smaller, they more often traveled by pack mules and horses than in covered wagons, and they were susceptible to robberies because highwaymen assumed they had struck gold. Though their experience provided information to those westward bound, the "go-backs" also spread rumors and misinformation, perhaps to justify their returning.

(1840–1860)   WOMEN ON THE OVERLAND TRAILS   723

Schlissel, Lillian. "Women's Diaries on the Western Frontier." *American Studies* 18 (Spring 1977):87–100.

Asserts that women pioneers resented overland migration because they thought the burdens they were forced to assume were a part of a masculine enterprise. Anxieties arose as women faced their new roles, but they still struggled to maintain the societal norms to which they were accustomed. The author suggests that the traditional study of the West, which emphasizes how the region was conquered, should be changed to examine the toll the experience took on the pioneers in such human terms as divorce, marriage, illegitimacy, sex roles, and class identification. The diaries of women who traveled the overland trails between 1840 and 1860 would provide an excellent source for such a study.

(1841–1847)   OVERLAND TRAIL ADVICE   724

Andrews, Thomas F. "'Ho! For Oregon and California!': An Annotated Bibliography of Published Advice to the Emigrant, 1841–47." *Princeton University Library Chronicles* 33 (Autumn 1971):41–64.

In his introduction to this 29-item bibliography, Andrews says published advice was written by actual emigrants for prospective emigrants to provide information about the routes and the outfitting necessary for the trip. The accounts of 1846 and 1847 ceased to contain detailed trail routes because the paths were more clearly marked by that time. This advice appeared as personal diaries, letters printed in newspapers, and published guidebooks. Andrews believes the accounts for the years 1841 to 1847 to be similar in that they were aimed primarily at emigrants to Oregon and they generally agreed on the requirements for making the trip.

He says the accounts were weak in providing sufficient advice on medical needs, and they did not keep abreast of the trails and cutoffs that were opening up. Andrews calls for students of American studies to utilize these guidebooks, together with overland diaries, to analyze the "emigrant mind" or the "pioneer impulse" on the far western frontier. His critically annotated bibliography is a contribution toward that goal.

(1842–1867) FAMILIES ON THE OVERLAND TRAILS 725

Faragher, John Mack. "Families on the Overland Trail." *Pacific Historian* 23 (Spring 1979):4–23.

Faragher relates how the routines of farm life and the sexual division of labor were smoothly translated into the work required by the westward migration. The decision to sell the family property and move was made by the men. The preparation for the trip—making clothes, wagon covers, and tents, and storing food—was taken care of by the women. What possessions should be taken was a matter of give and take between spouses. On the trail the men handled the jobs related to movement: driving the wagon, searching for grass and water, and crossing rivers. Women's work was geared to the timetable for travel and the needs of the family. Women were up before dawn and still up after dusk preparing meals, collecting fuel and water, and washing clothes.

Though the men almost always walked, guarding the train or tending the livestock, it appears women walked to lighten the load, but they also rode in the wagons when they tired of walking, or to mend clothes or care for babies and small children. For the men, recreation and relaxation came from hunting or perhaps playing cards in the evening. Women seldom used the evenings for anything but work. This division of labor on the overland trails, which was agreed upon by the men and women, sometimes found women performing men's work in emergencies, but seldom found men doing women's jobs. A chapter from *Women and Men on the Overland Trail* (New Haven, 1979).

(1842–1867) 726

———, and Stansell, Christine. "Women and Their Families on the Overland Trail to California and Oregon, 1842–1867." *FS: Feminist Studies* 2 (no. 2–3, 1975):150–66.

Migration on the overland trail was overwhelmingly a family undertaking. The decision to go and the work required on the trail fell into sex roles that reflected mid-nineteenth-century American culture. Men decided the move was necessary for economic reasons. Women followed because homemaking fell into their sphere of accepted behavior. Though the physical and emotional strains of the trip were undeniably taxing for both sexes, it was especially hard on the women, who were sacrificing the security and comfort of their homes in addition to assuming new duties. They cared for the children, fixed meals, and sewed as usual, but some traditionally male jobs were forced on women when the need for additional physical labor arose. The men, however, seldom assumed any "female tasks."

On the trail women tried to reconstruct their homelife, but the sheer amount of work and the need to discard personal items or household goods that were reminders of their former lives worked against them. This breakdown in the traditional division of labor should have provided women with expanded opportunities for social advancement. The authors believe it did not because women viewed themselves simply as draftees in an essentially male enterprise, and they saw it as a dissolution of their own autonomous sphere. The authors conclude that the "true cult of womanhood," which provided women with a sense of self-worth, female companionship, and independence from male dominance, had penetrated women's ideals far beyond New England, where it flourished at mid-century.

(1843–1853)   CHILDREN ON THE OVERLAND TRAILS   727

Moynihan, Ruth Barnes. "Children and Young People on the Overland Trail." *Western Historical Quarterly* 6 (July 1975):279–94.

Recreates everyday life on the overland trail from the diaries of eight young persons who traveled between 1843 and 1853. Toddlers and children could not be easily controlled on the trip, and Moynihan conjectures that they probably found the journey only a little more tiring than a day of play at home. If the children acted much the way they had at home, however, the consequences could be more serious. Wandering away meant they could easily become lost. Falling down in front of a moving wagon could result in a fatal accident.

Like adults, children wrote of the hardships of the journey—suffering, exhaustion, starvation, illness, and death—but their diaries have little about these dismal occurrences. Instead, they express excitement and curiosity. The children explored and played among the natural wonders along the trail. Their apprehension of Indians was usually overcome by their fascination. Even gathering buffalo chips for firewood seemed less odious to the young than to the women. Because accounts by young people about incidents of travel on the overland trail are written from a different perspective, "we may gain insights to the emigrant experience in general and into the psychology of children and families under stress." (p. 294)

(1846)   LUCY ANN HENDERSON   728

Strong, Roland Thomas, ed. "Young Adventure by Lucy Ann Henderson." *Nevada Historical Society Quarterly* 16 (Summer 1973):66–99.

In 1846 the family of 11-year-old Lucy Henderson was one of many that crossed the plains to Oregon, a journey of 2,200 miles and seven months. They traveled from Liberty and Saint Joseph, Missouri, to Fort Laramie (Wyoming) and Fort Hall (Idaho) by way of Sublette's Cutoff. They then left the Oregon Trail and traveled through Nevada across the northeast corner of California along the Applegate Cutoff to Yamhill, Oregon. The editor fills in substantial gaps in Henderson's reminiscences, recorded seventy-seven years after the trip, with other accounts to recreate what the trip must have been like.

(1848–1850)   JOHN A. HUNTER   729

Francis, David W., ed. "The Letters of a Missourian in the Gold Rush 1848–1850." *Bulletin of the Missouri Historical Society* 29 (October 1972):38–45.

These three letters are more important for tracing the motivation of some who sought to strike it rich than for what they tell us about overland travel. On December 31, 1848, John A. Hunter wrote from his farm in Washington County about the difficulties he was experiencing as a farmer. He says he would like to go back to selling goods, but he has doubts about his success in establishing himself in another town. In his next letter, from Fort Laramie (Wyoming) on June 18, 1849, he describes his wagon train and the impact of cholera on his company. In his last letter, February 21, 1850, he has not struck it rich and hopes to start a hauling business. During the winter of 1851, John A. Hunter died of cholera in California.

(1849)   JOSEPH WARING BERRIEN   730

Hinckley, Ted, and Hinckley, Carol. eds. "Overland from Saint Louis to the California Gold Field in 1849: The Diary of Joseph Waring Berrien." *Indiana Magazine of History* 56 (December 1960):273–352.

Although the editors admit that Berrien traveled the conventional trails to California and undoubtedly had experiences common to thousands of others, they believe his lucid descriptions make his account an outstanding record of overland travel. Shortly after leaving Saint Louis, Berrien's writing reflects his sense of urgency about getting to the goldfields as soon as possible. Even though his train let one group go ahead, he says they should not let many more pass. Before reaching Ash Hollow, the train was joined by more wagons, and at a Sioux village the wagon-train leader was able to exchange some worn-out horses for mules. The trail past Courthouse Rock and Chimney Rock and all the way to Fort Laramie (Wyoming) was good, as was the crossing of the Mormon Ferry on the Platte River. Berrien was aware that this was the easy part of the trip.

The train passed Independence Rock, Devil's Gate, and the South Pass, and then descended into Green River Valley, past Soda Springs, Steamboat Springs, and Fort Hall (Idaho) before the travel took its toll. Berrien's wagon broke and a mule died. When the wagon master refused to sell or loan Berrien replacements, he was deserted. Berrien then was able to procure another mule and joined an oxen train. The remainder of the trip south of the Great Salt Lake and across the desert of Utah and Nevada was an extremely difficult crossing. Berrien remarked at one point that not all the gold in California would tempt him to make the trip again. His diary ends in Sacramento, a city in name only; in reality, it was "a collection of tents or canvass screens." (p. 351) Diary kept between March 31 and August 15, 1849.

(1849) THOMAS EVERSHED 731

Barnes, Joseph W., ed. "The Gold Rush Journal of Thomas Evershed: Engineer, Artist, and Rochesterian." *Rochester History* 39 (January/April 1977):1–44.

An informative and interesting account of overland travel. Evershed's train started at Independence, Missouri, traveled along the Platte River Trail to Salt Lake City, north along the east side of the Great Salt Lake, then west to the Humboldt River, and southwest across Nevada to Sacramento. Evershed includes many aspects of the trek that one looks for in such an account—descriptions of the conditions of the trail and the land, comments about other emigrants, details of day-to-day living, the disposal and transfer of possessions to adapt to changing needs of travel—as well as revealing his own feelings about the experience. Contains lengthy descriptions of Salt Lake City and the California goldfields, and includes four watercolors. Journal kept May 21 to August 16, 1849.

(1849) EDWIN HILLYER 732

Holzhueter, John O., ed. "From Waupun to Sacramento in 1849: The Gold Rush Journal of Edwin Hillyer." *Wisconsin Magazine of History* 49 (Spring 1966):210–44.

After young Edwin Hillyer accompanied his wife from Wisconsin to her family in Ohio (a tiring trip in itself), he went to Council Bluffs, Iowa, to join a company of Wisconsin forty-niners. The most interesting aspect of this diary is that it documents the transition from the exhilaration felt at the beginning of the trip to the relief experienced at being alive at the end of it, a range of emotions experienced by many other emigrants. Hillyer was chosen colonel of the company. He realized the enormity of the task of leading sixty-three men who were all used to being their own boss. He describes them as "young and energetic and after gold." (p. 220) At first, Hillyer was obviously enjoying the adventure of tramping across the prairie. Perhaps he felt a little guilty at enjoying himself so much because once, after writing about his family, he confided to his journal, "I am not doing this for fun or from selfishness, but for the hope that I can secure more gold with which to give them more than the comforts of life." (p. 222)

No more than two weeks after departure, the sense of excitement leaves his writings. A companion was killed by the Indians. Near Ash Hollow he resigned his command and soon after the train began breaking up. Hillyer reports the great number of wagons on the trail. At the Mormon Crossing of the Platte River in Wyoming, he says ninety wagons were ahead of his.

Still, considering the large number of people on the trail he saw little sickness. Near Fort Bridger (Wyoming) he left the train and rode to Salt Lake City by mule. Hillyer says he slept most of the time he was there (three or four days), but simply could not get rested.

He rejoined his group when it arrived at the Mormon city and they all traded their cattle for pack horses. They returned to the trail north along the east side of the Great Salt Lake, then northwest and met the California Trail that came down from Fort Hall (Idaho). As they followed the Humboldt River across Nevada, Hillyer's horse gave out and he had to share one with a friend. Crossing the Forty-mile Desert by the Truckee River Route, he described the other emigrants: "Their faces all wear a woe begone look, and seem as though all hope had fled." (p. 241)

In California, Hillyer prospected only several days. As the journal ends, he is unemployed. The editor adds that Hillyer opened a packet-boat business between Sacramento and San Francisco and earned enough to return home in 1856. Journal kept between March and August 26, 1849.

(1849)   THADDEUS LEVI LOOMIS   733

Anderson, Niles, ed. "Grandfather Was a Forty-Niner." *Western Pennsylvania Historical Magazine* 50 (January 1967):33–50.

Letters written between May 20 and October 21, 1849, in which Thaddeus Levi Loomis tells of crossing the plains from Saint Joseph, Missouri, to Sacramento. He also relates conditions in California. Loomis's small train followed the usual emigrant route along the Platte River Trail into Wyoming. At the South Pass they cut over to Fort Hall (Idaho), then went southwest through Nevada following the Humboldt River to the Carson Sink, along the Carson River into the Sierra Nevadas, and through the Sacramento valley.

The young man tried to allay his family's fears about his safety and health. Early in this trip, after describing the Pawnees as the most bold and skillful thieves and the Sioux as being unmatched as warriors, he writes that he was sure he would hide in case of a fight. He assures his family, however, that his company could fight off five hundred Indians if necessary. Several times he tells his parents how healthy the journey had made him.

Loomis's writings contain a sense of adventure. He relates how, after the long march across Nevada, the mules got the scent of water and stampeded, pulling the wagons over an embankment twelve feet high. Then, after thirty-six hours without food, they quite fortuitously ran into another emigrant train that fed them.

His characterization of the Sacramento area is typical: fertile soil, a lawless, multiracial population, evidence of riches, and an expensive place to live. Upon reflection he advises against coming to California, but says if emigrants do come, they should travel by water because of the comfort and security. He estimates that of the eight thousand wagons that left the States that year, only a hundred had arrived, and only another twelve hundred would ultimately reach California. In his last letter, Loomis says California is unfit for civilized beings and he is trying to get up a company to go to the Mexican-American border to prospect the Gila River.

(1849)   ISAAC OWEN   734

Purdy, John R., Jr. "Isaac Owen—Overland to California." *Methodist History* 11 (July 1973):46–54.

Owen traveled overland to California from Indiana to assume his appointment to the California Mission of the Methodist Episcopal Church. The details of the journey (February 20-October 6, 1849) are pieced together from letters Owen wrote to the *Western Christian Advocate* and the diary of Sallie Hester.

(1849)   BERNARD J. REID   735

Van Trump, James D., and Reid, Alfred D., Jr., eds. "A California Gold Rush Letter From Bernard J. Reid." *Western Pennsylvania Historical Magazine* 44 (September 1961):217–35.

Reid's letter is a mixture of complaints about the trip across the plains and a description of life in California. He signed on as a passenger with a wagon train whose business was to transport forty-niners to California. Turner, Allen, and Company (Saint Louis) had advertised a comfortable 60- to 80-day trip from Independence, Missouri, to San Francisco. Instead, it became 165 days of misery, part of which Reid blamed on Turner's poor provisioning that led to scurvy and dysentery. They traveled the Platte River Trail west to Soda Springs, Idaho, then south on the Hudspeth's Cutoff through Idaho, into Nevada. After the train reached the Humboldt Sink, Reid left the train and traveled to Weber's Creek near Placerville, California, where he dug gold for a short time.

His sharpest impressions of the Sacramento goldfields were that everything, from mining gear to food, was expensive; lynch law was effective, and gaming tables and drinking were to be found everywhere. He thought it would take some time for the region to acquire the temper of a settled society. When the wagon train finally reached Sacramento, Reid reclaimed his passage money from Turner. In his last letter Reid offers a description of San Francisco, and sends his sister a little gold dust and a cactus flower as mementos of his trip. Written between October 24 and 31, 1849.

(1849)   **THOMAS S. WYLLY**   **736**

Wylly, Thomas S., III, ed. "'Westward Ho—In '49': Memoirs of Captain Thomas S. Wylly." (Part I) *Pacific Historian* 22 (Spring 1978):71–96.

————. (Part II) *Pacific Historian* 22 (Summer 1978):120–44.

————. (Part III) *Pacific Historian* 22 (Fall 1978):274–97.

————. (Part IV) *Pacific Historian* 22 (Winter 1978):327–52.

Wylly attributes his desire to leave his Georgia home more to wanderlust—a result of reading George W. Kendall's narrative of the Texans' Santa Fe Expedition—than to the lure of gold. He relates some dangers of the trail: a man was carried off by the swift current of a river, and a pregnant woman was jostled from her wagon seat and run over by the front wheel, but gave birth shortly after. Upon reaching Salt Lake City, his party found it was too late in the season to try one of the usual trails to California, so they decided on a route west of Salt Lake City and south along the Old Spanish Trail.

After arriving in Los Angeles, which he describes as an unattractive Spanish town with a sluggish stream running through it, his party moved on to the goldfields. He relates his brief experiences around Sacramento more as an adventure than a commercial enterprise. Any nuggets he may have gathered, he says, were left with the people of Central America he met on his trip home (perhaps the señoritas to whose alluring charms he refers), who made it their business to be hospitable to Americans with gold.

(1850)   **ADAM MERCER BROWN**   **737**

Kiefer, David M., ed. "Over Barren Plains and Rock-Bound Mountains." *Montana: The Magazine of Western History* 22 (October 1972):16–29.

Excerpts from the diary of Adam Mercer Brown, who traveled to the goldfields of California with a group of fellow Pennsylvanians. The train, which left Saint Louis, Missouri, on April 25, 1850, consisted of six wagons, twenty-six men, and fifty-five head of cattle. As he passed through Missouri en route to St. Joseph, he commented on how gold fever had nearly depopulated some Missouri towns. Brown's appraisal of the Sioux Indians was favorable; the men were robust and the women good looking. He cautions against accepting the appraisal of men who have been traveling too long on the prairie in the company of other men, however. As he passed Fort Laramie (Wyoming), Brown took note of the register of emigrants that had passed by: 18,790 men, 270 women, 271 children, and 5,122 wagons. Around Fort Bridger (Wyoming) rumors that Indians were attacking emigrants kept the men on the alert. One night a guard shot his mule twice thinking it was an intruder.

The company went into Salt Lake City, and then north along the east side of the Great Salt

Lake and west to the Humboldt River. Brown relates conversations with groups who had taken other routes—Sublette's Cutoff and Fort Hall, both north of Salt Lake City, and Hastings' Cutoff to the south of the Great Salt Lake—and indicates all had suffered. As they crossed the Nevada desert he saw many who had abandoned their wagons and goods and were entirely dependent on others. Brown's group left their heavy wagon and transferred their provisions to a lighter, abandoned wagon.

After reaching the Carson River valley they sold everything, bought horses, and headed for the Sierra Nevadas, reaching the California town of Ringold on September 9. The next January they booked passage back for Pennsylvania.

(1850)   JAMES W. DENVER   738

Meyer, Richard, E., ed. "The Denver Diary: Overland to California in 1850." *Arizona and the West* 17 (Spring 1975):35–62.

An interesting aspect of this account is the means by which the diarist was transported, although James W. Denver provides little detail about the uniqueness of the trip. He was a paying passenger on a train of spring carriages that seated six persons each. Provisions and baggage were in mule-drawn wagons that followed. Because of the relative comfort of these carriages and the speed with which they traveled (as much as fifty miles a day), the passengers were spared much of the usual tedium and hardship of such a trip. They began at Fort Leavenworth (Kansas) on May 20, 1850, and traveled along the Platte River Trail. At Salt Lake City they took the Hastings' Cutoff and continued on into California, although the diary ends near the Humboldt Sink on September 5, 1850.

(1850)   WILLIAM RILEY FRANKLIN   739

Franklin, Homer, Sr., and Franklin, Homer, Jr., eds. "Journal of William Riley Franklin to California from Missouri in 1850." *Annals of Wyoming* 46 (Spring 1974):47–74.

A party of gold seekers left from Clinton County, Missouri, on April 4, 1850, traveled the Platte River Trail across Nebraska and Wyoming, where they turned south on Sublette's Cutoff and then west across Utah and Nevada, and reached Weaver (Weber) Creek, California, on July 19. It was an uneventful trip, and good grass and water were generally available. Accidents, illness, and Indian attacks were absent, although somewhere along the trail one member of the party was shot by an intoxicated companion. A final entry dated December 2, 1850, reveals that the party returned home by way of Panama without any mention of their success as prospectors.

(1850)   WARREN HOUGH   740

Hough, Warren. "The 1850 Overland Diary of Dr. Warren Hough." *Annals of Wyoming* 46 (Fall 1974):207–16.

This terse record of a small group of emigrants bound for the California goldfields begins in Davenport, Iowa, on March 21 and ends in Nevada's Humboldt Sink on July 12, 1850. Hough makes brief mention of buffalo hunts, sickness, accidents, landmarks, varying amounts of grass and water for the animals, and incidents with the Indians.

(1850)   SAMUEL M. JAMISON   741

Jamison, Samuel M. "Diary." *Nevada Historical Society Quarterly* 10 (Winter 1967):3–27.

Jamison began this trip to the goldfields with a group of friends from Independence, Missouri, and traveled overland to Georgetown, California, along the Platte River Trail to South

Pass, Fort Hall (Idaho), the Humboldt River, the Humboldt and Carson sinks, and Genoa, Nevada. Although he is mostly concerned with the details of travel, Jamison's terse account mentions the many other emigrants, a fight between two men, and the cost of provisions. His diary covers April 19 to September 18, 1850.

(1850)   **CALVIN TAYLOR**   **742**

Williams, Burton J., ed. "Overland to the Gold Fields of California in 1850: The Journal of Calvin Taylor." *Nebraska History* 50 (Summer 1969):125–49.

———. "Overland to California in 1850: The Journal of Calvin Taylor." *Utah Historical Quarterly* 38 (Fall 1970):312–49.

An excellent account of a trek from Saint Joseph, Missouri, to Georgetown, California, between May 26 and September 30, 1850. While crossing Nebraska, Taylor frequently mentioned the many deaths from cholera, but in Wyoming he said that he saw much less evidence of the disease. He comments on the many emigrants who had changed their minds about going west and were returning home because of sickness, fear, or scarcity of provisions. Taylor provides great detail about the route and the problem of obtaining provisions along the trail.

They traveled along the Platte River Trail to South Pass, and then south to Salt Lake City to obtain supplies. Although the nature of the emigrants' relationship with "Wright and Company" is unclear, Wright was apparently supposed to provide provisions along the way. Since he did not, either because of ineptitude or crookedness, the future of the venture was threatened. In Salt Lake City, Taylor and several other men confiscated Wright's supplies and divided them.

They continued back north of the Great Salt Lake, then west, linking up with the road from Fort Hall (Idaho), and later with those who had traveled the Hastings' Cutoff south of the Great Salt Lake. They followed the Humboldt River until it disappeared into the sand in the Humboldt Sink.

In western Nevada, as they prepared to cross the Forty-mile Desert, they struck a bargain with another emigrant train to take their baggage and provisions to California in exchange for their wagon and team. Traveling across the desert on horseback, Taylor saw hundreds of emigrants in the same sad predicament—drinking muddy slough water and throwing away goods that their undernourished, depleted teams could no longer pull.

After they left the desert, the ride along the Carson River and the climb up the Sierras was relatively easy, but by the time they reached California they were completely out of provisions. Taylor and his companions sold their horses, replenished their supplies, and started for Georgetown. Like so many others, though, they earned only enough money from the gold they found to return home by ship.

(1852)   **WILLIAM CORNELL**   **743**

Offen, Karen M., and Duniway, David C., eds. "William Cornell's Journal, 1852, with His Overland Guide to Oregon." *Oregon Historical Quarterly* 79 (Winter 1978):358–93.

——— "William Cornell's Guide to Oregon, 1852." *Oregon Historical Quarterly* 80 (Spring 1979):66–100.

Already the owner of a successful farm in central Ohio, Cornell moved to Oregon Territory to claim a free 320 acres of land near Portland. His wagon-train trip from Saint Joseph, Missouri, to the Umatilla Indian Agency near the Columbia River in Oregon was routine, except that one of his two companions died shortly after the trip began, and the other was stricken with a kind of lunacy and died shortly after the trek was completed.

Cornell participated in the sort of justice commonly found on the overland trail. When a man was struck with a firebrand by another, the arbitrators decreed that the provocation was slight and the damaged man was awarded $27, or in this case, one cow. The journal covers May 4 to September 29, 1852. The "Guide" is a day-by-day description of the route, providing comments on and listing miles between significant landmarks and the total distance from Saint Joseph.

(1852) JAMES DAVID 744

Urbanek, Mae, ed. "1852 On the Oregon Trail." *Annals of Wyoming* 34 (April 1962):52–59.

Presents portions of a diary of travel to the California goldfields by James David of Wisconsin. Early in the trip, which began on April 7, he described the passage through Iowa and Nebraska in some detail. As the ox team inched farther west, the entries become less descriptive and philosophical and more concerned with grass and water. The writings are also abbreviated after June 15 because of David's illness in Wyoming.

(1852) OLIVE HARRIET OTTO TERRY 745

Baldwin, Orval F., II, ed. "A Mormon Bride in the Great Migration." *Nebraska History* 58 (Spring 1977):52–71.

Brief reminiscenses by Olive Harriet Otto Terry about how she, a non-Mormon, met and married her Mormon husband near Council Bluffs (Kanesville), Iowa. Shortly after their marriage they traveled to Salt Lake City during 1852, the year of the largest Mormon migration west.

(1852–1853) HARRIET STEELE 746

Steele, Harriet. "Gold Rush Letters Copied From an Old Letter Book." *Pacific Historian* 8 (February 1964):43–52.

The Steele family immigrated from England in 1852, traveled overland to Salt Lake City, where they spent the winter, and continued on to Prairie City, California, in the spring of 1853. They had intended to go to Oregon, but the hostility of the Indians and the belief that they could make money selling chickens and melons to California miners changed their minds. These three letters, written between September 26, 1852, and August 28, 1853, offer descriptions of the trip from Wisconsin and conditions in California.

(1852–1855) WILLIAM H. WOODHAMS 747

Martin, Charles W., ed. "The Diary of William H. Woodhams, 1852–1854: The Great Deserts or Around and Across." *Nebraska History* 61 (Spring 1980):1–101.

Woodhams was an English author who moved to Michigan in about 1844. Between October 24, 1852, and March 5, 1855, he made a trip to California around South America, a return trip to Michigan via Nicaragua and New York, an overland trip to California, and a return trip to New York. The editor believes the account of the overland trip, which began in Indiana on March 12, 1854, and ended in the goldfields of Elizabethtown on July 22, is important because few people traveled during that year and only a small number of diaries exist. Woodhams' description of the Beckwith Route in California is one of the few descriptions of this variant of the California Trail.

(1853) REBECCA KETCHAM 748

Kaiser, Leo M., and Knuth, Priscilla, eds. "From Ithaca to Clatsop Plains: Miss Ketcham's Journal of Travel." (Part I) *Oregon Historical Quarterly* 62 (September 1961):237–87.

————. (Part II) *Oregon Historical Quarterly* 62 (December 1961):337–402.

Rebecca Ketcham traveled with a party of fifteen led by William H. Gray, who was driving a flock of sheep to Oregon. Her journal begins at Independence, Missouri, on May 22 and ends near Pendleton, Oregon, on September 13, 1853. Rebecca's writing is filled with the usual details of such a trip: drenching rains, bad roads, unhealthy water, sunburned skin, sandstorms, snakes, prominent landmarks, and the beauty of the plains and the mountains.

The journal is unique because of the explicit revelation of the tensions that must have existed on many overland trips. Although Rebecca says she was prepared for the heartlessness she might find in people, the bad feelings manifested by everyone, especially by Gray, surprised her. She expected the group to act as a family, a cohesive unit, but it did not. She believes the unhappiness caused by those with whom she was traveling to be greater than that caused by all the dangers they faced. Rebecca's reserves of good will became so drained that several days of "the blues" (p. 340) prevented her from making any entries. Still, she tried to make the best of things. Even as the diary was drawing to a close, she was admonishing herself to try to be more good-natured and patient.

Ironically, Gray's sheep, around which many decisions of the trip revolved and which possibly caused much of his irritability, were drowned near the end of the trip.

(1853)   **NATHANIEL MYER**   **749**

Ham, Edward B., ed. "Journey into Southern Oregon: Diary of a Pennsylvania Dutchman." *Oregon Historical Quarterly* 60 (Summer 1959):375–407.

At sixty-six years of age Nathaniel Myer wrote this chronicle of settlers emigrating to the Rogue River of Oregon. They traveled from Council Bluffs, Iowa, along the north side of the Platte River Trail. After reaching Fort Laramie (Wyoming) they went to Soda Springs by way of Sublette's Cutoff, then southwest across southern Idaho to Goose Creek, along which they entered the northeastern corner of Nevada. They followed the Humboldt River to Imlay, Nevada, then into northern California and past Goose Lake, probably entering Oregon at Worden in Klamath County. Myer's first entry is March 21, 1853, from Van Buren County, Iowa, and his final entry is October 4, when illness restricted his writing in southern Oregon. The editor says that although fifteen thousand travelers passed westward during the first eight months of that year, relatively few wrote about their experiences en route to Oregon.

(1853)   **JOHN SMITH**   **750**

Reid, John Phillip. "Replenishing the Elephant: Property and Survival on the Overland Trail." *Oregon Historical Quarterly* 79 (Spring 1978):64–90.

Examines the attitudes emigrants held toward the value of property and rights of ownership. Necessity, circumstances, and convenience all helped determine what property was brought, retained, and replenished as the travel took its toll. Sometimes contracts for sharing services or goods were necessary, and these were often drawn up along formal lines. Reid says that the understanding and respect for the law of property indicates that nineteenth-century Americans were more law-minded than has generally been accepted. Reid illustrates these attitudes and characteristics by focusing on the journal of John Smith, who traveled the Oregon Trail to Portland in 1853.

(1854)   **WINFIELD SCOTT EBEY**   **751**

Baydo, Gerald. "Overland from Missouri to Washington Territory in 1854." *Nebraska History* 52 (Spring 1971):65–87.

Using primarily the diary of the son, Winfield Scott Ebey, Baydo details the 2,192-mile, 169-day journey (April 10-October 12, 1854) of the Jacob Ebey family from Plum Grove, Missouri, to Whidbey Island, Washington Territory. Their trip along the first Mormon Trail, the Oregon Trail, the Washington Territorial Emigrant's Road, and finally the Yakima River valley was uneventful. There were only three cases of cholera, a minor accident in a river crossing, and minimal contact with the Indians.

(1857)   **PHILIP ST. GEORGE COOKE**   **752**

Gardner, Hamilton, ed. "March of 2nd Dragoons: Report of Lieutenant Colonel Philip St. George Cooke on the March of the 2nd Dragoons from Fort Leavenworth to Fort Bridger in 1857." *Annals of Wyoming* 27 (April 1955):43–60.

Cooke relates his role as commander of a cavalry unit in the Utah Expedition. (See item 754.) By the time his dragoons left Kansas on September 17, 1857, the expedition was strung out along the trail, and it was very late in the season to attempt a march. The weather held until the unit reached Fort Kearney (Nebraska), but during the remainder of the journey the men and animals suffered from cold weather, sleet, and snow. On November 19, Cooke wrote from Camp Scott, a temporary winter encampment outside Fort Bridger (Wyoming), that he had lost 134 horses, nearly as many as had survived.

(1857)   **ARTHUR M. MENEFEE**   **753**

Menefee, Arthur M. "Arthur M. Menefee's Travels Across the Plains, 1857." *Nevada Historical Society Quarterly* 9 (Spring 1966):5–28.

A terse diary (May 13-October 15, 1857) kept en route from Ralls County, Missouri, to Carson City, Nevada, along the Platte River Trail through Wyoming and south from Fort Hall (Wyoming). Menefee mentions his poor health frequently. In her brief introduction, Helen S. Griffen speculates that his illness was the reason for halting in Carson City. Menefee died later that year.

(1857–1861)   **CHARLES A. SCOTT**   **754**

Stowers, Robert E., and Ellis, John M., eds. "Charles A. Scott's Diary of the Utah Expedition, 1857–1861." (Part I) *Utah Historical Quarterly* 28 (April 1960):155–76.

———. (Part II) *Utah Historical Quarterly* 28 (October 1960):389–402.

By appointing a new governor, President James Buchanan attempted to resolve the conflict in Utah between the Mormon territorial governor, Brigham Young, and the non-Mormon officials. In what has been called the Utah Expedition, federal troops accompanied the new governor, Alfred Cummings, to ensure his acceptance by the Mormons. Brigham Young retaliated by declaring martial law and ordering local militia to set up defenses. Because of the Mormons harassment, the federal troops were forced to stop short of their goal and to winter at Camp Scott, outside Fort Bridger (Wyoming). After negotiations brought peace, the army spent the next four years at Camp Floyd, near Salt Lake City.

Scott's diary relates some of his experiences in the East, his enlistment, the train trip to Fort Leavenworth (Kansas), and the expedition's departure on July 26 along the overland emigrant trail. Most of the journey was uneventful, except for a tragic descent into Ash Hollow. Once in Wyoming, Scott heard that the Mormons had burned a supply train, and he saw them burning grass to delay the troops. He describes the first cold winter spent at Camp Scott. The remainder of his entries cover the establishment of Camp Floyd, incidents with the Mormons and Indians during the next four years, and the troops' return to the East in 1861. The editors add that Scott's diary (March 28, 1857-October 22, 1861) is the only eyewitness account of these events that covers the complete expedition. (See also item 752.)

(1858)   **KIRK ANDERSON**   **755**

Wells, Eugene T., ed. "Kirk Anderson's Trip to Utah, 1858." *Bulletin of the Missouri Historical Society* 18 (October 1961):3–19.

Letters written in an interesting anecdotal style by a newspaperman for the *Missouri Republican* (Saint Louis) between August 17 and September 17, 1858. They describe a trip from Saint

Joseph (Missouri) to Salt Lake City with a mail train pulled by mules, whose unpredictable antics were a source of amusement and concern. Along the Missouri River bottom Anderson believed the mosquitoes were the fiercest he had ever encountered. He thought the noble Indians were so much of James Fenimore Cooper's humbug: "an Indian is an Indian and nothing else" (p. 7). All the way he comments on the famous landmarks on the Platte River Trail: Ash Hollow, Chimney Rock, Fort Laramie (Wyoming), Independence Rock, Devil's Gate, the South Pass, and finally Salt Lake City.

(1858)   GEORGE WILLIAM BEEHRER   756

Colyer, Julie Beehrer, ed. "Freighting Across the Plains." *Montana: The Magazine of Western History* 12 (October 1962):2–17.

Between June and September, 1858, George William Beehrer was a member of a group of teamsters carrying supplies from Fort Leavenworth (Kansas) to Camp Floyd (Utah) where the army anticipated a war with the Mormons. While his diary relates the usual hazards of life on the overland trails, as they neared Utah his apprehension increased. He heard rumors that the Mormons had attempted to poison soldiers, had dressed like Indians to participate in the Mountain Meadow massacre of an emigrant train in August, 1857, and had placed rocks high on passes to be pushed down on the soldiers. The only battles that occurred, however, took place in Salt Lake City when three of his friends were killed in brawls.

(1858–1859)   JAMES HERVEY SIMPSON   757

Beeton, Barbara. "James Hervey Simpson in the Great Basin." *Montana: The Magazine of Western History* 28 (January 1978):28–43.

The need to establish direct wagon routes between military posts in the West during the "Mormon War" brought Simpson to Utah. As a captain in the U.S. Corps of Topographical Engineers, he surveyed and established a road from Camp Floyd (Utah) to San Francisco during the fall of 1858 and spring of 1859. The road contributed to the development of the Great Basin because it was used by California emigrants and by the telegraph companies. It now approximates U.S. Highway 30. Although his *Report of Explorations Across the Great Basin of the Territory of Utah* . . . was not published until 1876, it was consulted earlier by scientists for the information it contains on the flora and fauna, the geology, and the Indians of the region.

(1859)   GEORGE SUCKLEY   758

Beidleman, Richard G., ed. "The 1859 Overland Journal of Naturalist George Suckley." *Annals of Wyoming* 28 (April 1956):68–79.

Suckley was a doctor and professional naturalist who was accompanying a troop of recruits to Utah as a contract surgeon. His diary begins on June 1, 1859, at Fort Leavenworth (Kansas) and ends on August 12 in Wyoming. Suckley was attracted to the wildlife and his diary contains a list of specimens he collected.

(1862)   JANE HOLBROOK GOULD   759

Lack, Philip K., ed. "Iowa to California in 1862: The Journal of Jane Holbrook Gould." (Part I) *Annals of Iowa* 37 (Fall 1964):460–76.

———. (Part II) *Annals of Iowa* 37 (Winter 1965):544–59.

———. (Part III) *Annals of Iowa* 37 (Spring 1965):623–40.

———. (Part IV) *Annals of Iowa* 38 (Summer 1965):68–75.

Mrs. Gould, traveling with her husband and two sons, began her journal in Mitchell County, Iowa, on April 27, 1862, and made the final entry near Stockton, California, on October 8, 1862. During the early stages of the trip, Mrs. Gould described her experiences matter-

of-factly as she reported the organization of a wagon train near the Platte River, amicable relations with the Indians, frequent grave sites, and such familiar landmarks on the Platte River
Trail as Independence Rock, on which the family wrote its name. After a train just ahead of
theirs was attacked by Indians near the Snake River and then their own train was attacked, the
tone of her writing changes to one of apprehension. During the remainder of the journey south
and then west through Nevada, they saw evidence of another attack, but arrived in California
by the Carson River Route unharmed. The editor adds that four months after her arrival in
California Mrs. Gould's husband died.

(1862)   **ADA MILLINGTON**   **760**

Clarke, Charles G., ed. "Journal Kept While Crossing the Plains by Ada Millington."
(Part I) "From Keosauqua, Iowa to Nebraska City on the Missouri." *Southern California Quarterly* 59 (Spring 1977):13–48.

––––––. (Part II) "From Fort Laramie to Salt Lake City." *Southern California Quarterly* 59 (Summer 1977):139–84.

––––––. (Part III) "From Carson City, Nevada to Santa Rosa, California." *Southern
California Quarterly* 59 (Fall 1977):251–69.

The editor defends the publication of yet another overland trail diary because it describes a
new route across central Nevada that had been only recently opened by the overland stage lines
and because it is written with a girl's sense of humor. The diary of young Ada, who celebrated
her thirteenth birthday in Nevada, also recommends itself because her writing retains a freshness
throughout that often dwindled in accounts written by adults when travel became difficult. Ada
relates some of the activities of children on the trail: studying spelling, playing, and gathering
buffalo chips, sagebrush, and berries. Once she and her brother knocked over a shotgun in the
wagon causing it to fire.

She also tells of the death of her baby brother in Nevada. Ada says her parents did not want
to bury him in the open. At first they wanted to bury him temporarily in Carson City, then come
back for the casket after they settled in California. After a few days of traveling with the casket,
during which her father sprinkled the corpse with camphor, they settled on a permanent burial
in Virginia City, Nevada. The diary was kept between April 29 and September 16, 1862. Also
included is an addendum written by Ada in 1878 that relates the subsequent activities of the
emigrants.

(1863)   **FLORA ISABELLE BENDER**   **761**

Bender, Flora Isabelle. "Memoranda of a Journey Across the Plains from Bell Creek,
Washington Co., Nebraska to Virginia City, Nevada Territory, May 7 to August 4,
1863." *Nevada Historical Quarterly* 1 (Summer 1958):144–73.

After young Flora Bender reached Virginia City, she summed up her journey by saying
that the family "have had a pleasant trip across the plains—endured none of those hardships
which we read of so often." (p. 173) During the first part of the trip across Nebraska, she
mentions frequent dances and tells of people she likes and others she dislikes. Except for sandy
roads, travel was easy as they passed such emigrant landmarks on the Platte River Trail as
Courthouse Rock, Chimney Rock, Independence Rock, and Devil's Gate. The train took the
route from South Pass, Fort Bridger (Wyoming) into Salt Lake City, then north along the east
side of the Great Salt Lake, and then west through Utah and Nevada. During the later part of
the journey the ground was covered with alkaline deposits, and adequate water and good grass
were found less often. Then, moments of gaiety are not mentioned.

Flora's diary records the frequency of emigrants joining and then leaving wagon trains.
Her family was seldom alone on the trail; another company was always close. The Civil War is
also evident in her writing. A captain of her train proved to be an escaped Confederate prisoner
who was recaptured because Flora told the Union troops he was traveling nearby. She also says

that after leaving Salt Lake City, all emigrants were forced to take an oath of allegiance or be taken as prisoners. Flora liked what she saw of Brigham Young's city and attended a church service. Although she liked the music, she did not approve of the religion nor of his resistance to the United States government.

(1863)   JAMES PRESSLEY YAGER   762

Harris, Everett W., ed. "The Yager Journals: Diary of a Journey Across the Plains." (Part I) *Nevada Historical Society Quarterly* 13 (Spring 1970):5–20.
————. (Part II) *Nevada Historical Society Quarterly* 13 (Summer 1970):19–40.
————. (Part III) *Nevada Historical Society Quarterly* 13 (Fall 1970):27–48.
————. (Part IV) *Nevada Historical Society Quarterly* 13 (Winter 1970):26–52.
————. (Part V) *Nevada Historical Society Quarterly* 14 (Spring 1971):27–54.
————. (Part VI) *Nevada Historical Society Quarterly* 14 (Summer 1971):33–56.

James Pressley Yager's diary includes much detail and is enhanced by extensive editorial notes. The diary began at Louisville, Kentucky, on April 22, 1863, and chronicles Yager's travels to Nebraska City, along the Platte River Trail to the South Pass, down to Fort Bridger (Wyoming) and on to Salt Lake City. The train then went north along the east side of the Great Salt Lake, then west to the Humboldt River, across Nevada and the Forty-mile Desert by the Truckee River route. Yager then left the train and went to Virginia City, Nevada. After about six weeks of work at chopping and hauling wood, he went to San Francisco but soon returned to Nevada.

While on the trail Yager observed the enforcement of informal "rules of the prairie." When another train tried to crowd into the space between the wagons of Yager's train, it was forced off the trail. Guns were fired and rocks thrown by Yager's group. He reveals the dependence of emigrants on river routes as trail marks: "Emigrants don't like to get out of sight of water" (p. 25, pt. II). In California and Nevada, Yager provided descriptions of San Francisco, Carson City, and Virginia City, and mentioned many other small gold-mining towns. As the diary ends on December 31, 1863, Yager has built a cabin at Antelope Flats, Nevada, and has begun to prospect.

(1865)   MARGARETTA FABER MCCLINTOCK   763

McClintock, Charles A., ed. "My Trip Across the Plains: Margaretta Faber Mc-Clintock." *Western Pennsylvania Historical Magazine* 40 (September 1957):13–20.

Mrs. McClintock reminisces about her trip from Saint Louis to Salt Lake City with her husband, an officer in the Eighteenth U. S. Infantry, between February and June (?) 1865.

(1865)   ALEXANDER MCDOWELL MCCOOK   764

Roberts, Gary L. "Condition of the Tribes–1865: The McCook Report, A Military View." *Montana: The Magazine of The West* 24 (January 1974):14–25.

Because relations between the Great Plains Indians and the settlers had deteriorated during the Civil War, Congress commissioned the Doolittle Committee to travel throughout Kansas, Colorado, and New Mexico in the summer of 1865 to investigate conditions. In his report, Major General Alexander McDowell McCook expressed the belief that:

> Our Indian troubles on the plains result from two flagrant causes. First, the almost universal bad faith of Indian agents toward Indians in defrauding them out of the annuities and presents granted them by law. Second, the inexperience and almost total ignorance of Volunteer officers of Indian character and the want of discipline in the Volunteer force serving on the Plains. (p. 22)

McCook offered recommendations for improvement, one of which was to transfer responsibility for Indian affairs from the Department of the Interior to the War Department.

(1867)   HENRY C. PARRY   765

Parry, Henry C. "Letters from the Frontier: 1867." *Annals of Wyoming* 30 (October 1958):127–44.

Dr. Parry was with General Grenville M. Dodge's Union Pacific Railroad Commission, which was charged with planning the route and protecting the builders of the first transcontinental railroad. At first, when the weather was good and water and wildlife abundant, the letters extol the joys of life on the prairie. After crossing the hot alkaline desert of Utah, however, Parry changed his assessment.

He described what he saw of Indian customs. Except for the Pawnee scouts, his opinion of Indians was unfavorable. These letters were written from Nebraska, Colorado, the Dakotas, Wyoming, and Utah, between May 16 and October 20, 1867. *Note*: Also published as "Observations on the Prairies: 1867," *Montana: The Magazine of Western History* 9 (October 1959):22–35.

(1871)   LEWIS RICHARD PRICE   766

Jackson, W. Turrentine, ed. "Journal of Lewis Richard Price: Voyage from London to San Francisco, 1871." *Pacific Historian* 4 (August 1960):96–112.

Price came to the West to visit and report on his British mining company's holdings in the Sierra Nevadas. His journal (April 20-July 15, 1871) tells of a railroad trip to Salt Lake City where he met Brigham Young, and of visits to New Almadén, the Napa Valley and Lake Tahoe in California, and Virginia City and the Comstock Lode in Nevada.

(1875)   GILES BARTON LUMBARD   767

Lumbard, Giles Barton. "By Train from Omaha to Sacramento One Hundred Years Ago." *American West* 12 (November 1975):114–17.

Describes a trip across the West in 1875, only six years after the Central Pacific and Union Pacific railroads had joined. Lumbard and two friends made a 2,000-mile rail trip in nine days. They traveled many of the emigrant routes across Nebraska and Wyoming, south near Salt Lake City and west across the Humboldt River valley, the Truckee River valley, over the Sierra Nevadas to Sacramento, and then to San Francisco. They were afforded the luxury of being able to observe the rugged terrain, the alkaline deposits, and the Great American Desert without having to walk through them.

(1877)   ISAAC MAYER WISE   768

Wise, Isaac Mayer. "Rabbi Wise: By Parlor Car Across the Great American Desert." *Pacific Historian* 11 (Fall 1967):117–27.

Relates a whirlwind trip from Cincinnati to Peoria, and then across Iowa, Nebraska, Wyoming, and Nevada. Wise does not seem to like train travel and comments only briefly on what he saw. His longest passage is about Salt Lake City, from which he offers a comparison between the Chinese and Indians that is more complimentary to the former. Newspaper articles written in July 1877 for the *American Israelite* (Cincinnati). (See also item 989.)

9

Rocky Mountains

GENERAL

(1833–1835)   BENJAMIN LOUIS EULALIE DE BONNEVILLE   769

McDermott, John Francis. "Washington Irving and the Journal of Captain Bonneville." *Mississippi Valley Historical Review* 43 (December 1956):459–67.

Presents the background of Captain B. L. E. de Bonneville's trip to the Rocky Mountains (1833–35) and a history of the document that Washington Irving published as *The Rocky Mountains: or, Scenes, Incidents, and Adventures in the Far West* . . . (Philadelphia: 1837). Although Irving believed the journal was lost, McDermott believes that it may well still exist.

(1873)   DAVID H. STROTHER   770

Eby, Cecil D., Jr., ed. "'Porte Canyon' in the Rocky Mountains." *Colorado Magazine* 37 (April 1960):108–21.

David H. Strother ("Porte Canyon") made this five-week excursion in July and August, 1873. He describes his train ride from West Virginia to Saint Louis, south to Texas, then back north to Kansas through Indian Territory, and west to Colorado and Utah. Because he was an experienced travel writer, Strother seemingly found something to describe about all he saw. The editor believes Strother observed the West at a time when civilization was just beginning to wear away some of the frontier's rough edges.

(1876)   GERHARD LUKE LUHN   771

Nottage, James H., ed. "The Big Horn and Yellowstone Expedition of 1876 as Seen Through the Letters of Captain Gerhard Luke Luhn." *Annals of Wyoming* 45 (Spring 1973):27–46.

Captain Luhn's role in forcing the Indians to recognize the authority of the United States government was to command a company that marched from Wyoming into Montana and South Dakota looking for hostiles. In letters written between June 9 and September 15, 1876, Luhn describes the march and the battles with the Sioux at Rosebud (Montana) and at Slim Buttes (South Dakota).

(1898–1899)   THOMAS E. HINSHAW   772

Groesbeck, Kathryn D., ed. "A Southwest Photographic Expedition, 1898–99." *Utah Historical Quarterly* 34 (Summer 1966):191–201.

Thomas E. Hinshaw, Orson Pratt Huish, and Huish's 10-year-old son Dave drove their wagon through Utah, Colorado, New Mexico, and Arizona on a commercial photographic tour between July 27, 1898, and July 10, 1899. Hinshaw's brief entries in his journal are supplemented by O. P. Huish's Day Book. The subjects for their photographs were Indian and Mexican villages, ranches, lumber camps, and obstacles to their own travel. Groesbeck says that many photographs of the trip and the original camera have been preserved by Dave Huish.

COLORADO

(1846)   LEWIS HECTOR GARRARD   773

Garrard, Lewis Hector. "In the Lodge of Vi-Po-Na: A Visit to the Cheyenne." *American West* 5 (July 1968):32–36.

The author traveled over the Santa Fe Trail in 1846 and published his observations in *Wah-to-Yah and the Taos Trail* (New York, 1850). Presented here are excerpts that tell of a Cheyenne village along the Purgatoire River in Colorado.

(1859)   EDWIN A. BOWEN   774

Smith, Duane A., ed. "Pikes Peak Fifty-Niner: The Diary of E. A. Bowen." *Colorado Magazine* 47 (Fall 1970):269–311.

Edwin A. Bowen left his job as a clerk in La Salle, Illinois, with a group from Michigan, Illinois and Indiana to join the thousands who stampeded to the Colorado goldfields. His diary (February 23-October 2, 1859) describes the trip to Saint Joseph by rail, then across Nebraska to Denver by wagon. Bowen purchased a claim at the "Gregory Diggins" and worked it with some success until he decided to return to Illinois in the fall. He writes at length about the hard work involved in prospecting, the business aspects of keeping the claim running, and the application of law (or justice) by miners' committees and vigilantes.

(1859)   JOSHUA MANWARING   775

Warner, Robert M., ed. "Journal of a Fifty-Niner." *Colorado Magazine* 36 (July 1959):161–73.

Joshua Manwaring of Lapeer County, Michigan, was financially secure and apparently settled for life when he was lured to Colorado by gold. After experiencing frustration in the Colorado goldfields, which he relates here, Manwaring soon became disillusioned. His final entry in his diary laments, "I was thirty-five today. Just came home from P.P. and am going home satisfied with bumming, and I think I shall stay home in the future." (p. 179) Diary kept from April 2 to October 2, 1859.

(1859)   WILLIAM S. SALISBURY   776

Lindsey, David, ed. "The Journal of an 1859 Pike's Peak Gold Seeker." *Kansas Historical Quarterly* 22 (Winter 1956):321–41.

William S. Salisbury went with a party from Ohio to Colorado to search for gold. His journal (April 4-September 1, 1859) describes traveling across Kansas and prospecting along the Clear Creek region west of Denver. By the end of the summer the miners had become discouraged and returned home through Nebraska.

(1859)   DAVID F. SPAIN   777

Morrison, John D., ed. "The Diary of David F. Spain: Gregory's Grubstakers at the Diggins." *Colorado Magazine* 35 (January 1958):11–34.

Together with eight other South Bend, Indiana, gold seekers, Spain set out for the Pikes Peak gold region on March 18, 1859. After surviving the muddy roads of Iowa, the group and their well-provisioned wagons crossed Nebraska, reaching Denver on April 30. Spain's diary describes building a cabin, a devastating forest fire, and on some days the amounts of gold taken. A miner they grubstaked, John H. Gregory, discovered gold in great quantities, causing a rush. The group returned home on July 27, 1859. A newspaper article reported that the men brought with them $8,000 to $10,000 in gold dust. (See also item 778.)

(1859) **778**

"The Letters of David F. Spain: Gregory's Goldseekers at the Diggings." *Colorado Magazine* 35 (April 1958):81–112.

These letters, from March 9 to June 26, 1857, tell more about the events of the discovery of gold in Pikes Peak. (See also item 777.)

(1859–1861) **MATTHEW H. DALE** **779**

Athearn, Robert G., ed. "Life in The Pike's Peak Region: The Letters of Matthew H. Dale." *Colorado Magazine* 32 (April 1955):84–104.

For two and a half years (April 27, 1859-October 21, 1861) Dale wrote letters to his family in Pennsylvania describing first his trip across Kansas and then his efforts to find wealth in Colorado. Traveling at the height of the Colorado gold rush, he reports the great numbers on their way to the mines. He tells about the makeshift living conditions, the rapid growth of towns, the discovery of quartz and lead mines at Arapahoe and New Nevada, the newspapers, the mail service, the politics, and the wages in Colorado. He also relates local sentiment about the approaching Civil War.

(1861–1862) **AMOS S. BILLINGSLEY** **780**

Danker, Donald F., and Riley, Paul D., eds. "The Journal of Amos S. Billingsley, A Missionary in the Colorado Gold Fields, 1861–1862, and Chaplain of the House of Representatives." *Colorado Magazine* 40 (October 1963):241–70.

The West as it appeared to a devout Presbyterian minister. Billingsley's brief entries (February 14, 1861-October 18, 1862) refer to his scriptural messages, the people he married and those he buried, the immorality of the area, his problems with collecting money from his parishioners, the bitter sectional feelings resulting from the Civil War, and his preaching jaunts throughout Colorado.

(1862) **HARRIET AMELIA SMITH** **781**

Fraker, Fleming, Jr., ed. "To Pike's Peak by Ox-Wagon: The Harriet A. Smith Day-Book." *Annals of Iowa* 35 (Fall 1959):113–48.

Harriet Amelia Smith accompanied her aunt and uncle on a seventy-day trek (July 21-September 30, 1862) from Saylorville, Iowa, to their homestead in Boulder County, Colorado. The route took them across central Iowa and Nebraska, then south into central Colorado. Nothing momentous occurred on the trip; it was filled with the day-to-day routines of travel. Her comments are concerned with food, repairing wagon wheels, and gathering cattle that strayed in the night. Apparently relations between settlers and the emigrants were good, since Harriet frequently baked her bread in homes along the way. Although she was afraid of the Indians, they were no problem; a gift of bread and they would leave. The final entries describe the first days of life in the new home.

(1866) **CHRISTOPHER CARSON** **782**

Gressley, Gene M., ed. "Report on Fort Garland Made by Christopher (Kit) Carson to Major Roger James, June 10, 1866." *Colorado Magazine* 32 (July 1955):215–24.

The editor says this report was dictated by Carson, who was colonel and commander of Fort Garland (Colorado), but written by a much better educated person. It describes the physical layout of the fort and the precariousness of being located at the edge of civilization with too few troops to protect the miners and settlers. Although Carson realized that the Ute and Apache Indians were driven to stealing by hunger and destitution, he urged that they be placed on reservations as soon as possible. He saw more realistically than many that before this could happen conflict was inevitable.

(1868) ISAAC NEWTON BARD 783

Bard, Isaac Newton. "Isaac Newton Bard Dug Potatoes, Not Gold in 1868." *Colorado Magazine* 33 (July 1956):161–76.

Bard tells of his everyday life in the gold-rich area of Oro City, Colorado. After he arrived from Iowa he worked mostly for other people, sawing wood, putting up hay, digging potatoes, and suffering from loneliness until his wife finally arrived. The diary relates events from August 12 to December 7, 1868.

(1868) JAMES S. BRISBIN 784

Anderson, Harry H., ed. "Stand at the Arikaree." *Colorado Magazine* 41 (Fall 1964):337–42.

In the Battle of Beecher Island, September 17 to 25, 1868, Major George A. Forsyth held out on an island in the Republican River (near Wray, Colorado) against a superior number of Cheyenne and Sioux Indians. On September 25 he was relieved by Major James S. Brisbin, who describes the battle and the condition of the troops in this letter.

(1871) ANNIE B. SCHENCK 785

Filipiak, Jack D., ed. "Camping Vacation, 1871." *Colorado Magazine* 42 (Summer 1965):185–215.

Annie B. Schenck of Erie, Pennsylvania, kept this journal of a camping trip to the Rocky Mountains (August 4-29, 1871). A single two-horse wagon and eight people left Creswell, Colorado, west of Denver, and made a loop south and nearly as far west as Leadville before ending up at Georgetown. She describes the group's experiences as they passed through the mining towns of Fairplay, Montgomery, and Montezuma, and across the Argentine Pass. Includes a list of provisions.

(1872) H. MARTYN HART 786

Arps, Louisa Ward, ed. "Dean Hart Pre-Views His Wilderness: Excerpts from the 1872 Diary of H. Martyn Hart." *Colorado Magazine* 36 (January 1959):22–36.

Denver's future Episcopal clergyman records a buffalo hunt in Kansas and his first visit to Denver in December, 1872. On this trip Hart was making a journey around the world for his health, but he later returned to Denver as minister of Saint John's Church in the Wilderness.

(1878) "T" 787

Glazer, Sidney, ed. "A Michigan Correspondent in Colorado, 1878." *Colorado Magazine* 37 (July 1960):207–18.

The five letters "T" wrote to the *Michigan Christian Herald* in 1878 provide travel advice and descriptions of scenic wonders. He writes about railroad construction, mining operations at the state's oldest mine in Central City, and visits to Pikes Peak, Denver, and Pueblo, among other places.

(1879)   **GIOVANNI VIGNA DAL FERRO**   788

Bohme, F. G., ed. and tr. "Vigna Dal Ferro's 'Un Viaggio Nel Far West Americano'." *Colorado Magazine* 35 (October 1958):290–302.

A portion of Italian traveler, linguist, and journalist Giovanni Vigna dal Ferro's collection of articles to *La Patria* (Bologna). In this selection he describes his train trip from the East Coast to Colorado in 1879. He tells of a visit to an Apache village and relates his impression of government policy toward the Indians. After the Indians were sufficiently tired of the white invasion of their territories to declare war, he says, the United States Army simply wiped them out. He also offers a description of the colorful life of Leadville. (See also item 990.)

(1881)   **GEORGE C. STOREY**   789

Storey, George C. "My Trip West in 1881." *Colorado Magazine* 49 (Fall 1972):314–25.

The author and his brother traveled from Iowa to the mines of southern Colorado, where they discovered many good sites but located no mother lodes. A diary kept between March 9 and September 15, 1881.

(1885)   **E. S. KASSLER**   790

Kassler, E. S. "A Trip to the Troublesome." *Colorado Magazine* 33 (January 1956):67–73.

The author reminisces about a sixty-three-day camping and hunting trip from Denver to the Bear River country of Colorado in the summer of 1885.

(1889)   **FRANK C. KENDRICK**   791

Stiles, Helen J., ed. "Down the Colorado in 1889." *Colorado Magazine* 41 (Summer 1964):225–46.

Frank C. Kendrick was hired by railroad president Frank Mason Brown to survey the Colorado River from Grand Junction, Colorado, to the mouth of the Green River in Utah. Brown intended to run the Denver, Colorado Cañon and Pacific Railroad from Grand Junction to the Gulf of California and on to San Diego to ship coal and other Colorado products. The project was doomed when Brown was accidentally killed. Kendrick's diary (March 3-May 18, 1889) tells of the survey trip of 160 miles and then a 116-mile trip up the Green River.

(1896)   **MARY E. FLOOD**   792

Riley, Paul, ed. "Cripple Creek Letters." *Colorado Magazine* 34 (October 1957):290–93.

Two letters from Mary E. Flood, a recent arrival from Trenton, Nebraska, describe job hunting in Cripple Creek, Colorado, during March and April, 1896.

(1905)   **H. L. A. CULMER**   793

Steen, Charlie R., ed. "The Natural Bridges of White Canyon: A Diary of H. L. A. Culmer, 1905." *Utah Historical Quarterly* 40 (Winter 1972):55–87.

In an effort to attract tourists to southeastern Colorado, a region possessing scenic beauty but not well known, Clymer was commissioned to measure, photograph, and describe the natural bridges that existed there. In his journal (April 1–30, 1905) he records travel through the canyons and over the rugged terrain, observes the potential for sheep grazing, and relates his relic hunting in the caves.

(1934)   **MARK T. WARNER**   794

Warner, Mark T. "Through the Canyon." *Colorado Magazine* 40 (July 1963):179–82.

The Reverend Warner describes his five-day trip through the Black Canyon of the Gunnison National Monument with the United States Geological Survey in July, 1934. Originally appeared in *The Montrose Daily Press* (October 1, 1934).

IDAHO

(1824)   ALEXANDER ROSS   795

Ross, Alexander. "The Adventures of Alexander Ross in the Snake Country." *Idaho Yesterdays* 14 (Spring 1970):8–15.

The adventures of a Hudson's Bay Company fur-trapping expedition in 1824 are pieced together from Ross's unpublished journal. Part of the time Ross was exploring unworked areas and is credited with discovering Sun Valley.

(1836–1854)   SODA SPRINGS   796

Munkres, Robert L. "Soda Springs: Curiosity of the Trail." *Annals of Wyoming* 43 (Fall 1971):215–35.

Soda Springs was a mineral spring located in eastern Idaho on the overland trail. The emigrants found it curious because of the cones that were formed by the mineral residue and the noises the pressure of the gases made at nearby Steamboat Springs. Opinions differed on the taste and smell of the waters of Soda Springs—some even used the water for a purgative and as an ingredient in baking bread—but the waters of Steamboat Springs were considered less palatable. Munkres consults diaries of travelers who wrote between 1836 and 1854.

(1850)   HOWARD STANSBURY   797

Stansbury, Howard. "The Bannock Mountain Road." *Idaho Yesterdays* 8 (Spring 1964):10–15.

Captain Stansbury reported to the United States Army that he had found a natural road for wagons from Salt Lake City to Fort Hall (Idaho). Most of his report describes the roads and the terrain over which he marched between September 12 and early October, 1850. By 1862 this road carried heavy traffic bound for the Montana mines.

(1853)   WILLIAM HOFFMAN   798

Taylor, Arthur S., and McKinney, William M. "An Accurate Observer: William Hoffman's View of Idaho in 1853." *Idaho Yesterdays* 8 (Summer 1964):20–25.

The authors provide extensive explanatory comment on brief excerpts from Hoffman's diary which describe a seven-month trip over the Oregon Trail from Covington, Indiana, to Jacksonville, Oregon, with an emigrant party. The entire text of Hoffman's travels on Hudspeth's Cutoff in Idaho is reproduced here.

(1861)   HENRY MILLER   799

Miller, Henry. "Letters from the Upper Columbia." *Idaho Yesterdays* 4 (Winter 1960/1961):14–25.

The record of a steamboat trip up the Columbia River from The Dalles to Pierce, Idaho, during the Clearwater gold rush in the spring of 1861. In addition to describing the river, Miller offers his assessment of the Nez Percé Indians. He found them to be aloof and not especially attractive, but admits that their horses and cattle did prosper. He emphasizes that they should not simply be given the accoutrements of civilization. Before they or any other Indians could become civilized, Miller believed that they must pass through first a pastoral and then an agricultural stage of development. These letters originally appeared in the *Oregonian* (June 1861).

(1862)   GEORGE A. HARDING   800

Tanasoca, Steven, and Sudduth, Susan, eds. "'A Journal Kept by George A. Harding'." *Oregon Historical Quarterly* 79 (Summer 1978):172–202.

    Harding, his stepfather, and his brother, all residents of Oregon City, Oregon, spent six months during 1862 in the Idaho mines looking for gold. His journal of May 7 to October 16, 1862, describes the trek from the Willamette Valley to Walla Walla, to Lewiston, and finally to Elk City, Idaho. They gained employment as painters and paperhangers in the town, but apparently achieved little success at prospecting. An incident that Harding witnessed shortly before his return home was an attempt to hang a murderer that was prevented when the rope broke. The prisoner was released. Harding also describes the trip back to Oregon in the fall.

(1863)   C. AUBREY ANGELO   801

Angelo, C. Aubrey. "Impressions of Boise Basin in 1863." *Idaho Yesterdays* 7 (Spring 1963):4–13.

    Angelo was a correspondent for the *Daily Alta California* (San Francisco) who joined the gold rush to Idaho and Montana in the spring of 1863. These three columns tell of the difficulties of travel in the mountains and the danger from the Bannock and Shoshone Indians. He describes Placerville, Centerville, and Fort Hogan, Idaho. In Bannack City, Montana, he says, lawlessness and disorder reached a peak of "perfect pandemonium" on Sunday. (p. 11) He writes: "There is no jail in Bannack City, but plenty of rope and trees." (p. 13) Angelo reveals the strength of southern sentiment in the area which, the editor adds, was created by Missourians drawn to the Boise mines. From what Angelo had seen, the gold rush was depopulating Oregon and Washington.

(1864–1865)   GEORGE FORMAN   802

Davis, William E., ed. "George Forman, the Great Pedestrian." *Idaho Yesterdays* 10 (Spring 1966):2–11.

    During this second period of his western experiences (September 25, 1964-August 17, 1865), Forman relates events that occurred after he left Montana and moved to the mines of Idaho. As Forman traveled west from Virginia City he reported that emigrants were having trouble with the Indians in the spring of 1865, just as they had in the previous year. He traveled in the company of southerners who were trying to avoid the Civil War. Forman gives a description of Idaho City, where he found strong southern sentiment, as well as a corrupt Democrat government. He was in Idaho City when the "secesh" (secessionists) burned the city to rob the Union businessmen. About fifty men were shot, but no one was punished because of the strong Democrat and southern political faction. In August, 1865, Forman returned to Ontario, Canada. (See also item 811.)

(1866)   ELIJAH CHANEY   803

Chaney, Elijah. "A Visit to Boise Basin, 1866." *Idaho Yesterdays* 16 (Spring 1972):26–27.

    A description of Idaho City and the nearby Chickahominy quartz mill. Originally appeared in *Ballou's Monthly Magazine* (July 1873).

(1874)   JOHN CODMAN   804

Codman, John. "A Trip to Cariboo Mountain." *Idaho Yesterdays* 19 (Winter 1976):18–24.

Writer John Codman went from Soda Springs to Cariboo (Keenan City) to inspect Idaho's recently discovered gold mines in August, 1874. What impressed him most was the beauty of the mountains, the mineral waters of Soda Springs, the amount of whiskey consumed by the miners, and the food and lodging, which ranged from excellent to awful. From his *The Mormon Country* (New York, 1874).

(1876)   GUSTAVUS CHEYNEY DOANE   805

Doane, Gustavus Cheyney. "Gustavus C. Doane's Military Expedition to Cariboo Mountain, December 16–22, 1876." *Idaho Yesterdays* 19 (Winter 1976):25–67.

While on his way from Fort Ellis (Montana) to Fort Hall (Idaho), Doane took a side trip to Cariboo Mountain. He relates the experience of going without food for more than three days in temperatures ranging from 10° to 40° below zero.

(1884)   EUGENE V. SMALLEY   806

Smalley, Eugene V. "The Great Coeur d'Alene Stampede: 1884." *Idaho Yesterdays* 11 (Fall 1967):2–10.

The Coeur d'Alene stampede occurred in the first three months of 1884 in the dense forests of northern Idaho, a region that was largely inaccessible by roads. From his trips to the gold strike, Smalley, a veteran travel writer, describes the routes that developed, the mining towns of Eagle and Murray, and the social life he found there. Originally published in *Century Magazine* (October 1884).

(1907)   ELMER PERRY MONAHAN   807

Sokolofsky, Homer, ed. "A 'Scientific Expedition' to Idaho Mountains, 1907." *Idaho Yesterdays* 14 (Winter 1970/1971):18–35.

Baker University of Baldwin, Kansas, hired biologist and taxidermist Elmer Perry Monahan to lead a ten-month collecting expedition to the Sawtooth Mountain region of Idaho and southwestern Oregon. These entries from Monahan's diary (June 22-September 17, 1907) tell of the party's camping activities and the specimens collected.

(1918)   ERNEST N. MAY   808

May, Ernest N. "'On the Line' in Idaho: A Reminiscence." *Idaho Yesterdays* 21 (Summer 1977):2–10.

The author recalls with fondness a summer he worked on a survey crew in central Idaho. Includes three letters written during the summer of 1918 that confirm his memory of a great time.

(1939–1940)   DONALD TANASOCA   809

Tanasoca, Donald. "Six Months in Garden Valley." *Idaho Yesterdays* 11 (Summer 1967):16–24.

A New Jersey boy remembers the time he spent in a Civilian Conservation Corps camp near Banks, Idaho, in late 1939 and early 1940. Strongest in his memory was the backbreaking work of chopping trees and clearing brush by men from the East who were unaccustomed to such labor. He also remembers the horseplay in the barracks and the acts of prejudice inflicted on the Jewish boys. Tanasoca praises the CCC experience for cultivating in him the virtues of hard work and independence. Elmo Richardson provides an introduction.

MONTANA

(1863–1865)　　　　MARY WRIGHT EDGERTON　　　　810

Thane, James L., Jr., ed. "Love From All to All." *Montana: The Magazine of Western History* 24 (July 1974):12–25.

Soon after Mary Wright Edgerton, the wife of Montana's first territorial governor, arrived in Bannack City, she began writing letters home to Ohio. During the years of her correspondence (October 18, 1863-August 27, 1865), the town bulged with gold seekers before giving way to a richer strike in Virginia City. Her letters reveal the problems of rearing six children on the rough frontier. The extreme cold, which once froze the bulb in the thermometer at 40° below zero, led to illness; schooling was a worry; and there was no suitable social life for her eldest daughter. During this period Mary had another baby. She writes about the lawlessness and the frontier justice in the form of a vigilance committee that once burned a villains' stronghold and threw bodies on the fire.

(1864)　　　　GEORGE FORMAN　　　　811

Larson, T. A., ed. "Across the Plains in 1864 With George Forman." (Part I) *Annals of Wyoming* 40 (April 1968):5–22.

———. (Part II) *Annals of Wyoming* 40 (October 1968):267–81.

Canadian George Forman left from Saint Joseph, Missouri, for the Montana mines as a bullwhacker (driving oxen) but within a few days he had joined an emigrant train because the oxen were going too slowly. Before he reached the Lander Cutoff, which he took part of the way into Virginia City, Montana, he had switched again and ended up riding alone. The editor adds that this was a rather dangerous act, considering the frequent Indian attacks that year.

In writing his "Biographical Sketch . . . " some nineteen years after these events, Forman consulted his trail diary. Although his writing suffers from mistakes and material added later (which the editor clarifies), his account illuminates the fear of Indian activity during that year. The editor says that Forman escaped the heaviest Indian attacks by only a few weeks. Several of the people Forman traveled with were secessionist sympathizers fleeing Missouri. Forman tells of the great excitment for Montana he found in Saint Joseph and along the trails. He says wagons with signs reading "Bannock or Bust," or wagons coming back from Denver, were never out of sight.

After arriving in Virginia City he left for Emigrant Gulch, where he prospected unsuccessfully. Later in the year Forman saw hundreds traveling to Fort Benton, Montana, to return home down the Missouri. He was dissuaded from returning after being warned of danger from the Indians. Instead, he went on to Idaho to search for gold. (See item 802.) This part of his reminiscence covers May 31 to September 25, 1864.

(1868)　　　　CHARLES GALPIN　　　　812

Pfaller, Louis, ed. "The Galpin Journal: Dramatic Record of an Odyssey of Peace." *Montana: The Magazine of Western History* 18 (April 1968):2–23.

In June, 1868, trader Charles Galpin accompanied Father Pierre Jean de Smet from Fort Rice, North Dakota, to the encampment of Sitting Bull and the hostile Sioux on the Powder River in southeastern Montana. Galpin acted as guide and interpreter and kept notes of the journey and the conference at which de Smet tried to convince the Sioux to accept the terms of the Treaty of Fort Rice. Pfaller believes that this journal shows Father de Smet, who was nearing the end of a thirty-year career in the West, at his best as a true friend of the Indians.

(1881)　　　　WILLIAM E. WILSON　　　　813

Wilson, William E. "Hoboing in the West in the 1880's." *Montana: The Magazine of Western History* 18 (April 1968):36–51.

"Limestone" Wilson's reminiscences of when he and a companion crossed the Black Hills through hostile Indian country to Montana in hope of finding work with the railroad in the spring of 1881.

(1881–1885)   FRANK BURKE   814

Burke, Charles T., ed. "Letters from the Wild West." *Montana: The Magazine of Western History* 19 (January 1969):2–23.

To Frank Burke, a young corporal from Massachusetts stationed at several military posts in Montana between 1881 and 1885, the West was a strange place. Yet his unfamiliarity with the region allowed him to make some interesting observations about the territory. For example, he writes: "A man's importance is judged by the number of horses and cattle he owns and anyone who wears a white shirt is regarded with the greatest suspicion." (p. 5) In another place he comments on the high-sounding names westerners gave places that he deemed insignificant. Burke also writes of vigilante activity and skirmishes with the Indians, although the editor was unable to find any official record of army action where Frank Burke says he was involved.

(1906–1908)   CHRISTIAN SCRIVER THORPE   815

Anderson, Avis R., ed. "Pastor on the Prairie." *Montana: The Magazine of Western History* 24 (January 1974):36–54.

Christian Scriver Thorpe, a Norwegian Lutheran minister, describes the difficulties of attending to his far-flung parish, which covered seven counties of eastern Montana and western North Dakota. His letters, written between August 12, 1906, and October 7, 1908, also provide information on Norwegian settlements, the high prices in Montana, the poor living conditions of settlers, and the state of religion on the frontier.

WYOMING

(1830–1857)   INDEPENDENCE ROCK AND DEVIL'S GATE   816

Munkres, Robert L. "Independence Rock and Devil's Gate." *Annals of Wyoming* 40 (April 1968):23–40.

Describes travelers' reactions to these two landmarks of the overland trail in central Wyoming. Independence Rock, an isolated outcropping of the granite that forms the mountains enclosing the Sweetwater River, was used by travelers to write, scratch, or paint their names. Devil's Gate, a steep gorge through which the Sweetwater River flows, is located about five miles above Independence Rock. Devil's Gate was acclaimed for its beauty and grandeur. Consults emigrant diaries written between 1830 and 1857.

(1867–1868)   GEORGE HENRY PALMER   817

Greene, Jerome A., ed. "'We Do Not Know What the Government Intends to Do . . . ': Lt. Palmer Writes From the Bozeman Trail, 1867–68." *Montana: The Magazine of Western History* 28 (July 1978):16–35.

George Henry Palmer was with the Twenty-seventh U.S. Infantry that was sent to Fort Reno (Wyoming), Fort Phil Kearny (Wyoming), and Fort C. F. Smith (Montana) to try to keep the Indians from shutting off travel on the Bozeman Trail, which was the short-cut across Wyoming to Montana's gold fields from the Oregon Trail. Palmer's letters to two newspapers, written over an eleven-month period, show frustration over the army's role in trying to hold the area against an overwhelming number of Sioux, Cheyenne, and Arapaho. He describes escorting supply wagons, skirmishes, and Indian fighting tactics, life at the forts, the efforts at a peace treaty, and the Crow Indians, who were on friendly terms with the whites. In March, 1868, the army left the area and it was awarded to the Teton Sioux and their allies by the Fort Laramie Treaty of April 29, 1868.

(1868–1871)   ADA A. VOGDES   818

Adams, Donald K., ed. "The Journal of Ada A. Vogdes, 1868–71." *Montana: The Magazine of Western History* 13 (July 1963):2–17.

The West had a shocking effect on the senses of a young, eastern-born, army lieutenant's wife. She thought the landscape of frontier Wyoming most desolate and the Indians primitive. These excerpts from her dairy give some detailed descriptions of the Indians she frequently had to entertain at Fort Laramie and Fort Fetterman.

(1869)   ALBERT GALLATIN BRACKETT   819

Peters, Joseph P. "March of the Montana Battalion, 1869." *Montana: The Magazine of Western History* 15 (April 1965):38–51.

The author uses the notes of Colonel Albert Gallatin Brackett to recount the 437-mile march from southwestern Wyoming to Fort Ellis (Montana) between May 19 and July 1, 1869, for the purpose of protecting settlements. Contains brief descriptions of Virginia City and Helena, Montana.

(1870)   GUSTAVUS CHEYNEY DOANE   820

Bonney, Orrin H., and Bonney, Lorraine, eds. "Lieutenant G. C. Doane: His Yellowstone Exploration Journal." *Journal of the West* 9 (April 1970):222–39.

Lieutenant Gustavus Cheyney Doane was coleader of the Washburn-Doane Yellowstone Expedition in 1870, which produced the first official report of the region. This article, which reproduces Doane's journal for the period August 22 to September 24, 1870, and which is extracted from the Bonney's biography of Doane, *Battle Drums and Geysers* . . . (Chicago, 1970), describes the natural wonders of Yellowstone.

(1878)   HARRY BOYER   821

Boyer, Francis, ed. "Harry Boyer in Wyoming, 1878." *Annals of Wyoming* 44 (Fall 1972):207–20.

Virginian Harry Boyer spent the months of June through October on an unfinished ranch near Fort Fetterman recovering his health. Most of his letters contain descriptions of camping at the ranch and his hunting experiences. At first he enjoyed his life immensely, especially the hunting, but by July he admitted there was an aimless waste of precious time. "There is nothing to do but hunt." (p. 214) He stayed for the fall season of elk and blacktail deer, however. In October he begged his father to send more of the *Lakeside Classics* to read and wrote that he was determined to return home soon.

(1881)   EDWARD HAYES   822

Hayes, Edward. "College Man on Horseback." *Colorado Magazine* 41 (Winter 1964):61–74.

These letters by Hayes, a recent arrival in Colorado, tell of a horseback trip from Colorado Springs to the Powder River region of Wyoming and of his experiences on a ranch there. Written between March 13 and August 4, 1881.

(1882 to 1887)   **RICHARD TRIMBLE**   **823**

Gressley, Gene M., ed. "Harvard Man Out West: The Letters of Richard Trimble, 1882–1887." *Montana: The Magazine of Western History* 10 (January 1960):14–23.

Trimble spent three years in Cheyenne working as comanager of a failing cattle enterprise. He provides a description of ranching from the perspectives of both a cowboy and a businessman.

(1889)   **RUDYARD KIPLING**   **824**

Kipling, Rudyard. "Kipling Among the Geysers: a Young Englishman's Adventures at Yellowstone, 1889." *American West* 15 (July/August 1978):24–27, 59–61.

The English author visited Yellowstone Park at a period when tourism was thriving. These reports to newspapers show that he viewed his fellow tourists with horror and decried American wastefulness and materialism. Kipling also found America with many beautiful, independent women, one of whom he later married. (See also item 467.)

(1892)   **HENRY A. KIRK**   **825**

Meschter, Daniel Y., ed. "Sixty Days To and In Yellowstone Park." *Annals of Wyoming* 44 (Spring 1972):5–24.

Reprints five letters that were first published in the *Carbon County Journal* (Rawlings, Wyoming) during July and August, 1892, that describe a vacation in Yellowstone taken by the Henry A. Kirk family.

(1899)   **FRANK L. MOORE**   **826**

Moore, Austin L., ed. "Fossil Hunting in the Big Horn Basin: The Diary of Frank L. Moore, 1899." *Annals of Wyoming* 36 (April 1964):22–33.

Diarist Frank Moore, a Minneapolis pastor, accompanied two University of Minnesota geologists into Wyoming and briefly described their discoveries.

10
Southwest

GENERAL

(1540–1542)　　　　**CORONADO EXPEDITION**　　　　**827**

Strout, Clevy Lloyd. "Flora and Fauna Mentioned in the Journals of the Coronado Expedition." *Great Plains Journal* 11 (Fall 1971):5–40.

Gleans the documents relating to the trek of Don Francisco Vásquez de Coronado, which passed through Arizona, New Mexico, Texas, Oklahoma, and into Kansas (1540–1542), for references to plants and animals. Although the descriptions were written by soldiers and not trained biologists, such references are plentiful because of the need to live off the land. The documents of the Coronado Expedition are Francisco Vásquez de Coronado's *Relación del suçeso de la Jornada . . .* , Juan Jaramillo's *Relación que dio El Capitan Juan Jaramillo . . .* , and Pedro de Castañeda's *Relación de la Jornada de Cibola. . . .* English-language translations of these reports may be found in *Narratives of the Coronado Expedition*, George P. Hammond, and Agapito Rey (Albuquerque: University of New Mexico Press, 1940). (See also items 833 and 874.)

(1825–1890)　　　　**SOUTHWEST BORDERLANDS**　　　　**828**

Noggle, Burl. "Anglo Observers of the Southwest Borderlands, 1825–1890: The Rise of a Concept." *Arizona and the West* 1 (Summer 1959):105–31.

Traces the growing appreciation by visitors to New Mexico of the unique culture that resulted from the blending of Spanish and Anglo heritages. Before 1870 the theme of racial superiority was predominant in the writings of American travelers. Later in the century the scholars who replaced travelers as the main source of information documented the way each culture had affected the other. The recognition of the uniqueness was complete when historian Herbert Eugene Bolton characterized the areas "the Spanish Borderlands."

(1831–1869)　　　　**MEXICAN IMAGE**　　　　**829**

Paredes, Raymund A. "The Mexican Image in American Travel Literature, 1831–1869." *New Mexico Historical Review* 52 (January 1977):5–29.

Emphasizes the effect American travel writings from this periood had on establishing a stereotyped, negative image of the Mexicans. Before 1831 few Americans had any contact with Mexicans. Later, the travel accounts written by Americans during the Texas Revolution and the war with Mexico transmitted a negative image of the Mexican. Paredes believes that the source of this negative image was partly latent hispanophobia and partly anti-Catholicism, but he also thinks that these American travelers observed the Mexicans at a time when they were most prepared to hate them.

(1854)   **M. H. ERSKINE**   **830**

Sanderlin, Walter S., ed. "A Cattle Drive from Texas to California: The Dairy of M. H. Erskine, 1854." _Southwestern Historical Quarterly_ 67 (January 1964):397–412.

Erskine's experiences differed from those of other travelers of the same route in that he found plenty of water and did not experience any Indian raids. Although the popular conception of the cattle trail across the Southwest is that it was filled with suffering, privation, and constant fear of Indian attack, Erskine's diary (April 23 or 24-November 1854) indicates an uneventful trip. The editor says that the trek was more consistent with the popular image of trail experiences in other regions.

(1858)   **PHOCION R. WAY**   **831**

Duffen, William A., ed. "Overland Via 'Jackass Mail' in 1858: The Diary of Phocion R. Way." (Part I) _Arizona and the West_ 2 (Spring 1960):35–53.

———. (Part II) _Arizona and the West_ 2 (Summer 1960):147–64.

———. (Part III) _Arizona and the West_ 2 (Autumn 1960):279–92.

———. (Part IV) _Arizona and the West_ 2 (Winter 1960):353–70.

In the first portion of his diary Way recorded his journey from Cincinnati to Galveston by way of the Mississippi River and the Gulf of Mexico. He then traveled from Indianola to San Antonio and across New Mexico to near Tubac, Arizona. His entries describe the conditions of his travel: the roads, heat, dust, food, and resting places, and the way the rugged travel affected the men. They were unwashed and unshaven and wore guns tucked in their belts. Indians were a constant concern, but they experienced no trouble. Once Way and his partners arrived in the mining country of southern Arizona, they began to build houses in anticipation of the arrival of other members of the Santa Rita Mining Company.

His impressions of the Mexicans were typical of American visitors to the Southwest during this period. Although Way blamed himself for his inability to converse with the Mexicans, he wrote, "even if I could their conversation would not interest me for they are very ignorant and not much better than savages." (p. 282) He thought their religion consisted of keeping innumerable holidays for the purpose of shooting guns and generally raising hell.

Mexican women drew much of Way's attention, although once he admitted that he could not determine whether his cook was an Indian or a Mexican. He believed the Mexican women had little virtue and were anxious to capture American lovers. He had been told, he said, that "Mexican women are affectionate, warm hearted to a fault and if they were brought up in good society and surrounded by proper influences, I have no doubt they would make refined and virtuous women, but the way they are raised here you cannot expect anything better of them." (p. 292) Diary kept between May 11 and October 17, 1858.

(1887)   **FOREST ROSE**   **832**

Rose, Forest. "The Diary of Forest Rose." _High Country_ 21 (1972):24–30.

Contains notations of the first, fleeting impressions of a young woman traveling from Missouri to southern California through the Southwest by rail in November, 1887.

Arizona

(1540–1542)   **MARCOS DE NIZA**   **833**

Schroeder, Albert H. "Fray Marcos de Niza, Coronado and the Yavapai." (Part I) _New Mexico Historical Review_ 30 (October 1955):265–96.

———. (Part II) _New Mexico Historical Review_ 31 (January 1956):24–37.

An attempt to discover the ethnology of Arizona at the time of Coronado's march by consulting the *Relaciṓns* of Fray Marcos de Niza, an expedition guide. Schroeder compares Niza's account with other primary sources of the Coronado Expedition (see items 827 and 874), secondary sources, and other studies.

(1698) EUSEBIO FRANCISCO KINO 834

Fireman, Bert M., ed. "Kino on the Arizona Border." *American West* 3 (Summer 1966):16–21, 94–95.

Excerpts from the diary of Jesuit priest and explorer Eusebio Francisco Kino in which he described his travels through the Papago country of Arizona and Sonora in 1698.

(1766) JUAN BAUTISTA DE ANZA 835

Kessell, John L., ed. "Anza, Indian Fighter." *Journal of Arizona History* 9 (Spring 1968):155–63.

This report by Captain Juan Bautista de Anza of a military expedition against the Apache in February and March, 1766, indicates why the editor believes Anza is deserving of the title of "Indian fighter." The expedition began near Benson, Arizona, and ended back in the presidio of Tubac, Arizona.

(1773) ANONYMOUS 836

———. "San José De Tumacácori—1773: A Franciscan Reports from Arizona." *Arizona and the West* 6 (Winter 1964):303–12.

Describes the deplorable condition of the Franciscan mission among the Pima Indians.

(1781) PEDRO FAGES 837

Ives, Ronald L., ed. "Retracing the Route of the Fages Expedition of 1781." (Part I) *Arizona and the West* 8 (Spring 1966):49–70.

———. (Part II) *Arizona and the West* 8 (Summer 1966):157–70.

Lieutenant Colonel Pedro Fages led a group of soldiers from Sonora to the Spanish mission at Yuma to put down a rebellion of the Yuma Indians. Ives uses Fages's diary, together with his personal investigation of the route, to establish the geographical details of Fages's 106-day, 980-mile march.

(1782) 838

———. "From Pitic to San Gabriel in 1782: The Journey of Don Pedro Fages." *Journal of Arizona History* 9 (Winter 1968):222–44.

Reprints the translated diary of Lieutenant Colonel Pedro Fages, who marched 545 miles from the royal presidio at Pitic, Mexico, across the desert trail of the Camino del Diablo of Sonora and southwestern Arizona, and then across the Salton Sink to the San Gabriel Mission near Los Angeles between February 27 and April 1, 1782. Ives adds to Fages's diary with his own investigation and other documents.

(1825) RAMÓN LIBERÓS 839

Kessell, John L., ed. "A Personal Note From Tumacácori, 1825." *Journal of Arizona History* 6 (Autumn 1965):147–51.

Father Ramón Liberós was a missionary at Mission San José de Tumacácori between 1822 and 1828. He exhibits displeasure with the actions of his superiors, tells of an Apache disturbance and of the Pimas' preparation for the day of the Immaculate Conception.

(1826)   JAMES OHIO PATTIE   840

Kroeber, Clifton B., ed. "The Route of James O. Pattie on the Colorado in 1826: A Reappraisal by A. L. Kroeber." *Arizona and the West* 6 (Summer 1964):119–36.

Although Pattie's *Personal Narrative of James O. Pattie* (Cincinnati, 1833) appears to be a prime source for the history of the Southwest, scholars have traditionally regarded it as extravagant and of little historical value. But when archaeologist A. L. Kroeber subjected Pattie's account of his 1826 trapping expedition in Arizona to a comparison with his own historical records of Indian tribes of the Gila and Colorado rivers, Kroeber's conclusions verified some portions of Pattie's narrative. Includes comments by Robert C. Euler and Albert H. Schroeder.

(1852)   JOHN R. BARTLETT   841

Faulk, Odie B., ed. "A Letter from John R. Bartlett at Camp Yuma, 1852." *Journal of Arizona History* 6 (Winter 1965):204–13.

Bartlett was United States boundary commissioner with the job of determining the boundary line between the United States and Mexico following the Treaty of Guadalupe Hidalgo. In this letter, written June 11, 1852, he tells of a twelve-day, 125-mile march from San Diego to Fort Yuma over country that he describes as "unquestionably the worst between the Atlantic and the Pacific Oceans." (p. 207) The temperature was 140° in the sun and 114° in the shade, and even muddy wells were found only great distances apart. Bartlett believed that the hostility of the Indians would make the survey like running a gauntlet to get to the Rio Grande.

(1853–1854)   AMIEL WEEKS WHIPPLE   842

Conrad, David E. "The Whipple Expedition in Arizona, 1853–1854." *Arizona and the West* 11 (Summer 1969):147–78.

A history of the survey led by Lieutenant Amiel Weeks Whipple from July, 1853, to March, 1854, to investigate a feasible route for a transcontinental railway. The expedition, which began at Fort Smith (Arkansas) and ended at Los Angeles, was also important for the scientific knowledge it gathered and for the information about the Indian tribes encountered. The period between December, 1853, and February 1854, was spent crossing central Arizona. The primary documents Conrad consults are Whipple's unpublished journal and volume three of his official report of the 35th parallel survey, *Reports of Explorations and Surveys to Ascertain the Most Practicable and Economic Route for a Railroad from the Mississippi River to the Pacific Ocean . . . 1853–4. . . .* (See also items 574 and 893.)

(1856)   RICHARD STODDERT EWELL   843

Hamlin, Percy G., ed. "An Arizona Letter of R. S. Ewell." *Journal of Arizona History*, 7 (Spring 1966):23–26.

Captain Richard Stoddert Ewell led one of the companies of United States dragoons into southwest Arizona in November, 1865, to establish the first American post in the recently acquired Gadsden Purchase. In this brief letter he expresses his opinions on why ladies should not travel with the army.

(1858)   BALDUIN MÖLLHAUSEN   844

Miller, David H. "The Ives Expedition Revisited: A Prussian's Impressions." *Journal of Arizona History* 13 (Spring 1972):1–25.

Balduin Möllhausen was a Prussian artist who served as the diarist and assistant naturalist on the expedition led by Lieutenant Joseph C. Ives to explore the navigability of the Colorado River in January, 1858. In this article Miller summarizes Möllhausen's comments from his

Reisen in die Felsengebirge Nord-Amerikas . . . (Leipzig, 1861), which is a primary source of information about the expedition. (See also item 845.)

(1858) **845**

————. "The Ives Expedition Revisited: Overland Into Grand Canyon." *Journal of Arizona History* 13 (Autumn 1972):177–96.

In March, 1858, after completing the hydrographic survey of the Colorado River by steamer, Lieutenant Joseph C. Ives of the U.S. Army Topographical Engineers started overland into the Grand Canyon. The purpose of this expedition was to gather scientific information about the Colorado Plateau, and to chart the sources of the Colorado River and its tributaries in present-day Arizona. This article is taken mainly from Balduin Möllhausen's *Reisen in die Felsengebirge Nord-Amerikas* . . . (Leipzig, 1861) and Ives's official report. (See also item 844.)

(1866) **JOHN A. SPRING** **846**

Spring, John A. "A March to Arizona from California in 1866, or: 'Lost in the Yuma Desert'." *Arizoniana* 3 (Fall 1962):1–6.

Contains Sergeant Spring's reminiscences of a march from Wilmington, California, to Fort Yuma (Arizona) to relieve California volunteers between March and May, 1866. On the trail they encountered coyotes so fearless that they stole pillows from under sleeping soldiers' heads, blinding sandstorms, and Spring had the frightening experience of being lost in the desert.

(1868–1869) **EVY ALEXANDER** **847**

Myres, Sandra L., ed. "Evy Alexander: The Colonel's Lady at McDowell." *Montana: The Magazine of Western History* 24 (July 1974):26–38.

Even though she was pregnant and homesick for the East, the wife of the commanding officer of Camp McDowell (Arizona) still thought the post was preferable to some other places her husband might have been assigned. Her letters, written between June 2, 1868, and February 25, 1869, contain information about army-Indian strife, but there is more about the dull, routine way of life, of which she and the other wives soon tired. Evy busied herself with church and welfare work among the Indians where she hoped to one day establish a mission. Includes a letter by her husband, whose attitude toward the Indians was not so charitable.

(1872) **"SABRE"** **848**

Splitter, Henry Winfield, ed. "Tour in Arizona: Footprints of an Army Officer." *Journal of the West* 1 (July/October 1962):74–97.

These letters, which were published by the *Los Angeles Star* in the spring of 1872, were written by an anonymous army paymaster known only as "Sabre" during a tour of military installations in southern Arizona. From such places as Fort Yuma, Gila City, Maricopa Wells, Tucson, and Camp Crittenden he described travel conditions and camp life, as well as the permanent inhabitants of the region. Both the Mexicans and the Indians were described in uncomplimentary terms that were typical of nineteenth-century American travelers to the Southwest. Sabre said the Mexicans looked sinister and cunning and were all unattractive. As for the Indians, he thought they could have easily overrun army defenses in Arizona had they not been so cowardly. Later in this issue (pp. 201–14) the editor describes his efforts to identfy Sabre.

(1872–1873) **HENRY R. PORTER** **849**

Gressley, Gene M., ed. "A Soldier with Crook: The Letters of Henry R. Porter." *Montana: The Magazine of Western History* 8 (July 1958):33–47.

A physician assigned to Lieutenant Colonel George A. Crook's staff tells of the hardships and loneliness endured on the military campaign against the Apaches in Arizona in 1872 and 1873. After describing his trip across the United States to San Francisco, Porter labeled his decision to come to Arizona as foolish. He thought the country was so miserable and poor that the government should let the Indians have it. His later letters provide some interesting descriptions of combat with the Indians.

(1873)   **ALEXANDER WYANT**   **850**

Dawdy, Doris Ostrander, ed. "The Wyant Diary: An Artist With the Wheeler Survey in Arizona, 1873." *Arizona and the West* 22 (Autumn 1980):255–78.

Between August 16 and November 7, 1873, artist Alexander Wyant kept this record of the survey team commanded by photographer Timothy H. O'Sullivan that explored the remote canyons and ancient ruins of northern Arizona and as far west as the Colorado River. As Wyant describes the duties performed and the hardships of the march, the editor suggests that Wyant's comments raise serious questions about the fitness of the civilian-led party to take the field in uncharted territory. At one point, Wyant says the train was so broken down that part of the cargo had to be discarded. In another place he complains of the lack of a professional herder for the mules and the absence of sufficient escort. Still later, "This is the 10th day and we were to do it in four—There are no disgusted persons about our camp. O-no!" (p. 274)

(1878)   **GEORGE H. R. MORAN**   **851**

Hagemann, E. R., ed. "Arizona Territory—1878: The Diary of George H. R. Moran, Contract Surgeon, U.S.A." *Arizona and the West* 5 (Autumn 1963):249–67.

These brief entries reveal that the dull garrison life at Camps Bowie and Thomas was enlivened by hunting and occasional patrols into Indian country. Diary kept February 1 to September 2, 1878.

(1884)   **JOHN G. BOURKE**   **852**

Casanova, Frank E., ed. "General Crook Visits the Supais As Reported by John G. Bourke." *Arizona and the West* 10 (Autumn 1968):253–76.

Bourke was the acting inspector general of the Department of Arizona who traveled with General Crook to visit the Havasupai Indians of the Cataract Canyon in November, 1884. He describes the difficult half-mile descent into the canyon and the Indians' homes, food, and customs.

(1886)   **LAWRENCE R. JEROME**   **853**

Stout, Joe A., Jr., ed. "Soldiering and Suffering in the Geronimo Campaign: Reminiscences of Lawrence R. Jerome." *Journal of the West* 11 (January 1972):154–69.

Jerome tells the story of Captain Henry W. Lawton's unsuccessful efforts to track down renegade Apaches under Geronimo in northern Mexico and southern Arizona in 1886. Jerome was a trooper with the Fourth U.S. Cavalry.

(1886)   **CHARLES F. LUMMIS**   **854**

Gordon Dudley, ed. "Lummis as a War Correspndent in Arizona." *American West* 2 (Summer 1965):4–12.

An author and promoter of the West, Charles F. Lummis reported the search for Geronimo by General George Crook for the *Los Angeles Times*. In this dispatch from Fort Bowie (Arizona) on April 4, 1886, Lummis criticizes the reportorial techniques used by the Associated Press.

Lummis says the A.P. reporters had not been within twenty-five miles of the Indian campaign, but instead had gathered their information from barkeepers. He tells his readers that the only way to get accurate reports is to be in the field.

Lummis describes the landscape, praises the abilities of the Apache warriors, and says that Geronimo was successful partly because he could slip into Mexico when pursued. Lummis also relates Geronimo's first capture and the conditions that contributed to his escape.

(1887)   JOHN MILLER STOTSENBERG   855

Wallace, William Swilling, ed. "Lieutenants Pershing and Stotsenberg Visit the Grand Canyon: 1887." *Arizona and the West* 3 (Autumn 1961):265–84.

While serving with the Sixth U.S. Cavalry in Arizona, Lieutenant John Miller Stotsenberg wrote this narrative of an exploration he made with John J. Pershing. The jaunt was meant to be recreational, but the canyon proved to be much more hazardous than they had expected. Stotsenberg's journal includes descriptions of the Indians and the white men who lived in the Grand Canyon.

(1889)   FREDERIC REMINGTON   856

Remington, Frederic. "A Scout With the Buffalo-Soldiers." *Pacific Historian* 12 (Spring 1968):25–39.

Reprints an illustrated article from *Century Magazine* (March 1889) about the artist's ride into Arizona Territory with the Tenth U.S. Cavalry, a unit of blacks.

(1902)   FLORA SMALLEY   857

Smalley, Flora. "'We Slept in the Wagon': An Arizona Camping Trip, 1902." *Journal of Arizona History* 12 (Autumn 1971):183–212.

In these seven letters the author describes a camping trip in southern Arizona in February, 1902. The trip, which began and ended in Tucson, made stops in Benson, Oracle, Mammoth, Dudleyville, Troy City, Florence, and Red Rock.

(1914)   EDITH S. KITT   858

Kitt, Edith S. "Motoring in Arizona in 1914." *Journal of Arizona History* 11 (Spring 1970):32–65.

A diary of a camping and automobile outing that began in Mesa and continued into northern Arizona before returning to Tucson. Preparations for the trip that took place between May 28 and June 2, 1914, included loading gasoline and water cans into a box on the running board, wiring a table to the bumper, and packing the extra hats that were necessary items. Contains details about the dusty, sun-filled trip, the conditions of early Arizona highways, mishaps with the car, and many descriptions of the Grand Canyon and its inhabitants.

(1924)   WARREN MCARTHUR, JR.   859

Hoober, David H., ed. "'Camping Delux': A Tour through Arizona in 1924." *Journal of Arizona History* 21 (Summer 1980):171–88.

Warren McArthur, Jr., and his brother Charles converted a Dodge truck into a coach, dubbed it "Wonderbus," and inaugurated camping tours of Arizona. This account describes the splendor and comfort of a 1,200-mile tour through northern Arizona in about 1924.

NEW MEXICO

(1756)   **BARTOLOMÉ SÁENZ**   860

Kessell, John L., ed. "Campaigning on the Upper Gila, 1756." *New Mexico Historical Review* 46 (April 1971):133–60.

In an attempt to quell Indian raids in the northern territories, Spanish soldiers launched a campaign against the Gila Apache from their base camp at Todos Santos, near present-day Cliff, New Mexico. While soldiers managed to kill some warriors and capture their women and children, they were unsuccessful in putting a stop to future marauding. Chaplain Bartolomé Sáenz, S.J., left this account of the expedition.

(1788)   **FERNANDO DE LA CONCHA**   861

Feather, Adlai, ed. "Colonel Don Fernando de la Concha Diary, 1788." *New Mexico Historical Review* 34 (October 1959):285–304.

A report submitted by the Spanish governor of New Mexico of his military expedition against the Gila and Mimbres Apaches in August, 1788.

(1820–1850)   **NEW MEXICAN WOMEN**   862

Lacy, James M. "New Mexican Women in Early American Writings." *New Mexico Historical Review* 34 (January 1959):41–51.

During the first part of the nineteenth century, American travelers in New Mexico had little good to say about the men, but they almost always praised Mexican women. Lacy stresses one factor common to all the men whose writings he has consulted: they had been away from home for a long time. New Mexican (and Texan) women were praised for their physical characteristics, their kindness and generosity, and their uninhibited natures. Lacy explains that those qualities contrasted greatly with those of the women the travelers were accustomed to at home, where puritanical restraint, decorum between the sexes, and clothing that hid feminine beauty were characteristic. Lacy also stresses that New Mexican women were attracted to men from the East because they were bigger and stronger than Mexican men, and they had more money to spend. The women's infidelity was considered a fault of marriage customs that forced girls to marry too young and without freedom of choice, of a society that placed greater emphasis on faithfulness by unmarried women, and of Mexican men who created their women's weaknesses. Lacy says that proof of the high esteem in which American men held New Mexican women is found in the great number of marriages between them.

(1820–1850)   863

Trulio, Beverly. "Anglo-American Attitudes Toward New Mexican Women." *Journal of the West* 12 (April 1973):229–39.

Argues against the familiar thesis that during the first half of the nineteenth century Anglo-Americans viewed Mexican men in less than complimentary terms but held Mexican women in high esteem. Trulio asserts that women of mid-nineteenth-century New Mexico also failed to escape the stigma of Anglo cultural, political, and racial bias. Trulio emphasizes that the greatest contact between American men and Mexican women was at the "end of the trail." She says that the qualities Anglo men praised in Mexican women were reflections of sexual cravings that served to enhance the male ego rather than being sincere expressions of approval. To reach these conclusions Trulio has examined a broad range of comments about New Mexican women regarding their dress, beauty, skin, hygiene, immodesty, and religion, as well as Anglo-American expressions of cultural superiority.

(1824–1850)   **GILA TRAIL**   **864**

Hufford, Kenneth. "Travelers on the Gila Trail, 1824–50." (Part I) *Journal of Arizona History* 7 (Spring 1966):1–8.

———. (Part II) *Journal of Arizona History* 8 (Spring 1967):30–44.

Part one is a discussion of travelers, routes, and general literature on the Gila Trail, which wound its way through New Mexico and Arizona, and in Chihuahua and Sonora, Mexico. The second part is an annotated bibliography of sixty-three items.

(1846)   **FRIEDRICH ADOLPH WISLIZENUS**   **865**

Porter, Eugene O., ed. "Down the Chihuahua Trail With Wislizenus." (Part I) *Password* 18 (Spring 1973):21–32.

———. (Part II) *Password* 18 (Summer 1973):66–74.

———. (Part III) *Password* 18 (Fall 1973):114–18.

———. (Part IV) *Password* 18 (Winter 1973):169–80.

Friedrich Adolph Wislizenus was a German physician who wrote of his travel experiences in two works. *A Journey to the Rocky Mountains in the Year 1839* (Saint Louis, 1839) relates a trip over the Oregon Trail. Several years later he joined a trading caravan to Santa Fe and then on to Chihuahua, Mexico, where he hoped to conduct a study of natural history. His work was interrupted by the Mexican War, however, and he had to be liberated by the American troops of Alexander Doniphan. This experience was recounted in *Memoirs of a Tour to Northern Mexico Connected with Col. Doniphan's Expedition in 1846 and 1847* (Washington, 1848).

Reprinted here are extracts from the second work that cover the trip along the Chihuahua Trail from Santa Fe to Chihuahua City. The editor recognizes the work to be the "first and only scientific investigation of the flora and fauna of the region." (p. 21) Wislizenus's day-to-day dairy (July 8– September 11, 1846) describes the terrain and the small communities, as well as Santa Fe, Albuquerque, and El Paso del Norte; anti-American sentiment in New Mexico, including his confrontation with a mob in Chihuahua; and his impressions of the people of the region. *Note*: Another account of Wislizenus's activities is Douglas D. Hale, "Friedrich Adolph Wislizenus: From Student Rebel to Southwestern Explorer," *Missouri Historical Review* 62 (April 1968):260–85.

(1846–1849)   **NEW MEXICANS**   **866**

Bloom, John P. "New Mexico Viewed by Anglo-Americans, 1846–1849." *New Mexico Historical Review* 34 (July 1959):165–98.

The author says that the negative attitudes American soldiers held toward New Mexicans during the war with Mexico were formed before their arrival in the region. He explains that because Americans had sided with Texas in its struggle for independence against the Mexicans, the American soldiers simply adopted the Texans' prejudices as fact. Also, there is evidence that many soldiers had read and apparently accepted the negative passages of earlier travel writers. Bloom believes that the American soldiers were typical of all occupation troops who, because their situation was forced on them, seldom went out of their way to find their own explanations for the conditions they observed. Unfortunately, the soldiers' writings provided continuity to previous accounts that also stressed the negative aspects of New Mexicans.

(1846–1861)   **NEW MEXICO**   **867**

Sunseri, Alvin R. "Anglo Attitudes toward Hispanos, 1846–1861." *Journal of Mexican-American History* 3 (1973):76–88.

During this period when Spanish New Mexico passed into American hands, "it is quite possible that the cultural cleavages would not have been formed had the Anglos been less disdainful in their treatment of Hispanos." (p. 76) The author uses travelers' accounts, along with other publications, to document the degree of disdain.

(1855–1856)   **CHARLES E. WHILDEN**   **868**

Moore, John Hammond, ed. "Letters from a Santa Fe Army Clerk, 1855–1856: Charles E. Whilden." *New Mexican Historical Review* 40 (April 1965):141–64.

During the trip from Fort Leavenworth (Kansas) to New Mexico, Whilden and his fellow soldiers encountered inquisitive Indians, stampeding cattle, and prairie fires. His comments about Santa Fe are typical of Americans of the period: the buildings were "unsightly," the children were constantly "jabbering" Spanish, the women were "ignorant" (but some beautiful), the men, the "worst specimens of humanity," and the priests were "rascals." (pp. 149–51) Nevertheless, he did think the sunsets beautiful and praised the crops.

(1861–1864)   **JOHN W. TEAL**   **869**

Walker, Henry P., ed. "Soldier in the California Column: The Diary of John W. Teal." *Arizona and the West* 13 (Spring 1971):33–82.

Teal, who served with the Second California Cavalry in the Civil War, describes his unit's march from California to New Mexico during 1862 and service in New Mexico. He also relates the return march to California and service on the San Bernardino Road in 1864. The march across Arizona was enlivened by a battle with the Indians and the capture of the "secesh" (secessionists). Most of his sixteen months' duty at Fort Sumner (New Mexico) as a scout and messenger was uneventful. On November 26, 1863, Teal had grown tired of routine duty. When he was made to clean the officers' cookhouse he was so disgruntled that he wrote: "I enlisted to serve the government as a soldier but instead of being a soldier for our government I am a dog or slave for the officers." (p. 56) After his discharge in San Francisco, he returned to Canada through the Isthmus of Panama, a trip he also describes. Diary kept September 24, 1861, to November 12, 1864.

(1873–1874)   **GEORGE MILLER**   **870**

Miller, George. "Ranching in Chicorica Park: A Diary Kept by George Miller, 1873–74." *Colorado Magazine* 33 (January 1956):52–66.

Englishman George Miller set up his ranching business in extreme northern New Mexico (Colfax County). His terse diary (October 8, 1873-May 28, 1874) tells of the weather, surviving the first winter, buying cattle, establishing the ranch, building a house, and the arrival of his family from England. (See also item 871.)

(1875)   **GEORGINA MILLER**   **871**

Miller, Georgina. "Ranching in Chicorica Park: A Diary Kept by Georgina Miller, 1874–75." *Colorado Magazine* 33 (April 1956):133–48.

Records Mrs. Miller's trip from England to join her husband in New Mexico and describes life on the ranch. This portion of her diary was kept from April 23 to January 7, 1875. (See also item 870.)

(1895)   **HAMLIN GARLAND**   **872**

Underhill, Lonnie E., and Littlefield, Daniel F., eds. "Hamlin Garland at Isleta Pueblo." *Southwestern Historical Quarterly* 78 (July 1974):45–68.

In June, 1895, writer Hamlin Garland visited Isleta Pueblo, an Indian village twelve miles from Albuquerque, New Mexico. This unpublished article is a firsthand observation of the homes, dress, farming practices, and daily life of the Isletans, who were in a transitional state. The editors say this essay was important in Garland's career because it indicates a new trend in his writing. For the next twenty years his work was as much sociological as literary. Garland believed the Isletans' quiet routine promoted a happier people, and he lamented the introduction of schools and threshing machines. This society had resisted the Navajo, the Apache, and the Spaniard, but was no match for the Yankee. He asked, "why 'civilize' these kindly folk" and "why disturb them with our problems?" (pp. 61–62)

(1898–1901)   ADAM CLARK VROMAN   873

Vroman, Adam Clark. "Zuni." *American West* 3 (Summer 1966):42–55.

Combines Vroman's essay, "The Pueblo of Zuni" (*Photo Era*, August 1901) with photographs taken in New Mexico beginning in 1898. He describes the pueblo, a performance of the rain dance, and the Zuñis' pottery making and blanket weaving.

TEXAS

(1540–1542)   CORONADO EXPEDITION   874

Williams, J. W. "Coronado: From the Rio Grande to the Concho." *Southwestern Historical Quarterly* 63 (October 1959):190–220.

Attempts to trace the explorations of Francisco Vásquez de Coronado on a modern map of Texas. Consults the diarists of the trip and other modern studies and reports. (See also items 827 and 833.)

(1716–1724)   FRANÇOIS DION DEPREZ DERBANNE   875

Bridges, Katherine, and DeVille, Winston, eds. and trans. "Natchitoches and the Trail to the Rio Grande: Two Early Eighteenth-Century Accounts by the Sieur Derbanne." *Louisiana History* 8 (Summer 1967):239–59.

François Dion Deprez Derbanne was a clerk at the newly established French military post of Natchitoches (Louisiana) and an early settler of the region. The first account is of his trip across Texas in 1716 and 1717 into Spanish territory. Derbanne thought highly of the land around the Rio Grande and believed that the Indians would be easy to trade with because of their hatred for the Spanish. The second account, prepared on June 12, 1724, is a report of the commercial activities of the post of Natchitoches with the Spanish and the Indians.

(1756)   BERNARDO DE MIRANDA Y FLORES   876

Patten, Roderick B., ed and tr. "Miranda's Inspection of Los Almagres: His Journal, Report, and Petition." *Southwestern Historical Quarterly* 74 (October 1970):223–54.

Bernardo de Miranda y Flores was sent on an official mission from San Antonio to Los Almagres, Texas, to inspect the fabled San Sabá silver mines in February, 1756. In the introduction the editor traces the development of the legend of the "lost mines" and summarizes modern attempts to locate them.

(1765)   JOSÉ DE LA FUENTE   877

Daniel, James M., ed. and tr. "Diary of Pedro José de la Fuente, Captain of the Presidio of El Paso del Norte, January-July 1765." *Southwestern Historical Quarterly* 60 (October 1956):260–81.

Nearly every entry in this account concerns the threatening presence of Apache Indians and includes an expedition that ended in an unsuccessful skirmish. The editor praises this document for being a day-to-day account of life in a typical Spanish frontier outpost.

(1767)   PIERRE MARIE FRANÇOIS DE PAGÈS   878

Sibley, Marilyn McAdams, ed. "Across Texas in 1767: The Travels of Captain Pagès." *Southwestern Historical Quarterly* 70 (April 1967):593–622.

In 1767, Pierre Marie François de Pagès began his trip around the world by crossing Texas. Did he really make the trip, and if so, how authentic are his descriptions? The editor discusses this controversy in the introduction. Taken from *Travels Round the World in the Years 1767, 1768, 1769, 1770, 1771* (London, 1791), which is conceded to be the first English-language description of Texas.

(1822)   JAMES CHAMBERS LUDLOW   879

————. "Texas in 1822: A Few Observations." *East Texas Historical Journal* 5 (October 1976):112–16.

A man identified only as J.C.L. (probably James Chambers Ludlow) authored this observation of Texas that first appeared in the *American Farmer* (vol. 4, February 15, 1823). It was based on a trip to Matagorda Bay, Galveston, and the Trinity River in the summer of 1822. He offers descriptions of a variety of grapes, of the stingray, and of the Corn Dance that he saw being performed by the Coushatta Indians.

(1830–1849)   TEXAS   880

Spence, Mary Lee. "British Impressions of Texas and the Texans." *Southwestern Historical Quarterly* 70 (October 1966):163–83.

In the 1830s and 1840s Britishers were fascinated by writings on independent Texas. Books, pamphlets, and newspapers printed a steady stream of information that was written by travelers, as well as taken from other sources. Interest centered on such issues as whether Texas had been stolen from Mexico and if Texas would join the United States. Englishmen were also interested in the character of the Texas people, but there was little controversy about their nature: Texans were considered crude and lawless. Spence also comments on literary works that were written during the period. She says that the conflicting testimony of the writings presented a confusing picture of Texas to the prospective emigrant, investor, or philanthropist.

(1835–1838)   MARY AUSTIN HOLLEY   881

Holley, Mary Austin. "The Texas Diary, 1835–38." *Texas Quarterly* 8 (Summer 1965):12–119.

The cousin of Stephen F. Austin made two trips to Texas that are recorded in this diary. The first between April and June, 1835, was spent at Bolivar. The second trip took her from Galveston, up the Buffalo Bayou to Houston, across to Brazoria, and then down the Brazos River to Galveston between December, 1837 and May, 1838. J. P. Bryan, who wrote the introduction and provided notes, says that the value of this diary is not that it adds any unusual historical facts to our knowledge, but rather that it provides glimpses of the early Republic, its prominent leaders, and social conditions on the coastal plains, near the mouth of the Brazos.

(1841–1843)   CAYTON ERHARD   882

Dixon, Ford, ed. "Cayton Erhard's Reminiscences of the Texan Santa Fe Expedition, 1841." (Part I). *Southwestern Historical Quarterly* 66 (January 1963):424–56.
————. (Part II) *Southwestern Historical Quarterly* 66 (April 1963):547–68.

Erhard was a member of a commercial expedition that left Texas in June, 1841, to establish trade between the coast of Texas and the Mexican city of Santa Fe. In a series of articles published in the *San Marcos Free Press* in 1882, Erhard recounted the hardships of the trip across Texas, the expedition's capture by Mexican forces in New Mexico, and the forced march back to near El Paso. Erhard was among those who were not released until March, 1843.

(1842)   JERRY B. ST. JOHN   883

St. John, Jerry B. "A Buffalo Hunt in the Texas Prairie." *Texana* 12 (no. 2, 1974):179–87.

For the readers of *The Sportsman* (London, January/June 1844), the author provided the details of a hunt in which he and several British naval officers participated in the spring of 1842. St. John says that buffalo were deserting the western prairies as civilization encroached upon their range pastures.

(1843–1844)   JOHN BELDEN BILLINGSLEY   884

Billingsley, John Beldon. "A Trip to Texas." *Texana* 7 (Fall 1969):201–19.

A young boy's reminiscence about a family's wagon trip from Missouri to Ellis County, Texas, between December, 1843, and May 1, 1844. Billingsley describes the journey across unbroken Texas prairie and the first year of settlement. He remembers hunting wildlife, farming, the establishment of the first mill, prairie fires, people that were important in his life, and the effects of civilization on Ellis County.

(1846)   JOHN POLLARD GAINES   885

Winfrey, Dorman H., ed. "Diary of Major John Pollard Gaines." *Texana* 1 (Winter 1963):20–41.

Gaines organized the First Regiment of Kentucky Volunteer Cavalry to fight during the War with Mexico. His diary records the march from Memphis to the Rio Grande, July 16 to October 20, 1846. For the most part, Gaines's diary provides extensive description of the terrain of Arkansas and Texas and reveals problems between some of the troops. He also offers reflections on what he has seen. For example, in passing through former Cherokee Indian country in southeastern Texas, Gaines criticizes the way the Texans took land away from the civilized Indians in 1839. Later, he offers a negative evaluation of the land in south-central Texas for settlement.

(1849)   ROBERTS S. NEIGHBORS   886

Neighbours, Kenneth F., ed. "The Report of the Expedition of Major Roberts S. Neighbors to El Paso in 1849." *Southwestern Historical Quarterly* 60 (April 1957):527–32.

The purpose of the expedition was to ascertain the practicality of a wagon route from Austin to El Paso that would be part of a permanent military road from the Gulf of Mexico to California. Neighbors's description of the topography indicates that he was in favor of this route.

(1849)   W. STEINERT   887

Jordan, Gilbert J., ed. and tr. "W. Steinert's View of Texas in 1849: May 22 to June 5." (Part I) *Southwestern Historical Quarterly* 80 (July 1976):57–78.

————. (Part II) *Southwestern Historical Quarterly* 80 (October 1976):177–200.

————. (Part III) *Southwestern Historical Quarterly* 80 (January 1977):383–301.

————. (Part IV) *Southwestern Historical Quarterly* 80 (April 1977):399–416.

————. (Part V) *Southwestern Historical Quarterly* 81 (July 1977):45–72.

Steinert was with a group of Germans who spent four months examining the prospects for colonization offered by the south-central part of Texas. What he saw was the poor conditions of travel and transportation, insects and plague, Indian attacks, difficulties of farming and cattle raising, and Anglo hostility to Germans. Therefore, his harsh description served to balance writings that portrayed the area more favorably. The editor adds that "in 1849 he was probably wise in emphasizing the undesirability of conditions for settlement in Texas." (p. 59)

(1849)   **J. TOLMER**   888

Jordan, Philip D. "J. Tolmer—Spurious Traveler." *Southwestern Historical Quarterly* 65 (April 1962):475–79.

Before the author's study, many accepted as authentic the description of Texas given in Captain J. Tolmer's *Scènes de l'Amérique du Nord en 1849* (Leipzig, 1850). Jordan insists that the work is fictional and filled with error, and, moreover, that there is no satisfactory proof that a Captain J. Tolmer existed.

(1850)   **FERDINAND ROEMER**   889

Biesele, Rudolph L., ed. and tr. "Dr. Ferdinand Roemer's Account of the Llano-San Saba Country." *Southwestern Historical Quarterly* 62 (July 1958):71–74.

Dr. Roemer, who was a German geologist, wrote this letter (April 3, 1850) to the Society for the Protection of German Immigrants in Texas. His purpose was to describe to the Society the lands it had been granted for settlement. Although he had formerly thought the land not suitable for farming, Roemer's recent visit to the Society's grant and other similar tracts made him think that the lands were desirable. He also reported that the Comanche Indians had become more peaceful.

(1850)   **EDWARD SMITH**   890

Smith, Edward. "Account of a Journey Through Northeastern Texas." (Part I) *East Texas Historical Journal* 7 (March 1969):28–49.

————. (Part II) *East Texas Historical Journal* 7 (October 1969):78–109.

————. (Part III) *East Texas Historical Journal* 8 (March 1970):29–91.

Smith was an Englishman who conducted a survey of northeastern Texas in May and June, 1850, to report on prospects for immigration. His document, reproduced in its entirety, takes into consideration the healthfulness of Texas, the advantages of each region, the quality of the soil, the availability of communication and transportation systems, the prices of products, the cost of labor, the laws respecting aliens and slavery, and the character of the inhabitants. Although his report was not as glowing as similar immigration reports, Smith wrote favorably about the region, especially with regard to security from Indian attacks. As a result of his report, the following year about a hundred English colonists established the short-lived colony of Kent, fifty miles north of Waco.

(1852)   **DUFF C. GREENE**   891

Tyler, Ronnie C., ed. "Exploring the Rio Grande: Lt. Duff C. Greene's Report of 1852." *Arizona and the West* 10 (Spring 1968):43–60.

Lieutenant Greene escorted the U.S. Boundary Survey Commission from Presidio de Norte south to Eagle Pass, Texas. His report from November 11-24, 1852, describes rugged country, hostile Indians, and the Mexican border defenses.

(1853)   **MARY JAMES EUBANK**   892

Nunn, W. C., ed. "A Journal of Our Trip to Texas, Oct. 6, 1853, By Mary James
Eubank." *Texana* 10 (Spring 1972):30–44.

Tells of an eight-week journey (October 6-December 4, 1853) by a family migrating from
Glasgow, Kentucky, to east-central Williamson County, Texas, across Tennessee and Arkansas.
A relatively uneventful trip that illustrates the routine activities of travel in the South during the
mid-nineteenth century.

(1853)   **AMIEL WEEKS WHIPPLE**   893

Archambeau, Ernest R., ed. "Lieutenant A. W. Whipple's Railroad Reconnaissance
Across the Panhandle of Texas in 1853." *Panhandle-Plains Historical Review* 44
(1971):iv–128.

Reprints volume 3 of Amiel Weeks Whipple's official report of the 35th parallel survey,
*Reports of Explorations and Surveys, to Ascertain the Most Practicable and Economical Route for a
Railroad from the Mississippi River to the Pacific Ocean . . . 1853-4. . . .* The purpose of this
article, with introduction and editorial notes, is to identify modern landmarks on Whipple's
route across the Panhandle of Texas. The complete survey ran from Fort Smith (Arkansas) to
Los Angeles, California, between July, 1853, and March, 1854. (See also items 574 and 842.)

(1854)   **ROBERT SEABORN JEMISON**   894

Reagan, Hugh D., ed. "Journey to Texas, 1854: The Diary of Robert Seaborn Jemison of Talladega." *Alabama Historical Quarterly* 33 (Fall/Winter 1971):190–209.

In April and May, 1854, Jemison and a party of friends traveled from Talladega, Alabama,
to Galveston, Texas, by way of Montgomery, Mobile, and New Orleans. Since their purpose
was to investigate the possibilities of moving, the group bought horses and visited a number of
places in southern and western Texas. Jemison paid particular attention to the soil, the grass, and
the water resources. He mentions a German colony and Alabamans who had moved to Texas.
Jemison praised Galveston and San Antonio, but thought the region around Austin was particularly desolate. He fell ill in Austin and spent most of May recuperating before his return home.

(1854–1856)   **ALBERT J. MYER**   895

Clary, David A., ed. "'I Am Already Quite a Texan': Albert J. Myer's Letters from
Texas, 1854–1856." *Southwestern Historical Quarterly* 82 (July 1978):25–76.

A military surgeon's letters (November 15, 1854-May 7, 1856) describe duty at Fort
Davis and Fort Duncan in southwestern Texas. Threats of Indian fighting and living conditions
in the field were among his chief preoccupations.

(1855)   **ROBERT WEAKLEY BRAHAN, JR.**   896

Boom, Aaron M., ed. "Texas in the 1850's As Viewed by a Recent Arrival." *Southwestern Historical Quarterly* 70 (October 1966):281–88.

In 1855, Robert Weakley Brahan, Jr., went to Texas ahead of his family to prepare for
their move from Mississippi. His two letters, written in January and May, are concerned with
conditions in San Antonio that would affect the family's future. He observed that the "Mexican
hovels" were giving way to American buildings and that the country was well stocked with
lawyers. (pp. 283–84) Brahan also comments on Mexican women, crops, and Alabamans he
met in Texas.

(1855)   **JOHN H. JAMES**   **897**

Smith, Ophia D., ed. "A Trip to Texas in 1855." *Southwestern Historical Quarterly* 59 (July 1955):24–39.

 John H. James of Urbana, Ohio, visited Texas to look after his legal affairs and to explore the possibility of permanent settlement. He thought the land around Galveston, Houston, and Austin was healthful, and found the people a pleasant mix of emigrants from other southern states. Although he felt he could establish himself in Texas, the editor says James was destined to remain in Ohio.

(1855)   **KALIKST WOLSKI**   **898**

Coleman, Marion Moore, ed. and tr. "New Light on La Réunion; From the Pages of 'Do Ameryki i w Ameryce'." (Part I) *Arizona and the West* 6 (Spring 1964):41–68.
————. (Part II) *Arizona and the West* 6 (Summer 1964):137–54.

 Chapters from the 1877 edition of Kalikst Wolski's work that relate his experiences with the utopian colony on the Trinity River known as La Réunion. Wolski, who had come to the United States as a political exile from France, was a follower of the French socialist Victor Prosper Considérant. At Considérant's request, Wolski acted as guide and interpreter for the first group of colonists. Wolski had previously seen and admired the North American Phalanx in New Jersey. (See item 101.) These extracts describe the journey from New Orleans to Galveston, and up the bayou to Houston, and the long march to near Dallas between February and May, 1855.

 During his stay at the colony, Wolski could see that the chances for its success were not good. Although the colony was planned as an agriculutral settlement, the Europeans did not know how to grow plants in the hot sun. Sickness, discontent, lack of provisioning, extreme heat, poor soil, and stockholders' foreclosures on their investments all contributed to the colony's decline by 1857. Wolski had left in November of 1855. Wolski blamed Considérant for his lack of planning and the Europeans for their inability to endure deprivation.

(1855–1856)   **MORRIS J. SNEDAKER**   **899**

Ferris, Norman B., ed. "The Diary of Morris J. Snedaker, 1855–1856." *Southwestern Historical Quarterly* 66 (April 1963):516–46.

 Snedaker was a Mormon who went to Texas from Salt Lake City on the North Platte, the Missouri, and the Mississippi rivers to pursue missionary work. His diary (September 11, 1855-November 8, 1866) is concerned with the initial trip and then tramping around southeastern Texas. The travel was arduous and sometimes hazardous, for not everyone was receptive to Snedaker's preaching.

(1858–1861)   **WILLIAM ESTE BURNET**   **900**

Estep, Raymond, ed. "Lieutenant Wm. E. Burnet: Notes on Removal of Indians From Texas to Indian Territory." (Part I) *Chronicles of Oklahoma* 38 (Autumn 1960):274–309.
————. "Lieutenant William E. Burnet Letters: Removal of The Texas Indians and the Founding of Fort Cobb." (Part II) *Chronicles of Oklahoma* 38 (Winter 1960):369–96.
————. (Part III) *Chronicles of Oklahoma* 39 (Spring 1961):15–41.

 Letters written by Lieutenant William Este Burnet of the First U.S. Infantry between October 11, 1858, and August 27, 1861. They describe the transfer of the Comanche Reservation Indians from the Brazos Agency in western Texas to a reservation near present-day Fort Cobb (Oklahoma). The removal was necessary because the white settlers blamed the reservation Indians for depredations and horse stealing. Burnet insists there was no proof of the reservation Indians' complicity in these crimes. On May 23, 1859, the soldiers were forced to protect the reservation Indians from the armed hostility of the Texas citizenry. Burnet had much more compassion for the Indians than did the settlers of West Texas.

The soldiers were in a precarious situation, for at this time they were also fighting hostile, nonreservation Comanches. Burnet predicted that once the reservation Indians were gone, there would be more hostilities from the Indians who were really creating the disturbances. He describes the difficulty of transporting fourteen hundred Indians, many of whom were sick and old, overland and then settling them into the new quarters.

The final letters relate events in Oklahoma Territory and include comments about the approaching Civil War. Burnet eventually resigned his commission and joined the Confederacy.

(1860)   JAMES H. HOLMAN   901

Rees, Beatrice Milhous, and Alderson, William T., eds. "A Tennessean, Texas, and Camels: The Diary of James H. Holman, June 11 to August 25, 1860." *Tennessee Historical Quarterly* 16 (September 1957):250–61.

Lieutenant Holman's assignment was to lead a mapping expedition, to try to find a better route from the Pecos River to Fort Davis (Texas), and to search for a suitable site for a military fort. The trip from San Antonio and back was made with twenty camels, which had much superior load-carrying abilities than horse-drawn wagons. Most of the diary concerns travel over rough, dry terrain with water in short supply.

(1864–1865)   JOHN C. GILL   902

Lupold, Harry F., ed. "A Union Medical Officer Views the 'Texians'." *Southwestern Historical Quarterly* 77 (April 1974):481–86.

John C. Gill, a surgeon with the 114th Ohio Infantry, wrote letters from Texas in which he expressed varying opinions of the people. In 1864, when he was held captive in Texas, he was pleased with the treatment he received. When he was a member of the occupying force in June, 1865, however, the conditions were so filled with unrest that he wished "the Union Army had laid it in waste." (p. 486)

(1866–1867)   ADAM KRAMER   903

Storey, Brit Allan, ed. "An Army Officer in Texas, 1866–1867." *Southwestern Historical Quarterly* 72 (October 1968):242–51.

In these letters, Lieutenant Adam Kramer (Sixth U.S. Colored Cavalry) tells about being stationed at Brazos Santiago Island when the French interventionists were shelling the Mexican town of Bagdad in January, 1866. The next month, he relates what he knew about the group of filibusterers from his unit that crossed the Rio Grande and plundered the town. In April, 1867, he describes the difficulty of keeping the Texans under control. He writes that the First Reconstruction Act has "desconconsertd [sic] the unreconstructed rebels here in Texas." (p. 250) He wishes the state would be placed under martial law again.

(1867)   JOHANNES SWENSON   904

Widén, Carl T., ed. and tr. "A Journey from Sweden to Texas in 1867, Johannes Swenson." *Southwestern Historical Quarterly* 62 (July 1958):63–70.

Describes the immigration of a party of Swedes for the purpose of working one year on the Texas cotton and sugar plantations of S. M. Swenson in exchange for payment of passage. The first part of the account covers the ocean voyage to America. The second describes the landing at Galveston, the trip up to Houston, and the train ride to Brenham, where some stayed while others walked to Brushy in Williamson County.

(1870)   **WILLIAM R. SHAFTER**   **905**

Sullivan, Jerry M., ed. "Lieutenant Colonel William R. Shafter's Pecos River Expedition of 1870." *West Texas Historical Association Year Book* 47 (1971):146–52.

The record of a forty-day scout by the black troops of the Ninth U.S. Cavalry during August and September, 1870. On this march the expedition located an Indian waterhole west of the head of the South Llano River from which Indian trails led to white settlements. This discovery allowed the soldiers to patrol the area and prevented the Indians from establishing a major camp.

(1873–1874)   **JAMES B. CLARK**   **906**

Sherman, Richard P., ed. "An Itinerant Mechanic Visits the West." *Journal of the West* 9 (July 1970):325–39.

On August 29, 1884 James B. Clark wrote to his aunt and uncle back home in Scotland about his activities during the past ten months. Since he left Pennsylvania in October, 1883, he had traveled more than five thousand miles. After passing through Chicago, where he was nearly taken in by confidence men, and Kansas City, he went to Georgetown, Colorado, where he worked in mine construction. Next, he went to El Paso in search of work, but finding none moved on to Chihuahua, Mexico, where he was employed as a stoneworker for the Mexican Central Railroad.

Following a lengthy description of his three months in Mexico, he says he went back to Texas, where he became ill and disgusted with the heat. "Never go to Texas. It is no place for a white man. . . ." (p. 338) In these letters, written from Saint Louis, he wanted his relatives to know that there was nothing particularly unusual in his travel because "The Americans are a nation of travelers." (p. 339)

(1874)   **THOMPSON MCFADDEN**   **907**

Carriker, Robert C., ed. "Thompson McFadden's Diary of an Indian Campaign, 1874." *Southwestern Historical Quarterly* 75 (October 1971):198–232.

McFadden was a civilian scout serving under Colonel Nelson A. Miles in the Red River War. The duty of the Indian Territory Expedition was to sweep the Texas Panhandle of hostiles. McFadden's eminently readable diary (August 6-December 25, 1874) describes riding from Fort Dodge (Kansas) to the Staked Plains, skirmishes with the Indians, and the recapture of two white girls who had been taken captive earlier.

(1875)   **S. S. PETERS**   **908**

White, Lonnie J., ed. "Letters of a Sixth Cavalryman Stationed at 'Cantonment' in the Texas Panhandle, 1875." *Texas Military History* 7 (Summer 1968):77–102.

During the Red River War, between February and June, 1875, Private S. S. Peters wrote these letters to the *Junction City Weekly Union* (Kansas) from Camp Supply (Oklahoma) and Cantonment (later Fort Elliott) on the Red River. The editor says that they constitute the only known record relating to events at Cantonment. Peters tells of marches between the two posts, as well as scouting parties that ensured the voluntary surrender of some Cheyenne Indians. His passages describing the prairie, buffalo hunts, the damaging effects of violent rainstorms, and Indian burial customs are informative and interesting.

(1875)   **NORWOOD STANSBURY**   **909**

Baughman, James P., ed. "Letters from the Texas Coast, 1875." *Southwestern Historical Quarterly* 69 (April 1966):499–515.

Norwood Stansbury was a displaced Louisiana sugar planter who was in north-central Texas looking for work. His letters provide a description of economic conditions in Texas in 1875. In Galveston cotton shipments were light because of bad roads and because the railroads were carrying what once passed through the city for ocean shipping. He reports that many sugar plantations were up for sale. He saw convicts being utilized for labor on the ship channel to Houston that was being constructed and thought the experiment was working well. Stansbury also describes the devastation caused by a hurricane in September, 1875. These letters appeared in the *Louisiana Sugarbowl* (New Iberia) during 1875, under the pseudonym "Sussex."

(1893) CHARLES A. CHAMBERLAIN 910

Smith, James Howell, ed. "Texas, 1893." *Southwestern Historical Quarterly* 70 (October 1966):321–23.

As the editor points out, this brief letter, written by Charles A. Chamberlain of Wisconsin en route to a California vacation, is notable for revealing the culture shock Texas effected upon the senses of a conservative middle westerner. Eastern Texas, especially the Dallas and Fort Worth area, was described in glowing terms. But, "of the country west of Fort Worth—the less said of it the better." (p. 322) The vegetation was poor and the heritage of bloodshed was lamentable. He spent an afternoon in Mexico (El Paso del Norte) and was so unnerved by all he saw that he thought he could not describe it in his letter. He and his wife were looking forward to a good night's rest, but "Mrs. C. says she is sure of visions of horrible Mexicans." (p. 323)

11

Far West

(including Northwest in general)

GENERAL

(1821)   **KIRILL KHLEBNIKOV**   911

Gibson, James R., ed. "Russian America in 1821." *Oregon Historical Quarterly* 77 (June 1976):174–88.

Presents a description of Russia's colonies in America written by an employee of the Russian-American Company, Kirill Khlebnikov. He lists the five subdivisions, describes the occupations of each, presents the figures that reflect their economic well-being, and tells of Russian contact with the Indians.

(1833)   912

————. "Russian America in 1833: The Survey of Kirill Khlebnikov." *Pacific Northwest Quarterly* 63 (January 1972):1–13.

After his stint as an administrative official with the Russian-American Company, Khlebnikov published this survey in a Saint Petersburg newspaper, the *Commercial Gazett*, in 1834. It describes the extent and the territorial limits of Russian America, the population, and the commercial activities of the colony.

(1850–1856)   **ZEBULON C. BISHOP**   913

Bishop, Zebulon C. "Letters of Zebulon C. Bishop, American Traveler." *Oregon Historical Quarterly* 66 (June 1965):161–70.

Between January 12, 1850, and August 21, 1856, Bishop traveled all over the West Coast and to Hong Kong. From Puget Sound, he complains that the climate of Oregon was not what had been represented—too much snow and rain and too many short days. From Salem, he writes about his experiences in the Oregon legislature. From Stockton, California, he tells of his experiences as a miner. Bishop found gold but not in sufficient quantities. Because of the seasonal nature of mining and the need for rain, he saw many idle workers in California and decided that ranch work was the only reliable employment.

(1855)   **SYLVESTER MOWRY**   914

Bailey, Lynn R., ed. "Lt. Sylvester Mowry's Report on His March in 1855 from Salt Lake City to Fort Tejon." *Arizona and the West* 7 (Winter 1965):329–46.

Mowry's mission was to explore the possibilities of a new military route from Utah across southern Nevada to Fort Tejon, California, a trip of 750 miles. The report describes the desolate terrain and offers advice on how to handle the Indians whose lands the route would cross. The march took place in April and May, 1855. (See also item 999.)

(1878)   **WILLIAM CAREY BROWN**   **915**

Brimlow, George F., ed. "Two Cavalrymen's Diaries of the Bannock War, 1878." "Lt. William Carey Brown, Co. L., 1st U.S. Cavalry." (Part I) *Oregon Historical Quarterly* 68 (September 1967):221–58.
————. "Pvt. Frederick W. Mayer, Co., L., 1st U.S. Cavalry." (Part II) *Oregon Historical Quarterly* 68 (December 1967):293–316.

The editor believes that these two diaries are significant because they trace General Oliver Otis Howard's pursuit of the hostile Indians and provide names of settlers, places, and distances traveled. The campaign against the Bannocks and the Paiutes covered nearly three thousand miles in Oregon, Washington, Nevada, and California between June and October, 1878.

(1881)   **ROBERT MCCONNELL**   **916**

Brown, John A., ed. "Businessman's Search: Pacific Northwest, 1881." *Oregon Historical Quarterly* 71 (March 1970):5–25.

A journal kept by Robert McConnell of Xenia, Illinois, who was trying to establish a mercantile business in the Northwest. He and his family traveled across the country by rail to San Francisco, and then took a ship to Vancouver. Leaving his family there, he searched for business opportunities in Portland, Tacoma, Seattle, Salem, and Corvallis, before eventually entering into a partnership in Moscow, Idaho. His terse comments tell something about the business climate of the region. For example, in Tacoma, "Property up" (p. 15) and "all living in Expectancy of a Big town." (p. 16) He went on to say that Seattle, Tacoma, and Portland were rival towns, but he liked Portland's prospects best. Journal kept between March 16 and July 5, 1881.

(1887)   **HENRY C. ELSING**   **917**

Elsing, Henry C. "Princetonian Out West." *Oregon Historical Quarterly* 74 (December 1973):333–44.

Armed with a fresh masters degree, Elsing canvassed the West for a job. His two letters (August 27 and September 11, 1887) reveal some details of a visit to Yellowstone and travel in Montana, Oregon, and western Washington. After a brief and unhappy experience at the Normal School in Weston, Washington, Elsing eventually accepted a teaching position at Vancouver Barracks, a school for army children. He reprints a poem from a Tacoma paper that reveals the rivalry between Tacoma, Portland, and Seattle.

(1915)   **FRED C. KNAPP**   **918**

Knapp, Fred C. "'Automobiling' on the Pacific Coast." *Oregon Historical Quarterly* 75 (September 1974):282–89.

Knapp describes a 2,000-mile car trip from Portland to San Francisco, then east to Reno, and back north through Oregon to Portland. The trip took place between August 20 and September 7, 1915. The Hudson Light Six, which was loaded with boxes of supplies, a table, blankets, and five people, weighed five thousand pounds. A broken spring was the only difficulty experienced. They cooked out, slept under the stars, and thankfully encountered no rain during the complete trip.

ALASKA

(1833–1834)   ANDREI GLAZUNOV   919

Vanstone, James W., ed. "Russian Exploration in Interior Alaska: An Extract from the Journal of Andrei Glazunov." *Pacific Northwest Quarterly* 50 (April 1959):37–47.

With the hope of opening up the fur trade, Glazunov embarked on a 104-day, 1,400 mile exploration from Saint Michael south to Stony River during 1833 and 1834. This article is a reprint of "Extract From the Journal of Andrei Gluzunov, First-mate of the Imperial Russian Navy, During His Voyage in the Northwest of America."

(1865–1867)   GEORGE RUSSELL ADAMS   920

Taggart, Harold F., ed. "Journal of George Russell Adams: Member, Exploring Expedition in Russian America, 1865–67." *California Historical Society Quarterly* 35 (December 1956):291–307.

The Russian-American Exploring Expedition was undertaken as a part of a Western Union plan to encircle the globe. Despite poor provisions, subzero temperatures, swarms of mosquitoes in the spring, and a constant longing to be in San Francisco, Lieutenant Adams writes of his Alaskan adventure with some humor. In this portion of his diary (December 25, 1866–June 30, 1867), Adams describes why "building telegraph line with dogs and sleds for transportation in the frigid zone is not as much fun as it is cracked up to be." (p. 296)

(1878)   IVAN PETROFF   921

Hinckley, Theodore C., and Hinckley, Caryl, eds. "Ivan Petroff's Journal of a Trip to Alaska in 1878." *Journal of the West* 5 (January 1966):25–70.

Following a lengthy biography of the Russian immigrant—an "enigmatic printer, writer, and prevaricator par excellence"—the editors present Petroff's account of his trip to Alaska to collect materials for historian Hubert Howe Bancroft. (p. 27) Petroff possessed considerable journalistic skill and his diary is interesting. Because he had been in Alaska when it was a Russian possession, his comments on changes that had occurred in the first years of adjustment to American rule were written with authority.

The round trip from San Francisco took place between July 11 and October 27, 1878. In addition to what he learned on this visit to Alaska, Petroff interviewed old-timers in San Francisco who had been associated with Alaska, and he translated documents of the Russian-American Company relating to Alaska. The editors say Petroff's contribution to Bancroft's *History of Alaska, 1730–1885* (San Francisco, 1886) was considerable.

(1885–1886)   VASILII ORLOV   922

Shalkop, Antoinette, ed. "The Travel Journal of Vasilii Orlov." *Pacific Northwest Quarterly* 68 (July 1977):131–40.

Presents the report of a journey along the Kuskokwim River in the winter of 1885–1886 by the deacon of Nushagak Missionary Church in Saint Peter and Saint Paul to the Ecclesiastical Administration of Alaska. The declining strength of the orthodox missions was caused by the inability of the priests to adapt to American ownership of Alaska and to the encroachment of other religions. Orlov's goal was to see if the mission at Kolmakovskii Redoubt could be rebuilt. He mentions the villages he passed through and the efforts of Americans to persuade the natives to reject Catholicism.

(1896)   WILLARD C. BEECHER   923

Miner, Ward L., and Miner, Thelma S., eds. "Gold Prospecting on Cook Inlet in 1896: The Diary of a Failure." *Pacific Northwest Quarterly* 64 (July 1973):97–111.

Willard C. Beecher, a railroad telegraph operator from Michigan, was lured to what proved to be a small Alaskan strike. His diary (March 5-November 3, 1896) describes storms, snow blindness, an earthquake, mosquitoes and prospecting the claim, but little success at finding gold.

(1896)   PHILIP CLAYTON VAN BUSKIRK   924

Monroe, Robert D., ed. "An Excursion to Wrangell, 1896." *Pacific Northwest Quarterly* 50 (April 1959):48–52.

The diary of Philip Clayton Van Buskirk makes it quite clear why this retired navy man went from Seattle to Wrangell, that is, to get a wife or even a concubine for "such a man as I am." (p. 50) Specifically, he was going to survey the possibilities for a mate among the Tlingit Indians. Although he returned home alone, he did leave his description of Wrangell during the off season. The diary covers August 9-23, 1896.

(1897)   JOAQUIN MILLER   925

Miller, Joaquin. "To Chilkoot Pass, 1897: An Uncollected Eyewitness Report." *Alaska Review* 2 (Spring/Summer 1966):43–54.

Four columns the "poet of the Sierras" wrote as a special correspondent for the Hearst newspapers between July 30 and August 30, 1897, describing the Klondike gold rush. They are: "Up the Inside Passage," "Juneau," "Skagway and Dyea," and "Chilkoot Pass." The editorial notes in this and the following item provide brief but interesting background on the circumstances surrounding the publication of these newspaper reports.

(1897)   926

————. "Klondike Gold, 1897: An Uncollected Eyewitness Report." *Alaska Review* 2 (Spring/Summer 1967):20–39.

Six columns Miller wrote for the Hearst newspapers between August 16 and September 4, 1897, that reported the conditions at the Klondike gold rush. They are entitled "Dawson City," "Bonanza Gulch," "Bear Creek," "Hunker Creek," "Sulpher Creek," and "Conclusion." (See also item 925.)

(1898–1899)   JOSEPH RUSSELL JARVIS   927

Probert, Alan, ed. "The Cape Nome Gold Rush: The Diary with Photographs, by Joseph Russell Jarvis." *Journal of the West* 9 (April 1970):153–95.

Joseph, his two brothers, their 65-year-old father, and a friend spent the fall and winter of 1898–1899 prospecting the Norton Sound-Seward Peninsula area of Alaska. In the fall they sailed around the beach area and up rivers looking for gold. When the winter came they built a sled to travel the frozen rivers. Prospecting was especially difficult in the winter because they had to chop ice to get to the gravel and then work quickly before the water froze in their pans. In February the father fell ill with rheumatism (or perhaps scurvy), and despite a variety of treatments, did not improve until the weather warmed. Much of the diary is concerned with everyday living. Such events as baking, skinning mice for nose protectors, reading *King Solomon's Mines* six times, and trading with the Indians helped Jarvis last out the winter in the small cabin. Diary kept between July 25, 1898, and June 9, 1899.

(1900)   EDWARD R. JESSON   928

Reat, Ruth, ed. "From Dawson to Nome on a Bicycle." *Pacific Northwest Quarterly* 47 (July 1956):65–74.

In February and March, 1900, Edward R. Jesson caught the gold fever and joined the stampede. Jesson traveled a thousand miles on his bicycle in temperatures as low as 23° below zero. He reminisces about the frozen tires and oil in the bearings, hard-packed snow along ice-covered roads, the food he ate, and the people he met along the way.

(1901)   **JOHN WHITECLAY CHAMBERS**   929

Chambers, John Whiteclay. "Under Steam for the Gold Rush." *American West* 11 (September 1974):30–39.

John Whiteclay Chambers was a crew member aboard a steam-powered schooner that carried prospectors to the Alaskan goldfields in 1901. Chambers describes the rough sea voyage from San Francisco to Nome with a stop at Seattle to pick up passengers who paid $100 for the trip. Travel was slow, about six knots an hour because of rough water, storms, and ice. When the captain tried to force his ship into an ice-filled Alaskan harbor, a rudder broke and passengers panicked, throwing Chambers into a fit of laughter. The goods were unloaded and no loss of life was suffered. Chambers ends his diary (May 26-July 7, 1901) with comments about Nome.

(1909)   **NED BURKE GOULD**   930

Maino, Jeannette Gould. "Six Months in Chignik, Alaska in 1909." *Pacific Historian* 20 (Winter 1976):475–83.

The author uses the letters of her father, Ned Burke Gould, to recreate his six-month experience in Alaska as a doctor and bookkeeper for a fish cannery.

CALIFORNIA

(1769)   **PORTOLÁ EXPEDITION**   931

Carrico, Richard L. "Portolá's 1769 Expedition and Coastal Native Villages in San Diego County." *Journal of California Anthropology* 4 (Summer 1977):30–41.

Focuses on the San Diego County portion (July 14–22) of Don Gaspár de Portolá's trek from San Diego to Monterey. Carrico consults the diarists of that expedition, Father Juan Crespí, Miguel Costansó, and Pedro Fages, as well as later studies, to present an ethnology of the area. Soon after the Portolá march, the Spanish mission system was established and the accompanying acculturation of the Indians marked the destruction of the native Californians' culture. (See also item 932.)

(1769)   932

Engstrand, Iris Wilson, ed. and tr. "Pedro Fages and Miguel Costansó: Two Early Letters From San Diego in 1769." *Journal of San Diego History* 21 (Spring 1975):1–11.

This correspondence provides an eyewitness look at Spain's first attempt to colonize Alta California, the Portolá Expedition. Fages and Costansó arrived by sea on April 29, 1769, before the arrival of the overland expeditions of Captain Fernando Rivera y Moncada on May 14 and Father Junípero Serra and Gaspár de Portolá on July 1. These letters describe the physical characteristics of San Diego Bay, the potential for trading with the Indians, military considerations, and other matters of interest to Spanish officials who planned the undertaking. (See also item 931.) *Note:* An article that describes the exploration and consults the writings of Costansó, Fages, Father Juan Crespí, and Commander Portolá is Theodore E. Treutlein, "The Portola Expedition of 1769–1770," *California Historical Society Quarterly* 47 (December 1968):291–313.

(1769–1772)   **PEDRO FAGES**   **933**

Treutlein, Theodore E. "Fages as Explorer, 1769–1772." *California Historical Quarterly* 51 (Winter 1972):338–56.

Presents Pedro Fages's diary of his exploration of the San Francisco area, March 20 to April 5, 1772. Treutlein credits Fages, who was accompanied by Father Juan Crespí, with leaving

> the first detailed description of the "Gate" and the main Islands of San Francisco Bay, the record of what they saw in their march along San Pablo Bay, their views of Carquinez Strait (which they discovered) and the confluence of waters of the Sacramento and San Joaquin systems (which they also were the first to see). (p. 338)

Treutlein reveals his discovery of Fages's diary and the uses other historians might have made of the document.

(1769–1776)   **JUAN CRESPÍ**   **934**

Brown, Alan K. "The Various Journals of Juan Crespí." *Americas* 21 (April 1965):375–98.

Discusses the history and fate of the several journals kept by Father Juan Crespí recording his participation in the expeditions along the California coast between 1769 and 1776.

(1774)   **FERNANDO DE RIVERA Y MONCADA**   **935**

———, tr. "Rivera at San Francisco: A Journal of Exploration, 1774." *California Historical Society Quarterly* 41 (December 1962):325–41.

Reprints "Journal of the Sally and Reconoissance of the Harbor of San Francisco Made by the Commandant of the New Establishments of California's Don Fernando de Rivera y Moncada." Captain Rivera y Moncada, who was the first explorer to visit the place where San Francisco now stands, kept this journal between November 23 and December 13, 1774. *Note*: Another article of interest that emphasizes Rivera's services in governing the Californias and his several overland expeditions between 1769 and 1776 is Ernest J. Burrus, "Rivera y Moncada, Explorer and Military Commander of Both Californias, in the Light of His Diary and Other Contemporary Documents," *Hispanic American Historical Review* 50 (November 1970):682–692.

(1782)   **PEDRO FAGES**   **936**

Ives, Ronald L., ed. "Retracing Fages' Route From San Gabriel to Yuma, April 1782." *Arizona and the West* 17 (Summer 1975):141–60.

Lieutenant Colonel Pedro Fages traveled from San Gabriel Mission near Los Angeles to Yuma, Arizona, to inform a contingent of troops that the planned military expedition to punish the Indian leaders of the Yuma uprising of 1781 was to be postponed until the fall. He then marched from Yuma to San Diego and left the first record of Spanish travel over the route. The complete journey took twenty-four days and covered about five hundred miles. In the late 1960s the editor retraced the march using Fages's diary, reproduced here, and modern maps.

(1786–1852)   **CALIFORNIA MISSIONS**   **937**

Weber, Francis J. "The California Missions and Their Visitors." *Americas* 24 (April 1968):319–36.

Examines the literary competence of twenty-four authors who visited the missions between 1786 and 1852. Their focus of attention was on the daily routines and the padres' character. The accuracy of the writings ranged from factual to fanciful. Weber provides brief quotations from each of the travelers and charts illustrating the years of their visits and the missions each visited.

(1800–1850)   RUSSIAN TRAVEL ACCOUNTS   938

Shur, Leonid A., and Gibson, James R. "Russian Travel Notes and Journals as Sources for The History of California, 1800–1850." *California Historical Quarterly* 52 (Spring 1973):37–63.

   Discusses the "sizeable and diverse legacy of journals, notes, reports, memoirs, and letters, many of which have been little used and some of which have only recently been uncovered" in Russian archives. (p. 37)

(1827)   GEORGE PEARD   939

Gough, Barry M., ed. "The Views of Lieutenant George Peard, R.N. on Alta California, 1826 and 1827." *Southern California Quarterly* 56 (Fall 1974):213–32.

   While on an exploring mission in the Pacific, H.M.S. *Blossom* called at California ports twice. In addition to describing the geographical layout of the San Francisco Bay area, Peard details the wildlife, vegetation, and commerce of California. He includes information about the administration of the Spanish missions at San Francisco, San Jose, and Santa Clara, the padres' attempts to civilize the Indians, and the crops raised there. Excerpts from a journal kept between October 23 and December 26, 1827.

(1827–1828)   JAMES OHIO PATTIE   940

Valle, Rosemary K. "James Ohio Pattie and the 1827–1828 Alta California Measles Epidemic." *California Historical Quarterly* 52 (Spring 1973):28–36.

   In his *Personal Narrative of James O. Pattie of Kentucky* (Cincinnati, 1833), Pattie attributed the epidemic that swept the California missions in 1827 and 1828 to smallpox. Valle has reviewed the mission records and scholarly writings on the disease, including those that have accepted Pattie's statement as well as those that doubt his veracity on this and many other points of his travel. Valle concludes that Pattie's account of the epidemic is just another of his tall tales.

(1827–1846)   CALIFORNIANS   941

Clark, Harry. "Their Pride, Their Manners, and Their Voices: Sources of the Traditional Portrait of the Early Californians." *California Historical Quarterly* 53 (Spring 1974):71–82.

   The traditional portrait of California before California became an American possession is that they were finely dressed people who lived life leisurely and nobly. The men were ruled by honor, and although sometimes cruel, were graceful and courtly. The women were virtuous and beautiful. The symbols of the Catholic Church, which ruled over all with benevolent tyranny, were everywhere. Clark traces the source of this characterization to travel accounts written by Americans who visited early California. The four travel accounts that he has gleaned contain all the elements for romanticizing the period and were read widely in the East. Clark says they were relatively free from the sentimentality that came in later writings. The editions of the accounts consulted are *The Personal Narrative of James O. Pattie of Kentucky* (new ed., Philadelphia, 1962); *Two Years Before the Mast*, by Richard Henry Dana, Jr. (New York, 1959); *Life in California*, by Alfred Robinson (Oakland, 1947); and *What I Saw in California* (Santa Ana, 1936), by Edwin Bryant. The men visited California between 1827 and 1846.

(1828–1847)   CALIFORNIA WOMEN   942

Langum, David J. "Californio Women and the Image of Virtue." *Southern California Quarterly* 59 (Fall 1977):245–50.

"One of the most recurrent popular and literary images of pre–American California concerns the beauty, grace, kindness and above all the virtue of, Hispanic ladies." (p. 245) Yet, among contemporary travel accounts (1828 to 1847) Langum finds enough evidence of moral laxity to question this image. He examines the social groups from which each observer gained his impression. Langum concludes that the reports of a lack of morality came from an acquaintance with lower classes. In the upper classes, however, where only a few Americans gained admittance, Langum concedes that the California ladies may well have been as virtuous as they were represented to be.

(1830–1849)   CALIFORNIANS   943

———. "Californios and the Image of Indolence." *Western Historical Quarterly* 9 (April 1978):181–96.

American travelers to California in the 1830s and 1840s frequently used the term "indolence" to condemn California men. Scholars have interpreted this attitude as being uniquely American, revealing our forebears' militant Protestantism, their Anglo-Saxon racism, and their dream of manifest destiny. By broadening the investigation of attitudes about indolence to include travelers of other nationalities, Langum finds similar comments by those whose motivation cannot be attributed to the American travelers' ideals. Langum hypothesizes that the critical attitudes came from the common European (and American) background of the Industrial Revolution, which praised industriousness and condemned leisure. *Note*: For a continuation of this discussion, see David J. Weber's critique, "Here Rests Juan Espinosa: Toward a Clearer Look at Image of the 'Indolent' Californios," *Western Historical Quarterly* 29 (1979):61–68. Langum's reply follows.

(1831)   HEINRICH VIRMOND   944

Weber, David J., ed. "California in 1831: Heinrich Virmond to Lucas Alamán." *Journal of San Diego History* 21 (Fall 1975):1–6.

Following a six-month stay in California during 1830 and 1831, this German-born merchant, who the editor says was probably an informal agent of the Mexican government, wrote a letter to the Mexican minister of relations. Virmond describes the unequal treatment of Mexican convicts who were being sent to California for rehabilitation, the growth of ranches and wine production, commerce with Russia and England, the bitter reaction of Californians to the overkilling of otter and beaver by both Anglo-Americans and Russians, the declining number of missionaries, and the growing hatred for Mexicans by some Californians. Translated by Ronald R. Young.

(1833)   FERDINAND VON WRANGELL   945

Gibson, James R., ed. "Russians in California, 1833: Report of Governor Wrangell." *Pacific Northwest Quarterly* 60 (October 1969):205–15.

Presents the report of Baron Ferdinand von Wrangell, governor of Russian California, following his inspection of Fort Ross in the summer of 1833. His analysis includes a description of the Russian-American Company's colony, the agriculture and cattle raising, and the population. Wrangell concludes that the colony was being operated at a loss and could succeed only if agriculture was expanded.

(1836)   IOANN VENIAMINOV   946

———. "A Russian Orthodox Priest in a Mexican Catholic Parish." *Pacific Historian* 15 (Summer 1971):57–66.

Presents the travel journal Father Ioann Veniaminov, a priest from Sitka, Alaska, kept during his trip to California between June 30 and October 13, 1836. The editor admits that the account is a disappointment. The priest was in a position to observe several important changes in California—the missions were undergoing secularization and the Russian-American Company was expanding its operations—but he provides only a brief description of Fort Ross and offers briefer comments about three missions he visited.

(1840)   JOSEPH DE ROSAMEL   947

Shepard, William Finley, ed. and tr. "California Prior to Conquest: A Frenchman's Views." *California Historical Society Quarterly* 37 (March 1958):63–77.

Captain Joseph de Rosamel sailed into Monterey Harbor on June 11, 1840, and remained about a month to protect the rights of French residents and to dissuade the Americans from taking any actions that would not be in French interests. Rosamel filed a report that provides a look at California in the final years before it changed hands.

He criticized the Mexican administration of California. He praised the work of the fathers in establishing the missions and deplored the way the missions had fallen into disuse after Mexico became independent from Spain. He observed that the Indians, who he felt had been treated well in the missions, were now wandering around without employment. Rosemel's report also contains references to American interests in California and a lengthy commercial report.

(1840–1850)   CALIFORNIA   948

Mann, Ralph. "The Americanization of Arcadia: Images of Hispanic and Gold Rush California." *American Studies* 19 (Spring 1978):5–19.

There exists an apparent contradiction between the writings of those Americans who saw California before 1849 and those who came during the gold rush. Earlier writers extolled California's virtues as a pastoral paradise where one could achieve relaxation and individual freedom, but writings of the gold-rush period praised the establishment of a structured society with American government and order. Mann resolves these contradictions by pointing out that though the earlier writers did praise California as a romantic wilderness, they also stressed how unrealistic those conditions were to future progress. The earlier writers were creating the ideology of Anglo-Saxon destiny in the West which the later writers believed was being realized with the establishment of American institutions.

(1841)   E. L. CHERNYKH   949

Chernykh, E. L. "Agriculture of Upper California." *Pacific Historian* 11 (Winter 1967):10–28.

The author, who was a Russian agricultural expert stationed at Fort Ross with the Russian-American Company, compiled this official report detailing the weather, the crops raised, and the prices of products. Originally published in the *Russian Journal of Rural Economy* in 1841.

(1847)   JONATHAN STEVENSON   950

Hughes, Charles, ed. "Military View of San Diego in 1847: Four Letters from Colonel Jonathan Stevenson to Governor Richard B. Mason." *Journal of San Diego History* 20 (Summer 1974):33–43.

The commander of the Southern Military District described the deterioration of relations between the Indians and the Californios, anti-American feelings, and the Americans' fear of attack by Mexico. Because of these conditions, Stevenson recommended the retention of a military force in San Diego.

(1849)   LEWIS RICHARD PRICE   951

Jackson, W. Turrentine, ed. "Mazatlan to the Estanislao: The Narrative of Lewis Richard Price's Journey to California in 1849." *California Historical Society Quarterly* 39 (March 1960):35–51.

An unpublished manuscript by an English businessman who was in California to investigate prospects for the establishment of a mint that would provide gold coins for the settlers. He describes his trips from Mazatlan, Mexico, to San Diego, San Francisco, San Jose, and Stockton, as well as to the New Almadén quicksilver mine and the gold-mining districts of Wood's Creek on the Stanislaus River and Hawkins' Bar on the Tuolumne River. It was Price's impression that the common dress of people from all walks of life, both in the city and the mines, wiped away social distinctions. In San Francisco he observed the overwhelmingly male population, the fog that lifted only once in the two months he was there, and the amazingly rapid growth of the city between August and September, 1849.

(1849)   SOCIETY OF CALIFORNIA   952
                  PIONEERS OF NEW ENGLAND

Richardson, Katherine Wood. "The Gold Seekers: The Story of 'La Grange' and the California Pioneers of New England." *Essex Institute Historical Collections* 115 (April 1979):73–122.

Relates the experiences of the Society of California Pioneers of New England, a company formed in 1849 by gold seekers from Massachusetts who sailed to California aboard the *La Grange*. When they arrived in San Francisco their hopes were buoyed by evidence of gold in the city. After sailing up the Sacramento River, however, mud and cold weather, illnesses, high prices, and an absence of gold conspired in the venture's failure. Most members straggled home overland. In 1883 the La Grange Company formed an organization of former forty-niners from the New England states. In 1890 fifty-six members made a nostalgic return to California aboard a Pullman coach. This article is based on the journals of four members.

(1849–1850)   JESSE HOLCOMB CHANEY   953

Chaney, William A., ed. "A Louisiana Planter in the Gold Rush." *Louisiana History* 3 (Spring 1962):133–44.

The editor considers the correspondence of Jesse Holcomb Chaney (December 31, 1849-July 10, 1850) important for two reasons. First, it concerns such matters as a trip to California by way of Panama, as well as information about prices, religious conditions, and abolitionists in California. Second, it illustrates the impact of the gold rush on Louisianians, even those of the planter class.

(1849–1850)   WILLIAM J. EMMET   954

Parsons, John E., ed. "Nine Cousins in the California Gold Rush." *New York Historical Society Quarterly* 47 (October 1963):349–97.

These letters from William J. Emmet and Herman R. LeRoy, written between January, 1849, and August, 1850, relate a family's experiences in California. The first letters describe the trip from New York around Cape Horn. Immediately upon arriving in California, a lawyer cousin saw that his fortune could be made by "hanging out his shingle" and quickly became successful. In Sacramento the rest of the group delayed going to the mines until they sold the provisions they had brought with them. After a trip to the headwaters of the Sacramento River proved to be a disaster, they found themselves back in San Francisco staying with the lawyer cousin. The two writers of these letters hoped to prosper in real estate in northern California near Trinidad Bay. An expedition to the Klamath River region led to an interesting confrontation with the Indians, after which William Emmet and Herman LeRoy returned home to New York.

(1849–1850)   **JAMES ROGERS**   955

Vail, Marie Rogers, ed. "Gold Rush Letters of the Reverend James Rogers." *New York Historical Society Quarterly* 44 (July 1960):259–95.

This New York minister never did get to the mines. Instead, he found a different kind of fortune in Sacramento, where he founded a private school and became a leader in Methodist education. His letters were filled with enthusiasm for California from the moment he entered San Francisco Harbor. Even though he did not like the dust and heat of the city and saw that gamblers, retail liqour dealers, and lawyers were making fortunes, he stressed the improvement of social conditions. He wrote that the bad elements of society were looked upon with disfavor, and he predicted that the Mexican sports would soon become illegal. Rogers saw more families arriving every day, and in Sacramento he observed how the tent city was quickly disappearing and being replaced by wooden buildings. Rogers also reported the devastating effects of cholera. These letters were written between October 16, 1849, and October 29, 1850.

(1849–1851)   **ISAAC ANNIS**   956

Parsons, John E., ed. "A Grandfather in the Gold Rush: Isaac Annis Writes Home From Auburn Dry Diggins." *New York Historical Society Quarterly* 41 (January 1957):5–23.

A 63-year-old blacksmith made restless by the discovery of gold in California in 1849 set sail around Cape Horn to seek his fortune. Annis made some money, but as a keeper of a boarding house. His letters, written between January 28, 1849, and June 30, 1851, provide descriptions of Sacramento and Auburn.

(1849–1851)   **GOLD RUSH ACCOUNTS**   957

Rotter, Andrew J. "'Matilda for Gods Sake Write': Women and Families on the Argonaut Mind." *California History* 58 (Summer 1979):128–41.

If recent studies that focus on the role of women and families in the westward movement project the idea that men functioned with a single-minded self-confidence in their decisions, then the diaries of men who traveled without women serve to correct that impression. Rotter reviewed diaries and letters written on the trail and in the goldfields between 1849 and 1851, years of heavy travel by overwhelmingly male groups. He found that these men were forced to come face-to-face with their reliance on their mothers or wives. They had to perform chores they regarded as women's work, and they were compelled to face doubt about the wisdom of their decisions without the psychological support of women. Rotter concludes that the gold rush was a male undertaking in head count only. The psychological importance of women, as revealed in laments of homesickness and melancholy, made them shadow members of every party.

(1849–1851)   **JOHN TURNER MILNER**   958

Milner, John Turner. "John T. Milner's Trip to California: Letters to the Family." *Alabama Historical Quarterly* 20 (Fall 1958):523–56.

Between 1849 and 1851 this Georgian made and lost several fortunes, but not in the same manner as many other forty-niners. Moreover, his comments about California do not reflect the disparaging attitudes of many other fortune hunters. In the fall of 1849 he was doing so well as a surveyor and owner of a boarding house that he sent $15,000 home. By winter, however, he had lost everything and began prospecting in the spring of 1850. Milner obviously had other financial resources (some Texas land?), for he bought a ranch near Marioposa and had machinery shipped from the East to start a series of stamp mills for processing quartz. By September, 1851, he had made $25,000 dollars, but not without some reversals, and was preparing to return to Georgia.

Although he wrote that California cities were "sickley holes," he believed that the mountains were healthy. (p. 535) Part of the reason so many men were dying was because of the lives they led: "if all men were to live in Georgia the way they do here they all would die and no mistake." (p. 524) He did not mention lawlessness and even commented that goods on Sacramento docks were safely left out in the open. Milner left California with mixed feelings. Partly he was glad to get out "ahead of the hounds," and yet he was "never better satisfied with the country and the prospects than now." (p. 555) Letters written between May 18, 1849, and October 14, 1851.

(1849–1852))   ROBERT GORDON   959

Stuart, Reginald R., and Stuart, Grace D., eds. "Journal of a Voyage from Baltimore to San Francisco by Robert Gordon 1849." (Part I) *Pacific Historian* 6 (August 1962):93–110.

———, and ———. (Part II) *Pacific Historian* 6 (November 1962):147–59.

———, and ———. (Part III) *Pacific Historian* 7 (February 1963):45–57.

———, and ———. (Part IV) *Pacific Historian* 7 (May 1963):79–93.

———, and ———. (Part V) *Pacific Historian* 7 (August 1963):124–37.

———, and ———. (Part VI) *Pacific Historian* 7 (November 1963):190–95.

This recent Irish immigrant first describes his sea voyage to California around Cape Horn between February 3 and September 14, 1849. Then Gordon tells of scurrying from camp to camp to locate a strike, spending what money he just made. He relates problems with Indians, high rivers and rainy conditions that prohibited him from finding a place to prospect, fights and murders, and the observance of Christmas and the Fourth of July in the mining camps. In his last entry, April 5, 1852, Gordon says that he has been storekeeping since the first of the year without much success. The editors add that he became a successful grocer in Auburn.

(1849–1853)   CHARLES C. BRADY   960

Price, Glenn, ed. "From Hannibal to the Gold Fields in 1849: Reminiscences of Charles C. Brady." (Part I) *Pacific Historian* 4 (November 1960):145–52.

———. (Part II) *Pacific Historian* 5 (February 1961):5–14.

———. (Part III) *Pacific Historian* 5 (May 1961):77–83.

As an 18-year-old boy in 1849, Brady followed his father overland to California. Young Brady soon gave up mining for a job in the post office. When his father had made enough money in 1853, the pair returned home by way of Nicaragua. Also included is a letter that was published in the *Hannibal Daily Journal* (April 29, 1853), in which Brady advises of the poor prospects of gold mining.

(1849–1856)   JOHN PAUL DART   961

Mitcham, Howard, ed. "A Mississippian in the Gold Fields: The Letters of John Paul Dart, 1849–1856." *California Historical Society Quarterly* 35 (September 1956):205–31.

As Dart worked without great success as a miner around Sonora, California, he wrote these letters that touch on a whole range of economic, social, and political matters. Although he apparently made some money, the inflated but always fluctuating prices of goods made it difficult for him to save. He wrote about problems with the mines, the danger of fire to the multitude of wooden houses, and how many had deserted California for a new strike in Australia. Dart seemed to thrive on the unsettled social conditions and the conflicts among such varied nationalities as Peruvians, Chinese, and French; French women are mentioned. He also kept his eye on matters of local and national importance. In 1850 he wrote that most people in California did not care one way or the other whether the territory was admitted to the Union; they just wanted to strike it rich and return home. Even though Dart may have found his life healthy and exciting, he often advised his brother against emigrating.

(1849–1875)   **CALIFORNIA**   **962**

Burchell, Robert A. "The Loss of a Reputation: or, The Image of California in Britain Before 1875." *California Historical Quarterly* 53 (Summer 1974):115–30.

The flood of people coming to California following the discovery of gold slowed drastically in the mid-1850s. Those concerned with the state's welfare, who originally thought people were arriving in numbers greater than the region could absorb, now worried about future population growth. One possible source of population was Great Britain, but California's reputation for lawlessness discouraged many potential British immigrants. It had not always been that way. Early reports about the climate, the soil, and the commercial and agricultural potential made the region seem like a paradise. During the turbulent years of the early 1850s, though, British travelers reported instability and insecurity. A campaign to improve California's reputation in Great Britain was unsuccessful; not until the 1880s, when the state was sufficiently ordered to assume progress, was the reputation changed.

(1850)   **JAMES BURGER**   **963**

Burger, James. "Letters from a Staten Island 'Forty-Niner', 1850." *Staten Island Historian* 30 (July/September 1969):23–25.

The pandemonium and the high prices in San Francisco caused Burger to write, on April 16, 1850, that he had not "seen the Elephant yet. But I think we have seen his taile." (p. 24) On May 26 he wrote that he was building houses for a living, but still hoped to get to the mines in the fall when the river waters fell.

(1850)   **PHILIP JOHN HINES**   **964**

Davis, Robert Ralph, Jr., ed. "An Ohioan's Letter from the California Gold Fields in 1850." *Ohio History* 76 (Summer 1967):159–63.

After three weeks of frustration, Dr. Philip John Hines wrote home from Yuba County expressing disillusionment. His health was poor, he had found no gold, he was unable to ply his own trade ("doctors are as plentiful as grasshoppers in a meadow"), and he could find no other employment to earn his return fare to Ohio. (p. 162)

(1850)   **L. R. SLAWSON**   **965**

Bidlack, Russell E., ed. "To California on the Sarah Sands: Two Letters Written in 1850 by L. R. Slawson." *California Historical Society Quarterly* 44 (September 1965):229–35.

Slawson tells a friend back in Ann Arbor, Michigan, about his trip around Cape Horn and his favorable impression of mining gold near Sacramento.

(1850–1851)   **HORACE BELKNAP**   **966**

Westholm, Woodrow, ed. "An Iowan in California, 1850." *Annals of Iowa* 36 (Fall 1962):462–65.

Reprints a letter by Dr. Horace Belknap from Mudspring (Eldorado County), California, on February 2, 1851, where he had accompanied a group of gold seekers the previous summer. He writes that the emigration in 1850 was very difficult because of sickness. Travelers failed to bring adequate supplies and were unable to obtain replacements along the way. He estimated that five thousand of the sixty thousand who started across the plains that year had perished. Belknap said that because the mines near Placerville were overworked, the group was going north to the Klamath River region.

(1851)   MATTHEW V. B. FOWLER   967

Elliott, Mary Joan, ed. "The 1851 California Journal of M. V. B. Fowler." (Part I) *Southern California Quarterly* 50 (Summer 1968):113–60.

————. (Part II) *Southern California Quarterly* 50 (Fall 1968):227–65.

Following an interesting introduction that includes preceding and subsequent facts of the writer's life, the editor presents Matthew Fowler's journal. Although he was previously a gold seeker, as the journal begins Fowler is a customs officer. After losing his position because of a change in political climate, he went looking for a farm in the Santa Clara Valley. He finally returned home to New York and ended his journal at sea beyond Panama.

Fowler comments on many local events: the lawlessness in San Francisco, the upheaval surrounding the Stewart and Burdue trial, and vigilante action. He attended the contempt of court trial of William Walker, the editor of the *San Francisco Herald*, as well as a meeting of the state legislature. Fowler tells a little about his duties as customs officer and about a pedestrian tour of the Santa Clara Valley. Journal kept between February 21 and May 6, 1851.

(1851–1852)   PETER Y. COOL   968

Clebsch, William A., ed. "Goodness, Gold, and God." *Pacific Historian* 10 (Summer 1966):19–42.

In Peter Y. Cool's struggle with piety and a moral life in the California goldfields around Fort John (Amador County), he writes that he has taken up public speaking and is lecturing for the temperance movement and religion. Journal kept June 15, 1851, to January 4, 1852.

(1852)   J. M. ALEXANDER   969

Hyatt, L. Paul, ed. "J. M. Alexander: A Gold Miner's Letter, 1852." *California Historical Society Quarterly* 49 (December 1970):353–58.

When Alexander obtained a pocket-sized letter book from an express company, he had the intention of filling it with one lengthy description of his experiences that would satisfy everyone back home in Alabama. He thought it would be an easy task, but about mid-way through he ran out of anything to say. He kept on writing, though. The gist of his letter is that he believes that he has hit it fairly lucky at Yankee Jims Diggins in Placer County. Despite his knowing there is a lot of gold around, he advises everyone else to stay at home.

(1852)   A. C. EDWARDS   970

Sherman, Richard P., ed. "A Gold Rush Letter from A. C. Edwards." *California Historical Society Quarterly* 43 (September 1964):247–50.

In a letter dated May 16, 1852, Edwards writes of his recent unhealthy trip from New York to San Francisco across the Isthmus of Panama. He opposes the mistreatment of the Chinese he found in California and the fervor to drive them from the mines. Edwards believes the Chinese to be more industrious than many other segments of the mining community.

(1852)   HILAND HALL   971

Barrows, June, ed. "A Vermonter's Description of a Sunday in Los Angeles, California, in 1852." *Vermont History* 38 (Summer 1970):192–94.

Hiland Hall, who was serving as federal land commissioner in California, wrote home to his minister in North Bennington, Vermont, that the celebration of the Sabbath in Los Angeles was much different from that to which he was accustomed. The day was highlighted by bell ringing, firing of cannons, drunkenness, and bull fights, or as Hall describes it, displays of horsemanship designed to irritate the bulls.

(1852)   MARTIN FRANCIS SCHWENINGER   972

McGloin, John B. "A California Gold Rush Padre: New Light on the 'Padre of Paradise Flat'." *California Historical Society Quarterly* 49 (March 1961):49–67.

A biography of Father Florian (the Reverend Father Martin Francis Schweninger), a German Benedictine missionary who ministered to the religious needs of gold seekers near the North Fork of the Salmon River. Includes a long letter in which Father Florian gives an assessment of California after his arrival in San Francisco on August 8, 1852. He describes his travels among the mining country where he saw much that was disgraceful: prostitution, gambling, poor application of the law, murder, and greed for gold. He tells of the mixture of nationalities that attended mass and how poorly the Catholic population supported him.

(1852–1854)   DEXTER HAZEN HUTCHINS   973

Stuart, Grace Dell, ed. "The Dexter Hazen Hutchins Letters." (Part I) *Pacific Historian* 2 (November 1958):5–8.
———. (Part II) *Pacific Historian* 3 (February 1959):5–6, 24.
———. (Part III) *Pacific Historian* 3 (May 1959):31–34.
———. (Part IV) *Pacific Historian* 3 (August 1959):64–67.
———. (Part V) *Pacific Historian* 3 (November 1959):85–89.
———. (Part VI) *Pacific Historian* 4 (February 1960):23–27.

Hutchins left his family in New York and traveled to California by sea around Cape Horn. His letters (March 8, 1852-February 26, 1854) indicate that he mined and hunted in Tuolumne County and farmed in the San Joaquin Valley. Hutchins describes his activities, the lawlessness that abounded, and the cost of provisions, but his letters also reveal the strain that separation put on his marriage. In one letter he pleads for his wife to write. He says that he has been disappointed in not receiving a letter during the past four months and that he has just about given up. His wife wants him to return home, and she implies that if he does not, it means that he cares more for money than for her. He assures her that is not the case. He reminds her that the only reason he came to California was to allow them to improve their lives. She does not relent, but Hutchins insists that he will not come home until he has earned enough to buy a home to come to. The editor adds that Hutchins did save money, returned home, and purchased land in Iowa.

(1852–1854)   GEORGE D. MAGOON   974

Throne, Mildred, ed. "The California Journey of George D. Magoon, 1852–1854." *Iowa Journal of History* 54 (April 1956):131–68.

Magoon's diary records the exploits of a young man from Muscatine, Iowa, who traveled to California from New York by way of Nicaragua, his adventures in California, and a return trip through Panama. His first six months in California were spent working in the goldfields sinking shafts for quartz mining. He returned to Sacramento before the end of the year and spent all of 1853 as a builder. Magoon offers a lengthy description of the flood on December 19, 1852, which devastated Sacramento. The editor points out that his rapid return home, when contrasted with his lengthy journey to California, reveals the improvement of transportation. Diary kept between February 9, 1852, and February 15, 1854.

(1853–1854)   EPHRAIM THOMPSON   975

Cantelon, Philip L., ed. "The California Gold Fields in the 1850's: Letters from Ephraim Thompson, Daviess County, Indiana." *Indiana Magazine of History* 65 (September 1969):157–72.

Thompson traveled to California from New Orleans by way of Nicaragua with high hopes of striking it rich, but his letters from December 4, 1853, to July 4, 1854, reflect disenchantment. He advised that others should not go to California in search of gold. His last letter says he is working as a clerk in Green Valley hoping to save money for his return home.

(1854)   CHRISTOPHER S. LOVELL   976

Frazer, Robert W., ed. "Lovell's Report on them Cohuilla Indians, 1854." *Journal of San Diego History* 22 (Winter 1976):4–10.

Captain Christopher S. Lovell, Second Regiment of Infantry (U.S.) reported on agricultural practices, recreation, and religion, as well as customs of birth, marriage, and death in this southern California tribe.

(1855)   WILLIAM HUBERT BURGESS   977

Kurutz, Gary F. "'California is quite a different place now': The Gold Rush Letters and Sketches of William Hubert Burgess." *California Historical Quarterly* 56 (Fall 1977):211–29.

William Hubert Burgess was an Englishman who first lived in New York, where he worked as a lithographer, before he and his three brothers sailed to California in 1850. This article contains excerpts from his letters and sketches, many of which originate from Mokelumne Hill (Calaveras County) in 1855. Burgess's writings indicate that he was thrilled by the beauty of the landscape and enjoyed the opportunity to hunt wildlife, but he was horrified at the mindless destruction of the wilderness and human life. In the five years since he first came to California, Burgess believed the society had undergone many changes, all for the worst.

(1855–1857)   ERNEST JAUDIN   978

Dietsche, Mary Lynn, ed. "'Mon coeur est gonfle d'esperance!'; Letters of a Young Frenchman in Early San Francisco." *California History* 59 (Winter 1980/1981):334–51.

The experiences of Ernest Jaudin provide a glimpse of life in California for the French as an ethnic group. Perhaps Jaudin was not typical, however, because he had a luxury that few French gold seekers had, family contacts to assist him in San Francisco. Jaudin, who first worked as a clerk in a grocery store and then plied his family's trade as a baker, writes glowingly about California. He tells about business conditions in San Francisco, about the fertility of California soil, and about increases in grain shipments. This selection of letters was written between his arrival in San Francisco on March 15, 1855, and December 4, 1857.

(1856)   FEDERICO BIESTA   979

Falbo, Ernest S., ed. and tr. "State of California in 1856: Federico Biesta's Report to the Sardinian Minister of Foreign Affairs." *California Historical Society Quarterly* 42 (December 1963):311–33.

Although Biesta was not the officially appointed Sardinian consul, the editor says this consular correspondence from San Francisco was written by Biesta. His reports focused on such commercial matters as imports, grape culture, liquor manufacture, clothing, foodstuffs, and a sluggish rate of business growth. Biesta thought the prospects for immigration were good, but he deplored local abuses of the Chinese which he felt placed them on the same level as the blacks. In his eyes the Chinese were more desirable than the mobs of other nationalities that were welcomed with open arms. Biesta's reports, which the editor says reveal most of what we know about Italians in California during this period, indicate that Italians were thriving and prosperous. Biesta adds that they found little need for the consul.

(1856–1859)   WILLIAM JACOBS   980

Smith, David P., ed. "A Texan in Search of Gold." *East Texas Historical Journal* 15 (no. 1, 1977):9–20.

William Jacobs spent most of the years covered by these letters (May 19, 1856-March 25, 1859) in the California goldfields, except for the time he followed a strike in British Columbia in 1858. In addition to a concern for his family and a continuing interest in the marital status of his hometown girls, Jacobs provides some information about the miners' political preferences in the 1856 election. In his camp, Shaw's Flat, he says the boys from Texas preferred the Democrat James Buchanan. When the whole camp was polled, the Democrats won by slight margins over the Know-Nothings and the Republicans.

(1858)   ALEXANDER HOLMES MACDONALD   981

MacDonald, Alexander Holmes. "A Year on the Yuba." (Part I) *Pacific Historian* 2 (February 1958):5–6, 11–16.

————. (Part II) *Pacific Historian* 2 (May 1958):11–16.

————. (Part III) *Pacific Historian* 2 (August 1958):3, 10–12.

————. (Part IV) *Pacific Historian* 2 (November 1958):13–16.

————. (Part V) *Pacific Historian* 3 (February 1959):17–20.

After three years in the goldfields, this Nova Scotian thought himself not much better off, except for the experience. MacDonald describes his social life at the Good Templars meetings. He relates such everyday incidents as the shooting of a man by a prostitute, a wife-poisoning by a "respectable citizen," and other routine murders and mining accidents. He also tells about seeing the blaze from afar when the mining camp of Downieville burned. The editors, Reginald R. and Grace D. Stuart, believe MacDonald's description of Orleans Flat may be the only existing record of day-to-day life there. Journal kept between January 1 and August 8, 1858.

(1858–1860)   JAMES MCPHERSON   982

Strobridge, William F., ed. "California Letters of Major General James McPherson, 1858–1860." *Ohio History* 81 (Winter 1972):38–50.

McPherson was sent to California to supervise construction of fortifications on Alcatraz Island. Although he did not initially find life in San Francisco appealing, McPherson soon became interested in local political affairs and society. Letters written between February 4, 1858, and December 18, 1860.

(1858–1861)   HARVEY TOWER   983

Posner, Russell M. "California Through English Eyes, 1858–1861." *Journal of the West* 11 (October 1972):663–69.

Integrates the observations of Harvey Tower (1858) and Sophia Cracroft (1861) during their tours of California. Both were critical of local manners but praised the scenery.

(1859–1860)   SARAH LINDSEY   984

Jackson, Sheldon G., ed. "An English Quaker Tours California: The Journal of Sarah Lindsey, 1859–1860." (Part I) *Southern California Quarterly* 51 (Spring 1969):1–33.

————. (Part II) *Southern California Quarterly* 51 (Summer 1969):153–75.

————. (Part III) *Southern California Quarterly* 51 (Fall 1969):221–46.

The editor believes this is the best account of Quakerism in California before 1880. Mrs. Lindsey reveals that at the time of her visit the Friends in that state were few, scattered, and not particularly devout. She and her husband traveled to Stockton, Sacramento, and Napa, and to the mining towns of Downieville, Marysville, Placerville, and Auburn, looking up Friends, speaking, and delivering religious books. Although much of her account refers to their religious activities, Mrs. Lindsey also describes the agriculture and mining procedures she observed.

Several of her comments about social conditions relate to the Chinese. She believed they made good house servants, but disapproved when they spit water on the clothes as they ironed. She writes that the Chinese were an unattractive people who inhabited the lowest level of society in California. The women, she says, were of loose character, but she does not elaborate. Mrs. Lindsey visited a Chinese temple and commented on their burial custom of sending the bones of men back to China but not those of women. She took this to mean that the women were presumed not to have souls. These excerpts cover only her California experience from June 20, 1859 to August 18, 1860, but some of her time was spent in Canada and Hawaii.

(1864)   **BENJAMIN SILLIMAN**   **985**

Webb, George E., ed. "Benjamin Silliman's Visit to California: A Letter to His Wife." *Southern California Quarterly* 59 (Winter 1977):365–78.

Professor Silliman of Yale College spent most of 1864 in the West examining mineral deposits in California, Nevada, and Arizona. In this letter of December 21, 1864, he provides some insights into the beginning of the California oil industry. He describes the events that led to the oil frenzy, and explains how he and his friends purchased tracts of land at low prices.

(1865)   **MARY C. MORSE**   **986**

Morse, Mary C. "A Trip to the Mines." *Journal of San Diego History* 13 (January 1967):8–18.

Mary recalls that San Diego appeared to be a dilapidated town surrounded by brown, barren hills when she arrived in June, 1865. She provides a lengthy description of a trip to the quartz mines near Julian City. After passing through the Peñasquitas Valley and staying at several ranches, her party reached the mining town. She describes her four-day stay, during which they slept in a miner's cabin and went into the mines to observe the operations before returning home through the Cajon Mountains. Originally appeared in the *San Diego Union* (September 29, 1870).

(1865–1866)   **WILLIAM BOWERS BOURN INGALLS**   **987**

Hayne, F. Bourn, ed. "A Boy's Voyage to San Francisco, 1865–66: Selections from the Diary of William Bowers Bourn Ingalls." (Part I) *California Historical Society Quarterly* 36 (September 1951):205–12.

———. (Part II) *California Historical Society Quarterly* 36 (December 1957):293–306.

Thirteen-year-old Willie accompanied his parents on a visit from New York to California by way of the Isthmus of Panama and stayed for the winter. His diary records school activities and his impressions of the sights in and near San Francisco.

(1877)   **MIRIAM FOLLIN LESLIE**   **988**

Reinhardt, Richard, ed. "On the Brink of the Boom: Southern California in 1877 As Witnessed by Mrs. Frank Leslie." *California Historical Quarterly* 52 (Spring 1973):64–79.

Favorable impressions of the area before the changes brought about by a real estate boom. Mrs. Leslie stresses the Spanish heritage of Los Angeles and Santa Monica, and describes a visit to the Mission of San Gabriel. Contains excerpts from a book Miriam Follin Leslie, the wife of magazine publisher Frank Leslie, wrote about the trip, *A Pleasure Trip from Gotham To the Golden Gate* (New York, 1887).

(1877)   **ISAAC MAYER WISE**   **989**

Wise, Isaac Mayer. "Rabbi Wise Sees San Francisco: 1877." *Pacific Historian* 11 (Summer 1967):10–25.

On his journey to the West Coast, Wise visited San Francisco in July, 1877. He was amazed at the city's tremendous growth and at the disparity between those parts of the city that were prosperous and those that were poor. He comments on the continuing prejudice against the Chinese, especially the violence against them by young hoodlums. Wise says that the white population blamed the Chinese for working for low pay and then sending their wages home. However, Wise noticed that at least some Chinese paid heavy taxes. He also describes the conditions of the Jews in the city and relates a visit to Santa Cruz. Articles written on July 18, 1877, for the *American Israelite* (Cincinnati). (See also item 768.)

(1879)   GIOVANNI VIGNA DAL FERRO   990

Bohme, Frederick G., ed. and tr. "Vigna Dal Ferro's 'Un Viaggio Nel Far West Americano'." *California Historical Society Quarterly* 41 (June 1962):149–61.

A portion of Italian traveler, linguist, and journalist Giovanni Vigna dal Ferro's collection of articles in *La Patria* (Bologna). In this selection he describes his train trip in 1879 from Colorado to San Francisco. He includes descriptions of the Mormons and Salt Lake City and of the Italian and Chinese colonies of San Francisco. While he thought the Chinese lived in deplorable conditions, he objected to talk by local politicians of placing limitations on immigration. (See also item 788.)

(1885–1886)   MARY E. LACEY HERREN   991

Hood, Brenda, ed. "'This Worry I have': Mary Herren Journal." *Oregon Historical Quarterly* 80 (Fall 1979):228–57.

Because Mary E. Lacey Herren was ill with tuberculosis, she and her family traveled by wagon from Yamhill County, Oregon, to Pasadena, California, in hopes of improving her health. Entries from her journal (September 5, 1885-May 23, 1886) tell of her illness, and of record traffic along the road; there is mention of Indians, Chinese laborers, and vineyards; some entries give her impressions of the countryside. She did not like Santa Barbara but was impressed with Los Angeles. She thought Pasadena the prettiest place she had seen. After her winter in the sun and an ocean trip home, Mary felt improved, but she died a year later.

(1906)   ED FLETCHER   992

Fletcher, Ed. "An Auto Trip Through San Diego's Back Country." *Journal of San Diego History* 15 (Spring 1969):3–14.

On May 5, 1906, the author and two friends began a trip in a four-cylinder touring car to convince one of the participants that the back country was not all desert. From San Diego they passed through El Cajon, Ramona, Warner Hot Springs, Mesa Grande, the Julian Country, Cuyamaca Lake, Descano, and back to San Diego. Throughout the trip Fletcher praises the fertility of the soil, the variety of crops, the availability of water, and the climate.

(1910)   EDWARD CHARLES PICKERING   993

Plotkin, Howard, ed. "Edward Charles Pickering's Diary of a Trip to Pasadena to Attend Meeting of Solar Union, August 1910." *Southern California Quarterly* 50 (Spring 1978):29–44.

Pickering, the director of Harvard College Observatory, attended the Solar Union's international meeting held at Mount Wilson. After describing his train ride from Boston, with a brief stop at Flagstaff to see the Lowell Observatory and the Grand Canyon, he relates events of the meeting and a return trip that included San Francisco and the University of California at Berkeley. Diary kept between August 20 and September 16, 1910.

(1913)   **U. S. GRANT IV**   **994**

Grant, U. S., IV. "A Midsummer Motoring Trip." *Southern California Quarterly* 43 (March 1961):85–96.

   The author reminisces about a camping trip that took him from San Diego to the San Bernardino Mountains and on to Palm Springs in the summer of 1913. He traveled in a stripped-down, two-seated Overland automobile.

HAWAII

(1778–1799)   **HAWAIIAN AGRICULTURE**   **995**

Moeller, Beverley B. "Some Eighteenth-Century Views on Hawaiian Agriculture." *Agriculture History* 41 (October 1967):397–404.

   Nearly every traveler to Hawaii from the time of its discovery by Captain James Cook on January 18, 1778, to the end of the century wrote in praise of the variety of crops, though Hawaiian agriculture was plowless. Moeller adds that as Europeans introduced new crops and cattle to promote civilization, they also brought pests that attacked plants and the cattle destroyed the watershed. The decline in Hawaiian agriculture continued until the late nineteenth century when it recovered because of the sugar industry and pineapple production.

(1852)   **JOHN SHEDDAN DAVIS**   **996**

Joesting, Edward, and Livingston-Little, D. E., eds. "A Scotsman Views Hawaii: An 1852 Log of a Cruise of the Emily Bourne." *Journal of the West* 9 (April 1970):196–221.

   The editors point out that this log, kept by an unidentified Scot (perhaps John Sheddan Davis) aboard a ship sent to buy food for the California mines, contains contradictions. The writer held most of the then prevalent attitudes about the inferiority of dark-skinned races and berates their customs, crafts, and activities in general. He does admire the women's headdresses and flower leis, and he praises the Hawaiians' taro cultivation, canoe-building, and seamanship. Log kept between February 8 and April 25, 1852.

(1855)   **C. AXEL EGERSTRÖM**   **997**

Conrad, Agnes C., ed., and Bengston, Caroline, tr. "Hawaii in 1855." *Hawaiian Journal of History* 9 (1975):37–59.

   After German merchant C. Axel Egerström visited Hawaii in March and April, 1855, he wrote *Borta är bra, men hemme är bäst* (Stockholm, 1859), a portion of which is reproduced here. He described the landscape, food, matters of commercial and agricultural interest, and current government affairs, but the editor says his account contains some inaccuracies. For example, he reported being present when the volcano Kilauea erupted, but actually there is no record of an eruption during Egerström's visit. He approved of nearly everything he saw and commended the "Kanakas" as being handsome people who had made excellent progress toward Christianity and civilization despite an "aversion to all kinds of labor." (p. 43)

NEVADA

(1845–1846)   **EDWARD MEYER KERN**   **998**

Hanson, Meri, ed. "From Walker Lake to Walker Pass with Frémont's Third Expedition: The Travel Journal of Edward Kern." *Nevada Historical Society Quarterly* 21 (Spring 1978):56–65.

"The purpose of this study is to locate the route and campsites of the Edward Meyer Kern party of John C. Frémont's Third Expedition (1845) whose winter journey from Walker Lake southward through the Owens Valley to Walker Pass recorded for the first time the true nature of the region adjacent to the eastern base of the Sierra Nevada Mountains." (p. 56)

Using Kern's three-month diary (November, 1845-February, 1846) and today's maps, the editor retraced the route through Nevada and California during 1975 and 1976.

(1855–1856)   **GEORGE W. BEAN**   **999**

Dees, Harry C., ed. "The Journal of George W. Bean." *Nevada Historical Society Quarterly* 15 (Fall 1972):3–30.

Bean was a Mormon frontiersman who began this journal as a scout for Lieutenant Sylvester Mowry's march from Salt Lake City to Fort Tejon, California. (See item 914.) Bean quit the expedition after about one hundred miles. He returned to Salt Lake City, was appointed as a missionary, and began another trip to Las Vegas Springs, New Mexico Territory. His diary is dated from April 6, 1855 to February 28, 1856.

(1865–1866)   **ROBERT WHEATLEY**   **1000**

Ball, Larry D., and Brodhead, Michael J., eds. "An Illinoian in the Nevada Mines and Mills: The Letters of Robert Wheatley, 1865–66." (Part I) *Nevada Historical Society Quarterly* 23 (Fall 1980):179–201.

———, and ———. (Part II) *Nevada Historical Society Quarterly* 23 (Winter 1980):262–82.

Wheatley's letters to the *Du Quoin Recorder* (Illinois) provide the itinerary of his trip from New York to Humboldt County, Nevada, to assist in the construction of a stamp mill. After his ocean trip to California by way of the Isthmus of Panama, he landed in San Francisco. Wheatley thought the city beautiful, although he complained that the air was constantly filled with dust. He judged California's agricultural prospects good where irrigation was available, but preferred Illinois farmland. He saw numerous "to let" signs on businesses and houses which he later learned was because miners had left the area to follow bigger gold strikes.

Wheatley was irritated at the presence of Chinese laborers because, he was told, they sent their money back to their mandarin lords in China. He believed the Chinese to be dishonest and the women particularly corrupt.

Wheatley was amazed at the immensity of the Sierras and thought the commercial possibilities of Lake Tahoe were unlimited once the railroad reached there. Once in Nevada, he writes of the progress of the stamp mill and of mining operations in general. He thought the alkaline flats the most dreary country he had ever seen and described the havoc of a Humboldt breeze as it swept across the dry land. Wheatley believed there were minerals in Nevada, but not to the extent that they were being promoted.

During the brief time he was in the West, Wheatley could see how quickly things changed. He used Virginia City's rapid transition from a wild, lawless setlement to a relatively civilized city as an example. Wheatley also describes his trip home and offers some opinions of Mexicans he saw in Acapulco.

(1869)   **JOHN MCQUIG**   **1001**

McQuig, John. "John McQuig's Diary, 1869." *Nevada Historical Society Quarterly* 6 (Summer 1963):3–27.

A record of a prospecting excursion in eastern Nevada by a resident of Murphys, California, between January 24 and July 23, 1869. The snow and wind, accidents in the mines, and fights in the towns made life hard for miners. Nevertheless, McQuig viewed it all with a sense of humor, for example, describing the time the floor of a saloon fell through because it was overloaded with men hoping to get a free look at two of the town's "fast women." (p. 16) Most of his time was spent in Treasure City, but he also describes the rapid growth of Hamilton, Austin, Virginia City, and Genoa.

(1870)   **JOHN AITKEN**   **1002**

Aitken, John. "An Englishman in Nevada." *Nevada Historical Society Quarterly* 20 (Summer 1977):110–21.

Excerpts from the journal Captain Aitken kept of his trip to Nevada in June, 1870, to investigate a mining investment. After leaving the train at Elko he boarded a stage for Hamilton. He describes the 120-mile ride over the rough roads and alkaline-covered terrain as the "most dreary, uncomfortable and fatiguing journey I ever took." (p. 112) The journal tells of the violence and vice of Hamilton, Aitken's visit to the peak of Treasure Hill, and the effect of the low humidity on his hair and skin.

He observed the neat, business-like appearance of the Chinese in Hamilton and contrasted it with the languid, ragged appearance of the Indians. He also describes Troy and the mines there, and his stay at the Blue Eagle Ranch. Of all the strange things he saw in the West, Aitken chose to condemn the open advertisement of fortune telling. He says astrology was an illegal practice in England at that time.

OREGON

(1846)   **ALEXANDER LATTIE**   **1003**

Lattie, Alexander. "Alexander Lattie's Fort George Journal, 1846." *Oregon Historical Quarterly* 64 (September 1963):197–245.

Lattie was a Hudson's Bay Company trader and ship pilot on the Columbia River. In this semiofficial report as company clerk at Fort George, he recorded the weather and the planting, trading, and other routine activities of the fort, including problems with American settlers.

(1849–1851)   **ISAAC A. FLINT**   **1004**

Van Arsdol, Ted, ed. "Golden Gate to Columbia River on the Bark 'Koeka': Isaac A. Flint's Journal. *Oregon Historical Quarterly* 63 (March 1962):41–54.

Records a harrowing voyage from San Francisco to Oregon in 1849, and a summary of all Flint had seen and done on the West Coast in 1851. Includes brief comments on conditions in Oregon and about the newspapers, settlements, prices, and marriageable women.

(1853–1855)   **CALVIN B. WEST**   **1005**

Stuart, Reginald R., and Stuart, Grace D., eds. "Calvin B. West of the Umpqua." (Part I) *Pacific Historian* 4 (May 1960):48–57.

———, and ———. (Part II) *Pacific Historian* 4 (August 1960):87–96, 112.

———, and ———. (Part III) *Pacific Historian* 4 (November 1960):129–43.

———, and ———. (Part IV) *Pacific Historian* 5 (February 1961):23–46.

———, and ———. (Part V) *Pacific Historian* 5 (May 1961):53–68, 86.

———, and ———. (Part VI) *Pacific Historian* 5 (August 1961):125–36.

From the Reverend West's diary, letters (April 10, 1853-June 25, 1855), and other sources, the editors reconstruct the life of an Oregon pioneer. Following his journey over the Oregon Trail, West established a land claim, taught school, and helped to establish the Umpqua Academy in Douglass County. In 1854, after returning to Ohio to bring his family west, he was stricken with cholera in Nicaragua and died at sea.

(1864)   CHARLES S. DREW   1006

Drew, Charles S. "Official Report of the Owyhee Expedition." *Ethnohistory* 2 (Spring 1955):146–82.

Lieutenant Colonel Drew led a reconnaissance of the area from Fort Klamath (Oregon) to the Owyhee region of Oregon during the summer and fall of 1864. He includes details of the terrain and the trails, and describes the wildlife, the mines, and the white settlers. Much of this report concerns the Indians, who, although they were constantly reported to be near, were never engaged in combat.

In Drew's opinion, the Indian concept of virtue was decidedly different from that held by the Christians: "among nearly all the Indian tribes of Oregon and northern California, murder, rapine, robbery, and theft are virtues of the highest order." (p. 167) He goes on to say that the degree to which one excels at these acts governs the Indian's status among the Paiute, Snake, Klamath, Modoc, and Pitt River tribes.

In his summary, Drew offers his recommendations for the best locations for a new fort. In an introduction, Erminie W. Voegelin says that Drew's report has been overlooked because of an incorrect evaluation in Hubert Howe Bancroft's *History of Oregon* (San Francisco, 1888).

(1864)   JOHN M. DRAKE   1007

Knuth, Priscilla, ed. "Cavalry in the Indian Country, 1864." *Oregon Historical Quarterly* 65 (March 1964):5–118.

Captain John M. Drake commanded several companies of the First Oregon Cavalry on a search for marauding bands of Snake Indians in eastern Oregon. His journal, written between April 20 and October 11, 1864, records that his unit saw no hostile Indians, although an accompanying unit did. Drake describes the Warm Springs Indians, who befriended the cavalry but who were bent on war with the Snakes, and he makes references to settlers and emigrants to Oregon that year. Drake also offers a number of pithy comments about his contemporaries and the internal dissension within the expedition.

(1865)   JOHN MARSHALL MCCALL   1008

Merriam, L. C., Jr., ed. "The First Oregon Cavalry and the Oregon Central Military Road Survey of 1865." *Oregon Historical Quarterly* 60 (March 1959):89–124.

The Oregon Central Military Road Company was given a land grant to build a road from Eugene to the southeast corner of the state. A railroad along the same route was projected for the future. The First Oregon Cavalry provided the military escort for the survey, and its operations are recorded by Lieutenant John Marshall McCall. Most of the entries between July 17 and September 17, 1865, describe the physical aspects of the land and the miles advanced. McCall also writes about the army's troubles with the Klamath Indians; he was present at Fort Klamath (Oregon) for the signing of a peace treaty.

(1866–1867)   WILLIAM MCKAY   1009

Clark, Keith, and Clark, Donna, eds., "William McKay's Journal, 1866–67: Indian Scouts." *Oregon Historical Quarterly* 79 (Summer 1978):121–71.

———, and ———. (Part II) *Oregon Historical Quarterly* 79 (Fall 1978):268–333.

McKay, a doctor at the Warm Springs Indian Reservation, commanded a troop of Indian scouts from the reservation in the campaign against the Snake Indians in central and southeastern Oregon. McKay was half Indian and half Scot. The editors review the controversy over the use of Indian scouts independent of the regular army and the order for a war of extermination against the Snakes. Included is a report objecting to the order, a list of the scouts, and a summary of McKay's later life. Journal kept between November 1, 1866, and November 29, 1867.

(1891)   **HAROLD DOUGLAS LANGILLE**   **1010**

Langille, Harold Douglas. "Across Oregon's 'Desert' by Buckboard." *Oregon Historical Quarterly* 59 (December 1958):326–37.

    The author reminisces about a round-trip journey taken in the fall of 1891 across that portion of central Oregon known as the "Great Sandy Desert." He remembers the dusty road lined with wagons filled with harvested grain, finding sleeping accommodations in lofts of barns, the rough social life of Prineville, and shooting ducks in an unsportsmanlike manner.

(1893)   **MARION B. RUSSELL**   **1011**

Russell, Marion B. "Our Trip to Mount Hood, 1893." *Oregon Historical Quarterly* 79 (Summer 1978):203–10.

    Relates an excursion taken by a group of fifteen persons from Portland to the Cloud Cap Inn between July 2 and July 5, 1893.

UTAH

(1828–1829)   **PETER SKENE OGDEN**   **1012**

Miller, David, ed. "Peter Skene Ogden's Trek into Utah, 1828–1829." *Pacific Northwest Quarterly* 51 (January 1960):16–25.

    Using extracts from Ogden's journal (December 10, 1828-April, 1829) and personal field trips, Miller traces this portion of the British exploration into Utah for new fur markets.

(1841)   **JOHN BIDWELL**   **1013**

Miller, David E. "The First Wagon Train to Cross Utah, 1841." *Utah Historical Quarterly* 30 (Winter 1962):41–52.

    In 1841 several members of the emigrant party led by John Bartleson and John Bidwell left the Oregon Trail at Soda Springs, Idaho, determined to skirt the north end of the Great Salt Lake and follow the Humboldt River across Nevada into California. In 1958 the author mapped the route from Soda Springs across Utah and on to the Humboldt River in Nevada. He consulted John Bidwell's *A Journey to California With Observations About the Country, Climate and The Route to this Country . . . May 18, 1841 to November 6, 1841 . . .* (San Francisco, 1937).

(1846)   **EDWIN BRYANT**   **1014**

Webb, Henry J. "Edwin Bryant's Trail Through Western Utah." *Utah Historical Quarterly* 29 (April 1961):129–35.

    In 1846, Edwin Bryant cut across the south end of the Great Salt Lake in an effort to find a shorter route to California. Following Bryant's description of the trek in *What I Saw in California . . .* (2nd ed., New York, 1848), Webb and a party of historians retraced the trail from Skull Valley to Pilot Peak on the Utah-Nevada border in the late 1950s.

(1848)   **ROBERT S. BLISS**   **1015**

Cooley, Everett L., ed. "The Robert S. Bliss Journal." *Utah Historical Quarterly* 27 (October 1959):380–404.

Concludes Bliss's account of the Mormon Battalion's march (January 13-May 2, 1848). He relates events of the winter at Salt Lake City and his journey back to the Mormons' winter headquarters in Nebraska. *Note*: The first part of the Bliss journal describing the Mormon Battalion's march from Kansas to California, garrison duty in San Diego, and then the march through California to Utah was published in the *Utah Historical Quarterly* 4 (July/October 1931):67–96, 110–28.

(1858)   C. E. GOULD   1016

Gould, C. E. "Soldiering on the Frontier." *Annals of Wyoming* 35 (April 1963):83–84.

A single letter written September 24, 1858, in which C. E. Gould describes life at Camp Floyd (Utah). He tries to correct the false impression that army life was filled with idleness and discourages his brother from enlisting.

(1858–1860)   WILL DEWEY   1017

Povlovich, Charles A., Jr., ed. "Will Dewey in Utah." *Utah Historical Quarterly* 33 (Spring 1965):134–40.

Five letters written between June 5, 1858, and July 10, 1860, that record experiences of a wandering Missourian. Dewey herded cattle and mined quartz, wounded his adversary in a shoot-out, and participated in a heated battle against the Paiute Indians before fading into obscurity.

(1860)   RICHARD BURTON   1018

Wilson, Laura Foster. "Richard Burton Visits the City of the Saints." *American West* 12 (January 1975):4–9.

Discusses the English writer and explorer's 1860 visit to Utah that resulted in *City of the Saints and Across the Rocky Mountains* (London, 1861), the most informed account about the Mormons of the period. Wilson summarizes the political situation between the United States government and the Mormons and explains Burton's support of polygamy.

(1866)   FRANKLIN B. WOOLLEY   1019

Crampton, C. Gregory, ed. "Military Reconnaissance in Southern Utah, 1866." *Utah Historical Quarterly* 32 (Spring 1964):145–61.

Reprints the official "Report of Reconoitering Expedition Mouth of the Green River, 1866" written by adjutant Franklin B. Woolley. The purpose of the mission in September and October, 1866, was to quell the warring Navajos and explore the canyon country eastward from the rim of the Great Basin and the high plateaus to the Colorado River. The soldiers saw hostile Indians only once when a single trooper was killed. Most of the report describes the terrain.

(1869)   JOHN COLTON SUMNER   1020

Marston, O. Dock, ed. "The Lost Journal of John Colton Sumner." *Utah Historical Quarterly* 37 (Spring 1969):173–89.

On May 24, 1869, Major John Wesley Powell and nine companions pushed boats into the Green River in Wyoming to explore the canyons of the Colorado River. Along the way the group encountered wild rapids, back-breaking portages, mishaps, short rations, and the defection of three men. On August 30, 1869, the six remaining men passed through the last three canyons and completed the expedition. The only extant journal is the one kept by the head boatman, John Colton Sumner, which describes the trip up to June 28. This issue of *Utah Historical Quarterly* is devoted to John Wesley Powell, his exploration of the Colorado River, and his contributions to the West.

(1871–1872) JOHN WESLEY POWELL 1021

Fowler, Don D., and Fowler, Catherine R., eds. "John Wesley Powell's Journal: Colorado River Exploration 1871–1872." *Smithsonian Journal of History* 3 (Summer 1968):1–44.

After sorting out the historical irregularities in John Wesley Powell's *Explorations of the Colorado and its Western Tributaries in 1869, 1870, 1871, and 1872* . . . (Washington, 1875), the editors present the journals of his second trip, May 22 to October 8, 1871, and another between August 17 and September 8, 1872. Contains maps and photographs.

(1877) CHARLES JACOB KINTNER 1022

Bidlack, Russell E., and Cooley, Everett L., eds. "The Kintner Letters: An Astronomer's Account of the Wheeler Survey in Utah and Idaho." (Part I) *Utah Historical Quarterly* 34 (Winter 1966):62–80.

———, and ———. (Part II) *Utah Historical Quarterly* 34 (Spring 1966):169–82.

Reprints letters Charles Jacob Kintner wrote to the *Ann Arbor Register* between May 14 and December 26, 1877. During this period he was employed by the Geographical Survey West of the 100th Meridian headed by First Lieutenant George M. Wheeler, U.S. Corps of Engineers. Kintner devotes most of his correspondence to descriptions of the terrain from Salt Lake to northern Idaho. He mentions the Mormons favorably.

(1905) ANNIE MONTAGUE ALEXANDER 1023

Zullo, Janet Lewis, ed. "Annie Montague Alexander: Her Work in Paleontology." *Journal of the West* 8 (April 1968):183–99.

A biographical sketch of Alexander and her personal account of a saurian expedition during 1905 to the Humboldt Mountains of Utah.

(1921) ELLSWORTH L. KOLB 1024

Rusho, W. L. "River Running 1921: The Diary of E. L. Kolb." *Utah Historical Quarterly* 37 (Spring 1969):269–83.

A 41-mile stretch of the Colorado River runs through Cataract Canyon in Utah, and has been called the "graveyard of the Colorado" because of the violence of its rapids. Emery and Ellsworth L. Kolb were two photographers who made the trip successfully several times. Presented here is Ellsworth's diary kept between September 3 and October 13, 1921.

(1921) WILLIAM E. OLIVER 1025

Oliver, William E. "Pilgrimage on Wheels." *Utah Historical Quarterly* 32 (Winter 1964):57–79.

An account of a ten-day, 1,000-mile automobile trip in 1921 in a Packard Roadster over the Lincoln Highway from Salt Lake City to San Francisco. The author retraced his drive along U.S. Highway 50 in 1962 and offers present-day photographs and comments on changes.

(1938) THOMAS WOLFE 1026

Cracroft, Richard H. "Through Utah and the Western Parks: Thomas Wolfe's Farewell to America." *Utah Historical Quarterly* 37 (Summer 1969):290–306.

In 1938 novelist Wolfe visited ten western parks by automobile as a guest of the Oregon State Motor Association. Cracroft says Wolfe's *A Western Journal, A Daily Log of the Great Parks Trip, June 20-July 2, 1938* (Pittsburgh, 1951) is not a typical tourist's account that records descriptions and routes. Instead, as these excerpts from the Utah portion show, it is a document that reveals Wofle's enthusiasm for the land and the people of the Rocky Mountains.

WASHINGTON

(1809–1811)   DAVID THOMPSON   1027

Smith, Allan H. "An Ethnohistorical Analysis of David Thompson's 1809–1811 Journeys in the Lower Pend Oreille Valley, Northeastern Washington." *Ethnohistory* 8 (Fall 1961):309–81.

David Thompson, an explorer, field geographer, and fur trader for the Canadian North West Company, was the first white man to come in contact with the Kalispel Indians. Primary sources used in this article include David Thompson's *Narrative of his Explorations in Western America, 1784–1812* (Toronto, 1916) and his *Journals Relating to Montana and Adjacent Regions, 1808–1812* (Missoula, Montana, 1950).

(1878–1879)   CHARLES ERSKINE SCOTT WOOD   1028

Wood, C. E. S. "Private Journal, 1878." *Oregon Historical Quarterly* 70 (March 1969):5–38.
————. "Private Journal, 1879." *Oregon Historical Quarterly* 70 (June 1969):139–70.

Charles Erskine Scott Wood, who was a young lieutenant serving as aide-de-camp to the commander of the Columbia Department (Washington Territory), relates a variety of experiences. He describes his travels with a company of touring actors and actresses, a close call with attacking Indians, several frontier characters, a long, snow-bound February, and a council with Indian chiefs. His account of the meeting between Wood, an Indian agent, and the Yakima Chief Moses presents the dialogue and arguments of the day-long meeting that was preliminary to the Indians' being granted a new reservation. Journal kept between June 7, 1878, and May 14, 1879.

Bibliography of Periodicals

Although the complete runs of 223 periodicals published between 1955 and 1980 were searched, not all contained articles pertinent to this bibliography. Listed here are the 170 publications from which articles were taken. Citations from periodicals that were searched selectively, found in periodical indexes, or located in other sources are indicated by S.

Adirondack Life, S
Agricultural History, vols. 29–54 (January 1955-October 1980)
Alabama Historical Quarterly, vols. 17–42 (Spring 1955-Fall/Winter 1980)
Alabama Review, vols. 8–33 (January 1955-October 1980)
Alaska Review, S
American Benedictine Review, S
American-German Review, vols. 22–36 (October 1955-August/September 1970)
American Heritage, vols. 6–32, no. 1 (December 1954-December 1980)
American Historical Review, vols. 61–85 (October 1955-December 1980)
American History Illustrated, vols. 1–14 (April 1966-February 1980)
American Jewish Archives, S
American Jewish Historical Quarterly, vols. 44–67 (September 1954-June 1978). Continued as *American Jewish History*.
American Jewish History, vols. 68–69 (September 1978-June 1980). Continues *American Jewish Historical Quarterly*.
American Quarterly, vols. 7–32 (Spring 1955-Winter 1980)
American Scholar, vols. 25–49 (Winter 1955/56-Autumn 1980)
American Studies, vols. 12–21 (Spring 1971-Fall 1980). Continues *Mid-Continent American Studies Journal*.
American West, vols. 1–16 (Winter 1965-November/December 1980)
Americas (Academy of American Franciscan History), vols. 12–36 (July 1955-April 1980)
Angol Filológiai Tanulmányok/Hungarian Studies in English, S
Annals of Iowa, vols. 33–45 (July 1955-Fall 1980)
Annals of the Association of American Geographers, vols. 45–70 (March 1955-December 1980)
Annals of Wyoming, vols. 27–52 (April 1955-Fall 1980)
Antioch Review, S
Apalachee, (1950/56-1971/79)
Arizona and the West, vols. 1–22 (Spring 1959-Winter 1980)
Arkansas Historical Quarterly, vols. 14–39 (Spring 1955-Winter 1980)
British Association for American Studies Bulletin, nos. 1–9 (April 1956-November 1959); New Series, nos. 1–12 (September 1960-1966)

Bulletin of the Friends Historical Association, vols. 44–50 (Spring 1955-Autumn 1961). Continued as *Quaker History*.

Bulletin of the Historical and Philosophical Society of Ohio, vols. 13–21 (January 1955-October 1963). Continued as *Cincinnati Historical Society Bulletin*.

Bulletin of the History of Medicine, S

Bulletin of the Missouri Historical Society, vols. 12–36, no. 2 (October 1955-April 1980)

California Historical Quarterly, vols. 50–56 (March 1971-Winter 1977/78). Continues *California Historical Society Quarterly*. Continued as *California History*.

California Historical Society Quarterly, vols. 34–49 (March 1955-December 1970). Continued as *California Historical Quarterly*.

California History, vols. 57–59 (Spring 1978-Winter 1980/81)

Chicago History, vols. 4–8 (Fall 1954-Summer 1969); New Series, vols. 1–8 (Spring 1970-Winter 1979/80)

Chronicles of Oklahoma, vols. 33–58 (Spring 1955-Winter 1980/81)

Chronicles of Smith County, Texas, vols. 1–19 (Fall 1962-Winter 1980)

Church History, vols. 24–49 (March 1955-December 1980)

Cincinnati Historical Society Bulletin, vols. 22–38 (January 1964-Winter 1980). Continues *Bulletin of the Historical and Philosophical Society of Ohio*.

Civil War History, vols. 1–25 (March 1955-December 1980)

Civil War Times Illustrated, vols. 1–19, no. 8 (April 1962-December 1980)

Colorado Magazine, vols. 32–57 (January 1955–1980)

Concordia Historical Institute Quarterly, S

Connecticut Historical Society Bulletin, vols. 20–45 (January 1955-October 1980)

Delaware History, vols. 6–19 (March 1954-Fall/Winter 1980)

Dickensian, S

Early American Literature, vols. 1–14 (Winter 1966-Winter 1979/80)

East Tennessee Historical Society Publications, nos. 27–48 (1955-1976)

East Texas Historical Journal, vols. 1–16 (July 1965-no. 2, 1978)

Ethnohistory, vols. 2–27 (Winter 1955-Spring 1980)

Essex Institute Historical Collections, vols. 91–116 (January 1955-October 1980)

Exploration, vols. 1–8 (December 1973-December 1980)

FS; Feminist Studies, vols. 1–6 (Summer 1972-Fall 1980)

Filson Club Historical Quarterly, vols. 29–54 (January 1955-October 1980)

Florida Historical Quarterly, vols. 34–58 (July 1955-April 1980)

Geographical Review, vols. 45–70 (January 1955-October 1980)

Georgia Historical Quarterly, vols. 39–64 (March 1955-Winter 1980)

Georgia Review, vols. 9–34 (Spring 1955-Winter 1980)

Great Lakes Review, S

Great Plains Journal, vols. 1–18 (Fall 1961-1979)

Hawaiian Journal of History, vols. 1–14 (1967-1980)

High Country, S

Historical Journal of Western Massachusetts, vols. 1–8 (Spring 1972-June 1980)

Historical New Hampshire, vols. 11–25 (April 1955-Winter 1980)

Historical Review of Berks County, vols. 21–45 (October/December 1955-Fall 1980)

Historical Society of Southern California Quarterly, vols. 37–43 (March 1955-December 1961). Continued as *Southern California Quarterly*.

History Today, vols. 5–30 (January 1955-December 1980)

Idaho Yesterdays, vols. 1–23 (Spring 1957-Winter 1980)

Indiana Magazine of History, vols. 51–76 (March 1955-December 1980)

Inter-American Review of Bibliography, S

Iowa Journal of History, vols. 53–57, no. 2 (January 1955-April 1961)

Journal of American History, vols. 51–66 (June 1964-March 1980). Continues *Mississippi Valley Historical Review.*
Journal of American Studies, vols. 1–14 (April 1967-December 1980)
Journal of Arizona History, vols. 1–20 (Spring-Winter 1980)
Journal of California Anthropology, S
Journal of Mexican-American History, vols. 1–3 (Fall 1970-1973)
Journal of Mississippi History, vols. 17–42 (January 1955-November 1980)
Journal of Negro History, vols. 40–65 (January 1955-Fall 1980)
Journal of San Diego History, vols. 12–26 (January 1966-Fall 1980). Continues *Times Gone By.*
Journal of Social History, vols. 1–13 (Fall 1967-Summer 1980)
Journal of Southern History, vols. 21–46 (February 1955-November 1980)
Journal of the Illinois State Historical Society, vols. 48–73 (Spring 1955-Winter 1980)
Journal of the Rutgers University Library, S
Journal of the West, vols. 1–19 (July/October 1962-October 1980)
Kansas Historical Quarterly, vols. 21, no. 5–43 (Spring 1954-Winter 1977)
Kansas History, vols. 1–3 (Spring 1978-Winter 1980)
Kansas Quarterly, S
Lincoln Herald, vols. 57–82 (Spring/Summer 1955-Winter 1980)
Louisiana Historical Quarterly, vols. 38–40, no. 1 (January 1955-January 1957)
Louisiana History, vols. 1–21 (Winter 1960-Fall 1980)
Louisiana Studies, vols. 1–15 (Spring 1962-Winter 1976). Continued as *Southern Studies.*
Maryland Historical Magazine, vols. 50–75 (March 1955-December 1980)
Massachusetts Historical Society Proceedings, vols. 71–92 (October 1953/May 1957-1980)
Massachusetts Review, S
Methodist History, S
Michigan History, vols. 39–64 (March 1955-November/December 1980)
Mid-America, vols. 37–62 (January 1955-October 1980)
Midcontinent American Studies Journal, vols. 1–11 (Spring 1960-Fall 1970). Continued as *American Studies.*
Military History of Texas and the Southwest, vols. 1–16, no. 2 (May 1961-1980)
Minnesota History, vols. 34, no. 5–47 (Spring 1955-Winter 1980)
Mississippi Quarterly, S
Mississippi Valley Historical Review, vols. 41–50 (June 1954-March 1964). Continued as *Journal of American History.*
Missouri Historical Review, vols. 50–74 (October 1955-July 1980)
Modern Age, S
Modern Language Journal, vols. 39–64 (January 1955-Winter 1980)
Montana: The Magazine of Western History, vols. 5–30 (Winter 1955-October 1980)
Nebraska History, vols. 36–61 (March 1955-Winter 1980)
Nevada Historical Society Quarterly, vols. 1–23 (Summer 1957-Winter 1980)
New England Galaxy, S
New England Quarterly, vols. 28–53 (March 1955-December 1980)
New Jersey History, vols. 85–98 (Spring 1967-Fall/Winter 1980). Continues *Proceedings of the New Jersey Historical Society.*
New Mexico Historical Review, vols. 30–55 (January 1955-October 1980)
New York Historical Society Quarterly, vols. 39–64, no. 1 (January 1955-January 1980)
New York History, vols. 36–61 (January 1955-October 1955)
Niagara Frontier, vols. 2–25 (Summer 1955-1978)
North Carolina Historical Review, vols. 32–57 (January 1955-October 1980)
North Dakota History, vols. 22–47 (January 1979-Winter 1980)
North Lousiana Historical Association Journal, vols. 1–11 (Fall 1969-Fall 1980)

Northwest Ohio Quarterly, **S**

Ohio Historical Quarterly, vols. 64–70 (January 1955-October 1961). Continued as *Ohio History*.

Ohio History, vols. 71–89 (January 1962-Autumn 1980). Continues *Ohio Historical Quarterly*.

Old Northwest, vols. 1–5 (March 1975-Winter 1979/80)

Old-Time New England, **S**

Oregon Historical Quarterly, vols. 56–82 (March 1955-Winter 1980)

Pacific Historian, vols. 1–24 (February 1957-Winter 1980)

Pacific Northwest Quarterly, vols. 46–71 (January 1955-October 1980)

Palimpsest, vols. 36–61 (January 1955-November/December 1980)

Panhandle-Plains Historical Review, vols. 28–51 (1955-1978)

Papers on Language and Literature, **S**

Password, vols. 1–25 (Fall 1956-Winter 1980)

Pennsylvania Folklife, **S**

Pennsylvania History, vols. 22–47 (January 1955-October 1980)

Pennsylvania Magazine of History and Biography, vols. 79–104 (January 1955-October 1980)

Phylon, vols. 15, no. 2–41 (Second Quarter 1954-December 1979)

Polish-American Studies, **S**

Polish Review, **S**

Political Science, **S**

Political Science Quarterly, vols. 70–95 (March 1955-Winter 1980–81)

Princeton University Library Chronicle, **S**

Proceedings of the American Antiquarian Society: New Series, vols. 65–90 (April 20, 1955-October 15, 1980)

Proceedings of the American Philosophical Society, vols. 99–124 (February 1955-December 17, 1980)

Proceedings of the New Jersey Historical Society, vols. 73–84 (January 1955-October 1966). Continued as *New Jersey History*.

Quaker History, vols. 51–69 (Spring 1962-Autumn 1980). Continues *Bulletin of the Friends Historical Association*.

The Quarterly Journal of the Library of Congress, **S**

The Quarterly Official Publication of the St. Lawrence Historical Association, **S**

Records of the Columbia Historical Society of Washington, D.C. (1953–56-1980)

Red River Valley Historical Review, **S**

Register of the Kentucky Historical Society, vols. 53–78 (January 1955-Autumn 1980)

Research Studies, **S**

Review of Politics, **S**

Revue de Louisiane/Louisiana Review, vols. 1–9 (Summer 1972-Winter 1980)

Rhode Island History, vols. 14–39 (January 1955-November 1980)

Rochester History, vols. 17–42 (January 1955-July 1980)

San Diego Historical Society Quarterly, vols. 1–10 (January 1955-April 1964). Continued as *Times Gone By*.

Smithsonian Journal of History, vols. 1–3 (Spring 1966-Winter 1968/69)

South Atlantic Bulletin, **S**

South Atlantic Quarterly, vols. 54–79 (January 1955-Autumn 1980)

South Carolina Historical Magazine, vols. 56–81 (January 1955-October 1980)

South Dakota History, vols. 1–10 (Winter 1970-Fall 1980)

Southern California Quarterly, vols. 44–62 (March 1962-Winter 1980). Continues *Historical Society of California Quarterly*.

Southern Studies, vols. 16–19 (Spring 1977-Winter 1980). Continues *Louisiana Studies*.

Southwestern Historical Quarterly, vols. 59–83 (July 1955-April 1980)

Staten Island Historian, **S**

Swedish Pioneer Historical Quarterly, vols. 6–31 (January 1955-October 1980)

Tennessee Folklore Society Bulletin, **S**

Tennessee Historical Quarterly, vols. 14–39 (March 1955-Winter 1980)

Texana, vols. 1–12 (Winter 1973-no. 4, 1974)

Texas Quarterly, vols. 1–21 (February 1958-Winter 1978)

Times Gone By, vol. 11 (January-October 1965). Continues *San Diego Historical Quarterly.* Continued as *Journal of San Diego History.*

Utah Historical Quarterly, vols. 23–48 (January 1955-Fall 1980)

Vermont History, vols. 23–48 (January 1955-Fall 1980)

Virginia Magazine of History and Biography, vols. 63–88 (January 1955-October 1980)

West Tennessee Historical Society Papers, nos. 9–34 (1955-1980)

West Texas Historical Association Yearbook, vols. 31–54 (October 1955-1978)

West Virginia History, vols. 17–41 (October 1955-Summer 1980)

Western Historical Quarterly, vols. 1–11 (January 1970-October 1980)

Western Humanities Review, **S**

Western Pennsylvania Historical Magazine, vols. 38–63 (Spring/Summer 1955-October 1980)

Western Political Quarterly, vols. 8–33 (March 1956-December 1980)

William and Mary Quarterly. Third Series, vols. 12–37 (January 1955-October 1980)

Wisconsin Magazine of History, vols. 39–63 (Autumn 1955-Summer 1980)

Yale University Library Gazette, **S**

Index to Travelers, Places, and Subjects

(References are to item numbers, not page numbers.)

This index has the names of all travelers, places, other persons, and subjects mentioned in the annotations. Italicized item numbers under regions and states indicate the concentration of articles about that area. In general, cities, counties, and physical features have been placed under their names. Battles may be found under the war in which they occurred, or if they took place in peacetime, under their distinctive names.

Forts are indexed under the identifying name of the fort, except where the designation has become attached to a city.

Although subject references have been made for themes that appear in the annotations, the reader should be aware that travelers usually addressed themselves to more topics than one could hope to include in a bibliography of this length. Book-length travel accounts from which articles were extracted are listed, but not periodicals or newspapers in which accounts originally appeared.

Index to Authors, Editors, and Translators

(References are to item numbers, not page numbers.)

This index includes all modern authors, editors, and translators cited in this bibliography.

Travels in America,
designed by Sandy See, was set in various sizes of Caslon by Graphic
Composition, Inc., and printed offset on 55-pound Glatfelter B-31 by
Cushing-Malloy, Inc., with case binding by John H. Dekker & Sons.